Modern Africa

Into Africa

Marq de Villiers and Sheila Hirtle

INTO AFRICA

A Journey through the Ancient Empires

KEY PORTER BOOKS

Canadian Cataloguing in Publication Data

De Villiers, Marq, 1940–
      Into Africa : a journey through the ancient empires

Includes bibliographical references and index.
ISBN 1-55013-884-7

1. Africa – Description and travel. 2. Africa – Social life and customs. 3. De Villiers, Marq, 1940– – Journeys – Africa. I. Hirtle, Sheila. II. Title.

DT14.D48   1997   960.3'2   C97-931294-9

THE CANADA COUNCIL | LE CONSEIL DES ARTS
FOR THE ARTS | DU CANADA
SINCE 1957 | DEPUIS 1957

The publisher gratefully acknowledges the support of the Canada Council for the Arts and the Ontario Arts Council for its publishing program.

Key Porter Books Limited
70 The Esplanade
Toronto, Ontario
Canada M5E 1R2
Design: Jean Lightfoot Peters
Electronic formatting: Heidi Palfrey
Cartography: John Sapsford

Distributed in the United States by Firefly Books

Printed and bound in Canada

97 98 99 00 6 5 4 3 2 1

In the beginning there was a river. The river became a road and the road branched out to the whole world. And because the road was once a river it was always hungry.

—BEN OKRI, *The Famished Road*

CONTENTS

NOTES TO READERS

In this book we have defined Africa as mainland Africa, with a few exceptions: Zanzibar is here, for its role along the Indian Ocean coast, and São Tomé, whose sinister place in the slave trade argued for inclusion. But the Canaries are not here, nor the Azores, nor the Comoros—all of them in some definitions "African." More strikingly, perhaps, we have omitted Madagascar, which in our view is neither African nor Asian, but something unique. We have stayed with the name Zaire for the newly named Democratic Republic of the Congo, if only to differentiate it from the other Republic of the Congo, across the river—a confusion that in the real world is sure to cause much diplomatic wrangling. And if we have passed lightly over the Maghreb and Egypt, it is not because those places are not crucial to African history, but because their rich stories have been often told—for our purposes we were more interested in their connections to the rest of the continent.

The "Bantu" are a group of peoples with a common linguistic origin who began in the Nigerian hinterland and whose great migrations throughout the continent have been one of the great dramas of African history. In later years the word was misappropriated by the architects of apartheid as a futile synonym for "race," which in their context meant inferior race. Nevertheless it is a good word, and we have given it back to the peoples it best describes. There are, of course, black Africans who are not Bantu: the Khoisan comes to mind, and the Nilotic and Kushitic cultures of the north.

Two of us have produced this book, though in the text you will find only the singular voice. This is mostly for convenience. We couldn't say (to take a trivial example) that "our great-great-grandfather was born in Africa," because it isn't true; nor could we say anything like "the great-great-grandfather of one of us was born in Africa," because that would be merely clumsy. Nevertheless, despite the first person singular, we are both equally responsible for this book. We divided up the duties. The on-ground travel was (mostly, and through an accident of birth and personal history) done by Marq de Villiers; the travel through time and into the archives was done by Sheila Hirtle. This book is a consequence of both these equal efforts.

—MARQ DE VILLIERS AND SHEILA HIRTLE

INTRODUCTION

I flew over the Kalahari into Johannesburg alongside a physician from Mauritius who had spent the night explaining his scheme—utterly persuasive and subtle—for transforming his country's medical insurance from its Marxist legacy of sclerotic bankruptcy to a privately funded system that rewards individual initiative. It was early morning, the plane, having left New York on a sweltering summer night, gingerly skirting a hurricane pounding the Carolina coast. Below, the soil of Namibia and the Kalahari, which had seemed in eviler times blood-red and brooding, now appeared leached in the thin winter sunshine, as though it had sucked up its violent past. There were game trails everywhere; here and there, clustered around the dry watercourses, little straggles of huts, the shelters of herders.

We had followed the coast for several hundred kilometres, and I'd seen dawn breaking where I imagined the mouth of the Congo to be. In times past that was the stamping-ground of the Kongo kings, come down from the interior in conquest eight hundred or more years ago. A little farther south, the Black Queen, Nzinga of the Mbundu, had fought her long and lonely wars against the Portuguese invaders, warfare that had persisted through all the endless years of slavery into modern times—not for nothing was Angola called "The Paths of the Dead" by travellers sickened by the carnage. I had in my notebooks a passage written by a liberationist fighter some thirty years earlier, when the enemy were still the colonizers, before Angola had collapsed into civil war: "... the cries of the wounded and the dying will fade," he wrote; "the blood will seep into the earth, the weeds will fill the hollows where we lay, waiting for the bullet that would end the pain ... The grass will come, and then a farmer, and his crops will know nothing of the blood that flowed here ... The pain will have departed, along with the dead ..."

He was an optimist, but he was describing something that had happened before in Africa. The continent was not at all what the West sometimes imagined it to be: merely a place with a long and melancholy history of violence and barbarism. Africa has had bad patches, true, as have all peoples—indeed, Africa could be said to be having one now, at least in part. Africa has also had its glorious periods, rich kingdoms, years of pastoral peace and prosperity. To see the real Africa clearly, you had to take the long view.

I pushed the window shutter up a little more to get a better look, flooding the darkened cabin with light. There was a chorus of hisses, and shouts of "Close the window!" from the rear seats. An elderly Sotho chief, on his way home to Maseru, tapped me on the shoulder and gestured at the movie screen, which was vainly trying to compete with the sunshine. He wanted me to close the shutter again. He was watching a movie based on Kipling's *Jungle Book*, and on the screen Mowgli was wrestling with a priggish British soldier. I protested feebly. "That's the real thing down there," I said, pointing at the earth passing below. "And *that's* only a movie!" But it was no use. I grudgingly lowered the shade to a sliver and hunched down in my seat to peer through it. Rasheed, the Mauritian physician, was yammering on about actuarial tables, and below was passing one of the grandest sights on the planet, while the old Sotho, on his way home to his fastness in the Maluti Mountains, was cheering for Mowgli, who was riding a trained elephant in a plastic Hollywood jungle. Later, all this seemed to me a fitting metaphor for the kind of Africa where a former Umkhonto we Sizwe guerrilla is now gainfully employed rummaging through bags at Customs, and the former militants of the African National Congress *toyi-toyi* to celebrate Afrikaners winning the World Cup of rugby.

A few days later I took to the air again and headed north, for the old Empire of Monomotapa, and as I passed over the Limpopo River I wondered where, in this boundless landscape and among these vibrant, turbulent, energetic millions, the "true Africa" was to be found. Sometimes I thought it was folly to look—perhaps the "real" Africa belonged only in a directory of imaginary places. Later, in a book shop near the Ngorongoro Crater, in Tanzania, I found a glossy photographic essay aimed at Outsiders. Its author, a German, had gone in search of this "real Africa" and had decided it must be located as far from modernity as he could get. He had pitched his tent in an "almost unknown corner of southwest Kenya" and set out to "win the trust of the mysterious and secretive Maasai," among whom he thrust himself. The Maasai, polite to a fault, put up with him, and the resulting book, despite its stunning photographs, had a cloyingly self-congratulatory tone. And what makes the Maasai in this "forgotten corner" (by which is meant "invisible to white people") any more real than, say, the Zanzibari performance artist who goes by the name of Shaka Zulu and every night has himself run over by cars as a symbol of the oppression of Africa by alien technology?

Africa's long past has been the story of the ebb and flow of kingdoms and dynasties, some great, some small, some exceptionally wealthy. All these empires rose and fell, flowered and decayed. Waves of immigrants, conquerors and peacemakers, swept across Africa for century after century. There were great migrations of people, Kushites and Nilotes down and up the Nile, the great boiling out of southeastern Nigeria of the Bantu people, west and south and east, and then north, then south again, until they filled up the continent. The old empires (Monomotapa, Kush, the Zanj coast, Mali, Benin, the Ashanti of Kumasi, the Kabakas of Uganda, Kanem-Bornu, the melancholy ruins of Tuareg Timbuktu, the Songhai of Gao) cut across modern national boundaries. They also cut across tribal boundaries. They were fluid, expansionist, organic, explosive—one of the great engines of African change. These empires were never tidy, with immutable boundaries.

Immutable boundaries are un-African. Like cloud patterns seen on satellite photos from space, Africa is always changing. Sometimes, of course, the continent seems chaotic, formless, tragic. Rwanda and Burundi are horrid lessons for all. Liberia has deteriorated into fetishistic savagery. Zaire has crumbled into corrupt anarchy, Nigeria apparently into a nation of thieves, Sierra Leone into murderousness. Lagos and Dakar, great and stinking slums, are widely seen as harbingers of the chaos to come.

But—I say again—to understand Africa you must understand the timeline and the pattern. Africa must be seen in long view, understood as a work in progress, in always-unfinished evolution.

Often, tyrants rose, and wise kings. There were times of peace, decades of decay and warfare. There were periods of savagery, periods of marvellous, fecund artistic flowering and prosperity. African history contains its own sources of optimism.

....

Each reader will draw his or her own conclusions from what follows. These are ours:

First, and most superficially, what should be utterly obvious: that Africa is more than warlords and tyrants and bloodshed played out in the stultifying embrace of tribalism, the Outsider cliché. Africa is going in all directions at once. There is also great political subtlety, in which Africans are working out new ways of governing; among the common people there is a yearning for education and political democracy that is infectious, and spreading, maybe not as fast as the dreadful scourge of AIDS, but as relentlessly. Despite crisis after crisis, all over the continent, in unexpected ways and in unexpected places, the rule of law is taking hold—now coups (and there are some and there will be more) are condemned by other Africans in ways that are new (only outsiders have failed to notice).

Second, that tribes are not what we think, the central fact in all African lives. In the long view, tribes have shifted and mutated, changed and evolved, been absorbed by others, with new tribes constantly emerging. That's the key: over Africa's long, long history, new tribes have been emerging all the time—it is another of the great engines of African change. It is a myth that in pre-colonial Africa political boundaries coincided with tribal boundaries: Africa was never that static. Only in the modern period has the notion of "tribe" taken on its quasi-permanent meaning.

Third, that the worst effects of colonialism, worse by far than economic exploitation, were twofold: the stultifying notion of the sovereign nation-state (the idea of the fixed boundary), and the ratcheting-up of the technology of murder. No remaking of Africa's boundaries could have come close to satisfying the complex and ever-changing demands of Africa's ethnic minorities—there were probably between six and ten thousand discrete political units in pre-colonial Africa, ranging from simple chiefdoms like the one inherited by Lesotho's founder, Moshoeshoe, to sophisticated empires run on federal lines by layered bureaucracies. It's true that the borders of today's nation-states take no account of geographical, ethnic, or commercial realities, and very small account of ancient kingdoms. But there is no ethnic group in Africa split by national boundaries that is demanding reunification; there is not a single secessionist movement of any consequence—even in Zaire, where Shaba province was by 1997 to all intents and purposes independent already, the rebel leaders were demanding reform of Zaire, not its partition. African leaders always assert the sanctity of borders: peculiar they may be, but all the alternatives, in their view, are worse. Nevertheless, Africa is still changing, despite the apparent inviolability of "borders." New power bases are emerging that cut across national boundaries. They include church and religious movements, attempts to revive ancient kingdoms, warlord-ruled fiefdoms, regional economic co-operatives and free-trade zones. African borders may erode from below and above. That would be consistent with ancient pattern.

Fourth, that it is impossible to underestimate the deadly effects of the European traffic in slaves. Hard as it may be to believe, there have even been attempts to "justify" the slave trade by pointing out that Africans occasionally enslaved each other long before Europe got there. But nothing—*nothing*—has ever equalled the European theft of thirteen million Africans.

Fifth, that hardly anyone in Africa any longer believes Africa's problems can be blamed forever on colonialism. New African leaders are weaning their countries from the addiction to foreign aid; they see Africa as an emerging market entirely capable of profiting through their own energy and their own efforts from global trade. Little noticed, Africa in 1997 was in the midst of an economic upturn—led by economic stars like Uganda and the Ivory Coast, but with many others following behind.

Sixth, that the richness of African culture has always been found in what we in the West think of as the Public Arts—music, dance, costume, religious art, storytelling. In every obscure corner of Africa, there are rich traditions of music and dance: from the jerky, shoulder-wrenching dancing of Ethiopia to the jump-dancing of the Kenyan steppe to the thunderous foot-stamping of the Zulus. In music, the drumming of Africa is well enough known, but there is a fecund tradition of hand-pianos, lyres, horns, and other instruments, and a millennia-long tradition of setting poetry to the complicated, contrapuntal cross-rhythms of the continent. But also that Africa evolves: the sophisticated writing of Ben Okri (from whom we have drawn our opening epigraph) is in direct descent from the storytelling of the Elder Days. "Authentic Africa" is found not only in the playful folktales of Anansi the Spider God, but also in the fictions of its urban cosmopolites.

Seventh, that the Elder People—the San and the pygmies, the last of the Stone Age peoples of Africa—have in many ways consciously rejected both Bantu and Western culture, preferring and preserving their own intimate connection to their universe. And among those peoples, as bereft of material goods as any on the planet, there are poetic traditions and reservoirs of legends as deep and as true as those of far wealthier cultures.

Eighth, how *old* Africa is.

Ninth, how ignorant the Outsider view that ancient Egypt somehow sprang up, fully formed, in Africa, and was somehow not "African."

Tenth, how *conservative* Africa is. Africa changes invaders more than invaders change Africa. Even Islam, that most infectious of religions, had trouble with tradition-inoculated African cultures. Africa *endures*.

Eleventh, how much more complicated African religion is than the dismissive Western word "animism" would seem to allow.

Finally, how much African wildlife has shaped African culture. And by "wildlife" we don't just mean the Big Five, or the great predators of the savannah. The deadliest of Africa's wildlife are much smaller: the liver fluke, the malaria mosquito, the hookworm, rinderpest, the tsetse fly . . . And now, of course, that latter-day plague, the AIDS virus.

Part I

Monomotapa

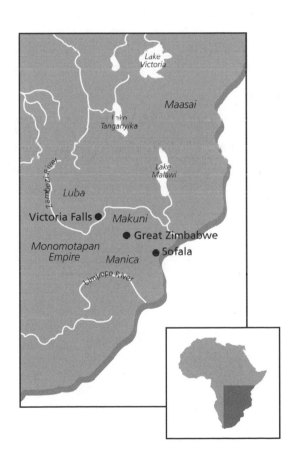

GREAT ZIMBABWE

O ther than the Temples of the Middle Nile and the brooding, enigmatic, African face of the Sphinx, Great Zimbabwe is probably the most romantic of all Africa's ruins. This has not been such a bad thing, over the years: romance breeds legend, and legend is still a more reliable guide to history than the boasting of victors. It's easy to forget, though, that at the root of the legends was a very real and formidable kingdom called Monomotapa, whose power in its latter days overlapped the modern countries of Zimbabwe and northern South Africa and stretched into Mozambique, Zambia, Malawi, and Tanzania; and whose skeins of influence wound up the Zambezi to the headwaters of the Congo, across the continent to the Mbundu kings, in what is now Angola, and to the Land of Zanj, where Swahili traders took Zimbabwean gold up the coast past Kilwa and all the way to the Gulf of Aden, and thence to Asia.

It's probable that Great Zimbabwe began as a cattle-herders' refuge from the tsetse fly. Religion and politics built it, gold and trade sustained it, power and ambition made it great, war and social exhaustion ended it.

It was glorious while it lasted.

The great granite stones of ruined Zimbabwe were grey, flecked with honey gold, flawed with patches of startling indigo. They were cool to the touch, much cooler than expected in the subtropical sun. Perhaps it was their age, I thought, thinking mortal thoughts; they had lain here in these massive walls so very long, the warmth pressed out by the weight of history. There were people here before the Merovingian kings ruled France, and Great Zimbabwe was at its height before the Crusades to the Holy Land had run their course, its rulers reaching out to Arabia Felix, and even to China—Oriental traders had sent their representatives up these precipitous, perilous pathways many centuries ago. I squinted along the wall. About a hundred metres (100 yards) away, it curved, skirting a rocky outcrop, and plunged into a small depression. Above, it towered 6 to 10 metres (20 to 30 feet) or more, thousands of stones, millions of stones piled row upon even row, with no mortar, into a massive, enigmatic ... something. I laid my cheek to the granite, feeling its roughness, closing my eyes, trying to feel its antiquity. Then, as instructed, I pressed my ear to the coolness.

"Listen," Tafirenyika said. "You have to listen very carefully. Be very still."

He squatted on his heels in the African fashion and began to draw idle patterns in the sandy soil. We were outside the largest ruin in Zimbabwe, what they call the Great Enclosure, a huge circle of stone containing other circles, mysterious conical towers. He was there as my guide. He'd grown up in the south of the country, on the South African border, but had spent all his adult life around Great Zimbabwe.

"What am I listening for?" I asked.

"Just listen," he said with a sly smile, ducking his head away.

At first I heard nothing. The wind did what the wind does in the grass, and from far away came the long ululation of a woman. Then that died away, and I pressed my ear hard to the flatness of the stone and I could just hear, on the edge of audibility, what sounded at first like a rustling, and as I caught the focus it resolved into clicking, millions of tiny clicks like a nest of carpenter ants in a wall cavity. I jerked my head away.

"What is it?"

Tafirenyika said nothing. He traced another pattern in the sand, then impatiently wiped it out and started afresh. He was trying to mimic the decorative friezes at the top of the walls of the Great Enclosure but couldn't seem to get it right. From what I could see, he was living proof that not everyone was born to art. The friezes were not difficult, after all—a simple chevron pattern breaking up the severity of the granite. I listened to the wall again. I could hear it plainly this time, the millions of minute clackings, and I thought I could just make out another, deeper, more subterranean sound that ground at the nerves because I couldn't quite resolve it, a sound like the distant basso rasping of shifting boulders, like the rumbling of far-away thunder, like the midnight coughing of a lion. Or so I fancied.

"What is it?" I asked again.

"Some say it's the sound of the spears of the armies of the Empire of Monomotapa," he said. "Others say it's the sound of the Wounded, all the dead since the Beginning, trying to climb out for Judgement Day . . . That's the Christian view." He squinted up at me solemnly, his face blank. But then, seeing that I wasn't buying this ersatz mysticism, he stood up and laughed. "Well," he said, "there are lots of stories. Who is to say some of them aren't true? The archaeologists believe the clicking sounds are the stones shifting minutely, trembling with their weight, pressing down on the earth, millions and millions of stones, billions of little shiftings. But then archaeologists aren't engineers. What do they know? The engineers came and punched markers into the stones, to see if they are shifting. See, here, brass nails in the rock? Every year or so they come, measure, and go away disappointed. Mostly, they don't even hear the sounds. They don't listen properly." He paused, fumbled for the right words. "They listen in a . . . a schooling way, which means they don't hear anything they can't measure." He looked at me to see if I was laughing, but I said nothing. "Why is it that not everyone can hear the hidden sounds of Zimbabwe? I myself believe it's just the wind finding its way into the deep centre of the Great Wall, the stones contracting and expanding as the temperature changes." He shrugged. "Who is to say? Great Zimbabwe has been here a very long time. Some things should remain a mystery."

I spent the rest of the day wandering around the Great Enclosure and following the broken walls, pacing the limits of the ancient city, and then, just before dusk, I climbed the kopje called Zimbabwe Hill. I looked down on the sprawling complex and tried to imagine what it would have been like when Zimbabwe was the centre of one of Africa's pre-eminent trading empires, a city of twenty thousand inhabitants, rich enough to attract the avarice of European and Oriental traders. This was one of Old Africa's grandest kingdoms, but when I had been growing up no more than a few hundred kilometres away I had known nothing of it. This history had been closed, obscured by a set of ingrained but wrong-headed assumptions about its builders that made it impossible to see.

At the summit, the archaeologists have spooned away the mud and uncovered a fifteenth-century homestead. A little farther down, there is one dating to the twelfth century. Today, the whole complex is grey stone and mud and vines, but when the king looked down from the high hill in the days of his magnificence, he saw flaming colours, sculpture, decoration, friezes, walls dipping and swooping in elegant curves, architecture as sculpture, architecture as art. Magical birds, carved from soapstone, were placed on great standards in niches in the walls. Small human figures decorated the small enclosures within the sweep of the walls. These great walls supported nothing; they were more like gigantic stone fences, and so, freed from the constraints of engineering, they could follow whatever forms their builders desired. Each new king, it seems, pulled down some of the walls his predecessors had built, and rebuilt them in his own aesthetic.

Archaeologists puzzle over the purpose of these mysterious curves and cones and sweeps. Were they there for defence? Ritual purposes? As an exhibition of raw power? The class system written in granite? (A learned thesis has been written on the notion that elevation above the plain was tied to status; there were charts purporting to relate hut size to metres above sea level.) Sitting up there on the high hill, I suddenly felt that the ethnographers were asking the wrong questions, or asking the questions of the wrong people. They should be asking the artists and the poets. After all, the *griots*, the storytellers and poets of their time, used to sing up here on the hill, as they looked down to the Great Enclosure far below. Near the summit there is a niche in the rocks where an ordinary speaking voice can plainly be heard 200 metres (200 yards) below, a magical place worthy of praise-poems, singing, and the invocation of spirits. The walls mimic the shapes of the gourds of the mbiras, of the cone huts, of female breasts; these buildings have nothing to do with power, everything to do with art. Great Zimbabwe is a living sculpture and, if it is also a temple, it is in tribute as much to abstraction as to ritual, to beauty rather than power. Or that's how it seemed to me.

The German Karl Mauch was one of the first Europeans to see, and excavate, the ruins, in 1871. Typically, if extravagantly, he "knew" what he had found. "I do not think I am far wrong if I suppose that the ruin on the hill is a copy of King Solomon's Temple on Mount Moriah and the building on the plain a copy of the palace where the Queen of Sheba lived during her visit to Solomon." Later, when Mauch found fragments of ancient Chinese pottery in the ruins, his theory was put into question, but he rallied gamely: Of course the Chinese would have gone in search of Sheba's legendary queen! Wasn't she, after all, one of the marvels of the world?

The theory persisted. When Thomas Baines, illustrator, scientist, explorer, and Livingstone's baggage master, happened on the ruins in the middle of the nineteenth century, he made a sketch of the largest conical tower. In his caption he reported that "the Portuguese are of the opinion that these Ruins are portions of the remains of the City and Palace of the Queen of Sheba."

Later, some European who couldn't conceive of a tower without a treasure drilled a tunnel to the interior—only to find it solid, and in danger of collapse from his excavations.

Historians now accept that it was the Bantu precursors of the Shona people, the political masters of modern Zimbabwe, who made their way here a millennium or two ago, presumably running the gauntlet of the tsetse fly–infested north, punching a corridor through to the fly-free highlands, and pushing out the Stone Age Bushmen who were already ensconced. Bantu were certainly living here in the second century. It was successive waves of Bantu who built this city, who developed the industries on which it was based and who opened up trading routes with the deep interior, with the Indian Ocean cities, and all the way across to the Atlantic. The current structures date from around 1100, were probably completed after 1300, and were at their greatest between the fourteenth and sixteenth centuries.

It was Nyatsimba Mutota, who according to legend was the great-great-grandson of Mbire, the semi-mythical founder of Zimbabwe, who was the first significant mambo, or ruler, of what was to become a great kingdom.

It was Mutota's son, Matope, king of the Karanga, who, in one of those African fits of organizational and military genius, burst like a typhoon out of Zimbabwe *circa* 1425. He set off on a campaign of war and conquest that saw him become master of the whole inland plateau between the Limpopo and the Zambezi rivers, the source of so much gold, and afterwards of the most significant trading port of the East Coast trade, Sofala. Matope was the sovereign of much of southeast Africa and was recognised as such by the rulers of the coastal trading cities. They called his empire Wilayuta 'l Mu'anamutapah, after his own title, Mwanamutapa ("Lord of the Plundered Lands" or, in another translation, "Ravager of the Lands"). This title was duly taken over and corrupted, in the European manner, by the Portuguese, who called it Monomotapa. Matope's networks of influence included the Swahili- and Arabic-speaking traders of the coast, and therefore the whole of the Indian Ocean, and stretched as far south as the mouth of the Umzimvubu River, in South Africa's Pondoland, where there were trading missions four hundred years before the Boers made their grim way to Natal.

I was trying to sense some of this as I stared down from the kopje in the rapidly gathering gloom. The Empire of Monomotapa had collapsed, Tafirenyika had told me earlier in a rare burst of fact-giving, in part as a result of Portuguese aggression that drove people from their homes, in part from a southward migration of the deadly tsetse fly after a climatic shift, and in part because the gold seams on which the empire had been built had been exhausted. With the gold went the trade, and with the trade went sufficient food, and with hunger came dissolution and desertion.

"Without manpower the kings found it tough," he had said with a grin, "to keep up a palace made up of so many millions of stone blocks, a palace that even the Egyptians would have been proud of. And without anyone to rule," he added, "you cannot have real rulers, can you?" He'd stared at me then, even more slyly. I wondered whether this was a commentary on current politics. He wasn't a Shona himself—I knew that; his ancestors had come to Zimbabwe as refugees less than two hundred years ago, fleeing the Zulu tyrant Shaka, and then the surly Boers of the northern Transvaal. I'd said nothing, judging it unwise to involve myself in this particular bout of tribal politics. He'd turned away, his face closed, and gone back to his art, such as it was. I'd wandered off into the ruins.

After the park closed, I slipped back through the gates and made for the lower end of the hill complex. Chivhu, a game warden who supplements his living by taking people through the ruins, was with me. It was dark, the half-moon no help at all,

---

Matope's grandfather, Mudadi, was no slouch himself in the grandiosity game. He was said to spend a considerable amount of time admiring himself in a mirror given him by an Arab trader. He bathed three times a day, and employed four hundred boys to fetch his water. He bathed publicly and in the nude, which caused endless gossip about the size of his genitals, and his potency, real or imagined. He turned down the Great Wife assigned him by the Elders on the grounds that a man as handsome as he should not be married to a plain woman. It was also Mudadi who ordered his men to bring him the moon as a stool, and who killed them when they didn't. From these genes came the Great King Matope.

From Mufuka, Dzimbahwe: Life and Politics in the Golden Age, 1100–1500

Chivhu's flashlight our only illumination. But I wasn't afraid, except of twisting an ankle. Save a few leopards, there were none of the great African predators here, and it was too cold for puff-adders. The path wound precipitously up Zimbabwe Hill, at times passing between great boulders so close together that they'd squeeze the portly, and through cracks in the cliff, until eventually it reached the summit. We found a low wall and looked into the blackness of the valley, south and east along the paths the traders had come, over to the Mozambican escarpment to the east, or down to the Sabi River, where it curved eastwards on its final run for the Indian Ocean. It was absolutely still. Chivhu, in the African way, respected the silence. Away, in the far distance, I could see the red glow of a fire, and once I heard a wail, a long sound chopped off, like the cry of the go-away bird. I listened to the silence and felt the gossiping clatter of the six thousand families who had lived on the plain below in the great days of this place. I put my hand down on a stone, cut and squared and set here so many hundreds of years before, and felt a kinship with that ghostly mason.

After a while, Chivhu began to talk about his family, which, like the country, was on the cusp between modernity and tradition. The previous week his father had demanded that he join them in venerating the ancestors. "And I told him, Father, to me the dead are just the dead. I don't believe in the dead." On the other hand, Chivhu made it clear that he rejects the Christian way, though he is nominally Christian, because he believes utterly in the spirits, that spirits animate every thing and control every aspect of life; it is why the diviners and the sorcerers are so powerful, because they represent the only way ordinary mortals have of interceding with the preordained passage of fate.

"In the old days," he said, "you never had to hide or lock away your goods in this country. No one would take them without asking first." I knew he was looking at me; I could see the moon catching the whites of his eyes. I think he was unsure whether I would understand, but the moon and the silence and the weight of history impelled him to try. "Everyone knew there were spirits watching, you see. If you tried to take what didn't belong to you, from a bag or a sack, your hand would freeze in the bag and you couldn't move it, no matter what you did. Or they knew that, if they succeeded in taking something, the goods would break afterwards, and not work, or would cause you misfortune. They believed, you see, and they were scared of the consequences of disobeying."

After another silence, he returned to the theme. "It's the same with this place. If a king told us now to build a wall, to put aside our families for a year, our herds for a year, and to build a wall, would we do so? No. But then … When the old kings said, 'The spirits tell us to build us a great wall,' the subjects said, 'Where do we start?' This is not really fear. But it is not persuasion either. It is more a belief in the inevitable. You see, the kings used belief in the system to get their political way, because the people believed the kings spoke with and for the spirits. Now, we have no such system."

"Is this such a bad thing?" I asked.

"The problem is," he said, "now the people are all English. By this I mean they believe in Jesus. Before, if there was a drought, you could talk to the spirits and get rain. If you hunted and got nothing, all you had to do was find the right tree, animated by the right spirits, and if you asked with the proper respect, the game would come to you, and your family would eat. Jesus can do none of these things. Jesus is consolation only for the dead. Death, and violence, and fear. Those things he can teach us to deal with. But what of the living?"

To this I had nothing to say, and we sat for a while in silence. I thought of the Christian critiques of "animist" Africa, which Christians regarded as a superstitious belief that mere things were animated with mysterious powers. Not being much of a Christian myself, I had always found it difficult to see the differences. Africans usually believe in a single supreme being, as Christians do. They believe in the power of prayer, as Christians do. True, they use fetishes to tap into the universal currents instead of verbal pleas or statues of saints (but, then, what was the communion wafer, mysteriously transmuted into the Flesh and the Blood of Christ—an act of ritual cannibalism?). I mulled over these thoughts without much result, then I began to think of the perilous staircase going downwards into the darkness, and the 2-kilometre (1-mile) walk through the African bush, back to where I could find a lift to the town of Masvingo, where I was staying. I stood up to go, and Chivhu rose with me. He promised to take me the next day to a soothsayer, someone he trusted.

On the way down, Chivhu told me of his youngest brother, who six months ago had walked 200 kilometres (125 miles) from his village to Harare to look for work, and didn't find any. Until the previous week the boy had been sleeping in a cardboard box outside a large factory, hoping they would relent and hire him after all. But then Robert Mugabe's police had scooped him up and put him in a camp, because foreign visitors were coming to the capital for the African Games, and beggars spoiled the President's image of his country as a paradise-in-waiting. It was a depressingly familiar political theme.

....

I reviewed what I knew of the long and turbulent history of this ancient kingdom. The Gokomere were the first people to cross the Zambezi and set up housekeeping here. By the fourth century they were already trading with the East Coast, exchanging ivory, copper, and gold for sea shells, china, cloth, and glass beads. Shortly thereafter they fade from history, to be replaced by the Ziwa, who fanned out over the territory, faded in their turn, were replaced by another wave of black immigrants from the northwest, and then another and another ... It was (so some current thinking goes) the Rozwi (or BaRozvi, as they are sometimes styled), who were culturally related but better organized, who finally gained ascendancy on the hill.[1]

When was this? Traditions differ. From some accounts Matope himself was Rozwi. From others, the Rozwi came earlier, or later. Names change; clans elide into others. The Rozwi later became the Shona or the Karanga. Or did they? For a while there were two empires, the Mwena-Mutapa and the Rozwi. Or were there? In the end, it doesn't matter: the Shona are their direct inheritors.

When the Europeans came, Great Zimbabwe was at its glorious height.

The Portuguese, like the Arabs, came primarily for the gold. As João de Barros wrote in the mid-sixteenth century, "These mines are the oldest known in this land and they are situated in open country. In the middle of [this region] is a square fortress built entirely of dressed stone both within and without and of stones of extraordinary size without mortar to bind them." He never saw these places himself; the description came from Arab traders, to whom these buildings had appeared "very ancient."

> During the monumental building phase, every visitor who came to Zimbabwe was required to bring with him three stones. Each chief who visited had to bring enough men to build a section of wall. They built like men obsessed. There are enough stones in the Great Enclosure alone to build a modern office tower ninety stories high.
>
> From Mufuka, Dzimbahwe: Life and Politics in the Golden Age, 1100–1500

In 1506, Diogo de Alcaçova wrote to the king of Portugal, responding to the royal whining about what proved to be a temporary drop in gold imports from Sofala. It was all explainable, de Alcacova wrote. "Your Highness is already aware that for twelve or thirteen years there has been war in the kingdom from which the gold came to Sofala; the war, Sir, was in this way. In the time of Mokomba Menamotepam, father of this Kwesaringo Menamotapam [king who now reigns], he had a favourite who was a great lord in his kingdom ... who was called Tshanganijr [Changamire], and was chief justice [also called Amir] of the king ... and this Amir had in the kingdom many towns and places which the king had given him ... and other favourites of the king, through envy, began to tell the king that the Amir wanted to raise himself to sovereign authority [and] that he should kill him." The King, taking their advice, sent him poison as was the custom, but he refused to drink it. Instead, he went to the houses of the King, "which were of stone and clay very large," and cut off the head of the King and slew all his children but one, and that one fled to the kingdom of an uncle. The Amir made himself king and reigned peacefully for four years, until the son of Mokomba came with an army to retake his father's kingdom and kill the chief justice, which he did. He "had the kingdom to himself," except the Amir's son was still fighting. "And for this reason, Sir, the gold does not come to Sofala as it used to ... and the gold is all found in the territory of the [chief justice] and round about it, although there is some in all parts of the kingdom but in small quantities."[2]

Thus, perhaps, the squabble between the Monomotapa kings and the Rozwi upstarts.

A 1631 French engraving "of the Great King Mono-motapa" has as its inscription: "Most powerful and so Rich in Gold that many call him the Emperor of Gold ... This Kingdom is of great Expanse—having nearly 800 leagues in circumference. He holds his Court at Zimboaé, where he maintains as his Ordinary Guard women and 200 large and fearsome dogs."

....

I wondered again why the place had been abandoned. Possibly for all the utilitarian reasons Tafirenyika had said—worn-out land, diminishing gold supplies, tsetse fly, ravaged forests. There is some suggestion it was the scarcity of salt that was to blame. Africans always valued salt more than gold, which was a European and Arab obsession. And possibly also because the very grandiosity of the buildings taught its rulers to believe in their own magnificence; the meagre agricultural and natural resources became attenuated, and finally collapsed, as the rulers struggled to maintain the opulence of the buildings and exotic imports. Chivhu believed that ultimately Zimbabwe was crushed by the weight of its own self-importance. By the early nineteenth century, Zimbabwe was a pathetic shadow of its great past. When Mzilikazi, former henchman of the Zulu tyrant Shaka, fled north over the Limpopo River and into Matabeleland, the incumbent rulers, by then a minor Shona dynasty called the NeManwa, were ousted in the turmoil that followed by a Karanga community ruled by the Mugabe dynasty, clan ancestors of the country's present ruler.

> **M**any of the early gold seams were located by a sophisticated and infallible prospecting device—termites. African termites will burrow almost a hundred metres to find water, and whatever they encounter in the soil, including the gold, is hauled to the surface to become part of the colony's mound. The old "bio-geologists" sifted through the mounds, and where they found gold, they dug.
>
> ....
>
> *From* National Geographic, *December 1996*

But, by then, the Great Zimbabwe was already in ruins.

....

The following day Chivhu took me to see the sorcerer who would tell me my fate. This demanded a little manoeuvring, as Chivhu wavered between his believing/not believing modes, and alternately warned me that nothing good would come of it (that is, he believed the sorcerer might be a fraud) and that nothing good could possibly come of it (we shouldn't meddle with matters that are too powerful for jesting).

The sorcerer's own position, it turned out, was equally ambiguous. In the Great Zimbabwe national park, there is a "Shona village," which has been re-created as a museum piece to show visitors the traditional way of life. One of the "exhibits" is a witch-doctor's hut. An elderly couple can usually be found here, sitting in the sun, passing the hours, a witch and a sorcerer, there to explain the old ways; they will tell you your future, as long as you cross their palms with the right amount of what passes for gold these days. The park authorities have set them up in business but don't pay them a salary. They are supposed to live off their earnings from tourists, and clearly their enthusiasm for any particular soothsaying varies in direct proportion to the amount offered. Fair enough. The park itself doesn't really care whether the shamans believe in what they are doing; ironically, perhaps, they've picked a couple who do.

I duly had my fortune told, and left. It was as perfunctory as I'd expected. Sure, the woman had gone into a "trance" and fiddled with some of her paraphernalia, which included a drum inset with Coke-bottle caps, but the whole thing had an off-hand manner, betrayed by a sly glint from her eye when she caught me watching. It was just about worth the two Zimbabwean dollars I gave her. Chivhu had worried about this. "They'll tell you a dishonest fortune," he said. It concerned him. Too many dishonest fortunes, and the spirits would be angry, because spirits hate lying. Later, after the tourists had gone, he took me back. This time, the rhythms of the affair were different. Now, there was no hurry. Before anything could be started, there was maize beer to drink, a fire to tend, conversation to be made, silence to be respected, news to be imparted and more silence in which to digest it. Money was not discussed, and never changed hands. And the "trance" was different in its intensity. It took much longer to come about, for one thing. The old woman pulled a tattered leopard skin over her shoulder, turned her back, and settled into a mumbling, grumbling, swaying monologue that took more than thirty minutes, before she began to twitch and shake, and her voice changed pitch, climbing higher up the register. She dipped a club into some evil-looking liquid and beat herself with it. She looked back over her shoulder at me, glaring. She began to shake, as though she had a violent fever. After a long while, she spoke to her husband. She couldn't do much for me, she said, because the spirits were strange ones. Not much revelation there— I had told Chivhu I was from Canada, and it was hardly a secret. But then she said something else, and her husband looked puzzled.

"What did she say?" I asked.

"She said they have lions there," he said. "Because there were lions nearby when you were born. A strange pride. Two females and three males, and no cubs at all."

"There are no lions in Canada," I said.

"Five lions, nearby, on the day you were born," she insisted.

How could she know this? There were indeed lions about when I was born, for I was born in South Africa, but I hadn't told her that. Even then, they were not wild lions, only lions in a zoo, but they had been nearby. When I was a child, I could hear them roaring at feeding time.

Then she said something unexpected. "Your wife is barren," she said, in an accusatory tone. "Why don't you get another one?" I didn't respond. It was true I had no children, but not for the reason she advanced. How did she know that? And the second part of her comment called for a discussion or for nothing at all, so I kept silent.

She watched me for a moment, then mumbled into her chin. Her husband translated again: My ancestral spirits were worrying spirits, he said, and I laughed, because this was true—my family are notorious worriers. She became offended, but when I told her I laughed because she was right, she relented and handed me a glass of maize beer. The spirits are never restful, she said, when they are far from home. It was the problem with the modern world. Everyone was restless, and therefore unhappy.

Later that night I met a Ghanaian professor sitting in the bar at the Flamboyant Motel, in Masvingo. He was there, improbably, on holiday. I told him about the lions.

"It's the difference between magic and religion," he said ponderously, after demanding another beer from the barman. "The religious believe that their intercession with the all-powerful will affect their lives, and that the lives they lead determine their fate in the hereafter. Africans believe in an entirely preordained universe, and the only way a person can alter his fate is to intercede with the spirits, who are the representatives on earth of the all-powerful. Witch-doctors and witches are powerful because they can attract the attention of these capricious spirits. That's why you propitiate witch-doctors as well as spirits. They govern your fate. Priests can't do that. It's why Christianity is skin-deep here. Its people are powerless."

I asked him if witch-doctors were always men, and diviners women.

"No, you have it wrong," he said. "It is not a question of names. Men deal with the spirits that affect public life, the crops, the weather, the fate of the young, wars and famines and droughts. Women deal with the matters of the family, of love and betrayal, sickness. Men do their work in public; women in the home, away from prying eyes. It's why men are suspicious of women. You never know what they are up to." He pulled gloomily on his beer. "If a woman falls out of favour in the village, it is easy to denounce her. After all, she comes from somewhere else, because a woman always lives with her husband's family. Her spirits aren't your spirits. If something goes wrong—a child falls ill, a baby dies, a man strays, a woman becomes pregnant when she shouldn't—there is always a witch to blame. Call her a witch and punish her."

"What happens when a woman is denounced?"

"They drive her out," he said. "She dies or becomes a prostitute. Don't you see them in the towns? It's the fate of the powerless."

After a gloomy silence, he told me this story: "I was sitting in a taxi, and the driver said to me, oh, we have to thank the whites for many things. They brought roads, bridges, tall buildings, things we didn't know how to do. Before, we lived very poor lives. Well, I didn't argue with him. What's the point? That would be an argument without end. I mean, it is now dogma in all our schools that the African people lived in mystic harmony with nature, that they somehow intuitively understood the interdependence of ecological systems, without ever having to articulate them. As well articulate the air you breathe, when it is merely self-evident! Huh! I come from such a village. Perhaps some people can watch someone smearing dung on a floor and talk about the sophisticated reuse of materials, but I tell you, once they try concrete they never go back to dung. Live in natural harmony with the African wildlife, did they? Didn't kill all the game? They would have if they could. They didn't because they couldn't. Look what happens when you give them AK-47s! No more elephants."

First let me hand over to you little things,
   my lady.
Lady Rows, let me hand over little things.
Rows, I have left you the husband;
   break me in two, yes.
Rows, I have left you the cowries;
   break me in two, yes.
Rows, I have left you the children;
   break me in two, yes.
Rows, I have left you the slaves;
   break me in two, yes.
Rows, I have left you the cotton goods;
   break me in two, yes.
Rows, I have left you the fowls;
   break me in two, yes.
Rows, I have left you the guinea-fowls;
   break me in two, yes.
Rows, I have left you the baskets;
   break me in two, yes.
Rows, I have left you the fire;
   break me in two, yes.
Rows, I have left you everything;
   break me in two, yes.
Let me hand over all the rows.

Extract from a Lenje (Zambia) folktale,
Radin, African Folktales and Sculpture

"What did you say to the cab driver?" I asked when he'd wound down.

"Oh, I didn't argue," the professor said. "I just asked him where he lived. He lived in a slum in Harare. I asked him if he preferred the village. He said he did. But he can't make any money there. So that's what I told him. That's what the white men really brought to Africa. The idea of money. The rest is all frills."

THE HIGH HILLS OF
CHIMANIMANI

F*rom Great Zimbabwe the Swahili traders loaded their porters with packs of
gold and ivory and strode out for the coast, first across the dry savannah, and
then down the escarpment into the coastal plains. Sometimes they headed south
before turning east to reach the Sabi River, and so to the tropical coast well south of
Sofala. Sometimes they headed northeast, through Mutare and a crack in the escarpment, to reach the coast that way. And sometimes they headed due east, through the
high and perilous hills of Chimanimani, home of the Monomotapa vassals, the
Manica ... So I followed them there.*

The Manica people have lived in the high hills of Chimanimani since ... well, presumably for millennia, though no one knows for sure. There are stone fortifications here
as well, some of them hundreds of hectares in extent, sprawling across rock and cliff,
plunging into ravines, guarding the *bomas*, the camps or kraals where the cattle are kept.
Most of these ruins date from the times of the Monomotapa emperors, and they were
clearly grafted on to much older local cultures. None of them is anywhere near as grand
as Great Zimbabwe, but they each have a power of their own nevertheless.

I spent a few hours in a Manica village hunched into a small wooded defile between
the alarmingly electrified fences of the bwana on the plateau above and the jagged
peaks that guard the approaches to the fertile plains of Mozambique stretching away
to the east. Somewhere down there is—was—fabled Sofala, now faded into obscurity
and ruin. Sometimes, though these days not often, the waspish rattle of a helicopter
can still be heard, and sometimes a band of assassins of one political stripe or another
slips over the border for a little blood-letting. This is nothing new to the Manica.
Monomotapa's kings were but newcomers in this matter of killing; and, in any case,
the politicals were not that different from the leopards that also slipped into the *boma*
at night to kill what they would kill, a kid or a calf. Killing was usual, or at least everyday; uncertainty about violence was commonplace, and so was resignation to it.
Often, the killers were other Manica, at least during the Mozambique civil war that
had ended, sort of, in 1990. They spoke Portuguese, mostly, and came from the poorest country on the poorest continent in the world. They were kin, but still they killed.

I'd wanted to learn something about the Manica history, and had found an old
man, the eldest of the elders, who was quite content to offer up the clan's lineages
for my scrutiny. I didn't make notes, not there in the dark, with the smoky fire flickering and the uneasy restlessness of the cattle beyond the brush walls—and, in any
case, I could neither spell nor remember the names. They scrolled past my ear a generation at a time, the old man squinting at me to see if I was listening.

(Later, I began to wonder about that squint. My Ghanaian professor had told me that twenty generations was the maximum reliable measure. "If the elders tell you more than twenty, they're making them up. Ask for lineages, they give you lineages, as many as you ask for. You have no idea how many social anthropologists' careers are based on false information acquired in just this agreeable way.")

There were five or six other people around the fire, which had been set among stones in the corner of an old fortification, now largely ruined. One of the men was still dressed in that prim English private-school uniform that is a bwana's vision of how a "houseboy" should dress. He'd stood patiently behind my chair in the bwana's dining-room all evening, waiting for me to finish so he could clear away my plate in preparation for the next in the interminable succession of courses, and it was he who had led me down the hillside when the bwana and his wife had finally put away the brandy bottle and had taken themselves and their guns off to bed. We had slipped out of the house, disconnecting the alarms as we went, giving the supposedly ferocious dogs a biscuit.

I had found the servants outside after dinner, smoking and gossiping, and made my pitch to see the elders. They had looked at me speculatively for a long time before making up their minds. I don't know what finally persuaded them. Perhaps it was the mere fact that I was out there, with them. The "houseboy" himself had thawed only when I offered him ten South African rand to take me to the oldest person he knew. He took the money, but warned me: "Old men," he said, "have no influence any more. It's not as it was. The men with the guns no longer listen to the wise."

I hadn't really minded the bwana's shrewish wife, Annabel. She had lost her brother when one of the killing squads had come up during the Rhodesian war, the war of independence; they had burned his farm and impaled him on his farm gate. She had stayed and rebuilt, only to see the farm burned again. In the end, she married her neighbour, Maurice,

> When we got to the gate, I offered to jump out and open it.
>
> "No," the bwana said, "it's on automatic."
>
> And sure enough, the gate swung open, and the worker, employed for just that purpose, closed it behind us. Not once did either of them acknowledge the other's existence.
>
> "I've been in Africa too long to change now," the bwana said when I pointed this out to him.

and merged their farms, their arsenals, and their bitterness. She spent her days brooding about the blacks who wouldn't ever learn not to destroy what hadn't been theirs to build. She called them "Munts," which was a derogatory corruption of the singular word for Bantu, "Muntu." Paid the Munts as little as she could, fired them when they got too familiar. Had them everywhere in the house. You couldn't run a farm properly without boys, dozens of them; they're no good for anything except being told what to do. Out in the fields, dozens more, picking the pineapples and the coffee.

"Why do you stay?" I asked.

She was uncomprehending. It was an Outsider's question. This place was theirs. They had built it. Without them, this lush border territory produced no food. With them, they exported coffee and tea and pineapples, and sent figs and prickly pears to European markets. "Before," she said—meaning "before independence"—"this country had plenty of farmers like us, and we exported food. Now ..."

Her voice trailed off. The servants standing around the table made no sign that they'd heard any of this.

A Muntu is one person; Bantu are people. A Sotho is one member of the tribe; the Basotho are the collectivity. And so it is with the Lunda, the Kongo, and many other Bantu people: a Makongo belongs to the Bakongo tribe; the Lunda people are collectively known as the Balunda, and so on.

The farmhouse was long, low-slung, with wide verandas and extended views over the escarpment into Mozambique. Years ago it had been thatched, but that was too vulnerable to passing terrorist whim, and it was now covered in corrugated iron. At the same time the teak doors had been replaced with steel, and heavy shutters installed both inside and outside the windows. The walls were thick enough to withstand an artillery shell. Outside, there were lush gardens, but care was taken that the planting not obscure the sight-lines. There was bougainvillaea everywhere, trails of blood-red flowers draping over the trees. Inside, surprisingly, the motif was African. Despite their personal dislike of the "Munts," they had a good eye for African sculpture—this was no African kitsch of the sort sold at roadside stands and in curio shops all over East Africa. There were animal skins artlessly arranged everywhere—zebra, springbok, impala, a kudu, two lions. For the rest, the art was sensitive watercolours done by the shrew herself, heavy teak furniture, deep cushions, duvets—a wonderful house, but filled with memories of hate, dismay, anger and bitterness, as well as stubbornness and pride. This is what it meant to be a bwana in Africa now. The nostalgia was palpable, but sundowners and gin and tonics had been replaced by satellite uplinks and constant vigilance. I wondered how they would react if Mugabe made good on his threat to "resettle" the white farmers. They had already asked me the previous night to show them ("Just show me one!") a black farm of comparable productivity, and I had to confess, *sotto voce* (for *I* was certainly aware, if they weren't, of the watching "houseboys"), that I hadn't seen one. (I called the Ghanaian professor later to ask him if he had an explanation, but he hadn't anything much to say. "I suspect because African culture has no tradition of employees," he said, "only of subjects. And families have had no tradition of producing beyond their needs. The family, after all, is everything, because it represents the clan." "But what of the Zulus? Someone had to keep those huge armies fed." "Ah, the discipline of the tyrant!") Yes, they wouldn't go easily into the Mugabean night.

It had been more than a decade since the Rhodesian war ended with the inevitable defeat of Cecil Rhodes's inheritors. Only the Mozambican bandits were to be feared, now. That and the ghosts of their own past. And the watchfulness of their staff.

The path to the Manica village wound past the outbuildings, cut through a hidden gap in a brush fence, and made its way along the rocks at the edge of the escarpment before dropping into the dark. In the black night we picked our way downwards. I tried to impress the path into my mind. It was, after all, one of the routes the traders to and from the Zimbabwean Empire had used to carry their goods down to the coast. How much ivory and powdered gold had passed this spot over the centuries, down this twisty path to the valley floor? It was lush here, much lusher than the arid plains around the ruins. On the way from Masvingo to Chimanimani, the vegetation had changed abruptly. Baobab trees appear, and mopane trees and all manner of strange carrion plants. Brilliant disa orchids are everywhere, the msasa trees drip with epiphytic orchids, and in the Vumba Mountains the vegetation veers wildly from alpine to tropical rain forest in a few hundred vertical metres. Lush, yes: it's why the great estates of the coffee bwanas are at the eastern end of the Honde valley, hard by the Mozambique border.

Down in the *boma* the elder reached the end of his recitation of the generations. The others had not interrupted him, merely punctuating his performance with what sounded suspiciously like amens. I closed my eyes and listened to the chanting, the crackle of the fire, the stamping of the hooves, the tinkling of a one-stringed lyre, and I smelled cut grass, dung, mud, smoky fires, sweat, the rank but somehow comforting and eternal smells of Africa.

The old man then told me the history of the Manica, but since it consisted of improbable exploits by unknown kings, none of it stayed with me, except that it seemed to go on a very long time, for it had been a turbulent history and there had been many wars, and conquests, and defeats. The others, who had clearly heard it all before, never got bored, but kept repeating their approving chorus of amens until the old man finally fell asleep, sitting upright by the fire.

In the years after Great Zimbabwe declined, the wars had become smaller, if no less ferocious. Horizons, too, shrank. History turned to legend, and then legend turned to folk-tale, until it ended up ... here, in the fading memories of very old men, to whom the youths with guns wouldn't listen. I looked around me at the village, which was jammed into a small corner of a once-magnificent fortress, and at the old man, who was poor and emaciated, dressed in tattered rags, and chewed leather sandals, his teeth broken and his skin as desiccated as old parchment. There was a large boil on his cheek. What a fragile repository for a people's history!

I slept that night under the thatch, and dreamed of scorpions. I was taken back "upstairs" very early the next morning, and was in my room when the bwana called, imperiously, for his first morning coffee.

THE MAKUNI OF ZAMBIA

For a few days I stayed there with those endlessly hospitable but fossilized bwanas, frozen as they were in the great sweep of time, and tried to decide whether I should follow the porterage trails to the coast. In the end, I chose to see Sofala in its context as a Swahili town, and to wait until I could do the whole coast in one sweep, from Mogadishu in the north to Umzimvubu in the south. So instead, I went north-west to the Zambezi, where the Mutapa kings had fled during the Rozwi wars. Zambia was, in its way, one of the key corners of Africa. The headwaters of the Zambezi are there, and just over the border, in Zaire, the mighty Congo passes on its 4,000-kilometre (2,500-mile) descent to the sea. I found myself sitting under a mango tree in a Zambian village David Livingstone had visited more than once in his extensive travels.

A newly installed chief at Makuni, for that was the village's name, accepts his burden of chieftainship by swallowing a small stone, which lodges in his gut and becomes the embodiment of his people—the rock on which his people's future is founded, a living stone. Perhaps this is why Livingstone, who spent some time at Makuni hobnobbing with the chiefs and trying valiantly (as his own journals plainly show) not to be a cultural chauvinist, made sure there was always a final "e" on his name.

The current senior chief used to be the marketing manager for BP Zambia. He's educated, Catholic, and only reluctantly chief. He hadn't been expected to succeed to the chieftainship, but his elder brothers either died or disgraced themselves, and he had had to quit his job, forgo his salary, and give up his friends in the village—partisanship must be scrupulously avoided; friendlessness is a chief's lot. He wasn't given any choice in this matter of succession. His duty was a heavy burden, but it *was* his duty.

Because he is Catholic, he has only one wife (and, by 1997, only two children, both of them daughters). In this he wasn't regarded as doing his chiefly duty—it was incumbent on him to produce a son, preferably many sons. It was coming to a point where his council might be forced to intervene. These elders would probably instruct him to take another wife or two to better the odds that he had sons; ensuring the succession was his principal obligation. It was uncertain how he would react. Often, in Africa, when modernity clashes with tradition, modernity yields.

The village, which is within walking distance of the Zambezi, only a few kilometres above Victoria Falls, has been rooted to its spot, as far as anyone knows, since the eleventh century. There is little reason to suspect that life there has changed much over these long centuries. Invasions came and went, waves of immigrants poured through, traders and slavers and missionaries and mercenaries and politicians and tax men showed up at the chief's door; even the name of the tribe changed and mutated and changed again; but life went on. The tribe is called Tokaleya now, but tribal names are not as permanent as the white ethnographers and missionaries assumed; they are instead fluid and malleable, changing with current political fashion.

Then, as now, the houses were rondavels, round huts made of mopane or mahogany poles, which are resistant to white ants. The floors are of mud, either polished termite mound or mud polished with cattle dung. This makes a shiny surface that is as tough as concrete, easy to clean, and sheds the rain, when there is rain, which is rarely. Rafters are made of the same woods, resting on but not tied to the circular walls, so the roof can be lifted off easily. The roof is of buffalo-grass thatch tied with bark strips.

Most households, which consist of three or four huts of related families, are surrounded by a reed fence. Everything is neat and clean. There is no debris and no garbage. Hens wander about. Children are playing underfoot. Everyone is effortlessly good-natured. The village now has two boreholes and one donated solar plant, but it's still the women who fetch the water. The women also sweep, endlessly. They are always cooking, cleaning, scrubbing, cracking nuts, stamping grain. There are no men in the village during the day, except a few lounging in the shade under trees. There are wild mango trees everywhere. The most prominent was the giant mango in the middle of the square, under which I took shelter from the noonday sun.

I sat there in the shade, looking up at the dense foliage to the harsh sun beyond, and contemplated what the tree had seen.

Dr. David Livingstone had sat there, too, in the same spot, under the same branches, to meet with the chief of the day—the good doctor, being an unbeliever (i.e., a Christian), wasn't allowed into the chief's compound. Years later, when he died near Bangweulu, after slogging around in malarial swamps near Lake Mweru, it was two men from this village, long-time retainers of the eminent missionary, who carried his desiccated body all the way to the coast. The grandchildren of these men still live here, enjoying their celebrity. A few years ago Dr. Livingstone's grandsons came to visit, and a wonderful photo-op was had by all.

Makuni's chief is a "senior chief," which in this case means he wields influence over many villages, totalling close to a million people, and is therefore a formidable political force. The village itself, the chiefly seat, contains about seven thousand people, and is partitioned into subunits run by headmen, who rule a cluster of families. In the kinship structure, there are no uncles or aunts; everyone is a mother or a father.

This is a sensible adaptation in times of hardship—at least orphaned kids will have someone to raise them.

Sadly, it hasn't turned out so well in the modern era, for, as soon as a man gets a salary, he is expected to share it with whoever in the family needs it. The consequence has been wholesale tax cheating—why pay taxes on a salary you never see?

Traditional notions of status have also become confused. High status in traditional society was the ownership of a large herd of cattle; high status was conferred on those (men, mostly) who no longer had to work. Work was for boys and women, and, as soon as a man married, it became women's work to look after him. And now? The village is still a cashless society operating in a modern or cash economy, where status is conferred on those who work at high-paying jobs. A common solution to this clash of cultures, how to get high status without having to work, is graft.

The tsetse fly is called Africa's great conservationist, because it keeps vast tracts of Africa free for wild game. As soon as the fly is cleared from an area, as it was, for example, from below Kariba, men move in with their livestock, cut down the trees for firewood, and the ecology changes. Forest changes to savannah, elephant and giraffe die or move out, grazers and browsers increase, but eventually all wild animals diminish under pressure from man and his cattle.

The village's governing structure is admirably clear. Decisions are made by the chief. But a wise chief uses his council of elders as a sounding-board. The council, a virtually universal institution among Bantu cultures, is a powerful force for conservatism and a brake on tyranny, since membership is hereditary and councillors cannot be removed by the chief. In the past, councils and kings often argued, and kings often gave way, because consensus was regarded as a higher virtue than consistency. A king or chief who seriously displeased his council for an extended period would be deposed. A delegation would take him a draught of poison, which he would then be obliged to drink. The last time this happened, more than a century ago, the king was such a strong man that he survived the poison and had to be buried alive. Now, of course, a chief would simply be pensioned off.

Historically, the chief's power was also circumscribed by a variety of other institutions over which he had little direct power, such as guilds, secret societies, religious organizations, and age-grade groupings. Traditionally, these institutions guaranteed a freedom of movement, association, and speech no longer common in modern Africa. Some countries have attempted variants of the council of elders at a national level, but they are generally ineffective. They are appointed and can be removed at the pleasure of the prime minister or president, which undercuts their independence.

The chief's many duties include resolving disputes, adjudicating property cases, judging criminal trials (these days only involving minor crimes), invoking rituals, and making regulations; he is both mayor and magistrate. In times of severe drought, he officiates at rain-making ceremonies. (Part of the Makuni rain-making ritual is to spit beer on the heads of everyone in the village, something of a trial for the current chief, who doesn't drink.)

The countervailing source of power, usually but not always an ally of the chief's, is the person variously described as diviner, sorcerer, or witch-doctor, whose function is to help keep social order. This person's tasks also include traditional healing through herbal medicines, using a fecund pharmacopoeia derived from native fauna and flora to treat headaches, sleeplessness, fevers, and cancers, as well as casting or removing spells, either through incantation or the invocation of artefacts (fetishes), or both.

The villagers, like most Africans, believe that their lives are preordained and pre-determined, but that the forces that do this, the spirits and the gods, can be influenced through the proper intervention of magic and through the intercession of a sorcerer. My Ghanaian professor had already told me this.

This sorcerer is to some degree a physician who uses psychiatric tricks to accomplish his means. But he (or she) can also be used as an offensive weapon, and in the repertoire is an alarming number of heavy-duty "attack fetishes" whose function can variously be to give people noxious diseases, cause their crops to fail, or prompt their kin to reject them. An interesting small museum in Livingstone has a significant collection of such fetishes. Among them is one carved from a zebra shin, and covered with twigs and human hair, whose function is to cause road accidents (the petitioner placed it on the highway where the hated one was likely to pass, and it would cause his car to crash).

It is the sorcerer's job to cure those social ills attributable to human wickedness as well as to the intervention of the spirits. It is also his job to extract confessions in those recalcitrant cases where the plainly guilty are stubbornly keeping silent. These days confessions are extorted mostly through psychic bullying rather than torture, though practitioners seem to agree that torture was a preferred, and highly effective, method of gaining information, and generally seem to regret its passing.

It is important for village justice that the guilty confess. Justice is believed to be fully served only when the perpetrator confesses and recants, because only then will the cultural balance, the village harmony, and the natural order of things be properly restored. One benefit of this system is the absence of contingency fee–hungry litigation counsel—Africans think it atrocious that anyone would willingly defend a person known to be guilty. Another is the absence of prisons. In practice, the social dynamic can be resolved in a surprisingly large number of cases; when people believe strongly that the spirits, who are all-powerful, speak through the witch-doctor, they tend to tell the truth.

With the exception of the chiefs, who are expected to produce sons, most Makuni men prefer daughters. Fathers get paid for daughters by sons-in-law, and four daughters can make a man comfortably off, if not rich. The custom of *lobola*, or bride price, stabilizes marriage and is one more powerful force in African society that militates against change. It also imposes on young men a certain social responsibility: to accumulate enough cattle to acquire a wife demands diligence, persistence, thrift—all virtues that help the tribe survive.

Senior Chief Makuni, the living stone comfortably in his gut, is watching as changes continue. He was too young to fight in the wars of liberation, but he has seen the white population of Zambia shrink in its aftermath. He has watched the economy drain away. He has watched Kenneth Kaunda's antics as president and disgraced ex-president, and listened to the speeches of his successor. These concern him. But they are transitory matters, and a chief has to take the long view. The task of his stewardship is the health of the tribe. Eventually he will have to choose. For himself: tradition or modernity. For his people: tradition … or what? How best to encourage the entrepreneurial spirit, the fecund creativity that seems latent in every African society and that can be seen working its anarchic way out in every African market? How to suppress, on the other hand, the endemic jealousies of the successful, the superstition that paralyses decision making, the iron chains of tradition? Is tradition compatible with politics? Is tradition compatible with liberty, even the anarchic liberty of modern times? It is a choice all Africa is making, one way or another.

"Mosi-oa-tunya," "The Thundering Smoke," is the Makololo name for one of the greatest waterfalls on the planet, the Zambezi River's Victoria Falls, which plunges more than a hundred metres into a narrow gorge. The falls are 1.6 kilometres (1 mile) wide, and carry 1,150 cubic metres (4,000 cubic feet) of water per second to the gorges below. David Livingstone, who named it after his queen, was disappointed the falls were there: he had hoped the Zambezi would be navigable to its headwaters, opening up the interior to commerce and settlement.

Victoria Falls hasn't forgotten its colonial past. David Livingstone stands proudly at the entrance to Zimbabwe's Falls' park, pith helmet in place, gazing over the Smoke That Thunders. The plaque accompanying the statue still refers to Rhodesia and Nyasaland, and, even more oddly, to Livingstone's "discovery" of the falls. The rulers of ancient Monomotapa would have a grim laugh at that; they had vassal states up here for centuries.

Livingstone's presence is still much evident in the Zambezi region, and although it is now fashionable to denigrate the missionaries, who are, in the current view, almost wholly pernicious in their past actions (redeemed only by their toiling in the fields of medicine and agriculture), Livingstone largely escapes the calumny. In part, he is exempt because he got on famously with most of the people he met and insisted on treating tribal rituals as useful and decent social customs rather than as the unchristian barbarism his fellow missionaries saw them to be. He is also deemed special because of his single-minded, ferocious, unforgiving assault on the slaving system.

The missionary was not without his self-doubts, worrying that his own exploratory journeys were opening up new routes to the interior for the slave factors. At Lake Nyasa, his journal noted grimly, "We are in the centre of the slave market." One party of Arab slavers, with their yoked and chained captives, tried to sell him some young girls. "It is against this gigantic evil that my mission is directed," he wrote. His diary became a record of atrocities: "19th June, 1866. We passed a woman tied by the neck to a tree and dead, the people of the country explained that she had been unable to keep up with the other slaves in a gang ... We saw others tied up in a similar manner, and one lying in the path shot or stabbed, for she was in a pool of blood."[3]

> "The strangest disease I have seen in this country seems really to be broken-heartedness, and it attacks free men who have been captured and made slaves."
>
> *David Livingstone*

Livingstone made several epic journeys in the interior, the first westwards to Angola and thence to the Atlantic coast, the second down to the Indian Ocean, where shortcuts caused him to miss the Kebrabasa (Cabora Bassa) Rapids, a sheer-sided gorge 30 kilometres (19 miles) long and at one point as steep as thirty degrees off the vertical, an omission that skewed his overall impression of the river's navigability and caused a subsequent expedition by steamer from the river's mouth to be a flop.

Livingstone, who had become a huge celebrity in England, focused European attention on the area, and it wasn't long before missionaries and settlers began to arrive in the country in considerable numbers. Rhodes intruded from the south, and farmers moved into the north; the gospel, in the cliché of the day, gave way to guns, and God's kingdom to administrative districts; it was the familiar litany of colonization (and a reason for the missions' ambiguous reputation in modern Africa). Coffee was introduced, plantations were established, land was expropriated, a hut tax introduced, and traditional slash-and-burn agriculture discouraged. As a result, increasing numbers of Africans in both Zambia (Northern Rhodesia) and Malawi (Nyasaland) were severed from their traditional ways, became destitute, and were forced to seek work in Zimbabwe and South Africa. And so it went.

MONOMOTAPA'S HEIRS

F irst there was Rhodesia, then Rhodesia and Nyasaland, then Northern and
Southern Rhodesia and Nyasaland, then the Federation of Rhodesia and
Nyasaland. Mutapa Matope, King of the Karanga, would have recognized the
boundaries easily enough. Of course, Matope's boundaries would have been wider than
the British managed. He would have included modern Mozambique, but the
Portuguese beat the British to that, and the Transvaal, but the Boers had that (until
they fought their own war with the British colonizers), and also Tanzania, but the
Germans hadn't yet been winkled out, and Queen Victoria, in any case, had relatives
involved, something else Matope would have been comfortable with—rank has its
privileges, after all.

The colonial-era history of Zimbabwe is, by comparison with the grandeur that went
before, rather lacklustre; but there are nevertheless marvellous characters in play—
Shaka of the Zulus, tyrant and military genius, a long way to the south; Mzilikazi,
henchman turned conqueror, who cut a swath through the placid inheritors of the
Rozwi; Cecil John Rhodes, with his overweening ambition for empire; Lobengula,
the philosopher king, whose fate was to trust too much to the invader; Ian Smith,
the rebel farmer, who against all the odds turned late in his life into a Beloved
Character, admired even by the former guerrillas whose soldiers he had so diligently
killed; and Mugabe, the bureaucrat, megalomaniac manqué (you could virtually see
the man suppressing the flood of self-adulation that threatened to rise in him every
few years like bile from a dyspeptic stomach).

Shaka became King of the Zulus in 1816. We will look at his history and character more closely in Part III. Here, it is enough to say that within a few years he controlled the territory from Delagoa Bay (now Maputo) in the north to Pondoland
(now part of the Transkei) in the south. His highly centralized military kingdom profoundly shook the continent as far away as Lakes Victoria Nyanza and Nyasa, in the
north and northeast, to Barotseland, in the northwest. The devastation he caused is
known in the collective psyche as the *Mfecane*, which is usually translated as "The
Crushing." The word reverberates in black memories the same way the word
"pogrom" does to Jewish ears, and the tribes to the north recall his predations the
way the Russians preserve the ghastly memories of the Golden Hordes.

Mzilikazi had been one of Shaka's most trusted lieutenants. When, after a major
campaign, he refused to hand over looted cattle, he was forced to leave Zululand with
three hundred followers. Over the next fifteen years or so, he moved westward, across
the Transvaal in flight from the Zulu armies, until, in 1837, after a triple conflict with
the Zulu, with Griqua raiders from the Orange River, and with the expansionist white

farmers from the Cape, he led his following, which had by now grown to upwards of twenty thousand, across the Limpopo, where they soon became dominant, calling themselves the Ndebele, or Matabele. A caste-like society evolved, with the Matabele at the top, the Sotho in the middle, and the unfortunate Shona at the bottom.

Mzilikazi set up his capital near present-day Bulawayo and was succeeded in 1870 by his son Lobengula. Meanwhile, European gold-seekers and ivory-hunters from the Cape were moving into Shona and Ndebele territory. The best-known of these was, of course, Cecil John Rhodes, who was pursuing his notion of a "corridor of British civilization" stretching along a Rhodes-built railway line from the Cape to Cairo.[4] Lobengula received the whites courteously, trusting that they would do no more than they promised, which was to look for gold and then disappear, and he amiably signed treaties with whoever would ask politely. He wasn't the first, nor has he been the last, to regret giving his word to the Europeans.

In 1890 Rhodes sent in the "Pioneer Column," an invading force of some five hundred heavily armed settlers, into Matabeleland. His excuse was the charter he had received for his British South Africa (BSA) Company from the British Crown. Finding only small amounts of gold in the north, the colonists contented themselves with taking all the best farmland.

Which is where matters rested until growing African militancy led first to the creation of the Zimbabwe African Peoples' Union (ZAPU) under Joshua Nkomo and the Zimbabwe African National Union (ZANU) under Ndabaningi Sithole, and then to Ian Smith's futile UDI, or Unilateral Declaration of Independence, and then to the war of liberation, which finally led to independence in 1980, after a decade and a half of fighting.

During that war, Robert Mugabe, who is Shona, operated out of Mozambique, and Joshua Nkomo, who is Ndebele, from Zambia. The Shona are in the majority in Zimbabwe, and still preserve Mzilikazi's invasions in folk memory. They won the first election, and Mugabe became president. Defying Western predictions that tribalism would never be overcome, Mugabe brought Nkomo into a coalition government, though not before there had been considerable persecution of the Matabele minority, and not until there had been riots and revolts, brutally suppressed.

> "Your Majesty, what I want to know from you is if people can be bought at any price... Your Majesty, what I want to know is why do your people kill me? Do you kill me for following my stolen cattle?... I have called all white men living at or near Bulawayo to hear my words, showing clearly that I am not hiding anything from them when writing to your Majesty."
>
> King Lobengula, Letter to Queen Victoria, quoted in Rhodes, by Sarah Gertrude Millin

The 1980s were characterized by scandal and corruption as Mugabe's ministers began accumulating their fortunes.[5] In the 1990 elections the opposition ZUM, or Zimbabwe Unity Movement, did well; soon after, one of its leaders was nearly killed in an assassination attempt, driving the rest into hiding. Mugabe was still threatening to "resettle" the white farmers by the year 2000. His dream of a one-party Marxist state remained, improbably, alive.

Late in the decade, everyone still watched his ebb and flow of paranoia. If it swamped him, Zimbabwe could so easily re-enter an era of instability. No one wanted another Mzilikazi.

This fragile peace was still holding as the millennium neared.

Zambia was, by the late nineties, pretty much of a mess.

As a country, it never made sense. It was created by Cecil Rhodes's British South Africa Company as a source of cheap labour for the mines in Johannesburg and Rhodesia, and its borders correspond even less to historic or tribal realities than those of most other ex-colonies. As a result, factionalism and tribal squabbling are a constant problem, exacerbated by politicians for their own ends.

It was only in the 1920s that Europeans detected anything worth having except labour in what was then Northern Rhodesia, with the discovery of vast copper deposits in the northwestern frontier district. The resulting accounting makes dismal reading: Rhodes extracted some $160 million (U.S.) in royalties from "ownership" of the country; the British treasury collected some $90 million in taxes and reinvested about $10 million of it; a further $200 million was extracted and reinvested in Southern Rhodesia, now Zimbabwe. The copper mines are still operating, but are run down and barely ticking over.

When Kenneth Kaunda, Zambia's president from independence in 1964 to 1991, took over, he had very little to work with. Not that his own actions helped much: his solution to "combating regionalism" was to set up a one-party state and become both its president and head of its armed forces; and, because of his commitment to liberation movements, he unstintingly supported at great cost a bewildering alphabet of freedom fighters—FRELIMO of Mozambique, SWAPO of Namibia, the ANC and PAC of South Africa, and both wings of the Zimbabwe liberation movement, ZAPU and ZANU.

It wasn't until 1980 that Kaunda was able to take his country off its war footing. But by that time he had consolidated his own position; and the country was accustomed to being run through sacrifice, fear of armed intervention, saboteurs, and spies. The economy was in ruins, there were shortages of food, foreign reserves were exhausted, and Zambia had a reputation among aid-donor countries as a national scofflaw.

Following violent street protests against food-price increases in 1990, there was a general demand for multiparty politics and a new election. Kaunda attempted to head it off with a snap referendum late in the year, but was forced to cancel it, amend the constitution, and schedule elections for October 1991. In those elections, he was resoundingly defeated and replaced by Frederick Chiluba, a former trade-unionist.[6]

Kaunda disappeared into a more or less indignant political oblivion. He was sharply critical of his successor, and in 1997 was still hoping to unseat him come the next election. Chiluba, for his part, wearied of the sniping from the sidelines and unveiled for the press a network of secret underground tunnels and bunkers below the presidential palace that he said had been built by Kaunda for the imprisonment and torture of his political opponents. Kaunda denied this, of course—the bunkers were there for the use of the liberation movements he had been supporting, he said. But it was hard to see how windowless cells with barred doors could really be dormitories for freedom fighters; and Chiluba subsequently produced other grisly evidence that seemed to support his contention.

I had already asked my Ghanaian professor why this pattern, this horrid progression from liberator though leader to tyrant and megalomaniac, was so common in Africa. So tempting, it seemed! *L'état, c'est moi!* Like most African intellectuals, he, too, was furious at it, regarding it as a betrayal of Africa by its own. "It's far too late in the game to blame colonialism," he said. "Have you noticed how often tyrants denigrate democracy because it's 'not African'? But nor is tyranny! There were checks and balances in traditional societies which these monsters have abolished."

"But it's true, isn't it, that the white colonialists made no attempt to prepare their colonies for independence?" I mentioned some of the dismal statistics, the looting of Mozambique and Angola, the economic rape of Zambia, the French reprisals against independence movements all through central Africa.

"True, all true! But there are countries that have made it work. It all depends on leadership. With honest leaders and determined effort, they would have been out of it by now." He referred me to a book by George Ayittey called *Africa Betrayed*, which deals with the subject of black African tyranny and corruption in chilling and depressing detail. The book, when I found it in South Africa—it's not available in most of the rest of Africa—carried an excellent foreword by Makaziwe Mandela, who said, "Blacks in independent Africa deserve not only liberation from the naked oppression of colonial and imperial powers, but from the brutal and harsh domination and control of their own black leaders." Jerry Rawlings, Ghana's president, has cited the same book, comfortable in the knowledge that, although he was hardly universally beloved at home, he at least had kept his country more or less free of the scourge of corruption.

There's little doubt that Kaunda helped to wreck his country's economy beyond what the colonialists did to it. Kaunda shamelessly milked the foreign-aid system, and largely because of the ineptitude, naïvety, and moral corruptibility of the aid industry, most of the money went to fatten his personal and political resources. He ruined his country's morale, too, so that violence, robbery, theft, and cynicism became rampant, along with a depressing sense of apathy.

The result is a dispirited country. Every city and every village has its "marauders," bands of looters, young men who will steal anything they can, often violently if they can get away with it. They also have their official counterparts. Whenever the police feel the need for some pin money (perhaps their salaries have been "withheld" yet again), they set up a roadblock and extract what they can. A tourist was recently fined the equivalent in kwachas of $50 (U.S.) for taking a picture of the country's most famous tourist attraction, Victoria Falls, on the grounds that the Zambezi River is the national boundary with Zimbabwe and frontiers are by definition military matters and everyone knows you are not allowed to take photographs of military installations. The tourist, an old Africa hand, paid up and went on her way.

By late in the nineties, all of Zambia looked run down, shabby. The Rainbow Falls Hotel, a state-owned establishment on the lip of the falls in a wonderful location, was operating at 10 per cent capacity; the service was surly, and the food awful. A foreign hotelier tried to buy the place. In the end, he threw up his hands in disgust. Three ministries controlled the site—Tourism, National Heritage, and Environment—and all three wanted millions of under-the-table kwachas for their approval. As a result, the hotel stood virtually empty. A tree fell on its phone line four weeks before I got there, and the line was still lying in the road. No one could be found to fix it, and the hotel staff hadn't even moved the tree—visitors had to drive around it. No one cared. In Livingstone, trash collection ceased years ago. In 1997, the streets remained unrepaired. The gardens—the city was famous for its gardens once—were gone. A local tour operator (who will fetch clients at the Zimbabwe border, some 10 kilometres [6 miles] away) was accused of "stealing" tourists from other operators, who preferred to sit in their offices waiting for customers. He "doesn't leave any business for us." They wanted to shut him down.

Malawi (Nyasaland) is an even less probable country than Zambia. Little more than a wide shoreline on Lake Malawi, with an extension that nearly cuts western Mozambique in half, the place had been on the periphery of the Monomotapan influence, and though it's possible the ferocious Zimbas originated here, the place was for centuries a relatively peaceful island in a less-than-peaceful ethnic sea. At least until the Ngoni, an aggressive though second-hand consequence of the Zulu rampages, got there early last century. Whites followed soon afterwards, suppressed the Ngoni and the native Yao, introduced coffee, and declared a protectorate to keep the planters from harm. All in all, a familiar-enough pattern, and one with little overt incident until Dr. Hastings Kamuzu Banda returned from forty years abroad to lead the independence movement in the 1950s. Independence duly followed in 1964; Banda suppressed his opposition, muzzled the press, and had himself declared president for life. The only curiosity in all this was his unstinting support of the apartheid regime in South Africa, a stance that earned him universal condemnation in Africa but blessed him with a flow of aid and money from the south, which he used to keep his people quiescent.

He usually travelled the country in a Rolls-Royce, and police cleared the roads half an hour before he went anywhere. The newspapers called him Messiah. He encouraged schoolchildren to sing him praise-poems and issued bizarre decrees: bell-bottomed trousers on men were forbidden. Banda was estimated at the start of the nineties to own personally about 30 per cent of the economic assets of his country. Nevertheless, his country had a balanced budget.

Still, as the Malawians, always a cheerful lot despite Banda's restrictive regime, used to say in the bars, even bad things don't last forever. The old man was well into his nineties when he was forced into an election, which he handily lost, just as Kaunda had lost his across the border in Zambia. A year later he was under house arrest, facing four charges of murder—four of his cabinet ministers, thought at the time to have died in an auto accident, were discovered to have been murdered by Banda's security forces at the "order of the authorities." The victor in the 1994 elections, Bakili Muluzi, came to power on a platform of less Banda but otherwise more of the same. Rapprochement followed with Mozambique, Zambia, and Zimbabwe; relations with South Africa, which had soured as that country went through its own re-examination, improved; and the economy began to show signs that it was coming out of its long coma.

Nevertheless, Malawi remains one of Africa's least developed countries. An expat who was trying to set up a business exporting dried mangoes and other fruits was for a while paying her workers in haemorrhoid cream and other nostrums, for the capital's hospital only had aspirins, and there were no drugstores.

And AIDS was still spreading, malignant and relentless.

"THIS DEADLY THING"

Just outside the crumbling Zambian city of Livingstone there is a truck stop. The signs say *Zambezi Rest Stop, Café, Good Food to Eat*. The forecourt is dirty and pitted, stained with oil. The café itself is crumbling concrete brick, tropical weeds spilling from the eaves. There are about thirty huge trucks parked haphazardly in the lot, some of them with motors still rumbling; others, with air-conditioning that should be rumbling, are quiet. Outside, the usual impromptu market, a few piles of tomatoes, bags of oranges, and stacks of Made-in-Kenya candies for sale. Knots of men stand around, shouting at each other, mostly in Swahili, the lingua franca of the Trans-Africa Highway. This is what Cecil Rhodes's great megalomaniacal dream of British Red from Cape to Cairo has come to: a thin ribbon of sometimes macadamized roadway peopled by the gypsies of our century, long-distance truckers. This is the only way to get by road from one end of Africa to another, from Cape Town to Cairo (almost—the road is still interrupted in Sudan, and in any case most of the trucks go no farther than Nairobi).

This is the AIDS Highway, the vector for Africa's latest deadly disease.

The Zambesi Rest Stop Café is next to the Zambian Customs extortion shed, where functionaries delay trucks, sometimes for days, while they search for something useful to steal. The truckers, of course, are well aware of this, but pay it little attention. Everyone understands that a little goes here and there for squeeze, for "duties" duly stamped and restamped. And they're in no hurry. Another day makes no difference. They spend some time in Livingstone's bars and cheap hotels, and with Livingstone's profusion of AIDS-ridden prostitutes.

I wandered into the café. The place was jammed. I had to shove my way past cursing, rank-smelling humanity to the bar, which consisted of planks across two crates and cardboard boxes of booze. At least a fifth of the crowd seemed to be hookers, with more milling around outside. Most of them were as unwashed as the truckers, and many looked ill. I pushed and shoved, and was pushed and shoved back, all good-naturedly, and yelled a few pleasantries and got a few back. It was impossible to have a conversation. Not that I needed to know much. The medical staffs of half a dozen countries and as many anxious aid agencies had all the information anyone required. I merely wanted to see for myself what the AIDS vector looked like.

AIDS began (or so at least one genesis myth has it) somewhere in Africa. It doesn't really matter how it got out of Africa (*ex Africa semper aliquid novi*, after all), or even if it did. What matters is the grim reality. In Africa, AIDS is a heterosexual disease, spread through prostitution and distributed throughout the continent ... right here, at the Zambesi Rest Stop Café. And other places along the highway.

In the towns and villages across Kenya, Tanzania, Uganda, Malawi, Zambia, Zimbabwe, and South Africa, the virus inexorably spreads. The disease made its way south to the Limpopo along this highway, spilling down into South Africa and into the teeming townships of Africa's most muscular city, Johannesburg. And this same highway is how it is making its way north, to the Muslim countries.

Thousands are dying in the villages, where AIDS is called "slims disease"—because that's what it does, emaciates. If you believe the most apocalyptic stories, a whole generation of young children are born infected, their parents dead or dying; travellers report villages in the countryside where no adults are left alive, the children running in starving packs. "This is a deadly thing," a public health nurse told me in Tanzania, pushing a sheet of mortality statistics towards me. "The deadliest thing, Africa's bane." How is it to be stopped? No one in Africa has the resources. Africa has so very many deadly scourges.

Late in 1996 there was an optimistic announcement: the incidence of new cases in Uganda, one of the worst hit, was dropping. But then the statisticians got busy, and the optimism faded: the drop was attributed to the fact that most people who could get the disease already had it.

AIDS is also spreading down the secondary trucking routes to Dar es Salaam and Mombasa, and thence along the coast. Mombasa is the port of entry for goods for Uganda, Rwanda, Burundi, and eastern Zaire. In Busia, on the Kenya–Uganda border, every trucker and hooker tested in a random survey was HIV-positive. Sixty per cent of the town was infected. By 1991, seven million people in Africa were infected, a third of them with full-blown AIDS. Throughout Kenya, in rural areas, one in eighteen is infected. In cities, the figure rises to one in nine. In some areas, Kenya's own statistics suggest that up to a third of adults are HIV-positive.

After I left Livingstone, I checked in with the truckers wherever my route intersected the highway—Mbeya, Morogoro, Dodoma, Arusha, Nairobi. The routiers, it seemed, had two conflicting views of AIDS, when they had a view at all. It either does not really exist—people die of all kinds of things in Africa—or, alternatively, it is a way foreigners have of putting another one over on Africans. Curiously, the villains of choice here seem to be the French, who are widely thought to have started it all.

None of the truckers seems to believe that you can be killed by doing what comes so naturally, so the prospects for prophylaxis are dim. There is no sex education to speak of. Indeed, in the villages there is hardly any medicine at all, only the occasional visiting immunization clinic. Making more children is a god-given right, and so are other women when one's wife is not available. As so often in Africa, the burden of change must fall on the women.

For too long, African governments denied the problem, sensitive to the implied Outsider slur of sexual promiscuity. I did visit one AIDS prevention clinic, in the village of Mto wa Mbu, in Tanzania's Rift Valley, run by foreign workers. They acknowledged the hopelessness of their task. AIDS posters and pamphlets miss the point, as do the now-endless conferences on AIDS. Everyone knows what to do— spend more money on education, more money on medical care, more money on everything. But where is that money to come from?

THE LUBA-LUNDA AND THE ZAIRIAN POGROMS

Some time later I passed a few days in the region I came to think of, in defiance of ethnic and geographic logic, as the heartland of Africa, the area of northwestern Zambia near the Zairian border that is neither tropical forest nor savannah, neither mountain nor plain, but that *is* the Great Divide: north and westward from here are the headwaters of the Congo, southeastward those of the Zambezi.

I was there at a time of great turmoil: Zaire seemed to be coming apart, both Rwanda and Burundi threatening once again to descend into ethnic slaughter, Uganda peering anxiously in from the north, Zambia and Tanzania bracing them-selves for another flood of refugees … It almost doesn't matter which crisis this was—there are so many, and they are so familiar.

I had flown in a little six-seater from Lusaka to Ndola, where I was met and bil-leted with an old Afrikaner, who put me up for nothing in exchange for practising his language, which he hadn't used for nearly thirty years. Ndola was the heart of the old Copperbelt, but since the price of copper plunged in the world recession of '83 the industry had been in a bad way. Now, the region was swelling with people, refugees from a dozen conflicts, so many that the border guards can't keep track. There were Zairian refugees streaming into Zambia, Burundi and Rwandan refugees streaming into Zaire, Tutsi refugees from the camps, Hutu refugees from the Tutsi.

In the morning two of the old Afrikaner's friends came for me at six in a battered jeep, open and reeking of fuel oil. The couple (I'll call them Hendrik and Anna) had been living in Zambia since they were children. I had told them the night before that I was less interested in current politics than I was in the Luba and Luba-Lunda story, a much older African story of conflict and conquest: the Luba-Lunda are one of the great expansionist tribes of African history. (We will meet them in Part IV.)

"You can't not be interested in politics around here," Hendrik said humourlessly, "or it will creep up and sandbag you. Besides," he added, "it is the Luba who *are* the politics around here."

What did he mean?

"You'll see," he said, and fell silent.

We drove past Chingola towards the Zaire border. There was a steady stream of people coming the other way. A Zambian soldier waved us over to the side. He was excited. Rumours were swirling about. Zaire was soon to shut the border again. Or, alternatively, it was going to open the border completely, and a flood of refugees would pour into Zambia. Among them would be Zairian soldiers bent on looting and take-over. They must be resisted. The soldier was shouting and waving his machine-pistol, and making me very nervous, though neither of the other two seemed to notice. He needed to requisition our car, he said. We argued. He became even more excited and pointed his gun at Anna's heart. Hendrik immediately became the soul of reasonableness, and offered to give the soldier a lift to the border. He stared at me, and then poked his gun into my pack, as though to frighten it into confessing something. He pulled back and fired a burst into the air, causing the refugees to dive for cover, and clambered in.

"What the hell is going on?" Hendrik demanded, as soon as the gun was safely stowed.

"Zaire is invading," he said; "in the north, in Uganda, they are already on the move. Here, we are told units are massing . . ."

"Why close the border then?"

"Who knows why they do what they do," the solder said, shrugging.

I asked him whether he'd ever been to Zaire.

"Once," he said, "a terrible place. Roadblocks everywhere, stealing everything. If you have a car, they just take it. If you are unlucky, they kill you, too. And if the soldiers let you go, the bandits will get you. They like to use their pangas. Even if you have nothing, they use their pangas."

"Three years ago," Hendrik said, "Mobutu started a pogrom against the Luba here."

"Why?" I asked.

He shrugged. Who knew why? The province of Shaba was restless. And the Luba were scapegoats. "Luba were killed, their property confiscated. The rest of the population was told it was their fault, they had been exploited for so long . . ." He shrugged again. "Why the Luba? They were in the way. They were pushed into Zambia then, which couldn't afford them. Most were shipped back, where they were killed."

"Not our fault," the solder said. "We didn't shoot them."

"No one paid any attention," Hendrik said. "The world was too busy with the Hutus."

"If there's a war here, who started it?" I asked.

"Not us," said the soldier.

Hendrik looked at me, as though it were a naïve question. "For what cause? To see who'll be in charge."

Mobutu may have started it, but now the war was being carried the other way— Zairian rebels were after his head.

The jeep ground on. The landscape was rolling, rocky, and looked exhausted, as though too many people had been using too few resources. There was red dust everywhere. We stopped near the border to let the soldier out. He disappeared into the throng. We sat on the banks of a ditch for a while, watching the human stream pass by. The vegetation behind us was scrawny. A chameleon eyed me beadily. At the bottom of the ditch, in a mud puddle, a hundred golden butterflies danced. Earlier, a mongoose had scurried by, unafraid.

Another stream of refugees went by, this one heading for the Zaire border instead of away. There must have been five thousand of them, herded by Zambian soldiers with machine-guns. They were Burundians, someone said, who had taken refuge in Zambia from Zaire and were being deported. No one knew whether Zaire would take them. But what was Zambia to do? Couldn't just send them back to Burundi ...

Every now and then a machine-gun chattered, just to keep the line moving. As far as I could see, none was aimed at anything but air, but the atmosphere was tense. We could hear the sound of heavier guns from the Zairian side, but had no idea what that meant.

Then, from the direction of the border post, a convoy of trucks pulled over a rise, grinding their gears, scattering the refugees going in the other direction. These trucks, too, were filled with refugees, but no one seemed to know who they were. They had been the last to pass the frontier before the border was abruptly shut, their Zairian escorts abruptly withdrawing and vanishing into the distance. So the border was closed—what were these Burundians to do when they got to the border? How were they to get across? What was the army going to do, shoot them all? The convoy seemed to have no end, nor did the convoy going the other way—the gates may have been closed, but the desperate Luba kept pouring out.

I pressed Hendrik for what else he knew about these Luba. It wasn't much, only that a collection of tribes calling themselves Luba—among them the Kazemba, "but no one uses that name any more"—had historically been running most of the commerce in Shaba province, along with the justice system, such as it was, and the police. Much, of course, to the resentment of the other inhabitants. Zaire's president, Mobutu, for reasons of his own, or maybe just because he didn't want any group to hold too much provincial power, had fomented a rebellion against them and, when the province seemed to be slipping away from him, unleashed a kind of bush-league genocide. No one noticed in the outside world. Zaire had too many other problems.

"What will happen?" I asked Hendrik. Anna answered obliquely: "Why shouldn't Shaba become an independent country, thirty years after Moise Tshombe?" Tshombe, I remembered, had been the Shaban (Katangan, then) leader who had declared his province's independence from the Congo. This had led to a civil war, the killing of the secretary general of the United Nations, and the murder of Congo's leader, Patrice Lumumba—now memorialised, sadly, in a second-rate Moscow university as a Marxist hero, a sad fate for a man who had tried to hold his improbable country together.

THE CROCODILE MAN

Meanwhile, in the remote villages and townships, life goes on as it always has, connected to the landscape and the fauna and the spirits and the ancestors in ways that the Kings of Monomotapa would surely have recognized.

One day in Ndola I read (in a borrowed week-old copy of the Harare *Herald*) about the man who rescues goats from the crocodiles. It seemed that villagers were always losing livestock (and occasionally themselves) to the voracious crocs, and this person set himself up as a rescuer. I had spent some hours not long before nervously contemplating the crocodiles sunning themselves on the banks of the Zambezi, and couldn't imagine anyone voluntarily slipping into the water alongside them. Didn't they kill their prey by drowning? Dragging them down to some slimy underground cavern? I resolved to talk to the hero.

The long drought in Zimbabwe had caused the Musangezi River in the Muzarabani district to stop flowing, leaving only a few perennial pools in which the villagers watered their cattle and did their washing. It was to these pools that the crocodiles had retreated. There were more than a hundred crocodiles, all competing for limited amounts of food. They were hungry, and the villagers, despite trying to fence off parts of the pools for themselves, had lost dozens of cows and hundreds of goats. Recently a young girl had been attacked and killed while she was washing dishes. Enter Ruwizhu Rufira, the only one who dared to venture into the water, and certainly the only one who consistently came back.

Every week, the *Herald* story said, Rufira was asked to try to help retrieve someone's goat—and, indeed, the picture accompanying the story was of Rufira and a man described as one of his trainees, Cephos Chipanco, emerging from the water with a rescued, if very dead, goat.

I arranged, through a complicated series of intermediaries and a good deal of patient negotiation, to talk to Rufira on the telephone nearest to him, which was about a kilometre away from the pool where he was working. He cheerfully walked there to take my call.

"What do the crocs do when you appear in their homes and start taking their food?" I asked. "Just watch?"

"I've got about eighty goats back so far," he said. "Never once had a problem."

"But how?" I asked.

"The villagers are still amazed at how I do it," he said.

"I bet! How do you do it, then?"

"My father in Mozambique taught me how to use traditional herbs to scare them away."

"But how? Do you eat these herbs? Smear them on your skin? What herbs, exactly?"

He affected not to hear, which was his polite way of refusing to answer. Why should he? Does Kentucky Fried Chicken give away the eleven secret herbs and spices? It was a trade secret.

"I've been doing this since I was a boy and have never been attacked," he said.

"Yes," I said again, "but how? What actually happens when a crocodile sees you?"

He wouldn't say, except to give the same answer he had already given the *Herald*, word for word, as though he had memorized it, as he probably had. "When they see me they become powerless," he said. "They just shiver all over, and swim away. I frighten them."

In the past, he confided, he'd made a living from incompetent hunters. How so? They would shoot the crocs but only wound them, and they'd swim away to die. "I fetched them up."

I was told by the interpreter later that these crocodiles had been allocated to the village under the Campfire Program, which sought to get villagers to protect their wildlife by beginning to understand what their potential was, in economic terms. In other words, the crocs "belong" to the village, which can then sell hunting rights to foreigners for hard currency. Campfire is an attempt to involve the villagers and rural people in conservation, and is much copied elsewhere in Africa.

It works straightforwardly, appealing to the villagers' acquisitive instincts instead of attempting to get them to buy into a theory of conservation that has small appeal and no relationship to their daily lives.

A farming village is in, say, elephant country. One day an elephant destroys a few hectares of maize field. First thing the villagers try to do, obviously, is to kill the beast. However, since they now "own" it, they can instead sell the rights to "cull" it to a rich American or German hunter at maybe $10,000 for a young bull, or $15,000 for a trophy bull. This way, they understand that the elephant is money in the bank—they could cultivate maize and sorghum all their lives and never make that kind of money. The villagers now understand that they should keep a few elephants around as a kind of savings account. The crops that get destroyed by the live elephants are, in this calculation, a version of banking charges that the villagers pay to nature.

This argument about conservation is constant in Africa. Many "green" tourists are horrified at the notion that southern African nations are going to have to shoot up to fifteen thousand elephants because of overpopulation—the elephants have been breeding almost as fast as the humans. But what else is there to do? No one has the money to take fifteen thousand multi-ton beasts elsewhere, and, even if they did, where would they go? Either to places where there is no poaching, where there are generally already too many, or to places where there is poaching, in which case they will be shot anyway.

Rufira waited patiently for more questions, but I had run out my string. I thought of asking him if he could teach me the trick, but resisted. What for? There was no way I would believe strongly enough in his prophylaxis. No croc would ever "shiver all over" because of me.

"Thank you," I said. "Good hunting."

We hung up the phones with mutual protestations of goodwill.

AMONG THE LIONS

A few days later I was out before dawn in a jeep with Clever Ndhlovo, a Ndebele. We had been skirting the banks of the Zambezi, looking for whatever we could find. As the sun came up, the game trail took a sharp turn inland to avoid a rocky out-cropping. Clever killed the motor. In the centre of the road ahead of us was a gigantic pile of elephant dung, still steaming.

I wished he would start the motor again, but he got out, prodded the dung with his toe. In the centre of the pile were two shiny nuts, undigested. He polished them on the grass and put them in his pocket. "Wooden ivory," he said. "Wonderful stuff. Easy to carve, yet very hard. Polishes to a glow. Elephants use them to aid digestion. I give them to the carvers."

Before we stopped we'd been talking about lions. Clever will kill his own lion one of these days. His father did, and has been teaching Clever the techniques.

Clever is no country peasant. He's a Fiat-driving, educated, sophisticated safari employee who was born in the national game park at Hwange in Zimbabwe. He had already killed his share of animals in the course of his professional life and had shown hundreds of hunters where the "game" is, so they could kill it, too. He is also a "green" in the sense that he understands balance and has a reverence for wild things that is as natural as breathing.

Still, he wants to kill his lion. It is a mark of manhood, a necessary rite, a challenge every man must pass. Or so the anthropology books say. Clever wanted to do it because his father had. And he knows he may be the last generation to be able to do so. Too many people, too few lions.

I spent some time with Clever in the bush. He showed me hippos, with their weary, cynical, mascaraed eyes; rhinos; ladylike giraffes with their luxurious lashes; ill-tempered baboons; vervet monkeys; wattle-nosed warthogs; crocodiles; bushbuck and waterbuck. A young male elephant appeared one morning from a thicket no more than twenty paces away, wary and hostile, ears flapping. He made a short charge in our direction. "Don't worry until he pins his ears back," Clever said, but just in case he kept the vehicle in gear with the motor running. "The first time I ever took guests out I was attacked by an elephant," he said. "Place where I couldn't turn around. Banged my hand on the side of the jeep and he backed off." If he hadn't? He just shrugged. The beast had retreated, after all. What use are "what ifs"?

A lion coughed and grumbled outside my tent a little after one midnight. It might have been a thousand paces away, but it sounded only an arm's length. Later it made a kill near the lodge kitchen, a young waterbuck, no more than 150 paces from where I was suddenly no longer sleeping. There was a ferocious roaring and the shrill squealing of the terrified victim. I gloomily contemplated the zipped mosquito net that separated me from the lion, and sat upright for the rest of the night. I heard nothing more except the angry barking of the baboons in the trees, alarmed at the racket the lion had made.

Do the predators come this close to safari camps? The operators are evasive. The night watchman at a Zimbabwe lodge once tugged at the garden hose and felt something tugging back. He tugged again, and again it was tugged back. He went to see and found a young male lion growling and pawing at the other end. He tiptoed away and spent the rest of his watch in the women's washroom, the only building in the place with a solid door, after which he was promoted to waiter, his nerves being shot.

> "Any person throwing litter into the crocodile pens will be asked to retrieve it"—sign at Victoria Falls crocodile farm

Another night two young elephants drank deeply from the swimming pool; fortunately it was unchlorinated.

Although the daily reality for Africans is increasingly urban, much of the African landscape is, well, wild. A leopard leaps through an open window to kill a sleeping tabby. Another does the same to take a dog, whose skull is later found nearby. I get up in the morning and an Egyptian banded cobra slithers into the rocks six paces from my tent. An elephant, annoyed by flapping laundry, demolishes a campsite and pushes over a large tree, causing the campers to flee into the bush in their skivvies. A hippo charges the camp manager, and she is last seen heading at top knots for high ground. There is a scorpion the size of a fist hiding under a rock. A spitting cobra can blind at 3 metres (10 feet), a very good reason to wear glasses in the bush. A black mamba can, very likely, slither faster than a man can run, and is very aggressive. A micro-organism in the water will cause bilharzia. The deadly mosquito comes out at dusk, stays till dawn. Mostly, of course, all these things kill each other, not us. Nature, red in tooth and mandible.

Clever would have to make his kill in a very defined way. No firearms are allowed. Only knobkerries (a kerrie is a long, heavy stick with a knot at the end), spears, or axes. Clever's father killed his lion armed with three knobkerries and an axe. You should carry more than one club, in case the first breaks. You must hit the lion exactly between the eyes with it, which will stun it, then you sever the neck with your axe. Those who are less sure of their kerrie work will generally carry a spear instead of an axe. A spear can use the lion's own charging weight to inflict a mortal wound. Many who try fail and are mortally wounded themselves. Clever, like his father, will use kerries and an axe.

"How will you feel," I asked, "when it is done?"

"Oh, very happy," he said.

There is a modern referent to this ancient rite of passage. Philippa, a young Zimbabwean training to be a professional guide, must demonstrate her coolness and her skill with firearms before being allowed to lead paying clients into the bush. How? She must, at a minimum, shoot and kill a buffalo, an elephant, and a lion.

"I'm going to hate doing it," she said, "but I must. I must show I can bring my clients back."

Like Clever, she will make her kills in all reverence.

There were echoes in that of the ways of Great Zimbabwe. The priests at the top of Zimbabwe Hill, chanting their incantations to summon the spirits, would have understood both the death and the reverence. I thought then of the people who had once massed below the hill, and the cooking fires, the red glare in the subtropical night, the restless stamping of the herds, the stories that were told in the smoke of the fires, the working out of rituals as old as stone: they would surely have understood the last strangled coughing of a lion.

NGORONGORO AND SERENGETI

A t Clever's insistence, I postponed my exploration of the Swahili cities of the Indian Ocean, and made a long detour into the great game parks of the southern Rift, in the Tanzanian interior. Clever was a chauvinist about Zimbabwe's wildlife, but conceded a little grudgingly that the migrations of Serengeti were among the natural wonders of Africa. "Besides," he said, knowing I was more interested in the people than the game, "it's where the Maasai live."

I went first to Ngorongoro, having booked myself into one of East Africa's premier game lodges—might as well do it right.

West of Arusha the countryside was savannah. But at the Rift Valley escarpment, near Lake Manyara, the land became lush and fertile. I crossed over the Mosquito River, and drove past a group of Peace Corps volunteers, who looked at me scornfully, with those I'm-a-member-of-the-community-and-you're-just-a-tourist looks that they all acquire after a few months in the field. Then we started to ascend the escarpment, and the roads became even worse. We swayed and rattled up a one-in-three incline as *the forest became lusher and lusher—lichens, mosses, ferns, and orchids trailing over the massive trees. Maasai herdsmen moved unconcernedly between their cattle and the herds of zebra and wildebeest. This was old Maasai territory. Halfway up the incline, a hyena darted off the road into the bush, then a pair of jackals. There was elephant dung everywhere, and as we rounded a corner on the lip of the crater we came on a young male lion trotting down the centre of the road, in the same direction we were going. He refused to give way, so we settled in to follow him, which we did for about a kilometre before he finally condescended to let us through, crouching in the bushes and snarling as we passed. It was unexpectedly thrilling to see a lion up close, in the wild, entirely unafraid and free.*

We were perched on the eastern lip of the Ngorongoro Crater, 100 metres (330 feet) or so from the lodge. It was black night, no moon, thin overcast scudding across the stars. In the far distance, out of sight even in daylight, were the Serengeti plains, stretching to Lake Victoria and Rwanda. Behind us were the lush hills of the great Rift Valley escarpment. In front was the crater itself, left over from some volcanic catastrophe, home to a wild assortment of African fauna, either in savagery or in some natural and harmonious balance with their environment, depending on your perspective. Home to the animals, but no longer to the Maasai. The Maasai were no longer part of the ecology. They were a part of the problem. Or so they were told.

I was squatting at the rim of the crater with a Maasai called Viola. I was doing so with difficulty with my arthritic knee, but it was still preferable, I was thinking, to lowering my buttocks onto a scorpion. Viola was apparently impervious to discomfort; he had been sitting, unmoving, for several hours, staring unblinkingly into the black, waiting.

He was called Viola ole Yaile, but he had told me to call him Viola. It wasn't his name, nor the name the missionaries had given him. Rather, it had been given by the schoolmistress to one of his female cousins, but he had thought it too good a name to be wasted on a woman and had appropriated it for himself. He came from a clan that had traditionally used the crater as hunting- and grazing-grounds, but they had been bundled out by the game wardens when the park was declared some years before. Until recently they could still come in, but only to graze their cattle. Now they were kept out altogether. They would disturb the animals and upset the tourists. The rest of his people were in Kenya. He had eight children altogether, so far. He was very talkative, for a Maasai.

There was a small fire flickering through the trees behind us, where Viola's family waited, and I could smell thorn bushes burning, acrid with a faint hint of thyme. The clan lived in a small cluster of circular huts, screened from the much larger circular huts of the lodge by a copse; they were singing this night as they always did, recounting their story—long, swelling melodies punctuated by the clavering treble of the women and the strings of a lyre. From the lodge bar came the chatter of tourists and the false bubbliness of some anonymous Zairian "percolator music." The rest of the lodge staff, of varying tribal backgrounds, went about their duties, dressed for no better reason than management whim in a designer version of Nigerian clothing, long flowing robes in bright colours. Viola wore only the red Maasai cloak, and carried a spear.

The lodge is on the eastern rim, looking westward, so the setting sun goes down across the crater, a magnificent sight poorly captured on film. It has been built in the currently acceptable international eco-style, its shape mimicking the vernacular architecture, the whole thing hugging the rim, keeping a low profile, or, in the case of the individual "guest pods," cascading down the rim. The main lodge consists of three interlocking rondavels, gigantic in scope; the restaurant and the bar have massive panoramic windows overlooking the crater. No expense has been spared.

Viola was the night watchman. His job was not so much to keep an eye out for predators—the great carnivores generally steered clear of the lodge's environs—or even for lesser wild creatures such as baboons. His real job, though unstated by management, was to keep blundering tourists from harm, and every now and then he would rise and lope away past the peacocks on the lawn to head off some hardy Scandinavian or German intent on "seeing the real Africa" at night instead of by day from the safety of a convoy of four-wheel-drive Toyotas or minibuses. Occasionally one got away from him and he'd have to go in chase; the previous night he'd been alerted by a mini lightning strike a hundred paces down into the crater, where an Englishwoman had used her flash to photograph what she imagined was some mighty hunter or other but had in reality been a rock, fortunately for her. She had been indignant when she'd been politely shepherded back, apparently not imagining that improperly behaving animals would contemplate eating *her*. She reported Viola to the management afterwards, and they later rewarded him by slipping him an English pound when she had gone off; they didn't want to lose a tourist any more than he did.

We had driven through the crater the day before, and it had been as rich in game as the brochures had said it would be; but for the moment I was more interested in the Maasai than the wildebeest, and I had seen him squatting there in the dark, and had sought him out. We hadn't exactly become chums, but through the long night we had become comfortable with each other, perhaps because I had learned the African trick that silence was a part of the art of conversation—the whites, in his experience, were always in such a hurry that their talk just became noise. He hadn't been interested in South Africa, not even after he learned I was an Afrikaner—he knew nothing of apartheid and hadn't heard of Nelson Mandela. But Canada interested him, and the idea of cold. He wanted to know the names of Canada, so I told him those I thought would interest him. He liked those ending with a *sh* best—Antigonish, Tatamagouche—but thought those with abrupt endings—Tuktoyaktuk, Quebec—

typical of a people in a hurry, always changing things, ever restless, never satisfied.

There were three kinds of tourists, he thought. The blunderers who would get themselves stupidly killed if he didn't head them off. The timid, who thought everything was either poisonous or dangerous. And the false-tongued, who said they liked everything.

But he didn't dislike them. On the contrary, he rather approved. They were stupid, but very rich, and they gave his children money to pose for photographs. His children earned more from stupid tourists than he did doing this job, and it amused him. Of course, he beat them and took the money away, but that was only right. What did they need money for? It also meant he had to make sure they were dressed up as miniature versions of himself—draped in a red cloak, earrings and necklaces and bracelets dangling, red ochre on the skin, cunningly scarred and adorned—so the tourists would think they looked adorable, but he didn't mind.

The Maasai were still numerous in Kenya and Tanzania, and therefore still, in theory, politically potent. But their influence was diminishing. They now occupy only a fraction of their former grazing-grounds, sharing them not only with some of Tanzania's most famous national parks and game reserves, but with farmers, both black and white. Although a few of the southern clans have built permanent villages and planted crops, their northern cousins have retained their pastoral habits and are the least affected by, or interested in, the mainstream of modern Tanzania. They were the one group that was treated with disdain both by the conservationists and by the government, and therefore could be dispossessed with impunity. As they had been.

It was easy to see why. In the "natural state" (B.C., or Before Conservation) Africa was not at all like a zoo, with animals in one place, humans in another. On the contrary, they mingled in a completely undisciplined fashion. I'd been reading Patrick Marnham's book, *Fantastic Invasion*, on the way to Tanzania, immensely enjoying his ferocious attack on officialdom of all kinds, and on loony Western policies in particular. Left alone, he wrote, "the creatures tend to mingle with the people, living off each other, coming and going, their numbers fluctuating in an undisciplined fashion; so before the animals can be controlled, they must be separated and placed in an area from which the human inhabitants have been removed. Then the people can be directed to take the place of the animals."

The Maasai, being nomadic pastoralists, refused to fit into this neat scenario. Nor did they endear themselves to nascent African governments skittishly trying to act as though Western political norms were safely in place. Nomads made politics devilishly difficult. For authoritarian governments, they were obviously anathema. But so were they for fledgling democracies. How can you count votes if you don't know where the voters are?

Just then Viola interrupted my musing by jerking himself erect and staring towards the lodge. A woman in a filmy white cocktail dress had emerged from the

Once upon a time a caterpillar entered the house of a hare when its owner was absent. On his return the hare noticed the marks on the ground and cried out, "Who is in my house?"

The caterpillar replied in a loud voice:"I am the warrior son of the long one whose anklets have become unfastened in the fight in the Kurtiale country. I crush the rhinoceros to the earth and make cow's dung of the elephant! I am invincible!"

The hare went away, saying, "What can a small animal like myself do with a person who tramples an elephant underfoot like cow's dung?"

On the road he met the jackal and asked him to return with him and talk with the big man who had taken possession of his house. The jackal agreed, and when they reached the hare's house he barked loudly and said, "Who is in the house of my friend the hare?"

The caterpillar replied, "I am the warrior son of the long one whose anklets have become unfastened in the fight in the Kurtiale country. I crush the rhinoceros to the earth and make cow's dung of the elephant!"

On hearing this, the jackal said, "I can do nothing with such a man," and went away.

The hare then fetched the leopard, but the caterpillar replied to the leopard in the same manner, and the leopard said, "If he crushes the elephant and the rhinoceros, he will do the same to me."

They went away again and the hare sought out the rhinoceros. The latter, on reaching the hare's house, asked who was inside, but when he heard the caterpillar's reply, he said, "What! He can crush me to the earth! I had better go away, then."

The hare next tried the elephant and asked him to come to his assistance, but on hearing what the caterpillar had said, the elephant remarked that he had no wish to be trampled into cow's dung, and departed.

A frog was passing at the time, and the hare asked him if he could make the man who had conquered all the animals go away. The frog went to the door and asked who was inside. He received the same reply as the others had been given, but instead of leaving he went nearer and said, "I who am strong and a leaper have come. My buttocks are like the post and God has made me vile."

When the caterpillar heard this, he trembled, and as he saw the frog coming nearer, he said, "I am only the caterpillar."

The animals, who had collected nearby, seized him and dragged him out, and they all laughed at the trouble he had given.

Maasai folktale, from Radin, African Folktales and Sculpture front door. She stretched her arms above her head and arched her back, enjoying the tropical air; she looked like a patch of blond fog against the night. She took a few tentative steps towards the edge of the escarpment, and Viola tensed. But after a while he subsided, grumbling away to himself, making tiny mock growls under his breath, like an irritated lion cub. The woman went back inside.

Viola wasn't interested in talking about the politics of game management. He only knew that when the rains came he would be gone. But he was thinking of leaving two of his daughters behind. They were learning tourist ways, which could be useful. The missionaries had all left, as far as he knew, though maybe the poor families pouring across the border from Rwanda would pull them back to Tanzania. Only the "Aids" people were left, he said. After some confusion it turned out it wasn't the disease he meant, but the U.S. aid volunteers, the people who built dams where there was no water and donated machines where there was no one to repair them. There was a group of them up near the border. They had a satellite dish on a flatbed and could download movies, which they showed on a video machine. People walked for 80 kilometres (50 miles) to see a movie. I wondered what they showed. Presumably not *The Lion King*.

After a while I made to go inside; we would be leaving at sun-up for Tarangire National Park, with lunch at Gibb's Farm along the way that would cost what Viola earned in a year or two. He stood up and leaned across to clap me on the shoulder in what I imagine he imagined was a white way of parting. He was half a head taller than I, strongly muscled, lean, with bony feet and knobby hands, skin even in the dark the colour of burnished chocolate, and the friendly clap was like a body blow. He looked magnificent. He told me to visit his brother's son in Kenya; he was near the end of his *moran* period, a fine young man. I promised I would. "Eeeerhhh," he growled, and said something in his language, something that sounded like a farewell. I clapped him back on his shoulder. His skin was oily to the touch. He smelled of grease and old sweat. Since my Swahili was less than rudimentary, I reverted to Afrikaans, the only language I knew really appropriate to Africa. *"Tot siens,"* I said, *"gaan't goed met jou."* Farewell, may it go well with you.

I left him then and slipped around the back of the lodge, making for my rondavel. As I passed the bar, I saw the woman in white, dancing. I wondered whether the American aid people would show *Pocahontas* on their video machine, and what Viola's daughters would think of that.

....

Earlier the same day we had descended the *en tiak*, the sheer drop into the crater, in two four-wheel-drive Toyotas, descending precipitously through acacia forests and into the grasslands covered with candle lilies, fields of buttercups, blue hyacinths, marguerites, flame gladioli, and clover.

Our comfortable trip from a comfortable lodge in a comfortable Toyota was called a safari, which meant that our driver would stop the vehicle every time we spotted an animal. This can get tiresome when travelling with others whose eyesight is better. Every few minutes the vehicle stops in the dust yet again, as someone sees a brown smudge that the knowing declare to be a rhino, or a black smudge they swear is an elephant. And how many buffalo, zebras, and gazelles is enough? Get out your list and tick them off as you see them—there a Gordon's bustard, here a crested crane, there an impala, and oh, look, a thousand or so wildebeest. Our driver-guide, who would identify himself only as Mike, was taciturn to a fault, but could spot a living smudge at a thousand paces and stopped for every one.

And yet ... cynicism aside, those herds of zebra and wildebeest sweeping across the plain, those ponds full of hippos, are exhilarating, and when, just before lunch, we rounded a bend and saw a pride of lions taking their ease by a small rock outcropping, cynicism seemed entirely out of place. Even though it is perfectly obvious that the crater and its wildlife are no longer "natural" in any really meaningful sense—those lions exist here only on sufferance, as a consequence of game management, bullying, lobbying, and political muscle. Ask the Maasai. The Ngorongoro Crater is as much a zoo as anything in the big city. Its denizens are freer, of course, to kill each other, and it is the humans who are caged in their moving vehicles, but the most omnipresent beast in the crater is becoming the four-wheel-drive Toyota. Are any of the great game parks of East Africa really "natural" any more? In the one around Great Zimbabwe, for instance, no predators are allowed, and the bushbucks, who look alarmingly like Bambi, are permitted to breed in peace. What's natural about this? As I had seen in the Zambezi National Park, elephants are being shot because they are destroying the trees and creating a new savannah where there was forest before—only because man allowed elephants to overpopulate through overzealous conservation. Even on the majestic plains of Serengeti, the big cats are allowed their god-given right to kill other species only because man has excluded from the park the lions' most deadly predator, that perfectly natural species called man.

AMONG THE MAASAI

A day or so later, I found myself at the Kenyan town of Narok. Viola had given me the name of his brother's son, and his address, as far as he knew it. The boy was going through the eunoto, the ceremony to signal that he was passing out of the state of being a moran, a warrior. There were a thousand morans going through the ceremony, he'd heard, one of the biggest groups ever. Much bigger than his own. In his time, only four or five hundred had gone into the bush. He thought I'd be interested in seeing the ceremony for myself.

I got to Narok two days after some of the *morans* had wrecked the town and killed a local citizen. They had also wounded a Kenyan policeman in an attempt to steal his watch, and wounding a cop is a dangerous thing to do anywhere—the town was crawling with cops.

It was easy to see what had happened. There were a thousand young men living out in the bush, all going through the *eunoto* ritual, all of them now aware that their carefree days as warriors were numbered; they were full of male bonding, high spirits, and excessive energy. They came into town to have a little fun with the townsfolk, and things got out of hand. When I arrived I was told a unit of the Territorial Army was also on its way. That was expected to be "entirely sufficient," as I guessed it should be against a group, no matter how large, armed only with spears. The *morans*, for their part, didn't seem to be at all cowed at this prospect. There were, after all, a thousand of them, thrice armed: by their numbers, by their male bonding, and by their impenetrable Maasai notion that the Maasai have an entitlement to take what should by rights be theirs but for some reason isn't. In older times this competitive edge was blunted by cattle-rustling and -raiding, even (especially?) from other Maasai. It was their god-given right as *morans* to grab as many cows as they felt they needed, both to replenish their own herds lost to drought, sickness, and other raids, and to build up enough of a reserve to be able to marry properly—only with enough cows could you get the woman you wanted. Raiding was something all your elders had done in their turn—they weren't going to tell you no.

The Maasai, Nilotic immigrants who are categorized by the ethnologists as half-Hamites, have a rich store of legends. One is that God first created the Maasai, and

---

Age-Set System

In East Africa, more than anywhere else on the continent, nomadic societies are ordered by the age-set system. This is a series of clearly defined stages through which every male of the tribe must pass, each state specifying the role and behaviour expected of him at that time. For most tribes there are three stages or sets—child, warrior and elder. The Maasai have five levels. The first, childhood, lasts until puberty. Boys have no rights but plenty of duties, most of them trivial and despised, although they are allowed to herd cattle and goats. Boys become warriors, *morans*, after the circumcision rite called *enkipaata*. Next they become junior elders or married men, then elders, then senior elders, each shift signalled by an elaborate ceremony.

From various sources, including Encyclopaedia Brittanica

then created cattle to keep him alive. Only after that were other people made. It's why all cattle are the natural property of the Maasai. They worship a single god, Ngai, and believe themselves his chosen people. They are also full of bravado, often reinforced by admiring Western commentary.

Today, as a culture, the Maasai, like the Samburu and the Turkana to the north, are barely on the threshold of survival. In colonial times the authorities had expro-priated most of their traditional grazing lands and had imposed severe limits on the size of their herds, which was greatly resented. But their way of life was other-wise left pretty much alone—in fact, it was somewhat romanticized. After inde-pendence, African governments rejected the pastoralist life altogether, and the Maasai were protected only by the fact that state authority hardly ever made its way seriously into the remote bush.

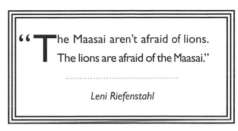

> "The Maasai aren't afraid of lions. The lions are afraid of the Maasai."
>
> *Leni Riefenstahl*

Well, times change. Like Viola and his kids, the Maasai are now tourist-savvy enough to station themselves at salient tourist sites in full regalia ("dress" Maasai, including head-dresses that should by rights be reserved for more ceremonial occa-sions). There they charge 2,000 Tanzanian shillings (about $3) to have their pictures taken. They know perfectly well that in the relatively colourless modern Africa they are as irresistible to tourists as a juicy Thomson's gazelle to a leopard. No matter that most Maasai, or at least the working Maasai who still tend their herds in the far bush, are wearing Timex wristwatches and shoes made from car tires. They are still attracted to red, and the brighter the better. Red tartan fabric is especially popular these days, as though the McMaasai had somehow joined the Scottish Register. The men carry spears and heavy sticks, as they always have. In the south, many Maasai have grudg-ingly accepted that they should settle down in more or less permanent villages, and their children almost all learn to speak Swahili, because they now almost all get at least a modicum of schooling (and also because the Maasai find it convenient to speak the language—a triumph for Julius Nyerere's universalist anti-tribalism).

They were once so fierce that the slavers never penetrated far into their territory, and so that scourge of Africa let their land be. It's also true that the Maasai are immigrants to this part of Kenya and Tanzania, driven out of their older homelands by a tribe even fiercer and more violent, the Turkana. What finally tamed them, to the extent that they are tamed, was not conquest but the relentless bureaucratization of life, along with the encroachment of the modern state with its rules, regulations, police—and jails.

Every night for more than a week the *morans* had camped out in the bush, going through the purification rituals, waiting for their time, growing ever more restless, ever more aggressive, ever more arrogant. They had marched to the appointed place, a *manyatta*, or camp, deep in the Olipito Forest, 20 kilometres (12 miles) from Narok, where they had built their *nkaji*, small traditional huts, and settled in to wait. There were so many of them it took 461 *nkaji* to house them. They had arrived in full and splendid regalia, and passed through Narok brandishing their spears, their locks flowing free, untrimmed in the decade since their circumcision, wearing head-dresses of ostrich (for those who hadn't yet killed a lion) or of lion's mane (for those who had). Thigh belts and ornaments jingled as they moved. Oh, they were a splendid sight, and they knew it full well, and so did the women, gathered in Narok's main square for the occasion.

Some of them had marched for more than three days to get there. They had been circumcised together years before, but there was still considerable tension—many of them hadn't seen each other since, except as enemies in cattle raids.

By the time they came back into town, they had pretty well run out of wild things to kill, and they weren't allowed to kill each other, though fighting was common enough, as was bragging.

"It is a very intimidating thing," the owner of a small shop told me, "to see a band of Maasai, with their spears and ornaments, their bodies painted, rattling the bars of your shop."

I walked around the town, which still seemed dazed from the events of days earlier, and afraid of it happening again, despite the massive police presence. In this atmosphere, I wasn't going to walk into the bush to find the *moran* camp. How, then, to find whom I came to find?

<hr>

A large group of boys had passed through the *enkipaata*, the circumcision ritual, only a week before. I wasn't sure whether to be relieved or regretful at missing this particular ceremony. It is performed on young men, not babies, for one thing. For another, there is no anaesthetic or painkiller—the pain is part of the process, and bearing it stoically is one part of growing up. And then there is the technique itself. The circumcision is performed with the sharpened edge of a spear point, left deliberately rough so that a sawing motion is used instead of a cutting one. And, worse, in this age of spiralling AIDS, all the thousand foreskins are sawed off with the same unsterilized blade. (Mary Anne Fitzgerald, whose book *Nomad* contains a splendid chapter on the people of the Turkana region, once described watching an elderly white Kenyan who had been helping out in such a ceremony actually performing a few of the circumcisions himself. She described him afterwards "shaking antiseptic powder onto the cut penises as though he were salting a stew.")

After the circumcision ceremony and other rituals, the young men become *morans*, the most exciting time of their lives, always looked back on with nostalgia. In theory, warriorship is a period of formal learning in the ways of the tribe, the rituals governed by the senior elders and imposed by the elders. But, in practice, as warriors they are free to roam the country, to hunt and to raid, to choose lovers from the uncircumcised girls (though causing pregnancy is taboo), to sing and dance, and to indulge in general troublemaking and carefree mayhem. There have been many complaints about the system from the Kenyan authorities, for obvious reasons—schooling, for instance, has little attraction for a young man with this kind of freedom, and there have been many calls to abolish the institution, some from Maasai politicians.

Morans are not allowed to marry, and the married men always try to delay their moving up to junior elder in order to give themselves more time to accumulate ever more cows and acquire a second or third wife before unleashing the warriors on the marriage market.

Raiding for cattle has always been a fact of Maasai life, and the British inadvertently reinforced the practice by "fining" the nomads cattle when they had transgressed some law or other. The Maasai, Turkana, and Samburu accepted this "fining" as another form of raiding by the more powerful, so they stole them back when they could. The British also set the Samburu to subdue the Turkana, which they did, but it took them twenty years. During this time the British upped the raiding ante by confiscating a quarter of a million cattle—raiding on a massive scale, a cause of some indignation, if also admiration. The Maasai were definitely impressed.

In the past twenty years, more than eight thousand people—many Maasai among them—have been killed in northern Kenya by cattle raiders, and the carnage is escalating—surplus AK-47s have been flooding across the Somali border (sometimes accompanied by often pitiless Somali bandits). Only a week before I was there, eleven men were ambushed and killed along the Great North Road by Somalis. Raiding usually takes place after the rains, because the cows are fat then and need less attention. The Maasai, as a rule, don't carry guns, nor do the Samburu or their cousins, the Redille. The Turkana and the Borana often do, and don't hesitate to use them. The Borana, particularly, are feared. They cut off raiders' penises and display them afterwards, grisly trophies of the cattle wars.

Still, the Maasai think all the other northern nomadic tribes are ridiculous, with barbaric customs.

....

The *eunoto* lasts for up to five days, and includes elaborate rituals of body painting with chalk and white mud from the sacred cliffs at Ungula Nalporr, the White Crossing, a limestone crag on the Maasai steppe. The designs they choose are supposed to reflect their prowess as warriors. They sing and dance wildly, to the admiration of the young women, who are themselves freshly painted with ochre and decked out in beads for the occasion. The next day, the painting ritual is repeated.

More dancing, more singing, more bravado, more giggling admiration from the wives-to-be, and, after dark, much coupling.

The climax of the transition is the shaving of the warriors' heads, which signals the end of their *moran*ship and the beginning of their new status as responsible adults.

With the *moran* group that had wrecked Narok, the good intentions went missing and the fun wasn't fun any more. They would go home in disgrace.

A day later, through a series of intermediaries, I was introduced to Viola's brother's son. He met me just outside town, swaggering up in his newly acquired adult's cloak, his glorious ornaments reduced to a few brass bangles and an aluminium necklace. His shaved head was gleaming. He was tall and muscular, and looked surly. At first, it didn't go well. Not only was I a *mzungu*, a white person, but I didn't speak Swahili. Indeed, as far as he was concerned, I didn't seem to understand anything at all. But he thawed when he understood that I brought greetings from the south, and after a while he relaxed and began, in English, a series of boastful and improbable tales of his exploits. He had brought down a buffalo with two knobkerries and a spear; he had frightened off lions and stolen their kills ... And no, of course he had been nowhere near town when the policeman was killed—the requisite "Who, me?" of any apprehended villain.

After a while, he abruptly lost interest, and stood up, swinging away into the bush, leaving me there in the inky-black African night. I sat for a long while, listening to the silence and feeling the many generations of Maasai nomads fading back into history. I wondered what would replace them—what would emerge as "African" from all the complex forces that were pressing them into the shabby "modern" cities. I couldn't imagine how the transformation could be made. But then the lights came on, the power company having fixed whatever the problem was, and I walked back into town.

In a village just outside Narok, the night after I had left the police and the *morans* rattling sticks and truncheons at each other, I was introduced to a family of Gabbra who lived in a tiny four-hut complex 2 kilometres (1 mile) from the nearest well. The woman, Manya, asked me to stay, and pressed on me unwanted gifts of food she couldn't afford.

In return, I picked up one of their yellow plastic pails and offered to help them fetch water.

They laughed, politely, but I could see what they were really thinking: *mzungu* are so *inept* ... Fetching water was woman's work.

So I stayed behind with the men, who were smoking on a wooden bench outside one of the huts, and that night ate corn and fried banana and sucked on a mango.

....

All over East Africa—and indeed all over Africa—it is normal for people to walk a kilometre or two or six for water. In the more arid areas, people walk even greater distances, and sometimes all they find at the far end is a pond slimy with overuse. More than 90 per cent of Africans still dig for their water, and waterborne diseases like typhoid, dysentery, and cholera are common—many Africans are a stew of parasites. In some areas the wells are so far below the earth's surface that chains of people are required to pass up the water.

So why, when aid workers drilled a borehole and installed a diesel pump in Manya's village just outside the Maasai Mara national park, was it wrecked and the corrugated-iron reservoir trashed?

When the pump was installed, the aid workers decided the local people would have to pay for the fuel (because aid money wouldn't last for ever and because "self-sufficiency is good for morale"). Then, when no one used the new borehole but kept going to the well instead, they cordoned off the well "for health reasons." (It *was* polluted.) When that led to resentment, they changed the fee structure. Only those who could afford it would henceforth have to pay. Naturally, those who did pay soon resented those who didn't, and first tried to keep them away altogether, and, when that didn't work, tried to ration them. In the end, some of those who couldn't afford to pay wrecked the pump and pierced the iron tank with their spears.

Thus it is that so much of the aid money sent to Africa is wasted. Much of it still goes to megaprojects—hydro-electric schemes, railways, highways, factories—and often a large proportion gets diverted to private pockets, and the projects are sabotaged; or the aid is tied to buy-back schemes in the donor country, in which case it is not aid at all; or, as is newly fashionable, the aid is given directly to the communities,

> Bodily ornaments in East Africa were traditionally made from ivory, bone, ostrich shells, feathers, hides and wood. Cowry shells, the traditional unit of currency, were stitched to garments as a mark of status. Trade beads were introduced by Arab and Indian traders sometime around the tenth century. More recently, brass earrings have been made from cartridges hammered flat, of which there is an endless supply. And in the last fifteen years, charms and jewellery in aluminium have been appearing. They first showed up after an aid shipment of cooking pots went missing in the border country between southern Sudan and Kenya; there are some fine pieces in the Kenya National Museum.
>
> *From various sources, including Fisher, Africa Adorned*

in which case the aid workers too often operate in the abysmal but altogether normal fashion indicated above. The donor attitude—"*Why can't they see what's good for them?*"—is almost guaranteed to cause the projects to fail.

Virtually everyone in Africa seems to believe that the aid industry has been a massive failure, that it has caused more damage than good, and that it has brought about a debilitating culture of dependency. The cynical go further, believing that the failure is deliberate—yet another colonial effort to keep Africa dependent so its raw materials can be painlessly extracted. The only dissenting voices I heard were from the direct recipients themselves (and not even all of them). About the only projects exempt from the general contempt were operations like Médecins Sans Frontières, the doctors' group, and famine-relief efforts. The United Nations was held in more contempt than any other agency, made worse by the Somali débâcle and its dithering over Rwanda.

This is hardly new. Alistair Graham, writing in 1973, had this to say: "In 1924 the [colonial] government established a famine-relief camp at Kalokol in the Northern District to give food to the many Turkana who were dying of famine. The camp was a great success and in subsequent years more and more Turkana became famished until gradually a permanent village of professional needy developed. Children were born and raised there who grew up knowing only a life of plenty in a mythical famine—a twisted parody of existence in a land where real and desperate hardship is commonplace."[7]

It needn't be so. There are small, unheralded projects, run by individuals and small aid groups all over Africa, that do work. A Belgian AIDS clinic in Tanzania. A Canadian-originated fabric workshop in Zimbabwe (so successful are the designs that they have opened a store in England). A private immunization clinic in north Kenya, financed by, of all things, the earnings of a free-lance journalist. Another, a pilot project in the arid Samburu region of Kenya, is entirely recipient-driven, and is becoming a model for small-scale development elsewhere in Africa.

So what are donor governments to do? Western solutions include rigorous accounting and other hard-edged fiscal measures.

The African solution, which I was to hear over and over, in every country, was much less complicated. It was simply this: Educate the girls and the women, and we will take care of it ourselves.

Part II

The Land of Zanj and the Birth of the Swahili

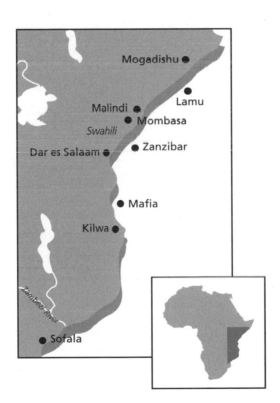

THE SHARKS OF MOGADISHU

The shallow gold seams of Zimbabwe are mostly worked out now, they say, though there are still prospectors in the rocky hills, chasing their futile dreams. Some of that gold was trucked down to the markets in Johannesburg in modern times, but for centuries most of it wound its way down to the Indian Ocean on the heads of porters, whence it was taken ... where? To the Swahili trading cities. And then? After a while I tired of the endless savannah, even the golden grasslands of Serengeti, and resolved to go see for myself.

The Swahili coastal culture, which stretches from Somalia in the north to Mozambique in the south, is very old. It is an exotic mix of the original inhabitants, often referred to as the Zanjj (or Zanj) in the old chronicles, and later arrivals— Arabs, Shirazi Persians, Indians and Indonesians, Portuguese and assorted other Europeans. The language, more modern than the culture, is Swahili, the old Zanji tongue with admixtures from a dozen cultures, a flexible, sophisticated language with a strong poetic tradition going back more than a millennium.

The History of Pate, a Swahili chronicle from the twelfth century, recounts how it all began (conveniently ignoring the Zanj, who were already there, and about whom very little was known): "In the beginning of these coastal towns, he who first made them was a ruler called Abdul Malik bin Muriani. The date was the seventy-seventh year of the Hejra [A.D. 699]. He heard of this country, and his soul longed to found a new kingdom. So he brought Syrians, and they built the cities of Pate, Malindi, Zanzibar, Mombasa, Lamu and Kilwa."[1]

A curious geographic order, but there they are. Reordering from the north and filling out, we would amend the list to read: Mogadishu, Brava, Pate, Lamu, Malindi, Mombasa, Zanzibar, Mafia, Kilwa, Sofala.

Somalian Mogadishu and Brava are in ruins, destroyed by modern explosives; Pate barely exists as a coherent entity. Lamu persists, unchanged and unchanging, but no longer powerful, a picturesque relic. Malindi has become a resort for acquisitive industrialists from Nairobi and wealthy Europeans. Mombasa, Kenya's second city, is torn between obeisance to the industrial heartland and allegiance to its Swahili past, a fine city with a slightly seedy and schizophrenic air. Zanzibar, too, persists—and persists in believing its time will come again. Mafia is a village. Kilwa is in ruins. And Sofala? I would try to find Sofala, now lost in legend. Below Sofala ... nothing. Some of the old *traders ventured on to Cape Agulhas, but saw no point in going farther. Beyond that were only storms hurtling out of the frigid waters of Antarctica, and there no men ventured.*

The first time I saw Mogadishu was after a tricky rounding of the Somali Horn and an uneasy stay in Yemen, where a security detail followed me around, their machine-pistols pointed at my knees, a queasy-making thing for an innocent traveller, such as I was then. I remember the dawn over Aden, and as we steamed into the Indian Ocean the dolphins joined us, surfing our wake, as hip and knowing as Hawaiian beach bums. Our cheap cabin was at the waterline, and sometimes in the late afternoons I could see them cruising alongside, exactly at my level, their curious eyes rolling in pleasure. Then one morning I came on deck to find a basket of nuns being lowered over the side.

This was not so surprising as it sounds, though the sight looked hallucinatory, if only briefly. There was no harbour in Mogadishu fit for large vessels, and people as well as cargo were winched overboard in giant wicker baskets to launches waiting below. The Somali mariners were careless of their own or their passengers' safety, and I remember staring at the nuns and wondering where they found the grit to tear themselves away from their homes in Umbria to venture among the heathen in this wild place.

Mogadishu didn't seem to me like much of a city, then. Nor did it the next time it came to my attention. I was in a dhow, heading north up the coast from Zanzibar. The Zanzibari who was with me looked gloomy. It was seven days to Somalia, and the last time he'd done the trip he'd eaten something rotten and spent most of the voyage strapped to a sling, his bare arse hanging over the side. "Damned uneasy," he said, "especially near Mogadishu." He pointed to the gunwales of the dhow. "Not very far above water. More sharks in Mog harbour than anywhere else in Africa." This, too, wasn't surprising: for centuries there had been a slaughterhouse on the shore in Mogadishu harbour, and the offal was thrown into the sea.

The frenzy of the sharks and the blood-red sea—a fine political metaphor.

Nevertheless, Mogadishu and Brava, its sister city a hundred or so kilometres to the south, were both flourishing trading ports in the days of Swahili hegemony. Their influence was destroyed by the Portuguese dismantling of the trans–Indian Ocean trading system in the sixteenth century, and they fell into decline. Hardly anyone bothered with them after that. Somalia was largely ignored in the European partition of Africa: the countryside was beautiful in an austere way, the nomadic cattle-herders and their camels exotic enough, but there were no minerals to speak of, and nothing much to exploit. True, Britain and Italy divided the place up between them, but as an afterthought: Britain took the northern half to protect Aden, across the gulf, and Italy got the south because it was another way into Ethiopia.

The post-colonial history of Somalia is depressingly familiar: independence in 1960, a military coup by Mohammed Siad Barré in 1969, the U.S. withdrawal after discovering Barré trading with North Vietnam, the Soviet arming of the Somalis until they had one of the most formidable arsenals in Africa, and the subsequent deterioration into civil war when the Russians withdrew.

The only truly interesting fact in this melancholy history is that the Somali civil war has nothing to do with ethnicity: the whole population shares an ethnic identity and a single language. The war has entirely to do with clan rivalries.

By 1997 many of the cultured and educated Somalis were either dead or had fled. There was no national government to speak of. Thugs ruled everywhere, no longer dignified with the name "warlords." One out of five Somalis was a refugee, most of them within the borders of their own country, such as it was. There were plagues among the cattle. There were famines and widespread starvation, most of it politically caused. The world had washed its hands. The capital city had been turned into rubble, and there was neither the money nor the will to repair it.

But the population was still expanding. There were babies everywhere. As soon as they were able, they'd pick up a gun.

LAMU AND SHELA

E lsewhere the Swahili culture is relatively intact. Some of the coastal cities are ruined and have vanished; others survive. They are part of sovereign nation-states now, but the coastal culture is still profoundly different from that of the interior. Lamu in Kenya has more in common with Mafia in Tanzania than with Nairobi; Zanzibar is part of Tanzania only in name.

From the top of the Friday Mosque in Shela, which is on Lamu Island, near the Somali border, you can see maybe 20 kilometres (12 miles) and at least eight centuries. The mosque, with its moon-rocket minaret, is Shela's most notable landmark—in fact, apart from Peponi's Hotel, it is pretty much Shela's only landmark. Fifty-eight steps lead to the top, and, since each one is a different height, it is treacherous to use. But from the top there is a grand view of Shela and the island.

I found a leper up there, praying. His right leg was covered in filthy bandages, and he had only one eye. He paid me little mind when I emerged on the roof, but kept himself prostrate, invoking Allah's mercy.

I stepped past him and looked out.

To the east are the massive Shela sand-dunes, which local legend says cover

Hadibu, Lamu's first seventh-century settlement. Beyond the dunes are 11 kilometres (7 miles) of unspoiled and uninhabited white-sand beaches.

To the north is Pate Island, Lamu's former great trading rival, whose power was obliterated in a famous massacre on these very dunes not quite two hundred years ago. (Over the centuries Lamu was frequently at war with its neighbouring city-states, Pate, Siyu, and Faza. Mostly these wars consisted of ritual taunting rather than fighting; the fleets would set out, banners flying, but would stay prudently out of reach of the opposition, hurling nothing more lethal than insults. In 1813, however, the Nabhani of Pate fatally miscalculated the tides. His boats were stranded and his men bloodily massacred at Shela beach.)

To the south, past another stretch of beach, past the dhow-builders and the mango-juice sellers, and past the bellowing and ever-erratic generating station, is the ancient town of Lamu itself. The *Lamu Chronicle*, a Swahili document, says the town was founded in the seventh century, which is probably so, though the oldest building still standing is the Pumwani Mosque, which dates only from 1370.

To the west, across the Manda Channel, is Manda Island and the ruined town of Takwa, now just broken coral-brick walls, a pretty little mosque, and an enigmatic tomb. The ruins are in poor shape and getting worse: elephants and the baobabs are not doing the remains any good. Takwa, like so much of the coast, has had a turbulent history.

In 1592, Father João dos Santos noted: "The Isle of Lamo hath great Asses, but of little service. This island was chastised when Ampaza [Pate] was destroyed, and Mombaça also, by Martin Alfonso de Mello. The King of Ampaza was slaine, and his head carried on a pole at Goa in triumph. When he was gone Mirale Beque [Amir Ali Bey] and the Turks came with foure Galleys out of the Red Sea, and infested the coast, till the Zimbas and the Portugalls ended the businesse with a new Armada, the Portugalls captiving and spoyling, the Zimbas eating the Turkes and inhabitants. The king of Lamo for betraying the Portugalls to the Turkes was beheaded. The Isle and Citie of Mandra [Manda] which had denied the Portugalls to land, saying, the Sunne onely might enter there, was sacked and two thousand Palme-trees cut down."[2]

The terrible Zimba and Mumbo came from somewhere east and south of Lake Malawi; no one really knows whether the rampages they made along the coast (and the cannibalism that accompanied them) were a response to being pushed out of their homes by invaders, or whether they were a consequence of the predations of slavers, a fevered revenge against those who were stealing their tribe's soul. Father João dos Santos was present at several Zimba incursions. He also visited a Mumbo town, Chicoronga, "neere which the Portugalls found many Negroes, men and women, bound hand and foot, destined to the slaughter for the next dayes food, whom with many others they freed ... All the ground before [the gate] was paved with men's Skuls, which [Quizura, the chief] had killed in that war, upon which they must passe which went in or out, a thing in his conceit of great Majestie."[3]

At the top of the Friday Mosque, the leper was still praying, but as I moved to go he looked up, his only eye squinting and blinking. He wore a kind of leer, which I took to be his happy face; it was so ruined it was hard to tell. He wanted to shake my hand, but I prudently refused, and he wandered disconsolately over to the parapet, where he leaned his head into his arms and began to mumble.

I went down to Lamu and sat in a café on the waterfront, watching the donkey traffic ambling by and staring out over the Manda Channel. Everything was peaceful. Indeed, apart from Somalia, a special case, the whole coast is as peaceful now as it has ever been. There had been mayhem here since the Middle Ages. Kilwa was ravaged twice, by the Zimba and by the Portuguese. Mombasa was also twice destroyed by war. In 1585, and again in 1589, Ottoman Turks tried to push out the Portuguese and failed, and sporadic warfare and raiding continued for generations. It wasn't until 1698 that Mombasa's Fort Jesus fell to the Arabs after a siege lasting thirty-three months. Twenty years later the Portuguese had effectively abandoned the coast to the Arabs. In 1805, Seyyid Said ascended to the Omani throne, and in 1822 he sent an army to subdue Mombasa, Pate, and Pemba, which until then were ruled by the Mazrui clan. In 1832 Seyyid moved his court to Zanzibar, where he had begun to lay out clove plantations.

In the mid-nineteenth century, Britain and Germany partitioned East Africa, but the Sultan of Zanzibar retained a 16-kilometre(10-mile-)-wide strip of the Kenyan coastline under a British protectorate. He retained it until Tanganyika's independence in 1963, which was followed by the ferocious Marxist revolution on Zanzibar that ended sultanate rule for good.

The next day I went over from Lamu to see the Takwa ruins on Manda Island on a dhow manned by four Swahili teenagers. The boat's name was *Hadija*; it was decorated in the traditional red, yellow, and blue, and its triangular lateen-rigged sail had a large but jolly skull and crossbones on it, and the Swahili words for "break the bull"—an expression that means something like "go for broke." These small dhows are infinitely manoeuvrable; the crew compensates for the boat's lean against the wind by clambering out on a heavy plank they wedge into the gunwales on one side, leaving it protruding 3 or 4 metres (10 to 12 feet) on the other. In a gust the three boys will scamper out, casually balancing on the narrow beam. We wound in past the coral brickworks and in among the channels of the mangrove swamps. While I looked at the ruins, one of the lads stayed in the mangroves, dipping for tropical fish, which he stored in plastic bags. Later, he would take them on an eight-hour bus ride to Mombasa and sell them to a broker for the export market. It was how he made his living.

Buzurg Ibn Shahriyar, a Persian Gulf sailor and collector of sailors' tales, recounts in A.D. 920 how some men from Oman, including one Ismailawaih, were shipwrecked on the coast of Zanj. The king there, "a young Negro, handsome and well made," received them with courtesy, encouraged them to trade, repaired their ships and went down to the harbour to see them off. Instead of gratitude, the Arabs kidnapped the king and sold him into slavery in Oman. The king later converted to Islam, made his way to Baghdad and then Mecca, and escaped to Egypt. In Cairo, said the king, "I saw the great river which is called the Nile. I asked: where does it come from? They answered: its source is in the land of the Zanj. On which side? On the side of a large town called Aswan, which is on the frontier land of the blacks. With this information, I followed the banks of the Nile, going from one town to another, asking alms, which was not refused me. I fell, however, among a company of blacks who gave me a bad welcome. I fled and fell into the hands of another company which seized me and sold me. I escaped again and went on in this manner until, after a series of similar adventures, I found myself in the country which adjoins the land of the Zanj ..." Well, the King walked home, all the way up the Nile from Cairo to its source, and down to the coast, where he found his people still kingless, for the diviners had told them he was still alive. But this was not the end of the tale, as Shahriyar recounts. Some years later the same sailors were again shipwrecked on the Zanj coast, and were terrified to learn that their erstwhile victim was once again king. Instead of revenge, however, he received them with courtesy, though he refused to accept gifts, saying, "You are not worthy for me to accept gifts from you; I will not sully my property with anything that comes from you." When they left, he instructed them, "Go, and if you return, I shall not treat you otherwise than I have done. You will receive the best welcome, and the Muslims may know that they may come here to us, as to brothers, Muslims like themselves. As for accompanying you to your ship, I have reasons for not doing that."

From Freeman-Grenville, The East African Coast p. 8

On the way back from Takwa, the dhow settled into a steady run before the wind. The crew, freed from their balancing act, fetched out yellow plastic cooking-oil pails, empty, turned them upside down, and started to drum, and then to sing, "Karibu Mena," the Swahili welcome song. The drumming picked up tempo in the wonderful crossed-rhythm harmonics of Africa, each pail adding its own syncopation that somehow magically merged into a single overlay, then they segued into a satiric song about white people, and without missing a complicated beat, they riffled through "My Bonny Lies Over the Ocean," "Frère Jacques," and "Guantanamera," before slipping effortlessly back into the poetics of Africa. I looked past the young drummers to the old port of Lamu beyond, and if it hadn't been for the plastic pails and a T-shirt one of them was wearing that had the Stars and Stripes and the words "Hello America!" stencilled on the back, it could have been ... any century. As we approached Lamu, they stopped singing to furl the sail, and across the water I could hear the muezzin calling the faithful to prayer in Lamu's mosques.

Later that night I sat at a table across the dusty roadway from the embankment where the dhows are moored. The lights were off (the generator had failed, again, and all of Lamu was dark) and candles were the only illumination. A boy on a donkey trotted past. Three women in black *bui-bui* glided by, veiled and hidden, their eyes glinting in the moonlight. Then another woman in black, her face unveiled, with henna "tattoos" on her cheeks—there are many studios in Lamu that specialize in henna face and arm painting. Children were playing with toy dhows made of string and wood with plastic sails; others were climbing on a rusty old cannon, left over from when the British subdued "Swahililand." Two donkeys, unaccompanied, ambled past, then a group of men in the long white robes called *kanzu*, and embroidered hats, *kofia*, their feet shuffling in the sand. The moon came up over Manda, full, orange, glowing, and as it did a dhow sailed by, its triangular sail intersecting the moon with a ghostly shadow, and I remembered a passage from Karen Blixen: "One night a row of Arab dhows came along, close to the coast, running noiselessly before the monsoon, a file of brown shadow-sails under the moon ..."

Lamu has turned its back on the twentieth century; the ambience is quite unchanged since the days of the war with Pate. There are still no vehicles permitted, and it is a routine sight to see a small donkey laden with a load of coral bricks, brought over in a dhow from Manda's brickworks. There are a dozen mosques, some dating back to the fourteenth and fifteenth centuries. It is Muslim, and conservative: many of the women are veiled, and alcohol is confined to the few tourist hotels. The town is a labyrinth of tiny alleys leading eastwards from the main street, sited that way so the monsoon rains could flush them out, the only cleaning the town ever got in the early days. (Indeed, the gutters still run with foul-smelling grey water.) The grander Swahili houses had sewers, but most of the town simply used the beach at low tide. The centuries-old Swahili houses are tall and elegant, built with coral-brick walls a metre thick. Inside, there is a series of curtained alcoves, their width dictated by the length of the mangrove poles used for floors and ceilings. Steep staircases lead to flat roofs, where the cooking is done and much of the household activity goes on. Each has a flower-filled courtyard, reflecting a gracious way of life that had running water and simple air-conditioning while Europe was struggling through the Dark Ages.

The maze of alleyways is lined with hole-in-the-wall stores, many with intricately carved doors. I sat on a stone bench in the main square with some old men playing dominoes, the market spilling out around us, baskets of squawking chickens and piles of mangoes and spices, patient donkeys, hawkers of *qat*, here and there a small brazier on which strips of chicken were grilling. A greybeard wandered past, clutching a garish poster advertising a Hindi movie playing at the local theatre.

On the quayside by the main jetty is Petley's Inn, founded by Percy Petley, a locally famous British officer who, it is said, could fell leopards with his fist. Nearby is the Lamu Palace Hotel, an especially remarkable place, run by a Swiss who had been in Kenya for forty years. He left Mombasa for the sleepier Lamu so he didn't have to work so hard, "so I could be pissed all the time." The hotel is air-conditioned, but since the power is off so frequently this is more a theory than a reality. Obviously there are no thieves—the Lamu Palace Hotel office doesn't even have a door, and there is no night clerk either. The money is piled in a heap in a box under the desk.

....

I spent a morning with a dhow-maker in the village of Matandoni, on the other side of Lamu Island. When I wandered by, he was squatting on his heels, chipping at a teak plank with an adze; he was repairing a dhow "some idiot" had damaged by ramming a marker buoy in the channel. Each chip with the adze removed less than a centimetre of wood; he was working without a chalk line or a straight-edge, but when he pushed the plank into place, it fitted perfectly. I asked if I could watch, and he only grunted, but after I had sat patiently for half an hour he put down his tools and leaned against the boat to rest. He accepted a carton of South African pineapple juice I had bought at a small shop nearby. Business, he said, was generally poor—mostly repair work these days, and most of the young people preferred the uncertainty of the outrigger dugouts called *ngalawas*, which took no skill at all to make. The *baggalas*, the ocean-going dhows, were less and less common, though he still built a few. The differences between the "true Arab," the Lamuan, and the Indian dhows were subtle but distinct, having

They caught a dugong one morning, the legendary mermaid. I watched them bring it ashore. It was about 2 metres (6.5 feet) long and weighed in at about 200 kilos (440 pounds), they said. It had human-like hair and astonishingly humanoid female breasts, so that when they were dragging it on board it did, indeed, look like an overlarge, dark grey female corpse. One of the Swahili fishermen told me they hate catching the things, not so much because they are destructive of nets (they are), but because they look disquietingly obscene, as though one should avert one's eyes. Men have to swear here, as the fisherman put it, "that they haven't done any family planning with it," or no one will buy it or eat it.

mostly to do with the superstructure; they all shared the lateen rigging with its tri-angular sail, and they could have either one mast or two, depending on their load and their purpose. He had made all kinds, but of course the Lamuan ones were best. Three years earlier he had worked with others on his largest dhow ever, and he was angry because the men who'd bought it had turned it into a restaurant in Mombasa called The Tamarind.

"It's supposed to be the best restaurant in East Africa," I said.

"It is supposed to sail, not spend its life tied to a wharf," he complained.

MOMBASA

I left Lamu for Mombasa by air. The Manda airstrip, called somewhat grandly Manda Lamu International Airport, has nothing that might be called a terminal, just a thatched hut with a few benches. Baggage handling is by human-powered trolleys, rather like clumsy rickshaws. There is a duty-free shop that advertises "drinks," which turn out to be Fanta and Coke; the shop is otherwise empty. The check-in clerk was a small worried-looking fellow with a clipboard, and he communicated with the incoming airplane via cellphone—there was no tower or radio beacon. The Air Kenya Twin Otter was captained by a cheery pilot who told us he was a "colonel, retired." There was no cabin crew—there was no room for a cabin crew—but that didn't matter; the retired colonel just shouted instructions to us over his shoulder. Including the fact that there was a Coleman cooler at the back with fruit juices and Cokes, and we should help ourselves.

Pedro Alvarez Cabral reported in 1500 that "along the coast [to Malindi] we found many islands inhabited by Moors. There is another city there, which is called Mombasa. The king is a Moor. All this coast is inhabited by Moors. Both on the island and on the mainland there are said to be Christians who wage many wars." Vasco da Gama, in 1498, was also impressed: "Mombasa is a large city seated on an eminence washed by the sea. Its port is entered daily by numerous vessels. At its entrance stands a pillar, and by the sea a low-lying fortress. Those who had gone on shore told us that in the town they had seen many men in irons; and it seemed to us that these must be Christians, as the Christians in that country are at war with the Moors. The town of Malindi lies in a bay and extends along the shore ... Its houses are lofty and well white-washed and have many windows; on the land side are palm groves, and all around it maize and vegetables are being cultivated."[4]

Impressed the early Portuguese might have been, but they knew who should be in charge. Duarte Barbosa, writing in 1501, was blunt: "The king of this city

[Mombasa] refused to obey the commands of the King our Lord, and through this arrogance he lost it, and our Portuguese took it from him by force. He fled away, and they slew many of his people and also took captive many, both men and women, in such sort that it was left ruined and plundered and burnt. Of gold and silver great booty was taken here, bangles, bracelets, earrings and gold beads, also a great store of copper with other rich wares in great quantity, and the town was left in ruins."[5]

Mombasa now is an industrial and port city serving the hinterland, Nairobi's outlet to the sea. But Fort Jesus, begun by the Portuguese in 1590 and added to almost as many times as it has been conquered, still broods over the harbour entrance, and there are still hundreds of old Swahili houses like the ones in Lamu, jumbled in a pleasant mix with the low-rise concrete and glass of modernity. Here is the best food in East Africa; even the roadside vendors sell excellent chapatis and tandoori chicken, fried plantains, mutton curries. The markets are busy, and so are the stores—Kenya's, after all, is the most robust economy in East Africa.

They say the prostitutes are the most beautiful in Africa. But then that's what they say in Conakry and Douala and Lomé too. It seems an odd claim to fame.

ZANZIBAR AND MAFIA

Zanzibar is part of the United Republic of Tanzania, which was formed from Tanganyika and Zanzibar at independence, but it's clear the separatist feeling is very strong. It took me five minutes after debarking and going through Zanzibar's "immigration" formalities (a sop to Island sensibilities) to find my first separatist. His name was Harry, and he insisted he wanted to be my "guide to the spice island and all its mysteries—we will see the spices where they grow and all the ruins you want and I will take you on a tour of the old Stone Town . . ." I interrupted this steady flow to tell him I didn't want or need a guide, thank you.

"All right," he said. "Let us go and have a drink now."

This was a very Zanzibari response. The island may be Muslim, but it is also flexible, free-wheeling, complicated, decadent. Zanzibaris regard themselves as tolerant, cosmopolitan, and well off. At least they did. They now seem to believe their wealth has been siphoned off to pay for mainland fecklessness and Julius Nyerere's harebrained schemes for self-sufficiency, and if only they could go it alone they'd be able to repair the town (now falling into ruin), their island, and the economy.

"Of course, we also speak better Swahili," Harry said. "The only pure Swahili. On the mainland, they make a mess of everything."

"But can you manage on your own?" I asked. "You're too small to be an independent country."

Harry wouldn't hear of it. They had been independent before, and were better traders than anyone else on the coast. They still exported spices, but the mainland got the money.

"That was then. You had slave labour on Zanzibar in those days."

"Sometimes I think slavery wasn't such a bad thing," Harry said darkly.

Zanzibar Stone Town, as the old city is called, is a UNESCO World Heritage Site and a protected area, which means there are strict regulations about what can be built, changed, or demolished. But there are obviously no regulations about sheer decay. The town is shabby, dirty, falling to bits, as well as exotic, colourful, and drenched in history. The sultans are the rulers who have most left their stamp on the place. There are few traces of the Portuguese, and though the British built some elegant colonial buildings, the character of the place derives strongly from the sultans and the great houses and palaces of the sultanate. The House of Wonders, the greatest building in town other than the fort, is now the headquarters of Chama Cha Mapinduzi (CCM), the governing party founded by Nyerere. The former royal palace is a museum. There are "Turkish baths" everywhere, mostly ruined. The sultan built his ninety-nine-person harem in a particularly fine spot on a beach outside town, with elegant bathing facilities as befits its purpose. Nearby is the ruin of another palace, saved only because the building was later used as a go-down, a warehouse, which it still is.

Meanwhile, there are foreigners, like the American Emerson Skeens, a former psychologist from New York, who is living out every foreigner's fantasy—running exquisite, if idiosyncratic, small hotels on the island of Zanzibar that have acquired cult status among sophisticated travellers (the kind that insist on being called travellers, not tourists). He had also acquired what amounts to a whole ruined village in the jungle on the island of Chole, part of the Mafia Island archipelago some 200 kilometres (124 miles) to the south; the ruins will soon become props for a lodge for affluent Western eco-tourists.

....

The day after I arrived, I gave in to Harry's importuning and allowed his brother to take me on a spice tour of the island, with a detour to see the red colobus monkey sanctuary; I collected entirely unwanted samples of cloves, peppercorns, nutmeg, cardamom, and coriander, which I abandoned in my hotel room. Later, Harry and I went to lunch at a Zanzibari institution called Two Tables, which was indeed just two tables set up on the second-floor balcony of a Swahili family home. The menu consists of whatever the family is having that day; the customers eat while the kids play in the living-room next door. We had soup, fish with fried banana, lentil and beef curry, and rice, and a splendid combination of juices, one-third avocado, one-third passion fruit, one-third mango.

That night, having shed the barnacle-like Harry, I went to see a locally famous performance artist who calls himself Shaka Zulu. His art is simplicity itself. It consists of dressing up in "native costumes" and getting himself run over by cars and station-wagons, which symbolizes Africa's oppression by the forces of alien technology. The most interesting thing is watching the faces in the crowd as the front end of a jeep slowly mounts the apparently dead figure—first an expression of glee; followed by apprehension, fascination, and anticipation; and then, when Shaka springs to his feet, a clear show of disappointment. The "native costume" he wears is not at all authentic, but this is precisely the point—authenticity in Shaka's view is of interest only to Outsider anthropologists, whose academic desire he believes is to imprison Africans in the folklore of their past.

....

Travellers have been visiting Zanzibar island for at least two thousand years; it was first mentioned in the first-century Greek handbook *Periplus of the Erythraean Sea*: "In this place there are sewed boats and canoes hollowed from logs, which they use for fishing and catching tortoises caught in a peculiar way, whereby the channel is blocked between breakers." These boats and this practice can still be seen on the island.

The original inhabitants were the Zanj, and Zanzibaris of Swahili origin believe the island name derives from the Persian word "Zangh," meaning black, and "Bar," meaning coast. (The Arabs think it comes from "Zayn Zal Barr," or "Fair Is the Island.") The Zanj, immigrants from the mainland, were followed in the seventh and eighth centuries by Arab and Persian traders. The first mosque built in East Africa was constructed here in 1107, and is still in use.

By the seventeenth century Zanzibar had supplanted Kilwa as the most prosperous city on the coast and had become the most significant trading city on the African Indian Ocean. It boomed even further after Seyyid Said moved from Oman, planting cloves and rationalizing the slave trade, until then haphazard and inefficient. The sultan organized a central slave market and massive slave auctions. The British explorer Richard Burton, not a man with a queasy stomach, was appalled at what he saw: "Slavery was rampant," he wrote, "for Zanzibar was a clearing house for the import and export of human beings. Since the sultan extorted a tax on each slave to pass through the islands, wretches were thrown overboard when sick, to prevent paying duty; and the sea-beach before the town presented horrible spectacles of dogs devouring human flesh."[6]

It wasn't until 1873, under the threat of a British naval bombardment, that Sultan Barghash (Seyyid Said's successor) signed a decree outlawing the slave trade. Nevertheless, the clandestine traffic continued; the secret caves where the wretched human cargo was kept are now on the Zanzibar tourist trail. They were confined in these dank caves until the ships came, then they were taken off, to Madagascar and the Indian Ocean islands (where French plantation owners ignored the British-led outcry against the traffic) and to the Gulf States and the rulers of Somalia, where life was unchanged. Indeed, the traffic continued well into the twentieth century and was widely rumoured to still be going on when Abed Karume waged his Afro-Shiraz revolution in Zanzibar in 1964. There are still slaves in the Sudan and Somalia and elsewhere in Africa.

....

A day or so later I flew down to Mafia Island, 200 kilometres (125 miles) to the south. There are perhaps thirty thousand people living on Mafia and its archipelago, almost all of them fishermen. On Chole, which is where Skeens's ruined village was being metamorphosed into a luxury lodge, the World Wildlife Fund has a mandate under the Ministry of Fisheries to set up and run a marine sanctuary. The local people support the project, mostly because they hope it will protect them from the dynamite fishermen from Dar, who are not only killing the fish, but ruining the coral reef—the resource on which the island's tourism potential is based.

The dynamiters were widely believed to have paid off the ministry officials who were supposed to be protecting the reef. The WWF, fed up with harassment by the interlopers, had bought a Boston Whaler fireboat with water cannon and were planning to deploy it against the fishermen from Dar. "They'll either leave or we'll sink them," the WWF guy said gleefully. "We'll have an unsigned confession ready. If they sign, we'll let them on board. If not, tough, fellows, swim to Dar ..." Meanwhile, the reef was rapidly disappearing. Threats and counter-threats were exchanged. An (unlit) stick of dynamite was thrown through the WWF window, and Mafia residents had been told dynamite will be used to silence opposition if necessary. Said to be hard-nosed street toughs, not real fishermen, the dynamiters have already destroyed the coral reef around Dar, but no one there seems to care, even now that the beaches are being eroded because their protection is gone. In any case, Dar pumps its sewage onto the beaches—who's going to swim?

Despite the explosives, the beaches of Mafia, Ungara, and Pemba are extraordinary, the best of the clichés—fine white sand, brilliant blue sea, coral, palm fringed, balmy breezes.

Back in Zanzibar itself there is a plan afoot to build umpteen 200-, 300-, 400-bed hotels and several golf courses. Most of Zanzibar consists of coral, which is poor for growing things. Of course, they want to site the golf courses near to town, which is on the little remaining land adequate for food crops. Again, no one seems to care except the NGOs and the people who take their money (who are also the people who circumvent the regulations). The island is much too small to support mass tourism, but no one is paying any attention.

DAR ES SALAAM AND THE TANZANIAN LITTORAL

Dar es Salaam, once a garden city, was by 1997 run down, depressed, and crime ridden. Everyone who could afford them had guards at home. Even middle-class people had two night watchmen, a day guard, and a couple of dogs, in addition to iron bars across windows and doors. Restaurants and parking spaces were also guarded.

The preferred guards were the Maasai. A Maasai guard is a guarantee of safety. Armed only with his spear and a red blanket and a whole lot of attitude, one Maasai is thought to be guard enough for a largish parking lot. Would-be perpetrators know that, if they attempt violence on a Maasai, they will soon have a dozen or a hundred hostile tribesmen on their case. This being so, the Tanzanian capital's affluent set up recruiting stations in the Maasai homelands at Arusha, near Mounts Meru and Kilimanjaro; the less affluent could only look on in envy.

Why was all this protection necessary in a country until recently renowned for its almost incredible civility? One reason was that crime had become more violent, in part because of the cheap arms from Mozambique pouring across the border in the aftermath of the civil war there, and in part because of the flood of refugees into the cities, both from the war-ravaged countries of Rwanda and Burundi and from the impoverished "self-help" villages set up by Nyerere's socialist government.

After thirty years of independence, Tanzania's economy was a basket case. The transport system was a wreck: many of the roads, even major ones, were virtually impassable, and the much-vaunted TanZam Railway, built by the Chinese at a cost of $400 million (U.S.), ran only haphazardly. The country had to import huge quantities of food despite its rich agricultural land, and the industrial base was operating at 30 to 40 per cent capacity.

....

Julius Nyerere, the first president of Tanzania, was known throughout his time in office as *Mwalimu*, teacher, and the pedagogical lessons he taught his new country were radical socialism, non-alignment, anti-racialism, and self-reliance. He was popular when he was first made president, and was just as popular when he stepped down in 1985 to become chairman of the party he founded, Chama Cha Mapinduzi, the Party of the Revolution. His policies were principled, rigorous, consistent, coherent, and economically disastrous. They were also enforced in a way entirely at odds with his professed love of liberty: during the 1970s, Tanzania had more political prisoners in its jails than the apartheid regime of South Africa.

The country Nyerere took over in 1965 had been explored, but hardly developed, by the Germans. It had been subsequently neglected by the British because, unlike Kenya, it seemed to have little to offer. At independence, there were few white settlers, the economy was lethargic, and there was virtually no black civil service—there were only 120 university graduates in the whole country. In 1967, in an attempt to shake things up, Nyerere and his party issued the Arusha Declaration, which was intended to transform the country, into a self-reliant republic whose basic unit would be the *Ujamaa* village, collectives that were in theory run along "African lines."[7] African lines they might have been, but the peasants, used to operating through networks of families and clans, resented the collectives bitterly and sabotaged them when they could. At the same time, Nyerere nationalized everything, expropriating the most productive citizens, the Asians, who until then had run most of East Africa's commerce. Many of those Asians have returned, now that Nyerere's successors are loosening their reins on the economy.

Nyerere did have his successes. The education system, poor and ill equipped as it is, manages to provide basic education for most of the country's citizens, including its women. And, in part because no tribe is dominant in Tanzania, unlike in Kenya or Zimbabwe, Nyerere's campaign to have a national consciousness free of tribal loyalties has been startlingly successful. As a result, Swahili is truly a lingua franca in the country, and is much more the official language than it is, say, in Kenya, where English is still much more common. This is a great source of strength and stability.

Nyerere's successor, Ali Hassan Mwinyi, edged ever so cautiously away from Nyerere's view that development is a northern calculation to entrap the developing, perhaps because he could see that the policy had left very little economy to develop. Village self-sufficiency, Nyerere's socialist dream, had simply evaporated available capital, never increased it. As some of the Asians returned, the economy started to pick up, though very slowly. What picked up a lot faster was, alas, that scourge of Africa, government corruption.

By 1995, the year of the country's first-ever multiparty elections, the situation was dire: a corrupt bureaucracy, no capital, a ruined economy, and a country that relied on foreign aid for up to 60 per cent of its current accounts.

Tanzania has become skilled in the guilt-manipulation that ensures an ongoing money supply without any attempts being made to scrutinize its uses or control its spending. That would be "intolerable interference." The only people who won't see this are the foreign NGOs who provide the money; but then they, too, are skilled at extracting funds, for which they often refuse to supply an accurate accounting.

I met a young woman in Dar who thought none of this mattered. She was earning only $50 a month, and sending some of it to her family in a village near Morogoro;

she had to repair clothes at night to get by. That didn't matter either. She was going to vote against CCM in the elections, but not with enthusiasm.

"If Nyerere was still president, I'd vote for him."

"Why?"

"Look what he left us. We may be poor—we are poor—but we've had peace for thirty years, ever since independence. We settle our differences in argument. Tribal differences don't matter. We're happy. Is that so bad?"

No, I said, I didn't think it was.

....

Then I talked to a woman called Mara, who every day buys a few fish at the Dar market and takes them out to a roadside stall she has set up in the industrial district. Her day starts before four, when she walks from the shantytown where she lives to the *daladala*, or minibus, stop, then walks again to the fish market, then takes another *daladala* to her stand, waiting patiently for someone to buy what she has. Sometimes she cooks the fish on charcoal, and if she is lucky she will sell it all. If not, she takes it home for her family to eat, but earns no money. In all, she makes maybe $1.50 a day, but sometimes less, because the fish spoils before it is sold. And sometimes she must pay the thugs who threaten to topple her stand. She has no capital, no reserves, no way out: it is all she knows how to do. She is terrified she will become ill, because, if she does, she doesn't think her children will survive.

I thought she was heroic.

I bought two fish from her, and gave them to an astonished beggar.

KILWA KISIWANI,
THE ROYAL CITY

For centuries Kilwa, or Kilwa Kisiwani, located in what is now southern Tanzania, was the dominant city-state on the coast. The sixteenth-century *History of Kilwa* gives a somewhat confusing account of its origins: "Historians have said, amongst their assertions, that the first man to come to Kilwa came in the following way. There arrived a ship in which there were people who claimed to have come from Shiraz in the land of the Persians. When they arrived in the ship that went to Kilwa, they found it was an island surrounded by the sea ... They disembarked on the island and met a man who was a Muslim followed by some of his children ... They asked the Muslim about the country and he replied: The island is ruled by an infidel from Muli, who is king of it; he has gone to Muli to hunt."

Whoever was there first, Kilwa's population was soon an inextricable mix of Arab, Persian, and Zanj, and the city controlled the coastal and Indian Ocean trade for centuries, even through the Zimba ravages, until it was sacked by the Portuguese in the eighteenth century. Thereafter it fell into decline, and Zanzibar become the dominant trading entrepôt.

In 1500, Pedro Alvares Cabral reported: "Then our captain inquired concerning Zaffalle [Sofala]. This Moor gave him the information that Zaffalle was a mine of much gold and that a Moorish king possessed it, that this king lived on an island which is called Chiloa [Kilwa] ... This island is small, near the mainland, and is a beautiful country. The houses are high like those of Spain. In this land there are rich merchants, and there is much gold and silver and amber and musk and pearls. Those of the land wear clothes of fine cotton and of silk and many fine things, and they are black men."[8]

In fact, Kilwa Kisiwani is not on an island but a high cliff on the mainland. To get there these days you must be ferried by a shallow-draft boat and dropped in the surf, to wade ashore. Then there is an arduous climb up the hillside to the plateau above, a grassland in which are scattered the sad remains of "the houses, high like in Spain," nothing much more than coral-brick foundations. Still, with some imagination you can pick out the streetscapes and wander through the courtyards of the merchants' mansions, and sit for a while on a bench made from the ruins of the sultan's palace and stare out across the blue of the Indian Ocean. Dhows plied those waters, and still do. But the merchants who grew fat on the profits of the traffic from Monomotapa are long gone. Perhaps their descendants are dhowmen still, plying the Arabian waters, conjuring the tunes of Africa on the phosphorus waters in the dark tropical nights. It is a melancholy place, Kilwa the Great, much given to thoughts of decay, entropy's child.

GOLDEN SOFALA

Which left ... Sofala, Monomotapa's home port. I flew to the fabled Sofala—or to where I thought it was, because no one seemed to know—in a twin-engined Otter with a man I knew only as Guy, who appeared to make his living flying tight-lipped people and unlabelled packages to inaccessible places. He'd got his training, he told me, with the Flying Doctors in Kenya (which they denied, when I asked them in Nairobi). He said he'd fly me down to Beira, as he had some business he could do there, unspecified. Beira is Sofala, or at least some think so. And Sofala is still marked on some maps, across the Pungue River estuary. Sometimes it's called New Sofala, sometimes not. No one really knows if it's the same place.

Guy only asked two questions: will you pay me $100 (U.S.), and do you have a visa?
"Yes," I said, "to both questions."

"Good on the visa," he said. "We're not landing anywhere they have Immigration,
but if you're stopped by soldiers and you do have a visa, all they'll do is fine you for
not having the proper entry stamp. Shut up and pay the squeeze; don't even try to
negotiate, not with that lot. Without a visa, it's prison for you, and you would not
like their prisons, believe me."

Indeed, that morning I'd read in the local paper of five Zimbabwean gold-
panners caught on the wrong side of the border by Mozambican police. Four of the
five had died in the squalor of a Mozambican prison before the Zimbabwean
authorities found out they were there, and the fifth was so traumatized by his
ordeal he refused to speak of it. They were all Manica, like my friends in the
Chimanimani village. The Manica in previous centuries hadn't paid much attention
to borders.

"Why don't we just go through Customs and Immigration?" I asked Guy.
"Waste of time," he said.

He obviously had interesting connections, because as we swooped low over the
escarpment into Mozambican air space we were briefly buzzed—or inspected?—by
an elderly Dakota prop plane bearing Mozambique markings and a military
demeanour. Guy waved as they went by, and they turned away.

"Who were they?" I asked.

"Mozzie air force," he said "No probs, I've done them favours before."

The flight down took an uneventful two hours. We swung in over the startlingly
blue Indian Ocean with its baking soda–white beaches. There was no sign of habitation at all on the coast, except for one resort on the mainland ("Mozzie army
camp—best-looking hookers in Africa") and one on an atoll of the purest blue coral,
a resort that looked oddly like a Howard Johnson's, with catamarans moored alongside ("Rich Boers, goggling").

Beira is on the north side of the Pungue estuary. The last time I'd seen it, many
years before, it was a modern industrialized city. Now, from the air, it looked normal enough. The harbour was filled with dhows and shipping vessels (it was only
later that I saw how many were hulks). There was a train, not moving, on the line
out of town, the terminal point of the Zimbabwe–Malawi railroad, and the streets
seemed to be full of traffic, swerving around stalled or abandoned cars. There were
people everywhere. We were coming in low, and I could see many of them looking
up—it wasn't so long ago that planes meant military, and military meant bombs, or
worse. The people hadn't adjusted to peace yet.

I'd checked earlier with the Canadian mission to see how safe Mozambique was
for visitors, and they referred me to the U.S. consular section. The Americans said
road travel between cities was "not recommended" but that Maputo was okay.

About Beira, they hadn't really anything to say. Why would I want to go there anyway? I didn't feel like explaining that I had no better reason than to see where the porters from Great Zimbabwe had taken their gold and ivory, so I hung up and called the South African trade commission instead. They were much more reassuring, in their way. South Africans have never been afraid of Africa. "Still," I was told, "remember that there are more than a million demobbed soldiers in the country, and many refugees pouring back over the border from South Africa and Zimbabwe, going home. And remember that there is 80 per cent unemployment in the country, that inflation is a mere 50 per cent or so, and some of these ex-soldiers are sure to feel the world owes them a living, and that means you. Avoid groups of young men, if you can. But it you are careful, and make local allies, you will be all right."

Vasco da Gama showed up in Sofala in February 1498, two months before Columbus set out on his third voyage to the Americas. He was on his way to "discover" the route to the Indies, and in Mozambique he looked for pilots to take him there—the Arabs had, after all, been making the voyage for centuries.

The whole coast, da Gama discovered, was under the domination of the sultan of Kilwa, which he described as one of its most celebrated ports, "having constant commercial relations with Persia, Arabia and India." Sofala, he was told, was in the country that furnished large and inexhaustible quantities of gold for the sultan's coffers.

A few years later, in 1506, Diogo de Alcaçova wrote to the king of Portugal: "The kingdom, Sir, in which there is the gold that comes to Sofala is called Vealanga ... And, Sir, a man might go from Sofala to a city which is called Zimbabwe which is large, in which the king always resides, in ten or twelve days ... and in the kingdom gold is extracted; and in this way: they dig out the earth and make a kind of tunnel, through which they go under the ground a long stone's throw, and keep on taking out from the veins with the ground mixed with the gold, and, when collected, they put it in a pot, and cook it much in fire; and after cooking they take it out, and put it to cool, and, when cold, the earth remains, and the gold all fine gold ... and no man can take the gold out without leave from the king, under penalty of death."[9]

Several centuries later Lyons McLeod, who in 1860 was British consul at Mozambique, published a short history of the place. The Portuguese discoverers, he said, "found in the interior a large Kingdom called Mocoranga, which reached to the coast, along which it extended from Delagoa Bay to the Zambezi. This kingdom was fast falling into decay, and appears to have been the remains of a much greater one, which was partially destroyed or broken up, by the invasion of a warlike people called the Lindens.

"They discovered that the kingdom of Mocoranga was very powerful, and the neighbouring vast territory under the Monomotapa more powerful still. They heard of people who had formerly inhabited these countries, who were far advanced in civilisation."

McLeod also published a list of the gold, silver, copper, and iron mines "which have been worked, but are now entirely neglected, as the country is destitute of labour, the Portuguese having entirely drained it to supply the slave trade of the Brazils, Cuba and America."

Sofala didn't impress him much, having deteriorated greatly since its glory days. "[It] is built at the mouth of the river of the same name, is divided into two portions, one of which contains the Moors, or labourers of the small settlement, and the other the governor and his subordinates, together with their slaves, who may, collectively, be well styled the drones, for they live by taxes and duties levied on the more industrious Moorish community.

"That portion of Sofala which is known as Portuguese Town is dirty in the extreme, while Moorish Town is but little better.

"Formerly the church was rich in gold and jewels of great value, which adorned the statue of the blessed Virgin; but the priests who sold their fellow-beings into slavery did not hesitate to rob the temple of their God.

> " **T**he juice of the India-rubber tree affords amusement for the little black boys of Inhambane, who chew it until it becomes plastic, and then inflating it with their breath, are pleased with the report which the bladder makes upon bursting."
>
> *From McLeod,* Travels in Eastern Africa with the Narrative of a Residence in Mozambique

"Of labouring Moors, groaning slaves and degenerate busybodies, there are said to be 125 persons.

"The military establishment of Sofala is from thirty to thirty-five soldiers, sent from [the town of] Mozambique for some misdemeanour while serving in that garrison; to these add a few Moors and Kaffirs, who are shut out of the fort at night, and do double duty by day.

"Sofala is admirably situated for commerce, and nothing but the baneful influence of the slave trade could have reduced it to its present state: a melancholy contrast to the flourishing Arab settlement which the Portuguese found there in 1505."

We landed at a small airstrip at the edge of a decaying industrial suburb. There was no tower, only a windsock and a small hut, around which lounged several groups of young men, dressed in that universal African gear—knitted caps or baseball caps, cheap windbreakers, nylon pants, Bata shoes. They seemed to know and expect Guy, which was reassuring. As Guy was securing the plane, a small Mazda pickup roared up in a cloud of dust. Guy squeezed into the cabin with three others and motioned me to climb onto the back. A dozen hands helped me up, and we roared away. Otherwise, I was ignored.

For about half an hour we made our way through the decaying city. There were shantytowns everywhere, often propped up against the walls of a locked or abandoned factory, row upon row of tiny huts cobbled together from scraps of corrugated iron and wooden crates. I saw what looked like an old fort, now in ruins. From the smell, there was obviously no sanitation. People were living in abandoned gas stations, overturned dumpsters, cardboard boxes tied together with twine. One man was fast asleep, or dead, his head and torso in an emptied garbage can. An astounding number were on crutches, or without an arm, an ear, an eye, a hand, fingers. They seemed astonishingly cheerful, and waved as we passed.

We roared through a "shopping district" of single-storey buildings, once whitewashed but now crumbling, storefronts with iron burgle-bars, most of them shuttered and dark. But on the sidewalks a lively market had sprung up. There were small piles of fruit, hoarded by large and tough-looking women. There were baskets of sugar cane, mounds of what looked like cabbage, caskets of sorghum and maize. Shoppers were milling about, the women, colourfully dressed as always, carrying their immense burdens on their heads. As in all African markets there was a chaotic vigour to the place, a lack of order, of tidiness, of any kind of system; even the market stalls were scattered at random, at varying distances from the curb and each other.

Finally, at a central square surrounded by one-storey official-looking buildings, also mostly abandoned, the pickup ground to a halt.

"Okay, out you get," Guy said, waving back at me. "Pick you up here an hour before sunset."

"Here?" I said dubiously, eyeing the milling throng, already crowding about, their faces upturned hopefully—and, I thought, greedily. "Where do I go from here?"

"Dunno," said Guy. "I'm not a bloody guide." And off he roared, leaving me to face the throng. The crowd pushed in, staring. One of them pawed at my holdall. I yanked it away. They began to mutter angrily.

At the far side of the square I saw what appeared to be a taxi stand. There were a few dangerously rusted vehicles and half a dozen bicycle taxis, some with sidecars, a few with only a spare saddle clamped over the rear wheels. I waded through the clutching hands and crossed the square, leaving a wake of grasping children and whining beggars. What little Portuguese I had deserted me utterly, and I couldn't even remember the word for *hello*.

I approached a group of taximen, who stared at me blankly.

"Sofala?" I asked, jerking my thumb in what I hoped was the right direction. This drew no reaction whatever, only more blank looks, and the odd murmur, which sounded like "*eyeyeey*," an approving sort of sound. I think they were agreeing with me that we were in Sofala, which wasn't what I had in mind. The bicycle taxis clustered around closely, shutting out even the beggars.

"Anyone speak English?" I asked hopefully. There was no response. "*Français?*" No response. "*Russki?*" I asked, exhausting my meagre store of languages. (I hadn't wanted to risk Afrikaans, knowing that South Africa had supported the rebel side in the recent war.)

"*Da! Da!*" one of the taximen yelled.

He was hopping up and down on one leg, the only one he had. About half the "drivers" had some limb or other missing. One of the consequences of the long, long civil war, apart from the obvious, were the land-mines still littering the countryside. Every now and then another hapless citizen would be blown apart. Mozambique has the distinction, if that's what it is, of having more one-legged people than any other country on the planet.

I eyed him doubtfully. How did a one-legged man ride a bike? And where did the Russian come from? I knew the Chinese had been active in Tanzania, but the Russians had been across the continent at Angola, and then mostly through their stooges, the Cubans.

"Where did you learn Russian?" I asked incredulously.

"Patrice Lumumba University," he said, grinning. "Army, then, until the Boers shot me. After the war, this"—he gestured at the bike; the crowd; his own stringy, one-legged body.

"Okay," I said, "let's go. The old port. Sofala. From before Beira was built. You know it?"

"Of course," he said, "We go quick quick. You pay in South African money?"

"Dollars?" I asked.

"No, no," he said, "dollars no good. Rands better. You can buy anything with rands."

"Okay, we go now," I said, eyeing the restless crowd. I didn't want to peel off any money until we had put some distance between us and them. They looked altogether menacing. He seemed to agree.

He strapped his left (and only) foot to the pedal and we set off, making very good speed on the flat. I was clinging to his back from the spare saddle. His torso felt tough and wiry, like an old rope doormat, and he smelled rank.

I was quickly lost. I had no idea in which direction the sea lay. I had no idea whether he knew where we were going, or what I wanted. I didn't see how I would ever get back to the square, at least without him. I resolved to cling to him as long as possible. We rounded a corner onto a long straightaway. Just then, a group of young men who had been lounging on the pavement started after us.

"I think we'd better go faster," I said to my furiously pedalling taximan. I didn't like the purposeful air of the running men behind us, strung out like the field in a 1,500-metre chase. There must have been a dozen of them, all about the same age. They looked fit and, from what little I could see, they weren't smiling. The taximan looked over his shoulder. "Faster, faster!" he agreed, using the Russian word *bistro*, standing up the better to pump his only pedal. I struggled to hang on to his belt, which was humping up and down like a ropy piston. The gang was gaining on us.

"Bistro!" I yelled. *"Bistro!"*

He said nothing, just continued pumping like mad, but he was clearly flagging. Another hundred metres and we'd be able to turn left. Then we could go downhill. Surely we could outdistance them on a hill?

I looked back. They were still gaining, the lead runner now only about ten paces behind. It was going to be touch and go. One of the pursuers was yelling something, but I couldn't make it out. They were sprinting hard now, seeing they could catch us with a last effort. We're going to make it! I thought, but I was wrong. The gang put on an extra burst of speed just as the driver ran completely out of juice. They surrounded us and we came to a stop, my taximan panting, a raw, ragged, gasping sound.

I got off the bicycle stiffly and stood upright.

"Who are you?" one of the men demanded, in perfectly serviceable English. There were about a dozen of them. They crowded in, standing close.

"Who are you?" I countered. Not very original, but then no one but Guy even knew I was in the city, and I doubted he'd make much fuss if I never showed up for our rendezvous. He'd think it was my own stupid fault.

"As to that, the stranger should declare himself first," another of them said, also in English. "But very well. We are the police here."

"The police?" I asked. "Without uniforms? Why were you running after me?" I didn't know if this was good news or bad—I remembered those Mozambican jails.

"As to that," he said again, "there are no more real police around here. We are the police now. You would call us vigilants."

"Vigilantes," I said, "that's great, just great. Vigilantes."

"As to that, we were running because we were giving you this back." He handed me my green Lunenburg Academy cap. "Now, who are you?"

I didn't believe a dozen men would run after me just to return a dropped cap. There must be something else.

"I'm not a political," I said, "I'm interested in the old Sofala, when Sofala had been a great port, before the Portuguese came. That's why I'm here, to see what's left of the old days."

The rest of the men were silent, listening intently. I didn't know how many spoke any English. Their faces looked blank.

"As to that," he said again, "do you have papers, passport, a visa? Where did you come from?"

"Yes," I said, opening my bag to show him my papers, but he pushed it away without looking.

"Yes," he said, "as to Sofala, I remember."

"No, you cannot. I mean much older than the war, much older than you, much older even than the Portuguese . . ."

"I remember," he said again. "My father told me and his father told him. But we never called this place Sofala. The Arabs called it that." He told me what they had called it, but I didn't catch it. It sounded like Pungara. I liked this conversation better; we were edging away from the whys and wherefores. His own name, he said, was João.

"There is nothing here of the old days" he said. "It is all gone."

"It was on the other side of the river," I said, pointing.

"There is no river that way," he said suspiciously.

"Okay, maybe that way," I said, reversing direction.

"As to that, there is no more Sofala," he said.

After more fruitless toing and froing, he said abruptly, "You have South Africa money?" I did, I said. "Good," he said, "now we go eat." And so we did. Behind a locked storefront nearby there was a canteen that had cases of lukewarm Zambezi beer from Zimbabwe and Castle lager from South Africa, and large stewpots of piripiri chicken, which may or may not have been chicken but which was in any case fiery hot and delicious. I guessed this was the real reason they had run after me. But I came to think I was wrong. I think the real reason was simple curiosity.

João was the only one who talked. The others ate, crowded around, listened, and stared. My taximan, who had been dragged unwillingly along, just ate. I ignored the others as best I could.

"Were you in the army?" I asked.

"For a while, yes," he said. "But I was RENAMO, and when we were losing, my family and I walked to South Africa. Because I was RENAMO, someone knew to turn off the fence, so I knew when the fence was okay, when it was hot, when it killed. They turned it off and we walked through." He walked all the way to Pietersburg, through the lion country of South Africa's Kruger National Park. He laughed, without bitterness. He knew perfectly well that the only really dangerous animal in Africa is man. In Pietersburg he got a job as a day labourer on an Afrikaner farm, and just waited.

....

Even by colonialist standards, the Portuguese stewardship over Mozambique was a disgrace. In the early days, they drained the country of its people, selling them to the

Americas, keeping just enough for a labour force of their own. When slavery was abolished in the nineteenth century, very little changed—"forced labour" substituted for slavery. Under this scheme, every man in the country had to put in six months' unpaid labour; in the south, most of them were sent to work in the mines of South Africa in exchange for the routing of some South African freight through Lourenço Marques, as Maputo was then called, and Beira.[10] Later, the system was "modernized," which meant that the men got paid (in local currency) while the colonial authorities got paid in gold by South Africa.

Resistance to this atrocious rule began in earnest with the forming of FRELIMO, the Mozambique Liberation Front, in 1962. Four years later they had driven the Portuguese from the two northern provinces, and finally won independence in 1975.

At independence, 90 per cent of the population was illiterate. Three dozen doctors served the whole country. Things were made worse by the massive exodus of Portuguese skilled labour, together with the wholesale looting and sabotage of factories, machinery, and whatever meagre infrastructure existed. The economy, of course, collapsed and there were serious food shortages.

A crash program to educate the population was begun at once; the target of a hundred thousand new people in schools each year being met with the help of hundreds of foreign volunteers. For the rest, FRELIMO's Marxist and radical leaders collectivized agriculture and nationalized what little industry remained. The economy nosedived even further.

There were successes: mass vaccinations and instruction in basic hygiene and sanitation were brought off by cadres of just sufficiently educated instant "doctors." Moves were afoot to bring as much local self-government into play as possible.

But by 1983 the country was, to all intents and purposes, bankrupt. Industrial production had virtually ceased. There was widespread starvation. Then, to make it worse, South Africa abruptly expelled Mozambican mine workers in retaliation for the country's harbouring Robert Mugabe in his fight against Ian Smith's Rhodesia.

Feeding on the discontent came RENAMO, a South African–backed guerrilla group who set out to systematically destroy what was left of the country, hoping to overthrow the government by making it impossible for them to govern or, indeed, to have much of a country worth governing. In the Cambodian fashion, intellectuals, teachers, and medical workers were shot out of hand. South African regular troops also gave support, when they could do so discreetly.

It couldn't possibly last. President Samora Machel was forced to do a deal with South Africa, and reluctantly signed the Nkomati Accord, in which Pretoria undertook to withdraw its support for RENAMO in return for the expulsion of the ANC and the opening up of the country to South African business. Machel abided by his commitment, but South Africa didn't even pretend to, and continued to supply arms and advisers to the rebels.

By the late 1980s South Africa abruptly lost interest; its rulers were preparing to deal with their country's own convulsion. The RENAMO rebels began to lose. At the same time FRELIMO officially abandoned its Marxist-Leninist ideology and switched to supporting a market economy, selling off state enterprises to anyone with hard currency to spare. They scheduled multiparty elections. After two rounds of South African— and Italian-sponsored talks, a cease-fire was announced in 1990, and while renegade RENAMO units were still attacking Beira and Maputo as late as 1992, the elections went ahead as scheduled. RENAMO took part, and lost.

The country held its breath. RENAMO said it would not recognize the election results. Then it said it would.

No more war. But not yet peace.

João came home.

When the war was over, or seemed to be over, he had walked back from South Africa, hoping to pick up the pieces of his family life from those dimly remembered times when there had been no fighting. But his village was gone, burned and bulldozed, those family members who hadn't gone with him dead as far as he knew. He came down to the coast, to the city, to see if he could find anyone he knew, or any work. He fell in with some comrades from RENAMO days, found much of the city in chaos, and without any prompting decided to do what he could to restore some vestiges of civil authority. They were being fed and housed by the community but received no pay, he said.

"Without authorization, without support?"

"None," he said. "There was no government here. They were busy elsewhere."

He didn't seem to think this so remarkable, or at least not so remarkable as I did. The government was too busy trying to see who would come out on top, who would "win the peace," whether they could live with each other. They had no time for local affairs.

Outside aid had vanished. Mozambique had been abandoned by the international-aid industry. It had already become a cliché that the country's new-found tranquillity was its worst enemy, because the aid people had left for more urgent catastrophes as soon as the Mozzies stopped killing each other. I wondered what behaviour they were reinforcing.

After our meal, I wanted to set off for Sofala again. I was well fed, and feeling safe in the company of these benign "vigilants." But no one was much interested in Sofala. "There is nothing there," João said again. "If you've seen the sea, you've seen what there is."

I wasn't sure—he didn't really seem to know what Sofala was, or why I cared— but there really wasn't anything I could do about it, and after a while the group of them escorted me back to the market square and left me there with great protestations of cordiality. My Russian-speaking taximan, who hadn't said a word through all this, vanished into the crowd as soon as he could.

....

Indeed, Sofala *is* Metropolitan Beira now. Some years back a typhoon exposed stones and rotting timbers from an ancient wharf, but before the archaeologists could do any serious work another storm came and carried the breastworks away. The porterage tracks have become a railway (repaired and running again after the war); the old wharves where the dhows docked are filled with rusting freighters of Panamanian and Liberian registry; but the only gold that moves through Beira is stolen, and the only ivory poached. Sofala of legend no longer exists, outside the history books.

....

I had waited at the rendezvous point for about ten minutes when I felt someone tugging at my sleeve. I looked down. It was a child of extraordinary beauty. She must have been about ten, with skin of golden chocolate and great fawn eyes. There were flies on her lip and she was covered with welts and sores. She tugged at my arm again.

"Please," she said in English, "we fuck for money?" I looked down in disbelief.

"What did you say?" I demanded, much too brusquely. She didn't understand the words, but she got the tone. Her eyes brimmed with tears.

"Please?" she said again. "You got rands? We fuck now?"

There was nothing I could say, but I bent down and took her hand. I gave her what South African money I had left, twenty rands, and told her to go away. She pressed into the crowd around me, looking back doubtfully. I turned away. But not before I saw a wizened adult hand grasp her by the shoulder, reaching for the money.

....

As the millennium neared, not everything was dark in Mozambique. South African and German money was pouring in. Resorts were being constructed on the magnificent Indian Ocean beaches (mostly, it is true, on islands easily defended against bandits). If Mozambique agrees to open its borders to South Africa's Kruger Park, wildlife, slaughtered for years by the starving or the merely trigger-happy, will once again flood into the country. The potential for tourism is striking. There were, indeed, a million demobilized soldiers around with nothing to do, but they were obviously not all resorting to mischief. As so often happens when a civil war runs out of patrons, the participants were merely sick of the killing and wanted to do something, anything, to stop it. Some, like João, were forces for stability, unheralded and unsung heroes. Mozambique's was a population weary of war.

Industry was barely ticking over, but there were factories in Beira brewing beer, making bedsteads, assembling Korean cars, employing workers at minuscule wages, but at least employing them. There were businesses, and railway workers, and affluent suburbs, albeit crumbling. Electricity worked, mostly. The Cabora Bassa Dam on the Zambezi was still generating power: no one had had the heart to knock it out. The central government was making valiant efforts to revive the coal mines at Moatize in central Mozambique, along with a rail line to what they hoped would be a revived port in the northern province of Nacala. The railway was running again, even if it still couldn't cross the Zambezi (the bridge had been bombed in 1986 and never repaired) and even though it was only going to Zambia, where they had no money to pay for anything. A business class still existed; I met a couple, she Mozambican and he Swedish, who ran a restaurant in Beira, and who said they were doing well. These were aspects of the city my taximan barely knew, a long way from the restless slums where João and his friends were keeping order.

There was also, for the moment, a fragile peace, just as there was in the whole southern end of this war-torn continent.

....

At the appointed hour, Guy returned. This time he was in a large van, unmarked, with stacks of boxes in the back, also unmarked. He wouldn't say what they were, but they were heavy enough to be weapons—and, with the war over, weapons are flooding across the borders into Tanzania, Zimbabwe, South Africa.

Once again we careened through the decaying city. And within the hour we were airborne.

"If you've got enough fuel," I yelled at Guy, "give me a look at the waterfront and the city, especially around the river."

"We're pushing our luck," he grumbled, but peeled away to the south and swung in a big arc over the ocean. I looked down at where I thought Sofala had been. There was nothing there that I could see, only more of the same dispiriting decay. Mozambique was a country that couldn't yet afford its history.

Part III
Towards Azania

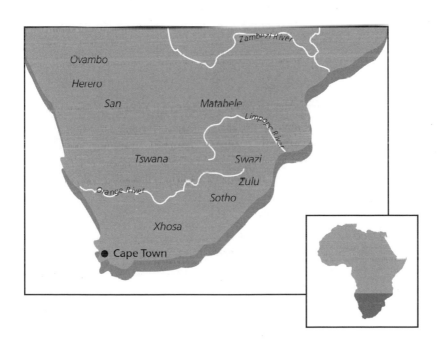

THE VIEW FROM THABA BOSIU

S outh of Monomotapa there were no ancient kingdoms. This is not to say there were no people, or that kingdoms didn't form later, but, when Matope ruled in Zimbabwe, southern Africa was still frontier country—the Khoikhoi, or Hottentots, were there, in the pastoral Cape, and of course the First Men, the San or Bushmen, had wandered the plains and lived in the hills for more generations than it is possible to count, but the Bantu were not much farther south than the Valley of a Thousand Hills, Zululand-to-be. (This is not to give legitimacy to the apartheid theorists, who believed the whites arrived in the south at the same time as the Bantu and the land was somehow theirs by right. The "I was here first, no you weren't, yes I was" of Afrikaners historiography now seems merely childish.)

The kingdoms that came to exist in the south were formed, in the African way, from shifting tribal allegiances, fluid migration patterns, conquests, accidents of history and personality, the deeds of tyrants, and—in at least two cases—the wise judgements of sensible kings, Moshoeshoe of Lesotho and the Khamas of Botswana. At least three of the kingdoms—the Zulu, the Swazi, and the Sotho—were created in historical times and were well documented, and so make a rare template for what happened anciently and is still happening in African politics.

The South owes much to the great movements of peoples set off by the iron will of the tyrant in Zululand, Shaka Zulu, in the early 1800s. So many of Shaka's henchmen fled, in the end. Matiwane headed west through Lesotho, where after desperate battles with Moshoeshoe, the Sotho leader, he was beaten off and finally destroyed by the British. Mzilikazi went north, and cut a horrid swath across the Transvaal before conquering the Shona and setting up the Matabele kingdom in present-day Zimbabwe. Shoshangane ruthlessly repressed the Tsonga between Maputo and the Zambezi, and set up a new kingdom he called Gaza. In the course of consolidation he overran and destroyed the Portuguese settlements at Maputo and Imhambane. Two others, Zwangendaba and Nqaba, became known as the Ngoni. They clashed with Shoshangane and were driven out. Nqaba was destroyed by the Makololo, whose descendants, the Living Stones, we encountered in Part I. Zwangendaba famously crossed the Zambezi during an eclipse of the sun, during which the local tribesmen fled and spread out on the western side of Lake Malawi as far north as Lake Tanganyika, 2,500 kilometres (1,550 miles) from his nemesis, Shaka. Sobhuza, not a henchman but a vassal, retreated north-east to the hills and created a new kingdom, Swaziland. Moshoeshoe, too wily to ever have been anyone's henchman, did the same in Lesotho.

The damned rain wouldn't stop. It blew in great drenching sheets over the Drakensberg Mountains to the northeast and swept across the Lesotho plains around Berea, turning the sand into glue, so the pony's hooves made a sucking sound at each step. And we had some way to go before we reached Thaba Bosiu, the "Mountain at Night," the legendary fortress of the wily old king, Moshoeshoe I, founder of the Lesotho nation.

Letlala, who was on the pony ahead of me, was impervious to the rain. His conical straw hat shed the water in a steady stream, and his blanket, tucked around him like a poncho, seemed almost dry. Mine, on the contrary, bunched around my armpits, was soaking wet. Water ran down my chest and pooled in my lap, before skidding off the saddle, turning it greasy and slippery to the touch. Water was filling my shoes. He wasn't wearing shoes, so it wasn't a problem for him. He seemed entirely at home in this place, as indeed he was, having been born in a neighbouring village some thirty-four years earlier, a great-great-grandson, he'd told me, of Moshoeshoe himself. (As I was to discover later, this wasn't such an impressive claim after all; half the Lesotho government and a good percentage of the population still avowed direct descent from the old king—how many wives had Moshoeshoe collected over his long life? Eighty? Ninety?)

We'd set out from Berea that morning at dawn, a beautiful clear early-summer's day. Strapped to Letlala's pony's withers was a large gunnysack containing our provisions: a spare set of clothing; some biltong, the cured venison that was the trail food of the frontier; and a huge packet of dried apricots, produced locally. Water we'd collect on the way; Lesotho is one of the few places in Africa where the streams are safe to drink from—or at least the mountain streams, and there was said to be a perennial spring on the summit of Thaba Bosiu. It was cold, the grasses still brittle from the frost.

For a few hours we passed across the plains in the increasingly warm sun; then, without warning, a bank of fog rolled over a koppie and descended on us, and with it a wind that chilled to the bone. Then the fog lifted, the sun came out—and so did a cloud of mosquitoes.

Well, the mosquitoes disappeared when the rains came.

I stared at the bobbing figure of Letlala, who was riding ahead of me. How much at home he looked! I grew up not more than 150 kliks (90 miles) from here, and as a child used to come often to Lesotho, or Basutoland as it was then; among my very early memories are the blanket-clad Basuto, or Ba-Sotho, with their marvellously efficient conical hats and their vigorous little ponies. It was so much a cliché of the place: the Sotho had taken to ponies as naturally as the Apache to horses in the Americas. Yet all the elements of the national cliché—the ponies, the blankets (still called Victorians), and the hats—were colonial adaptations. But then the Basotho nation itself was an invention. It was in some ways the most interesting thing about them. As a people, they had been invented no more than 150 years earlier by the man whose fortress we were going to see, Moshoeshoe the Great.

....

One of the great misconceptions that Westerners have always had about Africa is about the nature of tribalism. In the Outsider view, tribalism has been a permanent feature of the African political landscape, which is true enough; but they then assume that the tribes themselves are equally permanent. Scholars writing about African societies generally asserted that they changed, if at all, at a glacial pace. But this is not true. Permanence in this sense may be the result of a literate culture, of record-keeping—an essentially bureaucratic phenomenon. Africans keep their records in the heads of the elders and therefore have no need to be instructed who they are. They were *The People*. It didn't matter what others called them.

It can be frustrating for historians, already faced with a paucity of sources, to find that tribal names can mutate with surprising rapidity. Most of the tribes David Livingstone encountered along the Zambezi no longer exist, at least not under the names by which he knew them, though their descendants still inhabit the same villages and practise very much the same customs.

The Zulus, to take an example close to Thaba Bosiu, were merely an obscure Nguni subclan until the military genius of Shaka took hold of them; but, after his death, and the death of his murdering brother Dingaan, the Zulu name would, in the African way, have gone into decline or shifted to something else, except that by that time the missionaries and the settlers had arrived with their busy recording pencils. The Zulus remained the Zulus because the language they spoke was called Zulu by the missionaries and written down, codified for history. The word "Zulu" has now become synonymous with a much larger group, and the Zulus themselves, from King Goodwill to his councillor, Chief Mangosuthu Gatsha Buthelezi, would be indignant at the notion that they should think of themselves in any other way.

Lesotho, however, is the best extant example of this process.

....

I sat on the rock from which Moshoeshoe had conducted battles against the invading armies. Below was a steep cliff of about 50 metres (160 feet) or so, then a sloping, scrubby hillside treacherous with loose stones. To the northwest was the Khubelu Pass and its walled defences; just to the south the large cave where the King's wives took refuge during battles. The King's own cave was set into the cliff on the other side of the mesa, a long walk away, past his village and his home. If I stood up I could see Moshoeshoe's spring, and the burial ground where he was eventually laid to rest, marked by a cairn of stones. Letlala, who was sprawled on the edge of the cliff, pointed to a pile of boulders at the lower edge of the scree. Moshoeshoe's soldiers had hurled rocks down at the invading army of Sekonyela, the rival Sotho chieftain. They had hurled more rocks down at Matiwane, the Zulu invader and renegade from Shaka. Another set of rocks against the invading regiments of Mzilikazi's Ndebele, another Zulu renegade. And still more rocks against the British under General George Cathcart, and against the Boers of President M.T. Steyn's Orange Free State Republic. None of these invaders (except Sekonyela, and he only briefly) made it to the top of the hill where Moshoeshoe sat watching. And when they crept away, defeated, he sent after them tributes of cattle and humble apologies. For example, to the departing Ndebele, he sent several fat oxen and the message: "Moshesh salutes you. Supposing that hunger has brought you into his country, he sends you these cattle, that you may eat them on your way home." This was part of his political genius. Sometimes a king makes enemies, and Moshoeshoe had his share. But he saw no reason to keep them enemies. He understood the notion of countervailing forces, of having your enemies contend with each other instead of with you. He understood intuitively the diplomatic uses of conciliation. He was the statesman to Shaka's tyrant.

> In a protruding rock on the summit, not far from King Moshoeshoe's restored house, the footprint of one of the King's sons, Maleleka, can be seen. He was forbidden to marry a girl of lower rank, though he was in love, and, lamenting the loss of his beloved, he chiselled the print as an epitaph before leaping to his death on the rocks below.
>
> From Thompson, Survival in Two Worlds: Moshoeshoe of Lesotho 1786–1870

"Down there as boys we used to roll aside the boulders looking for human bones," Letlala said. "We wanted the skulls."

"Whatever for?"

He grinned. "We played a kind of soccer with them," he said.

Still, few skulls were found. Moshoeshoe's military stratagems were essentially defensive and, though the rolling stones were effective, they weren't always lethal.

Human habitation here is old, very old. Bushman (San) paintings have been found in caves and on rocky overhangs throughout Lesotho and South Africa; some of them have been dated back six thousand years and more. When I was a boy it became a game to find new ones, which even then, somehow, we knew better than to defile with graffiti or obscenities. I think they spoke to the romantic in us, for we found them beautiful, hauntingly so, these highly coloured, emotionally charged depictions of the natural world and their life in it. But there are no San left in these parts any longer, and their art is now no more "alive" than engravings on an Egyptian stele in a museum.

As for the Bantu ... Any country with eleven official languages, as South Africa has, will have a complicated history. But it is not so complicated as successive white governments (which emphasized the differences, and not the essential unity of culture) tried to make us believe.

Most ethnographers (David Hammond-Tooke, for example) now argue that the major groups that inhabit southern Africa (the Nguni, Tsonga, Sotho, and Venda) diverged, mostly for environmental and geographic reasons, from a single culture that drifted south over the Limpopo River; these were almost certainly the same peoples who built the city called Great Zimbabwe. The presumption is they had moved down from the Zambezi, and possibly before that had been part of the Great Dispersal of the Luba-Lunda of the Katanga basin, which in itself was but a part of the sweeping Bantu migrations that have been drifting across Africa for nearly two millennia.[1]

The ancestors of what was to become the Basotho nation settled in the region comparatively recently, possibly as late as the sixteenth century, only a hundred years before the white settlers arrived at the Cape of Good Hope, 1,000 kilometres (620 miles) to the southwest. Thereafter, for two hundred years or so, they settled into the folds of the mountains and made themselves at home, hunting among the crags and crannies, cultivating their grains on the plains around what was to be called the Caledon River. They were pastoral, and essentially peaceful. The culture they developed didn't lend itself to military adventure; it was too decentralized, and the chief's hold on his adherents depended on his ability to settle disputes more than on his genealogy or his military might. Tyrants were rare, because among the not-yet-Basotho it was a well-established custom that a citizen's allegiance could shift to another chief if his own became unpopular. The culture might be intensely conservative, but the politics were fluid in the extreme.

The system worked well until ... until the cataclysm wrought by the Zulus.

The rain had stopped. The sun came out, and the rocks glistened with moisture. It was warm, but there was a faint chill in the air as the breeze drifted down from the high mountains. I stared westward from the cliff face, towards the Orange Free State and its capital, Bloemfontein, where I was born. The Boer commandos who had besieged Thaba Bosiu (only to be repelled, to their great consternation and indignation) were my ancestors. But the Boers hadn't driven Moshoeshoe to this refuge. That had been a much more terrible scourge, the Zulu regiments from beyond the Drakensberg Mountains.

Letlala saw me staring at what remains of the old king's home.

"Yes," he said, "he was a great man. He was our father."

....

Moshoeshoe was a contemporary of Shaka's, born somewhere around 1790 in a small village in the high mountains of northern Lesotho. He was the son of a minor chief who ruled little more than his homestead—not an uncommon thing in Sotho governance, where "chiefdoms" ranged from hamlets to substantial towns.

But by the time he reached manhood, the peaceful pastoral valleys of the Maluti Mountains were already suffering the first of the long series of cataclysmic social tremors that were to last until the end of Moshoeshoe's life and much beyond. From the south, the white tribe that came to be called the Afrikaners was on the move, drifting steadily out of the reach of the British Empire and its (brand-new) anti-slaving ways. To the east, the great Empire of the Zulus was shaking itself awake.

....

The man who began the Zulu march to Empire was merely chief of a small clan called the Mthethwa, living near the coast at what is now Richard's Bay. Dingiswayo succeeded to the chieftainship of the clan in the closing years of the eighteenth century. Tradition has it that he was fed up with the jealousies and rivalries he saw around him and killed his brother, then the incumbent, on the grounds of incompetence. In any case, he took command, and in short order invented the military system that Shaka later perfected—merging the men into age-linked military units that placed members of diverse clans in single regiments, undercutting ancient clan and lineage loyalties. This was a change decisive enough to give his armies a crucial edge, and his power began to spread as he brought more and more subclans under his sway. One of these small chiefdoms was the Zulu, then numbering fewer than two thousand people. Its chief, Senzagakhona, had a lover outside marriage, Nandi of the Langeni tribe. In 1787 Nandi gave birth to an illegitimate child and called him Shaka.

The basic facts of Shaka's career are well enough known. He made a name for himself at Dingiswayo's court as a soldier, was installed as leader of the Zulus, and proceeded to revolutionize Zulu life along the lines his mentor had begun. He was a military tactician of genius. He used spies and covert action of all kinds, when he could. He introduced new weapons, particularly a short stabbing spear. He reinvented on his own the Roman "tortoise," a band of men who would creep forward under a "tortoiseshell" of shields. He banned sandals and hardened his men's feet by making them stamp up and down on thorns—those who didn't stamp down enthusiastically enough were clubbed to death. (In the latter part of his reign, when the tyrant's disease called megalomania was in full flower, he was having people impaled

From a praise song to Shaka from the Zulu poet Vilakazi:

Listen to me, you simpletons,

You who hear me speak

Until I waste to the thinness of a rake;

You let me wait and wait for nothing.

It is my duty to complete

The song to him, the mighty Cub

Of Phunga and of Xaba who was borne

Upon the shoulders of the sun,

Cared for and nurtured by the moon,

For he was destined to discover trails

Of Zulus bound for Pondoland.

From Zulu Horizons, *trans. D. Malcolmm and Florence Friedman*

for the most trivial of offences against the royal dignity—sneezing at the wrong time, not laughing, or laughing too much, at the royal jokes.)

After Dingiswayo's death—which Shaka engineered—Shaka became head of the Mthethwa confederacy, and his influence expanded rapidly. He set out systematically to conquer the territory of the present South African province of KwaZulu Natal, subjugating tribe after tribe and incorporating the remnants.

Three times in the early 1820s bands of marauders passed through the Caledon valley and the Maluti Mountains of what was to become Lesotho, destroying cattle and grain as they went, killing all they could reach, driving tribal remnants to take shelter in mountain caves and on sheer kopjes. By 1825 there was hardly a village in Sotho territory that hadn't been sacked at least once. Major towns were simply abandoned, their inhabitants drifting off, many of them starving. Reports from white explorers spoke of burned cities, heaps of bones everywhere. The early Boers caught sight of scrawny herds high up in the hills, which melted away when approached; there was no sign of the herdsmen. Lone refugees approached cautiously, fearful of being shot. They warned that desperate hunger had driven men to eat the flesh of others; a madness, they said, had passed through the land, turning good men into monsters, family against family, clan against clan, angering the spirits. Whole tribes disappeared.

A band of the dispossessed fell upon the village Moshoeshoe had recently founded below a mountain called Botha Bothe. He lost most of his cattle and retreated to his father's village, where he was attacked again. This time he prevailed, and as a bonus picked up a substantial herd of cattle and several new wives.

The key event that foreshadowed the end of the *Mfecane* and the beginning of reconstruction was Moshoeshoe's march in 1824 to his final fortress home at Thaba Bosiu.

Moshoeshoe undertook this now famous endeavour after a three-month siege by an ambitious Sotho rival called Sekonyela, who wanted control of the upper Caledon valley. The siege failed, but Moshoeshoe had seen the vulnerability of his home and, with his family and a mere two hundred followers, made a forced march of 100 kilometres (62 miles) to the south, where he had heard of a mountain that had perennial springs at the top and was suitable for defence. The march was made through frozen countryside in the dead of winter. Half-starved, chilled by the icy mountain air, they struggled through high passes. Several of the old, including Moshoeshoe's grandfather, were caught and killed by cannibals. The party reached its destination late one evening, and Moshoeshoe gave the mountain its new name: Thaba Bosiu, the "Mountain at Night," and set guards at the narrow fissures that pierce the cliffs and are the only way to the top.

He was to remain there for nearly fifty years, forming a constantly shifting network of ad hoc alliances, slowly expanding his influence and expanding his kingdom, defending it through diplomacy and war against Sotho and Nguni enemies alike, against missionary seductions, and finally against the white Afrikaner republics, skilfully playing the contending forces against one another. He was one of the few rulers of whatever colour to successfully manipulate Shaka and get away with it. Moshoeshoe's emissaries, bearing gifts and crafty plans of battle, persuaded the Zulus to take care of his rivals for him, and as a bonus Shaka, always ready for military adventure, detached a regiment to help Moshoeshoe deal with his neighbour to the south, a runaway Nguni chief called Matiwane. The Zulu army passed through Lesotho like a hurricane, leaving a trail of devastation behind them, but leaving the ruler of Thaba Bosiu the dominant power among the Sotho. Matiwane's power dwindled, and a British army finished him off.

Moshoeshoe's legend has almost certainly heightened his virtues and obscured his faults, but there is enough trustworthy evidence to confirm his remarkable qualities. Moshoeshoe and Shaka might almost have been invented by history to exemplify Diplomat and Warmonger, Statecraft and Tyranny. Shaka was an illegitimate child and had had a wretched boyhood. He never married and recognized no children of his own. He was violent, capricious, hungry for conquest. Moshoeshoe had had a happy childhood in a peaceful village; later in life he lost count of his many wives and children. He hated war and waged it only when he had to. He put a stop to the ritual killings of witches. He hardly ever imposed the death penalty, even for the most heinous of crimes. Even in his diplomacy he was unusual, resorting to deceit only after years of being lied to by the British. Shaka caused the *Mfecane*; Moshoeshoe's calm strength gathered in the tribal remnants, left them their customs and their chiefs, offered them the protection of the Mountain at Night, and imposed through his own moral stature a new way of living. It was typical of the man that, when he finally captured the cannibals who had eaten his grandfather, he refused to put them to death. In an apocryphal phrase, he is said to have remarked, "I will not defile the tomb of my grandfather," and sent them on their way with an injunction—thereafter strictly enforced—to abandon their flesh-eating ways.[2]

At the end, faced with a choice between conquerors, he had the wisdom to choose the one who wanted him least, the British. The Afrikaners to his west coveted his territory; they would have stripped him of his land and deprived him of his authority. Instead, by yielding to the British, he preserved his kingdom intact.

Lesotho is one of the smallest countries in Africa, and entirely landlocked. Quite unimportant, you might say. But from here you can plainly see all the turbulent, exotic, and melancholy history of the southernmost parts of Africa, from the mists of time until the uncertain but hopeful present.

What a complicated view it was from the summit of Thaba Bosiu! And yet, in some ways how very simple! How very simple, too, South Africa suddenly seemed.

From up here, the whites of southern Africa had presented to Moshoeshoe just another tribal incursion—complicated, to be sure, by their fearful weaponry and the sense that behind them, hidden from sight, were other powerful forces—but none the less somehow... familiar. And now? From up here, the great themes of Afrikaner history, the restless searching for the Land of Beulah, the mythical place where they could fulfil, at last, their grand destiny—all these were no different from the dreams of other tribes: they all wanted to make their way in the new world. From up here, the whole sour edifice of apartheid was just another episode of tribal hegemony; the Afrikaner chieftains believed in their manifest destiny, but then so did Sekonyela, so did the Xhosa's leading families (who ultimately produced the man called Mandela). South Africa, like all Africa, is still a work in progress.

The simmering angers over apartheid were altogether justified, but if you took the long view, which is the only view the land has, the petty squabbles of the Boer republics and the Afrikaners' later inglorious wrestling back of their land through political chicanery and sordid gerrymandering were not that important. That was over, a curiosity of history. It seemed to me, from up there on the Mountain at Night, that the historians of the future will look back on apartheid with bemusement but not very much interest. The only real issue, I saw, was this: How can cultures adapt? Can they invent new ways of dealing with the everlasting present, or must they remain imprisoned by the past, and stagnate, fade away into insignificance?

Meanwhile, of course, one lives when one lives, and finds important what one's contemporaries do. Men like Moshoeshoe, who understand the larger patterns of their contemporary existence, are very rare.

....

A few days after Thaba Bosiu, I headed a rental car away from Maseru, the sleepy little capital with its casino and burgeoning but still good-natured slums, and turned towards the historic mission station at Roma. I wanted to get to Thaba Tseka, for no other reason than that it was more or less at the geographic centre of the country. I hadn't decided what to do after that. I could either continue on, over what looked from my map like a perilous series of switchback roads, to the Sani Pass through the Drakensberg Mountains and into KwaZulu, or head north to Pitseng and thence to Maputsoe, on the Orange Free State border.

About 30 kilometres (20 miles) outside Maseru the road split. The Roma road, the better one, was on the right fork. I took the left. There was a signpost at the intersection, but it was broken and the larger half missing. I could make out the letters *CAUT*, which I took to mean "Caution," but what I was being cautioned about it was impossible to say. I spent a fruitless minute searching for the rest of the sign, but it was not there. Perhaps it had been seized for firewood, there being few trees any more. Still, I drove with Caut across the gully-eroded valley.

Like most of Lesotho, the landscape was magnificent—high mountains, rolling valleys, long vistas in the African palette of golden browns and hazy purples. For a long time the Europeans called Lesotho the Switzerland of Africa, but this does it a disservice. The Sotho themselves call it "The Land of Lost Horizons," for the view is always interrupted by another gaunt, spiny range of mountains. There are hardly any roads in Lesotho—fully two-thirds of the place is accessible only by bridle path. I looked around. Clusters of thatched huts clung to the hillsides.

The countryside seemed empty of people, as indeed it was; most of the men were in South Africa, working. Lesotho could no longer support its population, as it could in Moshoeshoe's day, and its only real export was labour. The coming to power of the ANC government in South Africa could do nothing about this, and in fact was likely to make things worse because they were under heavy pressure to ban "foreign" labour from taking "our" jobs—a litany familiar from, say, France or Germany. That Lesotho workers were foreign only by an accident of history would make little difference.

I crept over the Molimo Nthuse Pass, somewhat reassured by the rocky but stable roadbed. The road dropped steeply into a gully, but then began to climb again, heading for the summit of the Blue Mountain Pass. I'd been told this was the "most beautiful place in the country," but since this was confided by someone pulling on the arm of a slot-machine in Maseru's casino, I had reserved judgement. She was right, though. It was hard to see how there could be any place more beautiful than this. I stopped the car at the summit, just beyond a sign saying *Pony Trekking Centre*, and got out to sit on a stone on the edge of the drop. I looked eastwards, towards the Drakensberg Mountains, the Mountains of the Dragon themselves, fold after fold of misty purple beyond the golden grasses of the valley floor, a landscape imagined by a painter obsessed with the smoky colours of tobacco, ebony, and old ivory. I could just make out herdsmen hundreds of metres below; here and there smoke from a cooking fire rose lazily into the sky.

I turned to go, and saw three children staring at me no more than a few metres away. I hadn't heard them arrive, and they stood there solemnly, one with a thumb in his mouth.

"Lumela!" I said. Greetings.

They said nothing, just stared.

Another four children appeared out of the bush, then two more. They sidled closer to join the first three.

They came closer, still staring. Soon there were a dozen of them, edging closer, beginning to chatter amongst themselves. Two of the elder children were carrying sticks almost as large as they were. It was ridiculous, but a small alarm bell was going off in my mind—how many of them were there? Before I knew it, two were in the car, rummaging around on the back seat; others were pressing up against me, patting my pockets. The chattering rose in volume to a shrill yelling.

"Hey!" I said, ineffectually. "Hey!" I pushed my way over to the car—I had left the keys in the ignition, and I did not want my rental car rolling over the cliff, carrying small bodies with it. I felt a hand tugging at my wallet, slapped it away. *"Chelete!"* Money! the childish voices were yelling, *"Chelete chelete chelete chelete ..."*

Just then I heard a queer shuffling sound, surprisingly loud, as though an army were on the march in its bedroom slippers. A herd of cattle came ambling down the mountain road, filling the roadway completely. There must have been fifty of them. Two young men accompanied the animals.

One of the herders, seeing the crowd of children, walked towards us, raising his massive stick—more like a club, really—as he came. "Haikona!" he shouted at the kids. And again, "Haikona!" This word I knew. It's an all-purpose southern African word meaning variously "no!," "Absolutely not!," "Are you kidding?," "No way!," and "Get out of here!" The kids scattered, and melted into the bush.

The herdsman greeted me gravely. *"Lumela abuti!"* Greetings, brother!

"Lumela," I said. *"Keo leboha."* Thank you.

He said something else I didn't quite catch. I thought it was the ritual greeting, which translates to something like, "How did you get up?" I shrugged helplessly, and he switched to effortless English.

His name was Mopeli, and he lived in a small village down in the valley. It was a typical story. He had matriculated at a mission school in Teyateyaneng, but had been unable to find work. In former days, he would have drifted across the border to work on a white farm, or would perhaps have joined the swelling townships of Bloemfontein and worked for the South African railway system, but it was harder to cross the border than it used to be, so he looked after his family's cattle instead. Still, things weren't as bad as they could be. Things were happening at his village . . .

"What things?" I asked.

He was vague. Things . . . I should come and see for myself.

I spent that night in a candlelight-only lodge up in the mountains, and the next day at noon I met Mopeli at the foot of Blue Mountain Pass. From there, we walked to his village, a distance of about 5 kilometres (3 miles). Chief Tsapi, the headman, rented me a rondavel for ten maloti, about $3, a day. I could stay as long as I liked, he said. There were plenty of rondavels available: the population of his village had been steadily decreasing since . . . since what he wouldn't say.

Over a meal later that night of stewed chicken and store-bought beer, Mopeli veered back towards the subject that interested me most, the . . . things . . . that were supposed to be happening. But he was interrupted by the headman, and there followed several angry exchanges between him and his chief about the propriety of involving an Outsider (at least, I think that's what they were about; they were conducted entirely in Sotho).

It wasn't until the next morning, when I walked with Mopeli out to the cattle kraal, that he told me what the problem was. It involved, curiously, a local diviner and the World Bank. I was incredulous. What had the World Bank to do with his village? Nothing directly, he said, but the Bank had agreed to fund a massive hydro-electric scheme, and one consequence of it would be the flooding of the village. I'd heard something about this scheme in Maseru. It was the hottest topic around, pitting the government development experts against the traditionalists, mostly farmers and pastoralists, who would be the people dispossessed by the scheme. It was grandly called the Highlands Water Project, and it was intended to make Lesotho not only self-sufficient in electricity, but a net exporter both of power and of water. The World Bank's agreement to fund the thing elevated Lesotho bonds on world markets, and had given the capital a bullish sort of feeling. The consequence, though, would be the building of a massive series of dams, and the flooding of huge amounts of land. It wasn't as though Lesotho had good soil to spare: the country was mostly mountain. And what little agricultural land remained was badly eroded; the trees had all been cut down, and cattle dung was being used for fuel instead of wood, further deteriorating the soil. Now this . . .

How did the diviner come into it? Diviners were traditionalists. Indeed, in the past they had even resented Moshoeshoe's giving space to Christian missionaries. They absolutely didn't see the need for dams. But there was more, which took a longer time to emerge. Indeed, it was only after a long, looping, elliptical conversation that I finally got the point: there had been a killing, some distance away, up in the hills. Not just any killing. A ritual killing. The entrails used for divination, the heart drained of blood and preserved, a talisman, buried somewhere ...there were men searching for it.

Moshoeshoe, beguiled by the teachings of missionaries (though as much by their artefacts as their ideas), had tried to stamp them out witchcraft in his time, first through ridicule and then through threats, but had failed. Witchcraft was deeply embedded in Sotho society. Deaths without known causes were routinely ascribed to the malevolent intervention of witches with the spirits. Leonard Thompson, Moshoeshoe's biographer, recounts the King's efforts to end his subjects' dependence on witchcraft: "In 1843 a woman named 'MaMothepane, who was a relative of Moshoeshoe and perhaps a little mad, was dispossessed of a field by her immediate chief, Mojakisane, in south-western Lesotho. She cursed Mojakisane and soon afterwards he died—probably of typhus. The local people ill-treated her, supposing she was a witch, and Moshoeshoe gave her sanctuary at Thaba Bosiu. There, however, Moshoeshoe's wives were frightened of her and Mohale, Moshoeshoe's half-brother, encouraged them to intimidate her. Tempers rose. She shouted the terrible curse that their children would die and they themselves would become sterile. They then stoned her to death. Greatly shocked, Moshoeshoe convened a *pitso* [Sotho public meeting, where all men had the right both to hear their king and to criticize him] where he said: 'In my infancy I received the name Lepoqo [Dispute] because I was born at a moment when they were fighting in my father's village about a person accused of witchcraft ... I have never killed people, except on the battlefield. This is the first time that the vultures have eaten anyone at my home ... When disease takes a child from me, do I go out and consult a diviner, to find out who has bewitched my family? You say there are diviners who know how to discover the sorcerers; these diviners deceive you. Pretend to be ill and show them a fine present, and you will see they will not hesitate to identify the author of your sickness, even though you are quite well ... Hear me well today! Let no one ever have the audacity to come and tell me, "I have been bewitched!" May that word never again be pronounced in my presence!'"[3]

The people listened, and obeyed, but did not necessarily believe. Ever since, at times of great political crisis, witchcraft had been resurgent.

A surveyor's helper for the hydro scheme had disappeared. His body, or what was left of it, had been found, split from the throat to the crotch and ripped apart like halves of a bun. The entrails had been spread out on the grass nearby, arranged in neat patterns. The heart and sexual organs were missing; the killer would have taken those first—they were more potent if taken while the victim was still alive. The eyes were removed and then reinserted backwards.

Mopeli recounted these details with a kind of gloomy relish. He wanted the dams to be built—he was hoping for a job, though he'd heard they were insisting on importing skilled workers for most positions—but still! Nothing as extraordinary as this had happened in his village since he was born, and long before that, not even the furious arguments over polygyny, which the Church was still trying futilely to stamp out. Such killings were deplorable, of course. But it was thrilling to know that potent ideas were at work. It went to the heart of everything—here was someone who believed powerfully in something, powerfully enough to kill. Otherwise life was just ... politics.

"Do they know who the killer is?" I asked.

"Everyone knows but no one tells," he said. "It's a matter for the chiefs now."

....

It was British imperial rule that prevented Basutoland's disintegration after Moshoeshoe's death in 1870; the colonial bureaucracy made it impossible for the regional chiefs to split off to form their own chiefdoms, as had been their historic right in times past.

The Basotho, by now under British "protection," sat out the many annexations and de-annexations of white politics that followed in southern Africa. They watched the Cape colonial government's crushing of the Xhosa. They watched as the Zulus renascent delivered a sensational defeat to an Imperial Army at Isandlwana. They sat out the first Boer revolt against the British, and then the Boer War itself, although there were Sotho commandos helping the British learn the ways of African fighting. They managed to avoid becoming snared in the Act of Union that followed that war, but found themselves now entirely surrounded by a new country, the Union of South Africa. They watched with mounting dismay the radical social engineering the whites called "apartheid."

In 1950 the Basutoland National Council, a quasi-democratic body controlled by the regional chiefs, began agitating for internal self-government: no one any longer trusted the British to protect them. In 1960 a new constitution was in place and a legislative council was to be formed, half its members elected by the male population and half appointed by the King on behalf of the chiefs.

The first fully independent elections were held in 1966, and, with the open connivance of the South African government, were won by the unpopular autocrat Chief Leabua Jonathan—unpopular despite being a direct descendant of Moshoeshoe I. He became even more unpopular after his election, when he stripped the King, Moshoeshoe II (the former Constantine Bereng Seeiso), of most of the meagre powers the constitution had left him. When Jonathan lost the 1970 elections, he took power in a coup, suspending the constitution and banning political parties. He was later himself deposed by the military after he turned against his patrons, the apartheid regime in South Africa, and began flirting with Cuba.

In 1990 there was another bloodless coup, led by army Colonel Elias Ramaema. Three years later, the army permitted elections to be held and the BCP, the Basuto Congress Party, came to power, with Ntsu Mokhehle as prime minister. He helped his cause greatly by bringing King Moshoeshoe II back from his London exile to be chief of state in February 1995 (only to be killed in a car crash a year later).

Lesotho is now a "constitutional monarchy." The King (Letsie III), the prime minister, half the cabinet, and most of the regional chiefs claim descent from Moshoeshoe. Corruption is minimal. Ethnic and tribal tensions are absent (since other ethnic groups and tribes are also absent). The economy is poor but improving gradually, despite population pressure and the paucity of industry.

By 1997, after the South Africans had finally adopted their new (first post-apartheid) constitution, the Basotho were showing little inclination to join the new South Africa under Nelson Mandela's ANC. Mandela was a centralist, and de-tribalized to a fault; his country had no patience with ethnic nationalism—just ask the Zulus. Or the whites. If, as the Zulus were still demanding, South Africa were to devolve to a loose federation, Lesotho would probably join. Until then, they'd be content to watch.

AZANIA

I left Lesotho by a perilous mountain road (are there any others in this country?) heading south over the Drakensberg extensions into the Xhosa heartland, down to the Great Kei River.

I stopped the car in the middle of the road—there was no room to pull off, for the shoulder was soft mud eroding into the valley, far below—and got out to stretch, looking down once more at the land where I was born. What to say about South Africa that hasn't already been said? This curious, in-turned, obsessive place has been minutely examined from the beginning of its settlement by European colonists. I myself had more than four hundred books on the place, the earliest dating back to 1687, the most recent only weeks old. When my father died, my mother sent me his library—another five hundred books! At least half of these dealt with the complicated, poisoned relationships between the races in the brief era of white ascendancy. The meretricious theory of apartheid had been examined, dissected, defended, and demolished by dozens, hundreds, of writers—why, I had contributed to the flood myself!

But up there in the high hills of the Lesotho border it came to me again, as it had when I sat at Moshoeshoe's feet on Thaba Bosiu a few days earlier, that almost none of these hundreds of books had seen the place from the shrewd, calculating point of view of the wily old Basotho king. They had all been written from Down There, from the point of view of the white cities. Even those that had been written by black opponents of apartheid seemed to agree that the white nation was the key to the discussion, that black–white relations were the All of South African history—that what was Now was somehow permanent, and that the history of this place was the history of white incursions.

I got back into the car, shivering in the mountain air, and turned up the heater.

These lands had been called the Transkei and the Ciskei by the white settlers; in one of the tortured later rationalizations for apartheid, they were called "homelands," or Bantustans, a patently transparent excuse, under the Separate Development version of apartheid, to exclude blacks from any rights in the "white" cities: if they had their own homeland, in which they could vote and participate as full citizens, what need for rights elsewhere? Of course, typical of apartheid's theorists, they never consulted these suddenly manufactured ex-citizens, nor did they care that many of them had never been anywhere near the lands they were now obliged to call "home," or that there was no work there and never had been. None the less, the Kei lands were not declared home to the Xhosa for nothing: this was, in fact and in history, the heartland of the Xhosa nation.

I was still heading sharply downwards; the land fell away, in verdant folds of red earth, to the distant sea. Below, the road looked like string coiled on a lawn; there was mist in the valleys, and the mountains smelled of wet earth, dew, lush vegetation. Clusters of round huts clung to the slopes near the valley floor. With the motor stilled I could hear the lowing of cattle. There was no traffic at all. It looked utterly peaceful. Yet I knew that this had been the centre of resistance to the white tribe for two hundred years and more, ever since the first "Kaffir war" of 1793 brought simmering hostilities into the open, when the mistrust between Xhosa settlers and Boer settlers boiled into open warfare, and it remained so until the end. This was often where the Pan Africanist Congress and African National Congress militants came to take refuge when they were hunted by apartheid's enforcers. Sometimes they were betrayed by the stooge Bantustan governments; more often they simply melted into the population. As recently as the year of Mandela's release, armed gangs would descend into the valleys, cross the Ciskei border, and raid white farms. They seldom killed anyone—the whites were too wary and experienced and well armed—but many a farmhouse was riddled with bullet holes none the less, grim runes for human relations gone awry.

I remembered the extraordinary conversation I'd had with the Customs inspector when I flew into Johannesburg a year earlier. That time I had been on my way to visit Great Zimbabwe, but he had looked at my passport, newly minted for a re-minted citizen, and had given me a sly grin as he pretended to rummage through my baggage. "Welcome home," he said. "See you stay this time. There is a place for you here." Thank you, I said, but I clearly looked puzzled. This might seem common-place enough in other places—I could even imagine it as somewhat routine in Israel—but here? A black functionary welcoming a member of the white tribe "home"? He saw he had caught my interest, and he put aside his chalk, shoving my bag aside. "Only a few years ago," he said, "I was in training to kill people like you."

Yes, I thought to myself, an extraordinary thing for the vanguard of the state to say to a visitor, no matter how venerable his lineage. But then of course South Africa had long been an extraordinary place. And he had said his say entirely without mal-ice, as though it were the most normal thing in the world. So I merely said, "And did you get any?"

He grinned. "I was Umkhonto we Sizwe," he said, referring to the ANC's mili-tary wing, Spear of the Nation. "I was baptized Gordon, but I changed my name to Ndlambe. Ndlambe was a great chief of our history, a statesman. We trained in Mozambique, in Tanzania, in Libya. But of course we really didn't want to kill any-one. We just wanted our country back." This time the grin was a little more crooked. "Man, I got around. But when I came back, I spent most of my time up in the hills of the Transkei, near the Lesotho border."

By this time the press of people behind me was becoming restive, and he had to move me on. I had some time to kill before my Air Zimbabwe connecting flight, so I arranged to buy him a beer in the airport bar when his shift ended, an hour later.

He came, he said, from a village near Lesotho called Si-Sakwacha. There was, of course, no work there. True, there were cattle to raise and there was food to grow, but no real work, no cash employment. There weren't any jobs within 200 kilome-tres (125 miles) except a few government ones, and those always went to the Mantanzima clan, who ran this "homeland" with a single-minded devotion to their own welfare. So of course he had gone to work in the mines, leaving his womenfolk to till the fields. The mines employed only men, and put them up in bachelor bar-racks, which became a place for drinking, fighting, dancing, dreaming, and plotting. Unknown to the bosses, who cared nothing of what their labourers were up to, those barracks were fertile recruiting grounds for the Umkhonto soldiers, the nearest thing to the age-linked regiments Dingiswayo and Shaka had so cunningly conceived 150 years earlier: the mine owners had unwittingly reinvented regimental bonding.

"You know where I learned that? Libya! It's where I learned about my own his-tory, thousands of kilometres away. And you know what else I learned there? That the whites weren't the cause of all the misery in my world. That we ourselves were oppressing people before the whites ever got there."

There was a long silence. I was contemplating this notion of Libya as a school of political awareness. Curious. I had shared the almost universal assumption that the Libyans were training terrorists. Like most anti-apartheid observers, I had blamed the system for these "terrorist schools" but had never questioned the facts of their existence, or thought much about what they would be teaching there. "Libya" was just shorthand for violence.

They called my flight to Harare.

"Where's your village?" I asked as I stood up to go. "I'd like to visit some day."

"You'd never find it," he said. "It's up near the Lesotho border, in the hills. A dozen huts, with no name, no road, no shops, no post office, no bar, no bus, nothing."

"I'd still like to visit it."

"Perhaps some day," he said.

"Hlala gahle," I said in Zulu, the nearest equivalent I could come up with to Xhosa. "Go well."

He grinned quickly, and rattled off a sentence he knew I wouldn't understand. Then, as I turned to go, he said, "So we got our country back. Now what do we do with it?"

....

I drove cautiously down the muddy switchback that was the road into the Transkei, now once again merely South Africa, soon perhaps, in a misreading of African history, to be Azania (for the original Azania was thousands of kilometres away, up by the Somali coast). Late in the afternoon, I crossed the Kei River into the Ciskei. It, too, had been corrupt In fact, it still was   the "homeland" leaders were busy "alienating" the tribal lands, mostly to their friends and family, so that when reunification with South Africa was complete and the lands were redistributed to private farmers, as the Mandela government had promised, it would be too late—there would be no tribal lands left to distribute. The Ciskei government and its cronies would get rich, at their own people's expense. Nothing would be done about it, very likely. Not because the national government had bad intentions. But, in the short term, it was more important to worry about the thorny problem of redistributing white lands—that was where the real disparities were to be found. To this proposal, oddly, there had been remarkably little fuss. Years of drought and falling agricultural prices had meant too many white farmers were in debt to state banks anyway, and they'd be grateful enough to escape with some compensation.

The Ciskei looked no different from the Transkei, at least not here. There were misty mountains pierced by gullies, wooded with thorn trees. Near the villages the trees had been cut down and the surrounding lands were deeply eroded.

I stopped at the first real town to ask my way and to get fuel. But the only filling station in town was closed. I thought I had enough to get to the next town—but which road to take? My map wasn't helpful. I think the Automobile Association map makers hadn't really been up here themselves, and had yielded to the temptation to guess. In any case, they showed roads that apparently didn't exist. It was a small place, not much more than a main street with a few sheds out back. There had been a hotel, once, but it was closed. There was a post office in what had been the lobby. More than a hundred people thronged around the door, jostling to get in. Blanket-clad men lounged on the stoop, smoking. No one paid me any attention, and when I asked them a question, they turned their heads aside and ignored me.

I persisted for a while—I really did need directions—but so did their palpable hostility. There was no break in that sea of blank and angry faces; no one seemed uneasy at thus treating a stranger, in violation of ancient tribal custom. I retreated with as much dignity as I could muster.

It was the only place in Africa I ever felt ... locked out.

There was no need to ask why. Any library will tell you. Any newspaper archive. Any South African family legend. Anyone who was *here*.

The Bantu, in the form of the Xhosa, and the European settlers, in the form of migrating farmers seeking to escape the dead bureaucratic hand of the Dutch East India Company, collided about 800 kilometres (500 miles) northeast of Cape Town somewhere around the year 1770.

Xhosa tradition has it that there were several major splits in tribal organization in the hundred years prior to contact with the Europeans. At the beginning of the eighteenth century, several chiefs seceded from the authority of the senior chiefs and set themselves up in the fertile valleys between the Kei and Keiskama rivers. Fifty years later, the tribe split again, this time into competing chiefdoms named after their founding ancestors, Gcaleka and Rharhabe. The latter moved across the Fish River, but both claimed paramountcy over all the Xhosa, claims hotly disputed by almost everyone. Into this fluid and shifting polity came the whites, with their own hierarchical notions of authority; many of the wars that followed stemmed from their mistaken belief that a deal with the Rharhabe chiefs was enforceable on all the Xhosa, and that therefore a failure to comply meant wilful breaches of solemn treaties, which were grounds for "fines," as cattle confiscation was politely called. This state of affairs was complicated further by the wild variances in the competing sides' versions of land ownership.

For more than a hundred years thereafter, thieving Xhosa and thieving Boer, each with conflicting claims to the same land, stole each other's cattle, punished each other's people, occupied and plundered each other's land, settled down to farm near each other, quarrelled with each other, and occasionally ganged up with each other against factions of their own people (the Boers invoking Xhosa help against the hated British, the Gwali Xhosa chiefs enlisting the Boers to attempt a political hegemony).

In the end, neither the Xhosa nor the Boers prevailed. The Boers were driven from the eastern frontier by the British, and withdrew across the Great Karoo into the apparently endless interior (where they found only the chaos and disruption that had followed Shaka's *Mfecane*, which led them, in their political innocence, to believe that the land was "uninhabited"). The remaining Xhosa, for their part, were driven back across the Fish River into the present Ciskei by the British, and there they remained, unconquered and unbowed. So much so that even the architects of apartheid couldn't pretend to themselves that the land between the Fish and the Drakensberg Mountains was "theirs," and locked the Xhosa into the Bantustans of Dr. Verwoerd. But of course it didn't end there. Apartheid, from this perspective, was a transitory phenomenon, a last desperate effort at white tribal exclusivity, and it inevitably failed.

By the nineties, the Xhosa finally had their man in the presidential palace.

One of his jobs was to leech apartheid's poisons.

The process continues to unfold.

....

The Afrikaners were not, of course, the only whites in South Africa. The British had come as conquerors—mostly to spite the French—and only secondarily as colonists.

In 1856 a young woman called Nonqose, a young girl and apprentice witch-doctor, daughter (niece, in European terms) of the eminent diviner Mhlakaza, adviser to Kreli, announced that she had seen a vision of a strange people and their strange cattle; she foretold the resurrection of all former chiefs, members of their tribe, their cattle, and the miraculous filling of the pits with grain. The tribe would be strong and wealthy as never before. The strange people "from across the Sea" would come to help them. Mhlakaza, in turn, confirmed her vision, reporting that these strangers were "black Russians from the Crimea, on marvellous horses," and among them his own long-dead brother had been seen. They had commanded him to abjure witchcraft, to cleanse himself, to cause the sacrifice of all the cattle in the kingdom, to burn all the grain, and to refrain from sowing a new crop. If the Xhosa only did all this a great black wind would arise and sweep the whites into the sea. In a frenzy of religious enthusiasm—and despite the best efforts of Chief Kreli and his senior councillors, who prudently removed their own cattle closer to the Lesotho border—the cattle were duly slaughtered and the great day awaited. It was supposed to dawn with great signs and portents—the sun would rise blood-red and become stationary in mid-heavens. Within a few months there was widespread starvation. Entire chiefdoms dispersed, some members drifting onto white farms to work, others dying from hunger. Nonqose survived, living long enough to see the Boers themselves subjugated by the English in 1902.

From Soga, The Ama-Xhosa

It wasn't until 1820 that real English settlers arrived in any numbers, and after that they burrowed themselves into the fabric of South African life, just as the Afrikaners did.

Almost to the end—almost too late—the working out of "politics" in the South African context meant relations between English and Afrikaans. The two Afrikaner republics in the central South African plains were overthrown by the British Empire in the Boer War of 1899–1902. In the aftermath, there was the politics of accommodation: the British permitted a self-governing dominion to come into being in 1910 without a thought for its black not-yet-voters (only the "coloureds" were enfranchised, and then only in the Cape province); in turn, in 1914 the Boer general Jan Smuts helped steer South Africa into the Great War on the English side, somewhat to the fury of the Afrikaner hard-liners.

It was English-Afrikaans politics too, that led to the enthronement of the first National Party government of Dr. Daniel François Malan in 1948. The "English" had threatened to make an "English" government almost permanent by throwing the coloured votes of the Cape onto the scales on their side. (Well, it wasn't really the English—Smuts was still prime minister, after all. But he was written off by the racial purists as a pretend-Englishman, a mock Afrikaner, and to the hard-liners it amounted to the same thing.) This was threat enough. Conservative Afrikaners voted together to end the menace, and when they came to power they disenfranchised the coloureds and made sure non-whites would never vote again. Separateness was the watchword. Apartness.

Their lunatic scheme was called ... apartheid.

Even at the time we knew the apartheid laws were insane. The Group Areas Act, one of apartheid's underpinnings, was aimed at redrawing the ethnic map of the country, and it caused, in the words of a Dutch Reformed Church report of the 1970s, "suffering too deep to be imagined." The ethnic engineers in Pretoria wanted to remake three hundred years of history; in their rigid vision of an abstract "justice," they tried to undo three hundred years of mixing. Thousands of people were suddenly "unqualified" to live where they were living. In Johannesburg whole communities were uprooted and moved; what had been festering slums on the outskirts of the white city became festering slums dozens of kilometres farther out. In Durban, the Zulus were shifted from shantytowns in the cities to shantytowns on the fringes of Zululand. A few white farmers were affected, but the burden was placed on the backs of the powerless and the underprivileged.

The theorists of apartheid unveiled their perverted vision in a series of linked statutes: the Group Areas Act physically separated the races that the Population Registration Act had identified; the Job Reservation Act laid out who could do what and who couldn't; the Separate Amenities Act saw to social and informal segregation; and the notorious Suppression of Communism Act turned the secret police loose as enforcers. It was the complete bureaucratic system, chilling in its mindless efficiency.

Well, that's all gone now, at least in theory. The tourist amenities in Cape Town have welcoming signs in four of South Africa's many official languages, including Xhosa. The Group Areas Act has been tossed onto the rubbish heap of failed ideologies. By the mid-1990s (only a few years after Nelson Mandela's triumphant accession to the presidency of the country that had imprisoned him for so long) there was an almost eerie optimism in South Africa, a giddy disbelief that things were going so well. The blacks and urban whites were referring to Mandela as *madiba*, leader, but the Afrikaners in the Platteland were talking confidentially of *Oom Nelson*, Uncle Nelson, and acting almost as though they had invented him. The other countries of the region were looking covetously—and nervously—at welcoming South Africa to play a dominant role in their affairs (only Mugabe of Zimbabwe, whose paranoia is finely tuned to the nuances of power, was putting the contrary case, that giants take and don't give).

Yet when I stopped to examine it, the balance sheet in 1997 seemed almost entirely negative. What a litany of problems! An unemployment rate of better than 40 per cent. A black proletariat hungry for material goods, but with no education and few job prospects. The beginnings of disillusionment with the African National Congress government. Huge disparities in wealth. Shrinking capital investment. The hoped-for flood of foreign investment conspicuous by its absence. Factional violence, in the cliché of the time, rampant in KwaZulu Natal. Rising crime. Banditry in the rural areas.

Among his other political skills, Mandela has a natural genius for public relations. One summery afternoon he telephoned the widows of four or five of the apartheid-era Nationalist leaders, and invited them to tea. When one, Betsie Verwoerd, declined (she was both too old, at ninety-two, and an ensconced inhabitant of the Oranjestaat "boerestan"), he went to visit her instead—a decade's worth of goodwill, generated entirely uncynically in an hour or so. Later, out of the blue, the man who had prosecuted Mandela on behalf of the apartheid state got a phone call from the president. "He just wanted to chat about old times," this bemused and now smitten functionary said. "He wanted to assure me that I had just been doing my job."

Deteriorating medical services. Municipalities running out of money, and a crumbling infrastructure. And against this, what? A still-powerful economy, sure enough. And the formidable, overwhelming personality of an ageing leader with prostate problems. Mandela is a genius, but even geniuses have their limits. And he was an *old* genius.

In the muscular economic centre of South Africa, the central Witwatersrand, recently renamed Gauteng, the new South Africa is most obvious, the dislocation most violent. Downtown Johannesburg is now entirely a black city, but in the affluent malls and private enclaves of the Northern Suburbs hardly anything seems to have changed—the boutiques of Sandton Mall still sell their three-thousand-dollar frocks to the white wealthy. Gold financed everything here: industry, commerce, business, cocktail parties, literature, theatre, politics, revolution, and reaction. In the all-male barracks that housed the gold-miners they sang their songs and danced their dances and dreamed of liberation; now they have got it, and they still sing their songs and dance their dances. Nothing very much has changed. The Mozambicans and the Zambians and the Hereros from Namibia and the Tswana from Botswana and the Sothos and the Zulus all come here to work, and send money home. The economy of all the countries of southern Africa are driven by the engine of Johannesburg's vigorous capitalism.

> In a way, Jabulani Ntshangase could serve as a symbol for the new South Africa. He was born in Soweto and became an embalmer—always a growth trade in those perilous times. But he left in 1977, studied in Britain, arrived broke in the United States, and got a job in a wine shop. In the early 1990s he returned "home," to become by default South Africa's most knowledgeable black wine expert. Now he has been hired by Spier estate, an old Stellenbosch winery being aggressively marketed to become what the *Mail & Guardian* called a "dionysian disneyland," to sell its products to the new black élite.

On the vast white farms of the northern Transvaal, where the slow angers of a hard people simmered finally into war against the British colonialists, there was resentment and dismay, but no thoughts of revolt. Those early white trekkers had always fancied themselves as somehow attuned to the *bushveld*, to nature, but they had never noticed that people were part of nature too. It was a fatal mistake. For the Tswana and the Ndebele, the Venda, the Sotho, and the Shangaan, on the other hand, matters are mattering as they should; it was their land, after all (after they dispossessed its original inhabitants), and they are getting it back, one farm at a time. They're in no hurry now. The Boers can stay if they want, or drift away. It doesn't matter. There are more important things to hand: what kind of life to make? A modern Western state? An industrialized tribal culture? Some mix of the ancient and the modern? The boundaries are uneasy. The South African government in 1995 set up a commission of inquiry into the burning of witches. In the Northern Province alone, up near the Zimbabwe border, 150 witches, two-thirds of them women, were burned or stoned to death in the ten months before the commission began its work. A whole village, called Motonawabaloi, had been set up as a witch refuge centre. Most of the witches had been killed by mobs of the angry young—with the connivance, to be sure, of the village elders, but still the young. These were the children of apartheid. They could have been schooled, and nurtured in the ways of modernity. But they were refused. And now they have turned away, into superstition and fear.

An old Venda had once explained to me that disparities in wealth (by which he meant both material and spiritual wealth) were always caused by malice. There was a fixed amount of wealth to go around; if one person has more than another, it can only be at someone else's expense. Rarely, such success is earned. More often, it is a matter of witchcraft. It was no accident that witches were always materially successful, and usually old (for extreme old age, too, must be expropriation, this time of someone else's life force).

Reconciling these deeply rooted beliefs to the uncaring and mindless (but entirely necessary) efficiency of western capitalism is one of the great tasks for the future.

Not so long ago, as these things go, I was walking along a trail deep in the Thousand Hills, in search of a village I had heard of where there was a diviner who was familiar with all the old ways—his great-great-great-grandfather had "smelled out" witches for the Tyrant himself, until the smelling got too close to the royal kraal and he was killed by Shaka's thugs. The trail wound through some of the most fertile valleys of Old Zululand, gentle hills of sweet grasses and lush meadows, with cattle grazing peacefully. I was alone, and as I neared a curve in the track I heard the melodic tinkling of a one-stringed lyre, and saw a young woman striding towards me, the lyre to her shoulder. She was bare to the waist, bangled and necklaced, her hair braided with beads. *Dumela!* Greetings! she said as she passed, and her eyes laughed at me, because she knew I found her beautiful. I wondered often in the years that passed what had happened to her. I hoped she had never had to move into the squalid black townships of Durban, the sprawling, brawling capital of the province of KwaZulu Natal. I hoped her life had been happy. I hoped she had never raised boys who had joined the killing squads of the Inkatha Freedom Party as they battled Mandela's ANC in an almost-but-not-quite civil war. But of course I had no way of knowing. Frozen moments in time, no matter how beautiful, are an ever-unreliable guide to the future. Zululand was fluid, unstable, fraught with possibilities, doom threatened, blessed, violent, astonishing. Like South Africa. Like Africa itself.

SOBHUZA'S HEIRS

Before moving west and north, up through Botswana and Namibia to Angola and more of Africa's old kingdoms, I thought I'd better turn my attention to the other small enclave created as a refuge from Shaka. Swaziland is now mostly interesting because it's the last of the traditional African monarchies. There are peoples all over the continent (though, happily, diminishing in number) who are governed by putschists,

*military men, "democratically elected" tyrants, politburos, presidents for life and the rest,
who dream of returning to the old ways, the serene old ways in which the wise old kings
would listen carefully to their subjects and then, through consensus, would deliver
their judgements. They dream, in essence, of being governed in the way Swaziland is.*

*To be sure, there are other kings in Africa. For example, the new king in Lesotho.
But these are constitutional monarchs, figureheads without power, as useful as a hang-
nail. The Swazi kings are the real thing.*

*So it was interesting. In the rest of Africa they dream of some proto-Swaziland.
Swaziland, in turn, is peaceful, yet the students in the universities there dream of
Marxism and, late in 1995 and again in 1996, tried to fire-bomb the royal kraal. A
general strike in 1997 was another sign of unrest.*

Clearly, bucolic visions aren't always what they're puffed up to be.

Tom Mbelini, a young Swazi student, had been telling me about the sacred place
where the kings are buried, up in the tropical mountains in the west of the country.
He was making a political point, but I had become distracted by the tale of his scramble up a steep slope through the bush to look for the tombs. He had gingerly skirted
three of the charmless quartet of puff-adder, Egyptian spitting cobra, and green and
black mamba (only the deadly black mamba was missing). Oh, I knew those places!
He probably passed a few boomslang too, but the damn things look so much like
tree branches he wouldn't have noticed them. There are ticks in the long grass,
leeches in the swamps, and something like a chigger that burrows under the skin.
(You don't drink the water either—bilharzia lurks there, even up on the hillsides.
Never mind down in the valleys: crocodiles.) It is always stiflingly hot. There are
things that look like wasps that slither under the clothes and make for the dampest
places; you can feel them wriggling. I wondered—not for the first time—why the
people who live here weren't more ... irritable.

We'd been arguing, in a desultory but good-natured way, about the kings lying
in state there in the cave, buried after proper ritual in this place on the Pongola River,
where the great chief Ngwane II built his palace, of which there is now no sign. Tom
was studying public administration in Harare, Zimbabwe, where I first met him, and
he liked nothing better than to talk passionately about his country, its landscape, and
the way it was governed. The kings, of course, had lived in the royal village of
Lobamba, near Mbabane, the capital, while Tom himself had grown up in the dreary
little industrial town of Manzini. None of these places was very far from the others:
Swaziland is a small country. ("Smaller," Tom said, "than it was before the Boers
came and grabbed most of it," which was true enough. I refrained from pointing out
that the country hadn't existed at all a hundred years before that, and only came into
being because the Swazis had muscled out the locals, and then because Shaka was
"shaking the tree" down to the south.)

The argument wasn't one with any ending. Tom venerated the dead kings as military heroes, generals who had successfully defied Shaka and built their kingdom in the fastnesses of the Swazi mountains, and as wise rulers. He admired the ways they had governed their country, as a "consultative monarchy." He thought it was admirably democratic, or at least anti-autocratic.

"So why are you against it now?" I asked, gulping at an imported Castle lager, brewed down the road in South Africa.

"It's not the same," he insisted.

"But it is. King, royal council all of the royal line, head of government a prince of the blood, the council eminent men of the kingdom ..."

"It's not the same at all. In those days, it was a consensus. The king listened to his councillors. They listened to the headmen, who listened to their people. Grievances went back up the line. Anyone could have his say."

I mentioned the Sotho *pitso*, in which any citizen could have his say, directly to the king without any intermediaries. And among the Zulus, hadn't Shaka himself at first encouraged his men to speak out? Isn't that the way the Swazis still ruled, through the *liqoqo*?

About the Sotho, Tom was merely contemptuous. And Shaka ... "Only blooded warriors were allowed to speak."

"And you really think the Swazi councillors listened to their people?" I asked. "More than they do now?"

"Now they listen only to the king and for what they can get in return," he snapped.

....

The problem with a system that depends on wise old kings is that wise old kings themselves are rather hard to come by. Patrilineal descent and the death rate being what they are, most new kings are not old at all. And wisdom, as the world should attest, is mostly a fluke. Most kings are ordinary mortals beset with palace intrigues, infighting, conflicting advice, double-dealing among councillors, lobbyists, career civil servants, toadies, and the rest of the hazards of any state, no matter how governed. The Swazi kings have not only these to contend with, but a huge ruling clan that is contentious and impatient for its privileges. So far the Swazis have been lucky.

Still, Swaziland is governed in the old way, by the king and his ministers, the *liqoqo*, the traditional tribal advisory council. The *liqoqo* meets at Lobamba; "parliament" is close to the royal cattle kraal in the village, which itself backs onto the Mlilwane wildlife sanctuary. When the council is in session, the king, Ngwenyama (an honorific, meaning Lion) Mswati III, sits on skins on the ground with his senior ministers. They shed their three-piece suits for the occasion and wear traditional dress (more skins, gorgeous feathers, and considerable ornament), and they orient themselves to the sacred hills across the valley, the hills where the kings are buried.

Petitioners, who in theory can be of any rank and from anywhere in the kingdom, sit in front of the king, close enough to talk to him without raising their voices. They are permitted to broach any subject, air any grievance, discuss any policy. The king listens, debates policy, makes judgements.

Well, it's a nice theory. Tom Mbelini tried to go twice, but was turned away by security guards. Not that he was a security risk himself—Tom is more interested in hiphop than in political action—but eight of his fellow students at the university in Mbabane had been suspended not long before (for holding subversive, aka democratic, views) and the guards were just being cautious.

Swaziland was, until recently, occupied by Sotho-speaking people, who were conquered seven generations ago by the Nguni-speaking Dlamini, who came down from Mozambique. The founding father of Swaziland was Sobhuza I, of the Dlamini clan. His father, Ndungunya, had already held off attacks by Dingiswayo and Zwide and had begun amalgamating clan remnants into a new entity. Sobhuza I, who was king from about 1816, located defensible positions in the mountains, created a formidable army by following Shaka's own training manual, and created what is essentially still the Swazi state (named after Sobhuza's son, Mswazi).

> **From a praise-song to King Sobhuza I:**
> "I call Sobhuza, Sobhuza of the High Mountains
> Cast your shadow on the hills
> Cast your shadow on the huts
> You play with the waters
> And they speak
> You pointed a spear at the Sotho
> Black hero of the Swazi
> They hate Sobhuza and are right to hate
> Jaw that cracks all bones
> Spotted beast! Great conqueror!
> Hail! You of the inner house!

Sobhuza II was a young child when his father died, but his mother, Labotsibeni, proved a capable regent until he took over in 1921. He promptly started a campaign of buying back ancestral lands, and by the time independence was achieved in 1968 had regained two-thirds of the kingdom. Sobhuza flirted with the notion of a constitutional monarchy after independence, but his heart wasn't in it, and he finally condemned the notion as an alien import and, after opposition parties looked as though they might gain enough votes to take power, he used the excuse of the constitution's overt Britishness to revoke it. He dissolved all political parties and reverted to traditional rule, which meant in practice himself and his councillors. A new and more Swazi constitution was promulgated in 1978, but was never released, and in 1997 was still in suspension. Sobhuza died in 1982 after sixty-one years on the throne, the world's longest reigning monarch at the time.

The staircase that leads from the stony plain to the rock-ribbed summit of Zimbabwe Hill

The path winds precipitously upwards, at times passing between great boulders and through cracks in the cliff. Today, the whole complex is grey stone and mud and vines, but centuries ago when the king looked down from the high hill in the days of his magnificence he saw flaming colours, sculpture, decoration, friezes, walls dipping and swooping in elegant curves, architecture as sculpture, architecture as art. Magical birds, carved from soapstone, were placed on standards in niches in the walls. Small human figures decorated the enclosures within the sweep of the walls.

The austere huts of the Shona village at Great Zimbabwe are perched on a slab of grey granite, flecked with honey-gold

These "rondavels" with their conical roofs are no longer inhabited in a meaningful way; they are a show village, an interpretive centre for the curators of Zimbabwe's greatest monument. But they are nevertheless quite authentic, reconstructed from a pattern a thousand years old. I climbed to the summit of the hill at dusk, and looked down into the darkness. Away, in the far distance, I could see the red glow of a fire, and once I heard a wail, a long sound chopped off, like the cry of the go-away bird. I listened to the silence and felt the gossiping clatter of the six thousand families who had lived on the plain below in the glory days of this place.

Mask of a Shangaan dancer, Zambia-Zimbabwe border

The incised-wood and raffia masks of the Zimbabwean Shangaan can be found in many of the world's museums of ethnography (often masks of grand lineage and superior workmanship), and also hanging on the walls of suburban bungalows in every Western country (schlock art sold in roadside stalls all over East Africa). The dancers don't care whether they are "art" or "authentic"—Africans think authenticity is an imprisoning device urged on them by foreign romantics who never want Africa to change. Dance isn't performance art. Masks are role-playing devices, enabling the dancers to slip through into the real world, which is made up of everyone who has ever lived, and of the powers that move the world.

Market day in Lamu, Kenya

Lamu has turned its back on the twentieth century. There is no vehicular traffic—the only taxis and trucks are donkeys. The town is secretive and self-contained, a labyrinth of tiny alleys. The centuries-old Swahili houses are tall and elegant, built with coral-brick walls three feet thick. Inside, there is a series of curtained alcoves, their width dictated by the length of the mangrove poles used for floors and ceilings. Steep staircases lead to flat roofs, where the cooking is done and much of the household activity goes on. Each has a flower-filled courtyard, reflecting a gracious way of life that had running water and simple air-conditioning while Europe was struggling through the Dark Ages. The alleys are lined with tiny stores, many with intricately carved doors. In the market are baskets of squawking chickens and piles of mangoes and spices, patient donkeys, hawkers of qat, here and there a small brazier on which strips of chicken are grilling.

San ("Bushman") paintings in a shallow cave in the Cedarberg Mountains, not very far from Cape Town

No one knows when the San first arrived in southern Africa, except that it was a very long time ago. In millennia past they began to leave their extraordinary artistry everywhere there were rocks and caves, and continued to do so until recent times. Their early paintings celebrated nature and the hunt; only very late in San history did more menacing figures than elephants or buffalo appear in San iconography. From the eighteenth century the occasional men on horses appeared, with guns, more deadly by far than anything that had gone before. The Khoisan (the San, along with the Khoikhoi, once disparagingly called "Hottentots") were First Men hereabouts. As organised, coherent cultures they have long gone, destroyed by European avarice and European diseases. But as people, of course, they have not vanished at all. Their genetic roots are plain to see in the vibrant, vital culture still called by whites, blacks, and themselves the "Cape Coloureds."

Bamiléké figure in the royal museum of Bandjoun, Cameroon

The little museum is a small room, unlit, with a marvellous jumble of artefacts both historic and humble—it's hard not to trip over some ancient stool covered with leopard skin or, indeed, over a throne, for here they have managed to preserve the thrones of all the fourteen Fons (chiefs) in the known lineage of the community. The current Fon's throne is covered entirely in cowry shells, which the traditionalists scorn as a new-fangled invention, almost as bad as plastic. The Fon is called Ngnie Kamga, and when I was there had eleven wives but so far only twenty-two children, pretty pathetic next to his predecessor's two hundred and fifty.

Bandjoun Great Hall

Detail from a column at the Great Hall

The Bamiléké chief's compound at Bandjoun, a harmonious collection of traditional architecture, is one of the best-preserved royal residences anywhere in Africa. The supporting pillars and doorways are intricately carved; the ceilings and walls made from patterned bamboo. The buildings are massive and impressive, as befits a wealthy monarch. My guide was an old man who had helped reconstruct the buildings in the sixties (the ceilings were his work, and I made sure to remark on those).

People who know and love African art tell me Bamiléké carving is not what it used to be, that it has somehow lost its way. Of course, this could be said of much Western art too; and to the Bamiléké themselves the discussion seems irrelevant, for their art preserves its linkages to the past, in unbroken line for more centuries than there were observers to count. Bamiléké carving is still a living tradition, and has avoided the twin traps that have so punished art in so many places in Africa—the trap of aesthetic preciousness and the trap of treating art as a commodity, for sale to Western collectors.

Dogon diviner's plot

Here is a therapist's notebook: each small square in this dusty patch of earth represents a Problem brought to the diviner by a member of the community. Perhaps the crops are failing when they should not. Perhaps a man suspects his wife of bearing someone else's child, or perhaps someone's husband is being unfaithful. One square might represent an illness that needs curing, another an emotional knot that needs untangling. The diviner listens carefully to these tales of woe, then inscribes his symbols in the earth. At dusk, he will scatter peanuts on the ground. Overnight, the jackals, renowned in Dogon cosmology as intermediaries between heaven and earth, will come by to eat the peanuts, and their pawprints, unravelled and interpreted, provide the proper answers to the questions asked. Hit and miss? Not at all: diviners listen very carefully indeed, and learn much. A Jungian or Freudian analyst could envy the cure rate displayed so routinely here.

In accordance with Swazi custom, the death of a king meant an enforced seventy-five-day mourning period, during which no farming of any sort could be done—cattle couldn't be slaughtered and crops could be neither sown nor reaped. Sex was forbidden throughout the kingdom on pain of flogging. The mourning period was declared and enforced by the Great She-Elephant (the Queen Mother), as the King's most senior wife was called. The two-month respite was taken up with palace intrigues and political jockeying for power within the ruling clan. Sobhuza, after all, had somewhere around a hundred wives and well over six hundred children, of whom more than two hundred could be taken as serious contenders for the throne. Swazi custom rejects primogeniture; kings and chiefs are generally selected by the elders on the basis of the reputation in the community of the boy's mother, not of the boy himself. Eventually, power coalesced around a twenty-year-old prince called Makhosetive, who was promptly hustled away from the palace to a secret hideaway. The given reason was that he needed instruction in Swazi customs and traditions; the real reason was to protect him from the nefarious activities of disappointed losers. In the end, Makhosetive was crowned King Mswati III in 1986. His coaching in Swazi custom must have taken: he has shown as little sign as his father of having any affection at all for constitutionalism.

As the millennium neared, there was still no suffrage in Swaziland. It was "not needed," at least according to the king. By early 1997, no objective observer thought this could possibly last. Not just because of the lofty disdain of South Africa's newly democratic governors, but because the students and—more ominously—the trade unions were turning ugly.

It was Tom Mbelini who told me about hanging out with the Reed Girls.

The Reed Dance is the second of the major cultural festivals in modern Swaziland. The first, and most solemn, is the *incwala*, an ancient celebration of the new year and the first fruits of the harvest; it's a festival whose symbolism is potent: the ceremony, six days of song, dance, feasting, and ritual, acknowledges the king as the source of all fertility. The ceremony is described in all the tourist brochures as "a solemn and deeply religious festival" at which no photography is permitted. The Reed Dance, however, had neither the high religious significance nor the solemnity. And there was no way you could keep modern shutterbugs from photographing a ceremony at which hundreds of comely and exceedingly undressed maidens danced for their king. In generations past, the ceremony had been rather different, and much less "official." The *umcwasho* girls were simply a group of young women who got together, appointed one of themselves a princess, and had a more or less riotous sorority party. The *umcwasho* ceremony had traditionally been in two parts. In the first the girls, draped neck to ankle in drab cloth, brought reeds to repair the Queen

Mother's windscreen. During this part sex was strictly forbidden, even for the king, and anyone caught at it would be subject to the fine of an adult cow and—much worse—to elaborate forms of ridicule. In the second part, always a few months later, the decorum had been shed along with the garments, and the girls showed up at the palace dressed only in beads and ready to party.

A few generations ago the whole thing was captured by the monarchy and institutionalized. The Reed Girls, as they were now called, were said to be "symbolically" offering themselves as brides to the king. The modern reality is that the Umhlanga Dance, or Reed Dance, is an unofficial debutantes' ball for young women, a coming out into adult society after the enforced seclusion of the initiation rituals. The Reed Dance is not just a dance, or a series of dances, but a week-long festival of music, dance, feasting, and general merriment.

The young women perform their stylized gavotte for the king, swaying and stamping and singing in their tiny beaded skirts and bangles, anklets clicking, determinedly not looking at the young men clustered against the far gate, who are equally determined looking. Later, when the official dancing is over and the fires glow in the secretive night, the young men skip between the huts and the cars and the campfires and the storytellers with their circles of eager listeners, and set off to do what young boys universally do, which is to find the young girl who is willing.

Not for the first time, I thought of how much trouble the early missionaries had had with this notion of recreational sex, and the particular boundaries they placed around it. A great deal of spleen had been vented at the Swazi custom called *ukujama*. A mission document rather prissily described it as "a kind of onanistic connection," which was what young people did when they didn't want a pregnancy. In a sad but typical consequence, the missionaries succeeded in stamping out *ukujama*, and caused instead a dramatic rise in illegitimate births. Some of the more sophisticated Westerners, like David Livingstone, managed to understand how African propriety was merely different from Western notions, and in no way inferior (or, to put it another way, just as hedged about with rules and taboos). Conversely, the Christian or Paulist notion of linking sex to procreation seemed to the Africans merely perverse, and until missionaries understood this and began discreetly to shift their doctrinal interpretations away from Western Puritanism, converts were harder to come by than they might otherwise have been. By a neat reversal of fate, African notions of sex are now often more restrictive than the much more...decadent...Western norm.

Tom Mbelini began to dance what he said was the Reed Girls' dance on the sidewalk outside Greatermans (*Everything Must Go!*) Discount Store. He danced dreamily, swaying his hips from side to side, singing in the soft clicks of SiSwati, shuffling his feet on the dusty concrete. A couple of "delivery boys" who'd been sitting on the curb started to laugh, but after a while they were seduced by the rhythms rolling around in Tom's head, and they began to sing in counterpoint, and dance too, half a dozen of them, and I started to laugh in my turn, because the sidewalk came alive with music made entirely with imagination, and when I closed my eyes I could hear the shuffling of the bare feet and the soft rustling of the beaded skirts, and I could see the line of them, a hundred maidens all in a row, brown and beautiful, swaying in the sun before their king, their skin glistening with the marvellous muscle tone of the young and healthy, their teeth gleaming, heads bobbing, breasts maddeningly jiggling, crooning their songs of renewal and rejoicing. With my eyes closed I could feel the sun beating down, and I fancied for a moment that I fully understood this grand African notion of community inclusiveness, so attenuated among us in the West, where it has been traded for ideology. But then the Asian storekeeper came out the door and chased us away, and the song faded, and so did the dream.

THE KALAHARI

I used to think Botswana was the most boring country in Africa, Nowhere Land. All I ever saw of it when I was younger was the part Cecil Rhodes knew, the eastern corridor. For him, Bechuanaland was "the Suez Canal to the north," just a way of getting somewhere else, mostly from the Cape to Rhodesia, a short section of his grandiose dream of a British presence from the Cape to Cairo. It was the only place I knew whose capital, Mafikeng, was (then) not even in the country, but in neighbouring South Africa. To me, the rest was arid, flat, prone to great roiling clouds of dust driven in from the west.

What a canard! In reality Botswana is a place of great marvels. The Great Thirstland of the Kalahari. The Last Refuge of the San. The River without an End. The Okavango delta. Great herds of elephants, lions hunting at night, the "munu," the black tree baboons that the legends say stalk Okavango women, longing for the day when they might be men again. It is sunsets on the Chobe River, when the river boils with hippo. It is the greatest migrations of zebras on earth. And on top of all this it is the greatest curiosity of all: a democratically run, sensibly governed, economically sound country that has eschewed grandiose development projects in favour of small-scale enterprise, schooling, and decent housing. This alone would make it worth visiting.

People in Botswana say the San arrived thirty thousand years ago, though no one seems to know where the number came from. The San leave no traces but their enigmatic paintings and engravings in the caves; their own traditions are rich in legend and song, but very short on fact.

I remember an old San woman I met years ago outside Swakopmund, which is now in Namibia but was then called South West Africa. She was squatting on her heels in the sand, smoking contentedly on a pipe as long as her arm. Standing, she

was not more than a metre and a bit high, a dusty yellow-brown, wrinkled, the skin
hanging in folds like crêpe paper on her face and her neck, breasts as wrinkled as an
old granadilla and as long as razor strops. She wore only a tattered leather skirt and
a large pouch into which she stuffed her tobacco.

It was the tobacco she had come to town to fetch: the San were crazy for tobacco.
The town didn't intimidate her. But nor did it hold anything of interest for her,
except the tobacconist's. She had walked in from the bush that morning. Through
an interpreter I asked her where she lived. Lived? She looked at me blankly. What a
question! She lived where she was. If I meant where her band was, they were over
that way. She gestured to the east. Thirty kilometres (18 miles), the interpreter said
helpfully. I don't know how he knew, or, indeed, if he really knew. Maybe he just
wanted to give me an answer, any answer.

When her pipe was finished, we offered to give her a lift out into the desert, and
she accepted. She sprawled in the back of the four-wheel-drive open jeep, squeezed
between boxes of tools and a roll of carpet my interpreter had placed there for reasons of his own.

About 15 kilometres (10 miles) into the desert we saw a couple of women poking at the sand with sticks. We stopped, and our guest hopped out. The rest of her
band were a few kilometres away. They were preparing to leave as we pulled up, packing their meagre belongings (bows and quiverfuls of arrows, staffs, a few calabashes,
bundles of tattered clothing, and something that could have been a harp). They paid
us little attention.

I watched their purposeful actions with interest. They had done this hundreds of
times before, and there were no wasted movements. I stared, as politely as I could. They
were small, lightly built, their limbs skinny, with wiry muscles. Ages were hard to tell;
most of the adults were wrinkled. The men were beardless. There were thick folds of
flesh over their eyes. I had read about them before I went to Namibia, had seen the
technical descriptions by physiologically obsessed Westerners. I knew therefore that
steatopygia (protuberant buttocks) and "Hottentot apron" (elongated labia minora)
were common among Khoisan women. Well! The buttocks were certainly plump
enough, but you can't go around peering at the labia minora of women you've just met,
even among the uninhibited San. I also knew that "the penis of Bushmen [as the San
were then called] males and of many Hottentot [Khoikhoi] males extends outward
almost horizontally in a semi-erect position even when not tumescent," which at school
we'd always thought pretty interesting. Didn't look like that to me, but then they were
wearing bulky leather aprons knotted around the buttocks, so it was hard to tell.

Once, San roamed most of Africa. Probably the pygmies of the western rain forests
are close cousins, though ethnographers are still unsure. Most of the world's surviving
San live in the Kalahari sands of Botswana, though there are groups in Namibia and a
few have spilled over into southern Angola. There are traces of them in the Sahara and

the Arab North, and there are still San to be found in Uganda and the Rift. I was taught at school that they'd been driven to live in the Kalahari because they'd been hunted to extinction elsewhere, but this was a well-meaning falsehood. San had always been in the Kalahari; elsewhere they'd disappeared through war, disease, interbreeding, the reduction of their ranges by cattlemen, and cultural collapse: they were unable to adapt to a rooted way of life, and though many of them hired on in the south as cattlemen for Afrikaner farmers, they seldom lasted; the temptation to thievery (in the farmer's eyes) of cattle was just too great—all that meat on the hoof, going nowhere!

There are several distinct groups of San, the K!ung, the !xo and G/wi being the larger. (The *!* and */* marks are a Western orthographer's way of indicating the characteristic San clicks.)

How the San have been romanticized, though! The Western view has been shaped by a series of documentaries and novels from Laurens van der Post, the South African mystic. He anticipated the North American nativist movement by recounting many tales of the Bushmen's uncanny affinity for the natural world, and their intuitive understanding of how nature worked. More recently a French television documentary which showed a group of San hunters of the Botswanan Dzu clan "stalking" a helicopter, bows and poisoned arrows at the ready, delighted and fascinated audiences across Europe. Except that it was all stage-managed, a commercial fantasy. The San, recruited in Maun, the safari capital of Botswana, where they had been working as labourers on a cattle farm, had been paid to shed their Western clothing, and their "hunting" had been carefully choreographed by the television crew. *National Geographic* magazine later published a wonderful photograph that revealed the subtext of

The logic of the G/wi world view is that N!adima [the creator], having created man, intends him to survive and thus permits him to make use of what is available in the environment to that end, subject to the restriction that N!adima will be angered by wastefulness or greed on the part of those using his property. Man, at least G/wi man, must devise for himself the best means of survival that he can, including the regulation of interpersonal behaviour. Social usages and customs are therefore seen as man-made and not sacrosanct. The stability of behaviour and the predictability of others' actions require agreement by all concerned. Such agreement can be won only by persuasion and ensured by the fulfillment of obligation. It is therefore imperative that individuals and the community remain on good terms with everybody in the circle of social contact.

From Encyclopaedia Britannica 10:451, "Khoisan Cultures of Africa"

this shoot: the picture showed two bemused San, one with bow and arrow at the ready, both of them goggling at the antics of three colourfully dressed foreigners festooned with cables, wires, and remote mikes, who were staring at the world through the vacant lens of a camera. The picture left little doubt who the primitives really were.

As nomads, they carried their universe with them on their wanderings; and though they were forced to take refuge in remote caves to defend themselves first against animal and then human predators, they could never be dispossessed of their heritage, because it consisted, in the modern jargon, entirely of software.

A small universe, but never an impoverished one. Their art, of course, is well known. Their songs and word-games are complex and playful; their language is rich, evocative, allusive, metaphoric: they have the vocabulary of poets. They can coax music from stones. Their singing has been described as "not just contrapuntal but polyrhythmic, a playful weaving of four and more strands of short, flowing, canon-like melodies (each voice imitating the melody of the others), sounding wordless streams of vowels in clear, bell-like yodelling voices, in free counterpoint."[4] I've never heard it myself, but more than one trustworthy observer has come across them communally humming around a campfire, a complex double-syncopated melody originating deep in the stomach, while conversing normally with each other—the background music and the foreground words somehow, miraculously, remaining distinct and clear.

Maun is a frontier settlement, a dusty, chaotic, African village grown into a town. There are still clusters of traditional huts within its boundaries. Small, neatly painted concrete-block houses with corrugated iron roofs are built in family clusters, just as the traditional *bomas* were. Commercial buildings are scattered throughout, in an apparently random way. The whole place is as complex and organic as the remarkable Okavango delta itself, which lies just to the north.

I had a Coke and a meat pie with a Botswana government official in a café on the outskirts of Maun. He was there with a delegation from Zimbabwe to do some spot-checks on the elephant population, which was becoming as much a problem in Botswana as it was across the border in Zimbabwe. Gosetsemang had worked with the San years before, trying to settle them down. It wasn't easy, he said. Their culture was so fragile, you had to be careful. Cutting into one part of it risked destroying the rest; it was all so interdependent . . .

I reminded him of the irritation officials elsewhere in Africa felt at trying to push nomads into modernity, and how the nomads were generally subverting their efforts.

"It's not like that at all with us," he said. "If you push the San, they simply fade into the bush. We're trying to help them, not hinder them. We're thinking of their children. Their children's children."

The problem, he said, is that the San had little sense of time, of the future or the past. It was hard to explain to them how necessary it was for their children to adapt to new ways. The San had never seen the need for adaptability. It wasn't that they were ignorant of the modern. They actively rejected it.

Something in what he said struck me. I remembered a phrase in a column I had once read, by the American magazine editor Lewis Lapham. He had been talking about modern Americans, and how their schools had failed them, leaving them without a sense of their own or of human history. "People unfamiliar with the world in time," he'd written, "find themselves marooned in the ceaselessly dissolving and therefore terrifying present."

I recounted this to Gosetsemang.

"No," he said again, "it's not quite like that." He sat quietly for a long while, groping for meaning. "Elephants," he said finally, "are easy. You manage the population, and balance their needs against the needs of the human population, and out of that comes policy.

"But what is correct policy towards other cultures, fragile cultures, the nomads among us? We are not their guardians, their custodians or their keepers. Do we risk destroying them by changing them? This is one of the great dilemmas of all Africa — how do we preserve the old cultures while accepting the new?"

"Perhaps," I said, "these are loaded terms. Instead of speaking of the loss of culture, or the destruction of nomadic bands, why not speak of the adaptability of culture, the readiness to accept new ways? If a San throws away his bow and arrow and drives a tractor instead, is he any less San?"

He looked wistful. "It's easy for you," he said. "It's not your culture at risk."

I remembered something a history teacher of mine had once said. Monica Wilson, who had produced with Leonard Thompson the first credible history of all the races of South Africa, had had no sympathy with the romantic view of human affairs. She argued that it was the readiness of cultures to borrow inventions and accept new ideas and techniques that built civilizations. Peoples who failed to adapt to changing circumstances were dinosaurs, doomed to extinction. The more efficient economy always drives out the less efficient. Hunter-gatherers become pastoralists; subsistence farmers become migrant labourers in an industrial economy. In this definition the San, romanticized now as people who have lived in harmony with the land for millennia, were doomed by their own inaction, as fish die when drought dries up the streams.

"I'm still thinking mostly of the children," Gosetsemang said again, after a long silence. "That's why we intervene."

"My point is that traditional cultures are doomed whether you intervene or not," I said.

"Then we may as well do it right," he said.

Still, there was another way of looking at it. The "Hottentots" and the "Bushmen" in South Africa had in some ways mutated into the "Cape Coloureds," and *that* culture was still very much alive—not just alive but vibrant and modern, and was helping to run the banks and stores and corporations, those engines of Western capitalism. There are many ways to adapt. Perhaps all this fretting was for naught. History has its own imperatives.

Once the Okavango Swamp was a lake, but then the earth lurched or some slight tectonic shift in the crust drained the water into secret crevices; the Okavango River continued to pour down across what is now the Caprivi Strip from the moist hills of Angola as it always had, but the lake had gone and the river became tangled in thickets of reeds, giant papyrus, mud, mire and muck, and then it just … disappeared.

You can spend days poling through the Okavango's twisty hippoways in a *mokoro*, the little flat-bottomed swamp boat, and never see anyone. All paths look alike. You can clamber out of your *mokoro* onto an "island" of swamp grass a metre thick, but if you were to somehow plunge through—a very easy thing to do—there would be 3 metres (10 feet) or more of water beneath you. Crocodiles below, snakes above: an unholy choice. Everywhere improbable vegetation grows prolifically. Like the *nooientjie's been*, the maiden's thigh, a long, bare, silky-white stalk topped by a silly frond of leaves that does, indeed, look somewhat like a pubic bush. Every half-day's travel or so there are signs of life: slash-and-burn agriculture that has reduced the islands to ghastly stumps, herds of skinny domestic cattle (they've killed the tsetse fly with pesticides, of all things, in this most pristine of wildernesses), the throbbing of helicopters taking rich tourists from Maun to the lodges along the Savute and in Chobe; but, much more often, you'd just see the deadly logs that are swamp crocodiles, lurking among the thickets of 15-centimetre (6-inch) thorns. The Bayei people, swamp dwellers, can find their way through this maze as though they had a Global Positioning Satellite poised permanently overhead (a drifting leaf, a small ripple, a muddy eddy—these are the signs by which they navigate), but even they sometimes go into the swamp and never return. A legend says that there are legions of screaming skulls in the muck beneath the islands; at the end of the world, when the waters dry up, they will be exposed, and will cause the apocalypse so long forecast. At twilight, when the hippos return to the channels, their heavy, lethal bodies cutting *V*s into the water, it's an easy legend to believe.

In good years the waters still overflow into the Boteti River, and reach the parched and arid surface of the Makgadigadi Pans, and in the best years of all (alas, very infrequent) they seep north-eastwards through the Selinda Spillway into the even more remote, even more mysterious Linyanti Swamp.

Adjacent to the swamps are endless forests of thorn acacia and mopane trees, home to sixty thousand elephants. In a bar at Maun I had seen, spiked to a wall with a nail, a piece ripped from *National Geographic* magazine. A few paragraphs were circled. It was a piece on Botswana by Douglas Lee. I squinted at it, then took it down to read. Lee wrote well about elephants: "… from a bunker at Lloyd's Camp [in Chobe National Park] I watch elephant trunks dabble in water a yard from my face. With incredible delicacy they mouth small pebbles, swirl leaves, twine in intimate greeting. Butterflies dance among giant feet, bees clamber at water's edge. The air is filled with elephanthood, with a rich zoo smell of fodder and manure, with the rumblings of their speech and a sudden trumpet fit to break the walls of Jericho.

"I look up at faces like dirt-caked boulders embedded with thick-lashed hazel eyes. They have the knowing look of a race that has seen rivers come and go. In their minds are maps of far-flung clay pans and woodlands and swamps, linked by ancient trails written on the land by the feet of many generations.

"In northern Botswana they have found a haven where broad spaces are still open and where the government prohibited all hunting in 1983. [Triply underlined here.] Their numbers have grown into the healthiest, least molested population in Africa ... Their success is a heartening note in the doleful litany of disasters for African wildlife."

I don't know whether this piece was spiked there by someone who approved, or disapproved, of Lee's conservationist point of view. No one seemed to know. But a dozen years after the piece was written, things weren't so rosy. The herds had swollen alarmingly, and across the border the Zimbabweans were beginning controlled culling, as I had seen. Across the Caprivi Strip in Angola, the war was supposed to be over, but they were still shooting everything that moved, and if it happened to have tusks, so much the better. And from the south ... from the south came the worst enemy of all, growing human populations and their demands for more, more, more ...

In early 1997 there were already threats of a "water war" between Namibia, which wants to take 20 million cubic metres (700 million cubic feet) a year from the Okavango system (tripling by the year 2003), and Botswana, whose dams and reservoirs were critically low after ten years of drought. There were threats of sabotage if a pipeline proposed by Namibia was ever built—residents of Maun walked out of a conciliatory meeting called by the Namibian government.

....

The origins of the Bamangwatho, the Tswana tribe who rule Botswana, are simple enough, but full of melodrama. Around the end of the eighteenth century, the three main branches of the Tswana were formed when three brothers broke away from their father to establish their own followings. These were Kwena, Ngwaketse, and Ngwato. This was not an amicable family: Ngwato and Kwena fell to fighting; the legend has it that Ngwato was saved from death at the hands of his brother by a small deer, a duiker (*phuti*, in Setswana), which has remained the tribe's totem ever since.

Ngwato was followed as ruler of what were now called the Bamangwatho by Mathiba I, who was followed by Kgama I, the "one-eyed and cruel" king, who was followed in turn by Kgari, usually described as "brave, wise, and merciful." His successor, Kgama II, had his rule interrupted by the Zulu *Mfecane* and his people scattered into the Great Thirstland to the west and the secretive swamps to the north.

In this part of Africa, adversity often seems to bring out superior rulers. Kgama II was succeeded not by the rightful heir, Macheng, but by Sekgoma I, who rescued many small tribes and subclans from the ravages of Mzilikazi, and united them around a new capital he built at Shoshong. Within a few years there were fifteen thousand people living in this exemplary, orderly, well-regulated society, a time of golden memory in Tswana history—even the weather cooperated, for the winters were crisp and the springs pregnant with sweet rains. The salt pans filled with water, and the herds of giraffe, antelope, rhino, and elephant swelled.

Sekgoma was a tall, well-built man, capable, fearless, and somewhat unscrupulous. Like Moshoeshoe he was the "father of his people." In character, however, he was quite different from the Sotho king. David Livingstone, who visited him in 1842, found him "generous and friendly," but he remained adamantly "heathen," in the missionary's dismissive word, and closed his mind to alien ideas.

"Change my heart," he once challenged Livingstone. "Give me medicine to change it, for it is proud, proud and angry, angry always."

Livingstone offered him the Bible, but he pushed it aside.

"Nay," he said, "I wish to have it changed at once, for it is very proud and very uneasy, and continually angry with someone." The Word of God, he told the astonished missionary, was as little use as "going out to the plain and meeting single-handed all the forces of the Ndebele."

Still, a few years later, when he was exiled by his great rival, Macheng, he allowed Khama and Kgamane, his sons by his senior wife, to attend a missionary school.

Big mistake. Khama not only converted, but after some years began to teach in the mission school. He rejected the rite of initiation, and refused to take part in such chiefly duties as rain-making and the smelling-out of witches. Sekgoma ordered him to take a second wife. He refused. His refusal pushed Sekgoma over the edge, and warfare followed.

Once installed as king in 1875, Khama wasted no time. He established a new capital of thirty thousand people at Palapye, building it not at random but according to a meticulously thought out plan. First, he built his own household, then, immediately afterwards, the *kgotla* meeting-place, where the chief listened to the grievances of his people. After that the public cattle kraal was set up, and then clusters of thatched huts and kraals according to custom and precedence. He made sure that at least one classroom was built for each ten hut divisions. He built stores, a telegraph office, and a large church.

He also savaged ancient customs. He outlawed witchcraft, polygamy, bride-price, severe corporal punishment, the killing of a twin. He enforced prohibition. He elevated the status of the Masarwa, as the San were called in Setswana. He introduced laws to conserve game and birds.

And then, when all was done, he decentralized his own rule, creating satellite towns and villages so the rulers could be nearer the ruled.

That was unique. Even Moshoeshoe hadn't dared it.

....

Khama died in 1923 at the age of eighty-nine. After a series of nasty dynastic squabbles it became clear that the real heir to the throne was Seretse Khama, who was only four. His uncle, Tshekedi Khama, twenty-four, became regent, and ruled the country for the next twenty-five years—a period of stability, progress, and harmony.

After the First World War, Seretse went to England to study; there he met and married an Englishwoman, Ruth Williams, an act that dismayed almost everyone— Tshekedi Khama, the South Africans, and the British authorities, who moved to block his accession to power and exiled him from the Protectorate. It wasn't until 1956, when he renounced his claim to the throne, that he was allowed to return, as a minor official in the colonial government.

Patience, however, was its own reward. When general elections for the first independent Botswana government were held in 1965, Seretse Khama was elected president.

Botswana remained poor and sleepy until the discovery of rich diamond fields in 1967. There is still 25 per cent unemployment, and most of the people work at subsistence agriculture, but the country as a whole has a trade surplus, and Seretse Khama's successor, Ketumile Masire, has continued Khama's prudent, cautious, democratic, unflamboyant, but successful economic policy.

There are problems, to be sure. There is a chronic water shortage—85 per cent of the country is Kalahari. There is a political opposition that wants to introduce the kind of wealth redistribution so favoured by Robert Mugabe in Zimbabwe. The population is increasing at an alarming rate (though the rate has recently fallen slightly). Literacy is still far from universal, despite the efforts of the Khamas. There are still disputes (none of them violent) with Zambia, Zimbabwe, and Namibia over borders.

But the traditions of the *kgotla*, of good leadership that listens to the grievances of the people, persist.

THE THIRSTLAND AND THE SKELETON COAST

N*amibia is a grim place in many ways, a harsh place where the legends mostly speak of death and greed. But it is also one of the most startlingly beautiful places on earth. There were no great kingdoms there, in the Elder Days. The Namib was always a frontier zone.*

"Take off your shoes," the prim young man with the clipboard said, peremptorily I thought. "Take them off now."

In the Forbidden Zone, you tend to do what you're told. I slipped off my shoes and socks and stepped gingerly onto the Namibian desert, dirty red in colour and not quite hot enough to burn.

I looked around. What a grim landscape this was! This muddy red sand, rocky outcrops, gravel glittering in the relentless sun. There was not a blade of grass, a bush, or a thorn vine to be seen; nothing grew here but human greed. Behind me a group of workers leaned on their shovels and stared. They were all dressed in yellow or blue coveralls and carried what resembled a little domestic whisk broom tied by a thong to their wrists. They were expressionless, but I thought I could read their contempt.

"Just do it," he urged again, impatiently, gesturing at my feet.

I scuffed my toes through the gritty sand of the Namibian plains, flinching as a toe stubbed on a pebble. I moved the foot back and forth, experimenting. It wasn't too bad. Okay, in fact.

"What do you feel? Clipboard asked.

"Sand and gravel."

"What else?"

"Nothing else."

"Lift your foot up."

As I did so, one of the workers wandered over, and began whisking at my feet. I thought this was a bit much, but stood still as instructed. He brushed away, exposing the sand and gravel I had felt. But then he muttered something, and picked up a small pebble. He spat in his hand, rubbed the pebble back and forth. I stared. It was a muddy yellow colour. It looked like dirty glass.

"Is that what I think it is?" I asked.

"Yes," Clipboard said. "A diamond. Not a very good one, but a good size. Decent stone."

"Come on!" I said. "You planted it!" But I knew he hadn't, and he didn't dignify me with an answer.

The "lockbox boy" wandered over. He was carrying the lockbox itself, a small metal box the size and shape of a bank safety-deposit box. It was padlocked twice, and bound to his wrist with a steel-reinforced cord. On the upper surface were a series of graduated holes. He pushed my diamond through the appropriate hole and made a notation on a pad. The diamond wasn't "mine," not by a long shot. It belonged to the operating company, CDM, a part of De Beers of South Africa, and there were plenty of stories about how rigorously they were prepared to make sure no one walked off with their property—even to giving the miners X-rays and a very thorough enema before they left the diamond fields to go home. De Beers doesn't have a huge sense of humour about its role in the scheme of things.

"Who gets credit for it?" I asked.

"You. Us. No one."

"Give the credit to him," I said, pointing to the guy who had whisked my foot. "He found it."

For the first time I got a reaction. The whisk guy looked at me, still quite expressionless. Then one eye closed in a solemn wink, before he turned away.

On the brief drive back to Swakopmund I stared again at the unforgiving landscape. "My" diamond was one small part of millions of stones that had been brought out of Namibia, making the country the world's largest exporter of gemstone diamonds, a substantial proportion of national revenues. A few hours later, in the De Beers office, they spread out on a silky-soft stretch of karakul skin (another Namibian export for the luxury trade) a couple of days' take. There were trays of them, spilling carelessly onto the grey lamb's wool in glittering piles, Cape Yellows, pink and vulgar chartreuse, blue-whites, diamonds in the rough. Those diamonds had originated in the far interior of South Africa in the Cretaceous days; over the millennia they had been washed down the Orange and Fish rivers, over the Augrabies Falls, and out to the chilly Benguela Current that flows north up the African coast. There, tides and the restless desert winds had slowly driven them farther into the interior, where they just ... waited.

Before the whites came, no one really cared about diamonds. Neither the San nor the Nama, their close cousins, cared; water was much more precious. Nor did the Hottentots who pushed up from the south in the eighteenth century: they were cattlemen, and cared more for grazing. The Bantu weren't interested either. The Ovambos stayed in the north, inland from the Skeleton Coast. The Herero and their cousins, the still-exotic Himba, were agriculturists and found no use for glass beads that were harder than stone, impossible to string. The Portuguese, who came here in the fifteenth century, didn't stay.

It wasn't until the twentieth century that anyone cared.

And then they began to care a great deal.

The shifting sands of the Namib desert conceal and reveal with cruel whim. It is not uncommon for rows of grinning skulls to suddenly appear one morning, and then be gone the following week. Diamond prospectors who ventured inland have been found years later, buried with their ox, their cart, their worldly goods, macabre bas-reliefs preserved under shifting dunes. Once, not long ago, a row of miners' shovels, still upright in sand the colour of oatmeal, appeared near Lüderitz, only the upper third of the haft showing. In their straight rows, they looked eerily like grave markers, and in a way they were; they were all that remained of a German camp, abandoned during the First World War.

My first visit to the Forbidden Zone, the Sperrgebied, was years ago, when Namibia was still South West Africa and a Mandated Territory to South Africa under the United Nations charter. Security was tight, then, though not lethal. But a war has happened there in the meantime, a long and deadly war, and attitudes have hardened. The machinery has changed from men with shovels to gigantic earth-moving monsters that gulp tons of soil at a time; the landscape, always lunar, is now even more desolate, a nightmare from the post-industrial future. Fifty thousand square kilometres (19,300 square miles) of gravel pit, smoke, belching chimneys, and oil fires. If there was ever romance there, it has long gone.

This time, I was warned. There are armed patrols along the Sperrgebied boundaries. And they're not much for asking questions.

San have lived here for centuries, perhaps forever. At Twyfelfontein there are splendid rock engravings, a whole national gallery of San art, one of the largest in Africa, some of them dating back to the Stone Age, and depicting animals no longer found. Others are more recent, and show both white and black people with guns, an ominous icon. A little farther, near Brandberg, is the famous White Lady of the Brandberg, which is very old, some say as old as sixteen thousand years. This small figure, no more than 40 centimetres (16 inches) high, and clutching what looks very much like a bow and arrow in one hand and (to my eyes at least) a wine goblet in the other, is white only in the nether regions, and may or may not be a lady at all, but has certainly given rise to almost as many fanciful legends as the ruins of Great Zimbabwe. No one knows to this day what the figure means, if anything—

> In the northeast of the country is a curious piece of land called the Caprivi Zipfel, or Caprivi Strip, a 482-kilometre (300-mile) finger of Namibia thrust among Angola, Botswana, and Zambia, reaching for the Zambezi River. The Germans traded Zanzibar to the British for the strip, because they wanted access to their East Coast colonies. But in the end they were thwarted by Rhodes's annexation of Rhodesia, and the Strip never got beyond the Zambezi. The Zipfel was named after Georg Leo, Graf von Caprivi, Bismarck's successor as German chancellor.

perhaps it's nothing more than an unorthodox San artist's experiment in colour, the earliest of the avant-garde. It's as good a theory as any other.

The politically proper pan-tribalist view is that the early interactions among the San, the Khoikhoi (their close cousins), and the Bantu, mostly Ovambos, were harmonious, that they shared the land in a scrupulous way, each group interfering with the others as little as possible. Unfortunately, the San's own tales don't agree with this cosy interpretation.

Their view—filtered through the circumlocutions of tale-telling—is that they were minding their own business when the Ovambos moved in from the south and enslaved them, putting them to work herding cattle and fighting in their frequent internecine wars. Later, certain of the San became executioners for the Ovambo royalty. (This last seems to rankle more than the forced labour; historically the San have been pacifists, having no time for killing—the nature they faced every day did enough of that.)

A few weeks earlier I'd had dinner in Cape Town with a former South African reservist who had spent two years fighting a losing war against the Ovambos' SWAPO guerrillas and their Cuban (read: Soviet) backers in northern Namibia. He recalled how more than five thousand of the K!ung San had drifted in from the desert to work with the South Africans.

"We didn't have to recruit them," he said. "They just came. They wanted revenge. They remembered what had been done to them. They didn't care what the war was about. They just knew who the enemy was."

> As late as 1910 the farmers around Grootfontein petitioned a local magistrate to let them class the Bushmen as "*vogelvrei*"—as "game" to be shot all year round.
>
> The magistrate said, "No, they are human."
>
> This was not the prevailing opinion in the district at the time.
>
> ....
>
> *From Green,* Where Men Still Dream

In camp they'd discard their bows and poisoned arrows and receive training in captured Soviet weaponry much more deadly than their own. They became an élite squad of hunter-killers. South African commandos reported in astonishment that the best San trackers could pick out the hoofprints of a wildebeest they had wounded with one of their poison arrows, although it was stampeding in the middle of a large herd. Similarly, they could tell one jeep's tires from another, though they were the same make and had covered the same ground.

"They'd have worked for nothing, for the prestige of it. But mostly we used them as scouts. It wasn't so very different from what they did all their lives in the desert, finding game. Only this time the quarry was human—and more heavily armed than they were."

The Ovambos—a loose confederation of seven tribes—were the obvious candidates to fight the war of independence against the white colonists. As a confederation, they were strong enough to deter all aggressors, including the slavers of yore and the German invaders at the end of the last century. They were an aggressive culture themselves. When there was no one else to fight, they'd make war with each other. Their palisaded villages contained secret passageways and shifting gateways to confuse aggressors; they always lived in a state of heightened tension. Their heavy scarring of face and body was not just tribal markings, identity badges, or ornament, but the work of sorcerers to extract the evil spirits; Ovambo tribal myth was full of anger and malice. In olden times at the heart of each village was a sacred fire, *omulilo gwoshilongo*, burning mopane wood that symbolized the life of the chief and the welfare of his tribe. It was a disgrace for this fire to go out; it was therefore a target for raiders of all stripes, and was defended vigorously. (In this, as in all things, beliefs have atrophied. Now, if the damn thing goes out, you just toss a little paraffin on it and get it going again.) They were governed by priest-kings and a Queen Mother of great prestige. There was a hereditary aristocracy and endemic slavery. Even now, years after independence, in a relatively peaceful country, many village chiefs are guarded by squads of heavily armed thugs in camouflage fatigues.

The other major tribe, the aristocratic Hereros and their bucolic cousins, the Himba and the Tjimba of the northern Kaokoveld, claimed to have come to Namibia from central Africa, from an unknown country they call Raruu. Towards the middle of the eighteenth century, the Herero moved farther south, leaving their rural cousins behind. Their southward push and their battles with the Nama precipitated a bloody five-decade war that was stopped only by the arrival of the Europeans. But they were too few in number to fight a real war against the Germans.

> The Himba are a dark people given a wonderful buttery colour by smearing themselves with a mixture of butter and ochre, a rancid but powerful cosmetic which they say is essential to health and beauty. Good grooming demands that it cover every part of the body and every item of clothing. The Himba also have an intricate language of hair. At puberty, women shave the front of their scalps and braid the remaining strands with plant fibres. At marriage, they add locks of hair from their brothers and groom, each lock carefully positioned to indicate status.

The Germans, under Bismarck, were late entering the European colonial scramble for Africa. Bismarck had always been against colonies; he considered them expensive illusions. But he was pushed into it. In 1882, following the romantic exploits of German explorers in Tanganyika and Kenya, the German Colonial Organization was formed by such eminent personages as the Prince zu Hohenlohe-Langenburg. So when Adolf Lüderitz, a Bremen merchant who had founded a trading station in Lagos in 1881 and opened a second in 1882, which he "bought" for "one hundred rifles and £200, or two hundred rifles and £100," from a Hottentot chieftain, he at once applied for "protection." Bismarck, still trying to stay out of it, politely requested the British to say whether they had any interest in the matter. The Colonial Office didn't even deign to reply, so in 1884 Lüderitz was officially declared part of the German Empire. (After that, the Germans wasted no time. By 1914 the colony had been extended to take in territory larger than all of France. Within a few more years Bismarck had also added Togo and Cameroon and all the marvellous country around Kilimanjaro, called Tanganyika.)

Actually, Kilimanjaro should today belong to Kenya. But Queen Victoria gave it to her nephew, Kaiser Willie, as a birthday present. That's how things were done in Africa in those days.

After the First World War, South West Africa was turned over to the South Africans to rule as a "mandated territory," a mandate that was renewed by the United Nations after the next war. But they refused to allow South Africa to annex the country.

The Nationalist government of Dr. Malan in South Africa wasn't going to let a technicality stop it. The South Africans virtually sealed off the Ovambos and imposed the policies that had been so successful (they thought) in the south: hut and poll taxes drove the natives off their reserves; confiscation of native lands finished the job. The evil migrant-labour system that is still, to some extent, in place in southern Africa was instituted in South West Africa too. Tribal leaders were appointed with no legitimacy, and no consultation with the people.

The response was entirely predictable: bands of the disaffected, most of them Ovambos, gathered in the countryside, and the guerrilla warfare that was ultimately to drive the South Africans from their country began.

The South Africans tightened the system, and stories began to circulate about their use of "judicial torture." In retaliation, the guerrillas copied a trick they had learned from a chief named Mandumi, who had first revolted against the British as early as 1917, and who forced his prisoners to fry the evening meat over the campfire, using their own hands as cooking utensils.

The racial laws of apartheid were introduced, one by one. At the beginning of the 1950s miscegenation became illegal. Or at least cohabitation became illegal, but marriage was still allowed. On the "white" farms all over the territory lonely farmers married their Damara and Herero girls; but a few years later marriage, too, was forbidden.

> A newcomer to the colony under its early South African mandate was very popular, at first. But after a while she became aware that people were always finding ways of avoiding her dinner invitations. She finally went to a friend to beg an explanation.
>
> "My dear," the friend said, "do you ever go into your kitchen?"
>
> "No. Why should I?"
>
> "Because, my dear, your cook is a leper."
>
> *From Farson, Behind God's Back*

The mandate was revoked in 1966, and the SWAPO guerrilla war, backed by the Soviet Union through their surrogates Cuba and Angola, began to escalate. South

Africa reacted with calculated brutality. Torture and murder became commonplace; demonstrators were routinely shot in the streets. After Angola, to the north, wrested its independence from Portugal, a full-scale invasion followed, and was beaten back. A puppet government was set up in Windhoek, but it turned on its sponsors and demanded talks with SWAPO. It was fired and another puppet installed.

But the end of the Namibian fishing industry (from depletion of the stocks), falling world prices for minerals, especially uranium, a weakening diamond market, and severe drought caused the South Africans to lose heart. They had, after all, their own shifting fate to worry about. Negotiations finally began, a constitution was agreed on, and in March 1990 independence was granted under the leadership of Sam Nujoma, SWAPO's leader.

Nujoma was no Mandela, but nevertheless he steered a middle, sensible ground between his Marxist convictions and pragmatic dealings with the capitalists. None of the lurid forecasts of reprisal and massacre came to pass. By 1997 Namibia was a stable, well-governed country, relatively prosperous (if prone to drought). There was unrest, of course, it would be unrealistic to expect otherwise. There were demonstrations by groups of Hai//Om San, complaining that their ancestral lands had been stripped from them; seventy-three were arrested in early 1997, and released after protests from human-rights activists, the president indignantly denying that the San were being treated as second-class Namibians.

The contrasts were (and are) stark: In the far Kalahari, bands of San still roam as they have done since the Stone Age; but near Swakopmund is the world's largest (and most efficient) open-cast uranium mine: even in a depressed market, a hundred-car train leaves Rössing Mine, fully laden, every twenty minutes, twenty-four hours a day, all year.

> One of the symbols of change is the existence of a small but thriving stockmarket in Windhoek. A prudent recent buy would have been Namibian Breweries Class A stock. The plucky little brewery had 90 percent of Namibia's admittedly modest brewing market, but a recent public offering let it take on the giant South African Breweries, the Oppenheimer-controlled company that has become one of the world's ten largest brewers, in that company's home market.
>
> Namibian drove the SAB into a frenzy by alleging in its advertising campaign that its giant rival was putting "funny things" into its beer.
>
> It was an assault, as the British newspaper The Economist put it, on the "lager laager."
>
> From The Economist, February 8, 1977

Nujoma remained popular, and towards the end of his second term there was pressure on him from within SWAPO to have the constitution amended so he could run for a third term in the elections in 1999. Not everyone agreed, and *The Namibian* newspaper urged him to "leave office with his dignity intact and not go the way of Kaunda ... by turning ... the person and the office into one."

I had a talk about Namibian politics with Gert Viljoen, a farmer at Grootfontein, near Tsumeb in the Namibian northland. His farm was just off the main road to Rundu, at the entrance to the Caprivi Strip, and for a dozen years only the army had passed by. Then the tourists came, mainly South Africans, heading for the swamps on the Okavango, and for the Zambezi. Gert was a prototypical Boer: beefy, big-boned, a tough fellow who had defended his land ferociously. But he'd become a Nujoma loyalist. "The *kêrel* [fellow] fought for his country like a man," he said. "He won. Now he's doing his best. And we're going to help him." I found this more reassuring than all the promises of all the ubiquitous United Nations observers put together. This was not, as Gatsha Buthelezi once said of South Africa's white liberals, "making friends with the crocodile so he doesn't eat you first." This was a hard respect, hard won.

Part IV

Kongo

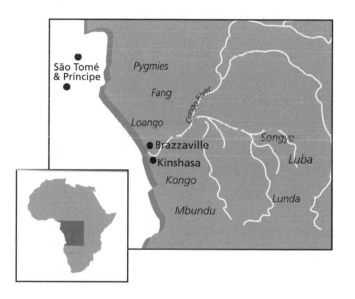

THE MANIKONGO KINGS,
AND THE DARK QUEEN OF
THE MBUNDU

I sat for a while on a rock, staring at the Congo River rapids southwest of the Zairian
capital, Kinshasa, watching islands of hyacinths come down from the deep interior
of tropical Africa dashing themselves to pieces on the glistening boulders, a strange
and exotic sight. A great log went over, cartwheeled once, and wedged itself between two
rocks. Then the corpse of a buffalo strangled in vines; I caught a brief glimpse of its eyes,
milky white in death, glaring up at the thunderclouds overhead. The water rushing by
was coming—or so Joseph Conrad had said—from the Heart of Darkness, but of course
he meant the blackness he saw in the souls of his Station Factors, there in the distant
jungle. The water had begun more than 4,000 kilometres (2,500 miles) away, near
Lubumbashi in Shaba province, almost on the continental divide, then drifted placidly
through Kisangani in Haute Zaire (where the rebels had started their 1997 drive to
wrest Zaire from its ageing and ailing dictator). A long and leisurely journey it was;
only here, at the rapids, did the river seem in any hurry.

I'd been reflecting on Beginnings that morning, as I shuffled through a thick sheaf
of notes on the Congo basin and the putative origins of the Bantu people. A river
might have a beginning, but people don't really—they only have a time and a place
where they finally impress themselves on history. So though the great arguments about
the origins of the Bantu are interesting, they are not necessary to resolve. (They are
interesting, nevertheless, for the painstaking detective work involved, tracing linguistic
fragments back to some kind of African ur-language, the tongue that started everything.) Perhaps the Bantu did, as one theory has it, "begin" somewhere in the Nigerian
interior, probably with the invention of iron smelting and the more complex agricultural techniques smelting made possible, which allowed them to spread out across the
savannah and seep down the great waterways to the coast. If so, it is equally "true" that
they "began" somewhere in the great bend of the Congo's upper reaches. Certainly this
is where their explosive and accelerated expansion commenced, two millennia ago.

I'd come north from the Namib into war-torn Angola, and thence to the Congo,
from the desert to ... to this rich gumbo of peoples, most of their kingdoms now lost,
ground into oblivion by the weight of history. Only here and there a few toy kingdoms

survive, have survived the crash of empires, the dreadful centuries of slavery, the bur-
den of modernity, cartoons of what once was, patterns of what might have been.

So many stories! I wanted to see the homelands of Nzinga, the Black Queen of Angola.
I wanted to see the Fang, among the greatest artists in Africa, and reputed to be cannibals,
who migrated down the Sanaga River from the savannah of northeast Cameroon; the
Kuba (whose ninety-third king, Shamba Bolongolo, according to the lineages, was a
Buddha-like figure who renounced all worldly possessions and travelled the kingdom like
a holy mendicant); the Chokwe, who arose like a fury as recently as 1850, dominating
Kasai and Katanga; the Lozi, who were overthrown by an invasion of the Rozwi from
Great Zimbabwe, who were convulsed in turn by the Mfecane of the Zulus; the Téké,
now the most bourgeois of the Congo Republic's peasant agriculturists . . .

One of the seminal events in the long and eventful Bantu history was the emergence
of the mythic warrior-king Kongolo, and the great Luba kingdoms his heirs founded.
Their successors and inheritors, the Songye and the Lunda, are the progenitors of many
modern peoples, from Zaire down into Namibia.

But Kongo's faded capital would be my first stop on this complicated journey.

When I reached Brazzaville, Congo, from Angola, I sat for a while in my air-conditioned hotel room, staring down at the Congo River and Kinshasa beyond. I ordered a bottle of wine from room service, but left it unopened. My suitcase was still red from the dust of M'banza Congo, once the capital city of the Kongo kings. I pushed it away, out of sight. After a while I got up and went downstairs and took a taxi to the Marché du Plateau, where they would know what to do.

"You want souvenir?" the taxi driver asked. I was sure he had a brother somewhere who made antique masks carved from newly imported Australian eucalyptus and stained with boot-blacking for the tourists, such few as they were.

"No," I said. "I need *grisgris*."

"For what you want *grisgris*?" he said, catching my eye in the mirror.

"I don't want it," I said. "I need it."

He stopped the taxi, then, and stared at me for a while. I said nothing more, and after a minute he started the engine and threaded his way through the town, heading for the Plateau. I'd been told that this was the place to go, that, despite being in the commercial centre of Brazzaville near the tourist hotels, it was where authentic items could be found, if you were persistent enough and your need was pressing.

I stared blindly at the passing city, leafy, green, benign-looking, the trees dripping with scarlet flowers. We passed the house where de Gaulle had stayed in his Free French days. Free for whom? I wondered. The French had abolished slavery in the Congo only in 1948, after de Gaulle had satisfactorily freed the French. Okay, so they called it "forced labour," and not "slavery," but it had amounted to the same thing—

how many thousands had they killed building the infamous Brazzaville–Pointe Noire railroad? And so Pointe Noire could become a notorious den of mercenaries, rene-gade Legionnaires, and bitter Brits and Boers from the Zuurveld, fleeing their own demons and becoming demons in their turn. Of course, that's all gone now. The mer-cenaries have moved on. Pointe Noire is a petroleum centre. And also a resort, where the Europeans go to show they can bare their breasts too.

It turned out I could have easily walked from my hotel to the Plateau, but I didn't mind the rip-off city tour. In a collapsing economy, cabbies have to make a living somehow. I had no more energy for resentment.

I felt feverish, but it wasn't the fever that filled my mind.

So many dead!

I lunged into the market, the usual chaotic jumble of stalls and sheds and con-tainers turned into retail outlets, and made my way to where the artisans were. Most of the stuff they offered the "patron" was junk, of course, and though there were some good pieces and some real antiques, I wasn't expert enough to always know the difference. In any case, I wasn't looking for art.

I stopped at a likely vendor, an old man, grizzled and leaning on a cane. Surely the old would know?

"I need *grisgris*," I said again.

The old man leaned forward and stared at me for a long time. Then he nodded, and jerked a thumb over his shoulder. That way.

I was passed from hand to hand. In the end, I found myself at the blackened entrance to a small hut cobbled together from scraps of corrugated iron. We were down in a gully somewhere, and it smelled rank, as though a sewer had overflowed. Somewhere down here, among the sorcerers, there are magic potions to be found, birds' feathers (symbols of power), the teeth of "phacochères," monkey skulls, dried baboon testicles. There are philtres for gastro-enteritis; "vaccines" against virtually all known diseases, including AIDS; prophylactics against this or that; aphrodisiacs; charms against thieves, against car accidents, against impotence, against any mis-fortune. I peered into the darkness of the hut. The small man inside, seated on a stool, didn't at first seem like a man of power. He was short and very black and dressed in a torn workshirt and beach flip-flops. I repeated my request.

"What is your trouble?" he asked. "You have an enemy who wants to defame you? A lover whose heart is not sure? You want to be rich?"

"No," I said. "There is a smile I want to forget."

"Is this a smile from your nightmares?" he asked.

"No," I said, encouraged that he saw so quickly. "This is a smile I should remem-ber in my nightmares, but do not."

How to explain? My French wasn't good enough. How to explain that this wasn't the rictus smile of a screaming man, the smile of a crazy man, a monkey smile, a thing of cruelty and pain. No, it was the simple smile of a man happy in his work. That was what haunted me.

I should have nightmares about that smile, but I don't.

In the end all I said, lamely, was this: "I saw a man smiling where he had no right to smile."

"Ah!" he said. "You have walked the paths of the dead."

The paths of the dead! Where had I heard that phrase? It had the ring of old poetry, a saga somewhere, some time long forgotten. Yes, I suppose I had walked the paths of the dead.

He scratched himself. "For the dreams I have only the smoke," he said, pulling a battered Nescafé tin from under a shelf, and stuffing weed into a paper cone made of newspaper. "The mind is afraid of the dead," he said. "This will give it courage."

"No," I said, "you have it wrong."

But how to explain? It was the living I fear. Or don't fear. Should fear. It was just a smile!

"I know," he said, "but you're wrong. A man like that is not part of our world. He is already one of the dead."

I took the weed, if that's what it was. I had no intention of using it. In my world, I thought, the dead are more removed from the living than they are here in Africa, though later, when I thought about it, I was not so sure. I thought he still hadn't quite understood. It wasn't the living I feared. It was the emptiness.

He saw my hesitation. Then he reached down and brought out what looked like two ivory chess pieces. He put them down on the counter gingerly, as though they were fragile. "They're not much," he said, "but they come from Gabon and they're what you want. It's a telephone fetish. They do have power. If you keep one with you, and someone who has your trust keeps the other, your troubles will seem smaller." They were not ivory, he said, but carved from the teeth of a hippopotamus: "This is a beast that lives in the river, and the river reaches down to the sea, and the sea envelops us all . . ."

I took them gratefully, paid him, and left. I had no heart to argue further.

That night I put them under my pillow. Even though I had both ends of the "telephone," I thought it might help. I tried to believe what the old man had said. *A man like that is not a man. He already has one foot on the paths of the dead.*

I slept that night soundly, like before.

No nightmares. Nothing.

Troubled only when awake.

....

It had begun simply enough, in the Bar Chez Martine on the Marginal, the boulevard that curves around the bay of Luanda, Angola's capital. The skies were gloomy and overcast—there had been thunderstorms along the Congo Basin and in the Cabinda enclave. I had come into town over the Morodora di Lua, the jagged hills that look down to the sea, and Luanda beyond. Even from a distance I could see the city decaying. But the waterfront cafés were still crowded. I had checked with the American consul before I came, and gotten almost the same answer I'd been given in Mozambique: the war was over, but the peace hadn't yet begun. The killing had been going on for ... what? Fifteen years? Seventeen? In some ways, as we shall see, for more than three hundred. It was too much to think it could simply stop. The day before the government leader, Jose Eduardo Dos Santos, had flown to Libreville, Gabon's capital, for a "summit" meeting with Jonas Savimbi, the insurgent leader, who was angling for a complete amnesty for his troops before agreeing to disband and join the new merged army urged on him by the United Nations. Good luck, I thought, looking around the waterfront, crowded not with tourists or the colonists, as it had been in the old days, but with mercenaries, waiting for their deadly work to resume.

The capital's curving Isla de Luanda waterfront would have been beautiful once, a small Lusitanian town in the tropics. The beaches, too, look beautiful, but they aren't really. They're filthy and poisoned, like much of the land, with human detritus. There is a dreadful smell of decay everywhere. Naked children wander the streets, dazed, beyond tears; on the beaches the fevered ones lie, dying alone. Corpses are rolled by the incoming tide, and ... things ... not yet corpses. I had wandered through the Roque Santiero market, but it was unlike any other I had visited in Africa. There was hardly anything there, and the people were hostile, squabbling over scraps. No food, though you could buy guns aplenty. The city was jammed. It was only designed to house and feed fifty thousand or so, but there were more than a million living there now, most of them penniless refugees.

It was easy enough to find what I was looking for. Chez Martine was a hang-out for large and weathered young men in combat fatigues, with hair too long and eyes too hard, mercenaries for sure. They were talking Afrikaans. No doubt of it. I had expected them to be there, or somewhere there, waiting. I had considered the mercenaries some weeks before, when I first started thinking about this trip, about getting inland from Luanda to where the great queen, Nzinga, had spun her webs and waged her wars, so long ago, and also north towards the Congo, towards M'banza Congo, Kongo's capital. Still, I hadn't really expected to find South Africans fighting for the government forces. Hadn't South Africa propped up Jonas Savimbi's rebels for so many years, and gone to war with Cuba? But I shouldn't have been surprised. These weren't regular soldiers—they were "mercs." As a soldier-for-hire had said to me years before, "Loyalty is not an asset in this business." The mercs had abandoned Savimbi. This was a bad sign for him, and I wondered whether he knew. He probably did. That's what this summit to discuss general amnesty was about. He wasn't going to fold his men into some amorphous U.N.–government force without assurances.

The U.N. peacekeepers—a mixed bag of Ukrainians, Uruguayans, Brazilians, and Romanians—had come back in 1995 to monitor the so-called Lusaka Protocol setting up, in theory, a unified government, and were supposed to be gone by 1997, but no one expected that to happen. In some ways, peace (as opposed to an end to the fighting) seemed farther off than ever. The mercs all agreed there'd be work for years yet.

I sat down in an empty chair and ordered myself a beer. It was just before nine in the morning, and the tables were already filled with bottles. I nodded hello, made polite greetings in Afrikaans. This perked up their attention. They'd taken me for one of those NGO do-gooders, or (worse) a U.N. observer.

We sat for a while and chatted. Mercs are usually pretty astute about politics—they have to be. Negotiations took a while, but eventually one of them, Theunissen by name, agreed to take me upcountry. "Why the hell not?" he said. "Nothing doing here this week. Might as well go take a look-see." He'd be flying into Zaire later on, he said. As that country disintegrated Angola was going to try a grab for the Zairian diamond fields. "Entirely unofficially, of course," he said without a trace of humour.

We settled on a price, and on the ground rules: I do what he said to do. The price was $150 per day, plus costs for provisions and other expenses. He'd find the gasoline and the travel papers.

"Actually, you don't need papers," he said. "Your visa's okay, I think, outside the city. My army pass is what we'll need. That and these," he said, pointing to a rack behind him in his four-wheeler, where there were two automatics, a hunting carbine with telescopic sight, something he called a "worrier," really just a shotgun with explosive pellets, and several pistols. In a case in the back there were neat rows of ammunition. There were also grenades. Theunissen was a walking arsenal. The vehicle had bullet-proof windows. "No good against the armour-piercing stuff," he said cheerfully. "But then we're unlikely to need it anyway. If we do, we've already made a bad mistake."

The road out of Luanda to the east wound through gullies and dumps and shantytowns; even here the irrepressible commercial instincts were popping up, and there were rudimentary bars and small shops and "service stations," where piles of rusty auto parts yanked from wrecks could be purchased, ground down, and somehow made to fit.

There were militia checkpoints at nearly every intersection on the outskirts of town, but Theunissen's army pass took us through with no trouble. No one even wanted to look at my documents, which was just as well—what was a "tourist" doing travelling with the army in a war zone? I had prudently not brought my camera. Cameras are for spies or, at best, inquisitors.

This good karma, if that's what it was, didn't last. Less than an hour out of town on the Dondo road we came to a more serious roadblock. This was not just a truck with a few more or less indolent soldiers. This was a real military affair. Theunissen sat up straighter and pulled a tarp over the beer. "No sense giving them ideas," he muttered.

No amount of persuasion would allow us to go on. We turned around and headed back to Luanda. I was just as happy. I didn't like the look of the lieutenant in charge, with his unsmiling face and mirrored shades.

From Luanda, we tried again. We headed northeast on a minor road. If we could get to Uige, we could possibly head south and hit our original route beyond the army checkpoint, closer to a town called N'dalatando, and so on to our destination, Malanje. Malanje was where the Dark Queen had set up her capital. But a little later we ran into trouble. Just beyond Caxito we found another barricade, and were turned back again.

"I guess they don't want anyone heading for Lunda Norte," he said.

"Why not?"

"That's where the diamond fields are. Lots of fighting up there. Mostly miners killing each other—good place to stay away from. Strikes, riots, changing sides . . . I wouldn't go there without a battalion, and then only in APCs."

"Me neither," I said. "Nzinga'll have to wait."

"Who's he?"

"She," I said.

"Oh, it's like that is it," he said, misunderstanding.

"No," I said impatiently. "It isn't. She's been dead more than two hundred years."

"Oh," he said, losing interest.

We made one more try, but this time we were turned back, not by the army, but because the road simply stopped. On my Michelin map it went through all right, but on the ground there was no sign that the road continued.

Theunissen turned the truck around and shut off the engine. He spread the map on the hood.

"I don't think there's any way of getting there unless you fly," he said.

"Problem is, I don't really have a 'there' in my mind," I said. I just wanted to poke around the plateau where Nzinga's Mbundu kingdom withdrew after their run-in with the Portuguese.

"In any case, renting a private plane is going to cost you plenty," he said. "And there are no scheduled flights there. Unless you know someone in De Beers?"

He'd showed me De Beers's ultra-discreet Angolan headquarters on the way out of town—in an alley that looked like a slum, behind an unmarked door.

"No" I said, "I don't think that would work. You're expensive enough for me."

He grinned and passed over a beer. We were suddenly chummy, two Boers in red-hot Africa. It turned out he came from Wepener, a little town close to where I was born, and knew someone I had known. I peered at the map, looking for a way around the problem. I couldn't see one.

I was going to have to give up on Nzinga. This was too bad, for she seemed an appropriate monarch for Angola—a fierce, even terrible, warrior queen.

"Okay, look," I said, "let's instead go take a look at the old capital of the Congo Empire, M'banza Congo. It's up here"—stabbing at the map with a finger—"M'banza Congo originally, then São Salvador, now M'banza Congo again."

"I've been there," he said. "There's nothing there. Nice country. That was the capital of the Congo at one time?"

"Yes," I said, "before the white man got here. When the ManiKongos ruled here, from the Kwanza all the way to Loango, north of the Congo River."

"Christ," he said, "I didn't know. When was this?"

"Fourteen hundred or so," I said.

"There was nothing here in fourteen hundred but bush and cannibals," he said, dismissively.

"Yes there was. The city had more than a hundred thousand people then, bigger than Luanda until recently. And cannibals were as rare as they were in Europe ..."

"Christ," he said again. And, in an unconscious imitation of Pliny's famous aphorism, "Always something new ..."

So we set off again, heading north up the coast towards N'zeto, where we would turn inland for a run of about 250 kilometres (150 miles) to M'banza Congo on what appeared to be a decent road (although, ominously, it was dotted in spots on the map).

It was there, somewhere south of the town of Ambroz, struggling up a pitted road in rolling countryside, that we came up behind a truck of human corpses, heading who knows where. It was a large dump truck, and its tailgate was flapping loose. Arms and legs could be seen sticking through the slots. Men and women. One of the women was stylishly dressed, the colourful *aba* knotted around her head stained with blood; I saw a hole where her ear should have been. On the top of the heap was a pile of legs, attached to no body. The truck stank with a sickening abattoir odour, and a vile black liquid seeped from the rear and dripped to the road. We tried to pass for 10 kilometres (6 miles), but the driver wouldn't let us—he wanted us to stay in his carrion wake, I guess, another object lesson in African *realpolitik*. Or maybe he really didn't care. Theunissen, who has seen everything, was unfazed. Eventually he found his chance, and as the truck veered to avoid a pothole he swept past, giving the death lorry the finger as he did so. I caught a glimpse of the heap of bodies as we swayed alongside for a few seconds. I remember the smell, and a head rolling about on the pile, its tongue hanging out like a dog's, its eyes missing. As we swept by, a man standing on the running board and clinging to the window post waved at us with his free hand. I looked up at him as we passed, and he waved again. His face was wreathed in a smile, a happy smile, the smile of a man well content with his life and his work, the dazzling smile of a man whose conscience is clear and who hasn't a care in the world. We went on by, and gradually the terrible stench of death dissipated; very faintly through the reopened windows I could smell the fresh air of the sea, only a few metres to our left.

The stench disappeared. But that iconic smile—that goddamn cheerful smile—never did.

It was against that smile, and the grim history that it represented, that I needed the *grisgris*.

The paths of the dead! A passage from a book called *A Modern Slavery*, written from the other end of Angola in the early part of this century by an American journalist, came into my mind. Henry Nevinson was his name. He was writing about the melancholy slave caravans that wound their way down to the sea; those who were too weak to carry their burdens were lashed to a tree and left to die. The country was heavy with the weight of the dead.

"In front of me a deep stream is flowing down to the Zambezi, with a strong but silent current in the middle of a marsh. The air is full of the cricket's call and the quiet sounds of night. Now and then a dove wakes to the brilliant moonlight, and sleeps again. Sometimes an owl cries, but no leopards are abroad, and it would be hard to imagine a scene of greater peace and of more profound solitude. And yet along this path there is no solitude, for the dead are here, neither is there any peace but a cry."

We drove on up the coast. I stared at the ocean off to my left; it glittered with the false lure of a tropical paradise, fecund and corrupt. For a long while, I could neither think nor not think of what I had seen. But then I hid myself in the past, remembering what I could about the Kongo kings.

Kongo had been one of the greatest kingdoms of Central Africa, rivalling Great Zimbabwe. In its glorious centuries, which stretched from the European Middle Ages to the Renaissance, it covered more than 300,000 square kilometres (115,000 square miles), and took in much of today's Angola, coastal Zaire, Gabon and across the Great River to the Batéké of the Congo, and as far as the vassal state called Loango. To the south, it reached the River Kwanza; to the east, the Kwango. Four million people and more were ruled by the ManiKongos, as the rulers were called. The capital city, M'banza Congo, was built on a hill in the healthy highlands. Afonso, perhaps the greatest of the Kongo kings (and the second to take a Christian name), once signed a missive to the Portuguese royal house as follows: "I, Afonso, by the grace of God King of Kongo, of Loango, of Kakongo, and of Ngoyo, this side and the other side of the Zaire, lord of the Ambundu and of Angola, of Aquisima, of Musuru, of Matamba, of Mulilu, of Musuku, and of the Anzico, of the conquests of . . ." and so on and so on, the vassal statelets rolling off the pen, so many he could barely recite them.[1]

There have been many attempts to trace the beginnings of the kingdom, with some success, though the origins are shrouded in legend and heroic tales. Still, the eighth king, Nzinga a Nkuwu, can be accurately dated from Portuguese records—he received baptism sometime in May 1491. The Founding is therefore placed somewhere in the twelfth century.

It began, as so many of Africa's empires did, in conquest.

At the time the country was divided into a number of more or less independent communities, each ruled by its own chief. One of these was a religious leader called ManiKabunga.

The invaders came from the north of the territory of ManiKabunga and his fellow chiefs, on the far side of the Congo River, from a small kingdom variously called Bungu or Vungu, in the region of Benin. The story—familiar from the founding myths of other African peoples—was that the King of Bungu had so many sons that the youngest, Mutinu Mbene (Motinobene), realized that he was unlikely ever to succeed to the throne, and would perforce have to create his own kingdom. He was, of course, a strong and fearless warrior. At first he and a band of followers acted more like brigands; they set up "toll-stations" at the Congo River crossings and exacted tribute and booty. Then, in an episode of high symbolism, he murdered a pregnant aunt, and was proclaimed *mutinu*, chief. Georges Balandier, the French ethnographer, explains the event this way: "By killing his kin, Mbene acquires the state of solitude necessary for the domination of men and the consecration of power. He is comparable to the heroes of Greek legend who seek the royal succession only after they have ceased to respect the prevailing laws. This defiance of the fundamental laws of any society is the mark of an exceptional being. Sacred violence remains the privilege of a sovereign with two faces: one brutal and tyrannical, the other justice-loving and conciliatory."[2]

Mbene crossed the Zaire and conquered the chiefs who ruled to the south of it, in what became part of his province of Mpenda. Within a few years he dominated a large part of the future Kongo kingdom, and divided it among his captains, instructing them to marry the daughters of local chiefs. He himself married the daughter of ManiKabunga and founded the dynasty of the Kongo kings. Of the indigenous chiefs the only one never to be conquered was Mbata; instead, Mutinu Mbene made an alliance with him. In future, all the Kongo kings should marry a daughter of the ManiMbata.

The first capital of the kingdom was at Mpemba Kazi. When Mbene moved his capital farther south to M'banza Congo, he left a woman to rule at the old capital; she was given the title Mother of the King of Kongo.

....

In 1483 the Portuguese navigator Diogo Cão, still diligently following the Portuguese obsession with a passage linking the Atlantic and the Indian oceans, came upon the Congo estuary. He soon learned that the country was governed by the ManiKongo, a great king several days' march east. He stayed with his ship, and sent ambassadors to the king. The embassy was well received, but greetings cannot be hurried, and they remained there several weeks. Cão, believing them to be forcibly detained and wanting to return to Portugal, picked up a few hostages on the shore and set sail for home.

A year later the hostages returned to the Kongo. Having been feted and celebrated in Lisbon, they were full of praise for Christianity and things European. Their stories, and the fact that the newcomers had been borne to them out of the sea—the domain of the sacred—"in ships with wings, which shone in the sun like knives," persuaded the ManiKongo of the time, Nzinga a Nkuwu, that the Portuguese *grisgris* was greater than his own. He immediately ordered that gifts of fine-woven and delicately dyed raffia-cloth and carved ivory should be sent to the king of Portugal. He also made haste to be baptized (becoming John I), and, craftily, demanded the presence of Portuguese artisans to instruct the Kongolese, and for his sons to be sent to Portugal to learn to read and write and to become Christians.

Eight years after First Contact a commercial armada set out for the Kongo—missionaries, priests, armed soldiers, traders, masons, and carpenters, and a few women, purpose unspecified. Three vessels, loaded for bear—building materials, sacerdotal objects, lavish gifts. Despite an ominous outbreak of plague on board (which killed the ManiKongo's returning ambassador, among others), the flotilla landed at Mpinda, the port of the province of Soyo, in March 1491. "The ManiSoyo called his people together. Three thousand warriors, armed with bows and arrows, had gathered at the call of the drums. Another group had been formed by the musicians who carried drums, ivory trumpets, and instruments resembling violas. They were naked to the waist and were painted with white and various coloured paints, a symbol of great joy. On their heads they wore head-dresses made of the feathers of parrots and other birds. The chief wore on his head a kind of night-cap decorated with skilful embroidery representing a snake."[3]

The ManiKongo, John I, hurriedly built a church. He had an urgent need: there was revolt in the kingdom and he wanted the foreigners to help him prevail. He therefore set off against the two rebellious provinces "under the sign of Christ"—a banner with the Cross embroidered on it. This no doubt helped, but the firearms almost certainly helped more. The rebellion was crushed.

But this new-found amity—during which the king, at the missionaries' urging, issued an edict that his people "cease to honour fetishes or to believe in amulets, now that we have seen the Cross of the Son of God ...""—didn't last. The King had already defected from Christianity by 1492. Politics, in the end, superseded religion. There had been rumblings all over the empire from traditionalists that the ancestors had been dishonoured and that calamities would surely follow. But it was probably missionary opposition to polygamy that tipped the matter: here the conflict between Church and royal policy was absolute. As Georges Balandier explains, "[the conflict] happened not so much because the king thereby lost one of his privileges and instruments of prestige—for in fact his wives refused to stop serving him—but because he thereby destroyed the alliances resulting from his numerous marriages. The precarious balance of the Kingdom depended on relationships that transformed formidable powers into in-laws. A prime requirement of politics was a skilful matrimonial policy."[4]

John's death in 1506 precipitated a bloody succession struggle eventually won by Afonso, a provincial captain allied with the Portuguese. His victory was naturally attributed in mission accounts to divine intervention, though the truth was more mundane: Afonso was a pretender to the throne who took it by violence, executed or banished his rivals, and put his own mother to death for refusing to renounce "pagan customs." Shortly thereafter the Pope himself was in contact with the ManiKongo, calling him "our most beloved son." In 1518 the Pope named Afonso's son Henry the first bishop of black Africa. Henry had been educated in Lisbon with the sons of other African nobles.[5]

Afonso was wilier than his predecessor; he managed to graft Christian customs and ceremony onto traditional ones without entirely alienating either side—a neat trick. (Subsequent rulers did the same, with mixed results, for Angolan history is filled with heresies, the most famous being Kimba Vita, Dona Beatrice, sometimes referred to as the Congolese Joan of Arc, who late in the seventeenth century helped restore the king to his throne, and was rewarded by being turned over to the Portuguese and burned as a heretic.)

Afonso became disillusioned in his turn. He wasn't looking for advice on how to run his country, thank you—he considered his own judicial system more humane than that of the Europeans, as indeed it was. He wanted teachers for the schools he was setting up, schools even for girls. He wanted craftsmen to pass on their technical knowledge. He wanted his own ship so that he could trade on his own account. All of which was contrary to Portuguese policy. All they wanted was to break the encirclement of western Europe by Islam by doing an end-run to Asia. They wanted trade. There was trade to be had in the Kongo itself, to be sure—Duarte Lopez, ambassador from the Vatican, wrote home that it was "necessary to describe the wonderful art of this and nearby countries, of weaving in different kinds of cloths such as velvets with and without pile, brocades, satins, sendals, damasks and similar cloths ... [woven] with finesse and delicacy."[6] The Kongo, though, wasn't enough to satisfy their appetites. They knew there were trade routes across Africa. A missionary,

Father Gouveia, held captive at the court of the Ngola Ndambi in the Kingdom of Ndongo, to the south of the Kongo king's borders, writing to his king in 1563 said that the "Dambia Songe," who lived in a large kingdom seventeen days' journey to the east of Ndongo, came to buy salt and copper in the Kasaba market and talked of the eastern seaboard as though familiar with it. Later, Joao Dos Santos, writing in 1609, said, "I have seen in Sofala a Commoditie bought by a Portugall in Manica ... which had come from Portugall by the way of Angola."[7]

As early as 1512 the Portuguese Crown made it clear it expected payment for its services to the Kongo. A *regimento*, sent to the king of the Kongo in that year, stated that the goal of the Portuguese is not "material gain" but only the propagation of the faith. Still, why miss a bet? It went on to recommend that the ships returning to Europe be "as heavily laden as possible with slaves as well as with copper and ivory" in order to repay the necessarily high expenses incurred in the said propagation.[8]

At Afonso's insistence, the Portuguese did set up a scheme for technical aid and education, but from the beginning slave traders followed the priests and teachers.

Portugal was a relatively small and underpopulated European country. However, its American colonies were huge, and hungry for manpower. So was the colony of São Tomé, just off the coast, where cocoa had recently been planted. It soon became clear to the resident Portuguese that their best hope for wealth was to forget about the gold they had believed was so abundant in the interior and concentrate on slaving. The most that the Kongolese could do, and that not always successfully, was to prevent the enslavement of their own.

Soon, the demand for slaves outstripped anything known to traditional Kongo society.

And soon after that, the demand outstripped anything the country could bear. The flourishing empire that Afonso had inherited was being undermined by the draining away of the nation's people. The countryside was leaking men and women. Slave-trading routes opened to the interior. Caravans of slaves came down to the coast, transshipped by the Kongolese. By the 1530s, nearly half a million had been shipped from Mpinda to the Americas, most of them from outside the kingdom (caught in raids, or by trade with neighbouring kings) but not all.

Hundreds of thousands more poured out of the Angolan and Zairian interior. Many thousands never made it to the coast. They died on the way.

On the routes that became the paths of the dead.

....

The growing hostility in Kongo towards the Portuguese and their predations erupted into open warfare in 1622, 1665, and again in 1681. By the end of the eighteenth century, the once mighty Kongo had been reduced to a series of fragmented and virtually autonomous villages. Its power had dissipated, vanquished by superior technology and an undefeatable sense of righteous purpose. In 1795 only about a hundred people were living in M'banza Congo, in twenty-two huts scattered among the imposing but decaying ruins of the many Portuguese-built Christian churches.

Still, the ManiKongos were complicit in the slave trade. They profited from it. They helped set up trading routes to facilitate it. They helped raid their neighbours and poured them into the pipeline. They saw nothing wrong with it, except, at the end, its very scale. They were, after all, slaveholders themselves. There have been attempts to portray the native slavers as somehow more benign, and the practice somehow more "natural" because balanced, in an ecological sense. However, the revisionists never sought the opinion of the slaves themselves.

A few kilometres beyond N'zeto, a half-hour after I had seen the man with the terrible smile, the road turned inland. There we ran into yet another obstinate army roadblock. Theunissen had had enough. "Might have known," he said, "though it was worth a try. Take you to the airport if you like. Easy enough to beg a seat up there. Lots of flights. No reason for you to be there, but no reason not to be either. Should be okay."

We turned and went back to the city. We never saw the truck with the corpses again. Maybe they had tipped them into the sea, and they'll drift up, bleached and bloated, to the pristine beaches of Pointe Noire, where they'll be picked clean by gulls, and the children of diplomats will find them and use them for beach croquet.

M'banza Congo is only about 100 kilometres (60 miles) from the Congo River. It's not much of a town, now, but it's pleasantly situated on its hill in rolling savannah cultivated by peasant smallholdings. Unless you knew, there was no sign that this had once been the capital of a huge trading empire.

It had been different, in its glory days. The Dutch explorer Olfert Dapper "reconstructed" from memory a detailed drawing of the capital. This shows the city dramatically perched on the edge of a cliff overhanging the River Lunda. Boats are plying the river; the royal palace is a massive fortress; there are churches everywhere. From what I could see, Dapper's memory was playing him considerable tricks. Or perhaps the reality was simply too mundane.

True, the city is located on the highest elevation in the plateau country; ten days' walk from the port city of Pinda, where the early European visitors disembarked. Those ten days' walking were all uphill; the plateau on which the city was constructed was more than 50 metres (160 feet) high and about 7 kilometres (4 miles) long, sloping up from west to east. As I could plainly see, the Lunda was a good way off, and Dapper's dramatic cliff simply did not exist.

Nevertheless, the city's population once exceeded a hundred thousand, and it was surrounded by numerous small villages that drove the metropolitan population up closer to the quarter-million mark. Now, it has all crumbled. There are several small churches, but nothing that looks like the magnificent cathedral that once existed here. And nothing at all of the indigenous architecture. All the buildings in town are run down; many show evidence of shell fire and grenades.

There is, however, a Customs post, since this is the last place of consequence before the Zairian border town of Songololo. They wanted to see my passport, even though I wasn't headed anywhere near the border. And after they'd seen it, they called in the army.

The army guy was surly. "Why are you here?"

I thought fleetingly of giving the excuse given so often by travellers in Africa, "I'm here to look at birds." This is almost always a good excuse, because you are usually written off as an idiot, and idiots are harmless—exactly the feeling you want to engender in suspicious authorities. But I didn't have a bird book or binoculars. I figured it would be best to stick to the truth.

"I'm interested in the history of ancient times," I said. "And this was the capital of a big empire." Even to me, this sounded like a really lame reason. Come to a war zone to look at ruins that weren't there anymore?

"Why here, so close to the border?" he demanded.

It seemed pointless to explain that there wasn't a border here, then. Because there was. This was always frontier country. The Batéké had been pressing down from the northeast. Kongo certainly kept a garrison on the river. Now . . . that was collapsing Zaire over there . . .

"I don't know," I said eventually, truthfully.

"Are you a spy?" he asked.

I didn't like this word at all. I was suddenly glad not to have brought my Nikon or my birdwatcher's binoculars.

"No," I said, "I'm from Canada."

For some reason, he seemed to buy this argument. My adopted country's benign image has served me well in the past, but never as well as this.

"So you're a journalist?" he demanded.

"Me! Never!" I repeated my Canadian line, and he turned and left.

I was in something of a quandary. Was I free to go? Who to ask? I was alone in a room with an unlocked door. My taxi had disappeared. I added up the money I had left, wondered if it would be enough. I could see a squeeze coming.

I poked my head outside. There was a line-up of people waiting to have their documents stamped. Or not a line-up exactly. Lines in Africa, like the borders of old, are always fluid. There were two lepers in the crowd, in an advanced state of disrepair. No one paid me any mind. There were soldiers, with bayonets fixed. The bayonets looked rusty, stained.

I could still smell the stench of corpses.

In the end, they came for me in an army jeep and took me to the airport, where they put me on a military plane.

"What's happening?" I asked a crew member.

"You're leaving," an officer said. And then, without much sense of humour, he added, "You're way too much trouble to shoot, and we have nowhere to keep you." I guess he was being helpful.

....

As the Kongo's power dwindled, the Portuguese interlopers were already turning their attention to the other kingdoms of Central Africa, Ndongo to the south and Loango to the north. Ndongo was inhabited by the Mbundu people and ruled by a dynasty of kings called Ngolas. For some centuries the Kongo kings had claimed dominion over the Mbundu—"Master of the Ambundos" was one of the titles in the 1512 letter from the ManiKongo Afonso to the Portuguese king, but in reality the Mbundu paid no tribute and little real attention. The Dande River was the effective border between the two states.

The Mbundu came from the Luba heartland, between the Congo River and the Great Lakes. The best memory of Mbundu history is retained by the Pende, a vassal tribe that left Angola in the seventeenth century to avoid domination by the Portuguese. According to their version, recounted in David Birmingham's excellent book *Trade and Conflict in Angola*, the earliest ancestor of the Mbundu, Ngola Kilaji, lived in Tanji ni Milumbu, which they maintain was somewhere near the upper Zambezi. Ngola's people were hunters and warriors who used only wooden and stone weapons. One day Ngola decided to leave his home. He destroyed his camp and set out towards the sea in the west. Along the route he left groups of men who settled and founded villages. When he reached the Kwanza he followed its course down to the coast at Luanda. He settled on the plains of Luanda, where he met the people of Bembo Kalamba, a blacksmith, who had come to Luanda with his followers and their cattle. From Bembo, Ngola learned how to smelt and forge iron, make pots, and weave. Bembo Kalamba's wife, Ngombe dia Nganda, taught Ngola's people agriculture and cattle-rearing. The followers of Ngola married the daughters of Ngombe, who became mothers of the Mbundu clans. Together they lived comfortably and prosperously in the Luanda plains, until one day the Europeans arrived and drove Ngola away with guns.[9]

Whatever the truth, it seems clear that Ngola brought to the peaceful settlements of the coast the concept of kingship, and all that it entailed. The kingdom was well established before the first Europeans arrived, but for most of its history is inextricably linked with coastal trading. And thus with the slave trade.

The kingdom's capital was on the northern bank of the Kwanza. It was up this river that the Portuguese came.

Individual Portuguese had been trading along the Angola coast and possibly with Ndongo since at least 1504. We know this because it was then that Manuel I of Portugal, attempting to assert a little royal protectionism, tried to forbid it, and decreed heavy penalties for traders sailing beyond the River Congo. None of them paid any attention.

In 1520 a *regimento* of royal instructions was drawn up, ordering the traders Manuel Pacheco and Balthasar de Castro to visit "el Rey d'Amgola," convert him to Christianity, and prepare a full report on his country. The *regimento* was in response to a request for Christian missionaries sent by the Ngola via Kongo. The Ngola presumably wanted to gain prestige by having European advisers resident at his court and may have hoped to open trade links with Europe, if possible, thereby putting a stop to the slave raids from across his northern border.

The *regimento* was unambiguous. No hope of trade was to be held out to the Ngola unless he accepted the Christian faith. Once the royal court had been converted, the process of "redemptions" could begin. This slippery word was the current euphemism for enslavement. Heathens would be given the opportunity to lead a Christian life as slaves in a country far removed from the temptations of their old environment. Although slaves, they would have gained the priceless privilege of saving their souls from condemnation.[10]

The Pende folk memory recalls their arrival:

"The Ngola and his people had been living for a long time on the plains behind Luanda, where they raised cattle and crops and bananas. One day the Tukusunia Tungunga (white men) arrived ... They fought hard battles with the Ngola and spat fire at him. They conquered his saltpans, and the Ngola fled inland to the Lukala River. Some of his bolder subjects remained by the sea and when the white men came they exchanged eggs and chickens for cloth and beads. The white men came yet again. They brought maize and cassava, knives and hoes, groundnuts and tobacco. From that time until our day the whites brought us nothing more but wars and miseries."[11]

A first attempt by the Europeans to establish an embassy with the Mbundu foundered on mutual suspicion and misunderstanding. The initiative for a second attempt in 1557 came from the Ngola himself, Ngola Inene. In that year an embassy he had dispatched to Lisbon finally arrived (nine years after it set off, having been held up by hostile traders in São Tomé). Queen Catherine responded by organizing a Jesuit religious mission with a lay leader, Paulo Dias, who would act as her ambassador.

By the time they got to Africa, Ngola Inene had died, and the much fiercer and more suspicious Ngola Ndambi was in charge.

Dias's party of seven sailed about 150 kilometres (90 miles) up the Kwanza River in a small boat. The barren coastal country gave way to more populous regions with rich valleys and lush vegetation. Numerous palm trees produced wine, oil, and fruits, as well as building materials for houses. At the limit of navigation, the party was welcomed by one of the Ngola's tributary chiefs. They marched for several days, passing through twenty villages before reaching the royal city. When they arrived they were received by an official called ManiDongo and accommodated in substantial straw huts. The city was large and well built; the Jesuits considered it not much smaller than their own city of Evora, in Portugal.

After waiting a few days, as was customary, the Ngola sent word that he would like to speak to the envoys. When Paulo Dias and his Jesuit companions were ushered into the central square, the Ngola was seated among his courtiers, drinking palm wine out of a horn, which he filled from a large calabash at his side.[12] Everything seemed cordial, but the Ngola had already received a friendly warning from the king of the Kongo that the Portuguese, despite their protestations of peace and offers of baptism, were really only interested in gold or silver and slaves. The Ngola obviously found this persuasive, for he took the mission hostage. Dias was eventually sent back to Portugal in 1565, but his spiritual adviser, Father Gouveia, was kept in Angola until he died, in 1575.

The good Father had an excellent reason to be annoyed with the Ngola, but still, his letter home in 1563 was wonderfully revealing of European colonialist attitudes. He argued that the only way to convert a heathen people to Christianity was by subjecting them to colonial rule. The example of Kongo had shown how weak and superficial Christianity became in a country which was not politically dominated by a Christian power. Furthermore, the refusal of the king of Ndongo to allow preaching in his lands was ample justification for the Portuguese to declare war and take away his kingdom. He felt the Ngola should be punished at once for accepting presents from the Jesuit mission and then refusing to listen to the word of God. His pique growing as he wrote, Gouveia referred to the "insolence" of the Mbundu in their treatment of white men—they had lacked respect for the ambassador of the king of Portugal, whom they had robbed even of his personal clothing; they had accused him of spying and inferred that the Jesuits were a mere cover for his activities.

This is not to say that Ndambi himself was a sweetheart. The Pende, Mbundu themselves, remember Ndambi as a terrible chief who repressed revolts without mercy. Their tradition represents this cruelty in a legendary form. When Ndambi wanted to make a surprise raid on a village, he first raised himself up into the air on two spears planted on the chests of two slaves. When the spears pierced their hearts, Ngola Ndambi disappeared on his raid.[13]

In 1575 the Portuguese, giving up on the notion of embassies, established a fort at Luanda, from which they made vain attempts to find mines of salt and rumoured but non-existent silver; once again slaves proved the most lucrative export. The slave trade grew, helped, no doubt by the Mbundu's expansionary wars, which provided a rich source of saleable manpower.[14]

The Portuguese attempted several times to overthrow the Ngolas, with mixed results. In the early part of the seventeenth century they drove the incumbent, Mbandi, away from his capital. The Ngola took refuge on an island.

He left his sister, Njinga Oande, in charge. She became Queen Nzinga, and generalissimo of the armies—the men listened to her because of her force of will and obvious intelligence. Until her death in 1663, she remained the most important personality in Angola.

The Portuguese first took notice of her when a new governor arrived at Luanda's fort in 1621, full of protestations of friendship. He attempted to persuade Mbandi to leave his island and make peace. The Ngola, suspicious, sent his sister as his ambassador.

Nzinga walked into the chamber at the fort where the governor waited, reclining in a large, throne-like armchair. His advisers and courtiers stood around him. There was no other chair in the room. The queen was not at all put out. She said nothing, but merely clicked her fingers, and one of her maiden attendants obediently dropped to all fours, forming a comfortable human chair on which the queen could repose. Only after that could business begin.[15]

The governor's reaction was not recorded, but can be guessed from the results of the meeting: Nzinga persuaded him not only to stop the Portuguese predations but to recognize Mbandi as an allied king of equal status to other independent monarchs, and not as a subject of the Portuguese Crown. Afterwards, with her usual political finesse, she allowed herself to be baptized, under the name of Dona Ana de Souza, and graciously permitted the governor to become her godfather.

The smitten governor, alas, was recalled in 1623, after a quarrel with the Jesuits, before carrying out his promises. Nzinga demanded satisfaction from his successor, without result. A year later, she went to war.

The Portuguese poured money, men, and arms into Luanda in a vain effort to suppress her. After an inconclusive battle in 1626, Nzinga made a strategic withdrawal to the interior, around the present Malanje. There, she conquered the somnolent state of Matamba, and developed it into an independent trading centre, with networks reaching north to the Kongo, west to Luanda, and eastward to the Lunda of Katanga. At the same time as Nzinga's migration, the Imbangala (aka the ferocious Jaga) established their new state of Kasanje to her west, in the Kwango Valley. Like the earlier Jaga raiders who had disrupted the Kongo kingdom in 1569, the Imbangala originated in the Luba-Lunda kingdoms of Katanga, somewhere around the late fifteenth century. By the end of the seventeenth century, Kasanje had become the leading slave-trading kingdom in the area and the chief entrepôt between the coast and the Lunda in the east.[16]

Nzinga was not at all disturbed by the Jaga's ferocity or ritual cannibalism. She made common cause with them, renouncing her Christianity to placate them and adopting, as a matter of statecraft, if not of preference, a few of their cannibal habits. In the end they, too, followed her, and for the next thirty years Nzinga outguessed, outgeneralled, and outfought the increasingly frustrated Portuguese. She imposed Jaga discipline on her own troops, and by building up a hardened corps of followers with a strong religious element in their political association, she was able to effortlessly conquer new territories.

The Portuguese, meanwhile, were lamenting the loss of trade Nzinga's warfare was causing them. In 1633 Father Goncalo de Souza reported to Lisbon that very little business was being conducted and the slave fairs had dried up. The factors were now having to travel several months' journey to buy slaves, costly both in time and in the numbers who died on the road. It also meant that the factors, often half-castes, travelled beyond the limits where their Portuguese masters could effectively control them. Some set up rival businesses, cutting into the profits of the coastal traders. The city of Luanda itself began to decline.

In 1639 a new Portuguese governor opened negotiations with Nzinga on the question of returning runaway slaves to their masters. The queen sent him an emissary carrying presents for himself, the chief justice, and the bishop, as well as a few runaways who were so old that no one knew who their masters had been. Her motive was predictably devious: her delegation was charged with obtaining first-hand intelligence on Portuguese troop movements.

In 1641 the Dutch, who had been nipping at the Portuguese heels, took Luanda and drove the Portuguese out. Like the ManiKongo, Nzinga welcomed the Dutch conquests, but by 1648 the Portuguese had reconquered Luanda, and for the next dozen years they systematically laid waste to the countryside, determined to bring the recalcitrant queen to what they fondly considered justice. But it was only after her death that they finally succeeded in taming the Mbundu. In 1671 Nzinga's successor was finally conquered and his kingdom completely dismantled.

Nothing was left. In the countryside, there was famine and mass starvation. Still, the fighting went on. And on. And on. For the next hundred years caravans of sullen slaves were captured and taken down to the coast, to be shipped away to the brave promise of the New World. The Portuguese stayed for centuries, finally departing a mere thirty years ago. Even then, the fighting went on.

Now it has stopped. At least that's the diplomatic assumption.

And the countryside is groaning with the dead and wounded.

....

The military flight from M'banza Congo back to the capital was an ancient DC-3. There were no seats, and I sat on the floor on a pile of old uniforms. My "captors" dozed on an old foam mattress at the rear of the aircraft, their guns carelessly slung from a hook, banging against the bulkhead whenever the plane lurched. To my right there was, incongruously, what looked like a picture window instead of the normal porthole. On the other side, the door was simply left open. I tried not to think of it. After all, pushing me out would be a much simpler solution than taking me to the airport. Less bother all round.

We flew at no more than 90 to 120 metres (300 to 400 feet). From the air, the countryside looked lush, prosperous, peaceful; the thatched villages sparse but orderly. No one was to be seen. There were numerous trails through the bush, wandering game trails converted by humans into paths. I remembered Nevinson's description of such a path, and finding ancient spikes driven into the oldest trees, where the slaves had been left to die. A grim passage from a Belgian missionary seeped into my mind. "Three thousand natives had been captured by this expedition, but only two thousand reached their destination. The rest had been murdered by their captors, who would not leave any laggards behind them, for fear lest they should secure their liberty. At each halting-place, ten, twenty, and sometimes fifty, of the sick were massacred. At one stage on the march three hundred women and children who could not proceed any farther were thrown into the river."[17]

David Livingstone, for his turn, had been travelling the headwaters of the Zambezi in 1853, still looking vainly for the source of the Nile. He noted the skittishness of the people, so unlike the hospitality of the eastern tribes. Most of the locals had never seen a European, but their lives had nevertheless been fatally disturbed by the half-caste slave traders coming in from Angola. There were deserted houses and frightened faces everywhere he turned.

We passed over a few small hills, and a larger village with a concrete-block building behind it, its windows barred. There was a banana grove in the yard, for once neatly planted in rows. Prisoners were cultivating a field off to the right as we swept overhead.

Abruptly we were going down. The wind whistling through the open door turned to a shrill whine. The plane lurched and dropped 15 metres (50 feet), 30 (100 feet). I caught a glimpse of the Atlantic glittering off to the right. We kept falling.

"Are we landing or crashing?" I said to no one in particular, hanging on to a stanchion, trying not to panic. The sleepers continued sleeping, and the pilots paid no attention. I peered out my picture window; the slums of Luanda were coming into view, and then the pastels of the centre core.

We landed with a jar, but safely, and taxied over to the terminal. The sleepers awoke and prodded me out. No one brought any steps. We had to jump to the ground.

I was hustled into the departures hall and marched with my escort to the Air Afrique desk. Air Afrique personnel are helpful and polite even at the worst of times, but now they outdid themselves in speed and efficiency. Yes, Monsieur's ticket can be arranged. Yes, Monsieur can pay in American dollars, no problem. No, there are no more flights tonight. Yes, there is a flight to Kinshasa at seven tomorrow morning. Yes, yes, he can get a visa on arrival. Yes, yes, of course we will take him.

I offered this effusive clerk some money, but she refused. That was new.

We went through security without any problems—the soldiers had so many weapons that the X-ray device, had they used it, wouldn't have blinked at my meagre stock of metal. I was pushed into a holding cell, where I spent an uneasy, and mosquito net–less, night.

....

In the modern period Portugal ran its African territories—Angola and Mozambique— not as colonies or "dependencies," but as provinces of Portugal itself. The Salazar dictatorship grandly called Portugal an "Afro-European power." As at home, the press in these overseas departments was censored, the secret police were omnipresent, and political parties were ruthlessly suppressed. Even so, things were worse in the colonies: the metropolitan provinces were not subjected to forced labour, which was used throughout Angola and Mozambique.

"Forced labour" is already a euphemism, but the Portuguese doubled the euphemism by calling it "directed labour" and maintaining that "every man should work, as an essential part of the civilizing process." How civilizing the process was could be judged from the fact that at independence there were sixty-eight black high-school students in Angola.

Gangs of forced labour were also taken to work the cocoa plantations on São Tomé and Príncipe, from which few ever returned.

The recalcitrant were beaten on the hands with a paddle until the bones were crushed. There was no capital punishment, but serious criminals had iron shackles welded to their ankles and were then turned loose in the deep bush, there to fend for themselves against nature's predators.

All was justified with the notion that the "fully civilized" could be "fully assimilated," and then become, legally and officially and socially, European. Why, Africans could get to sit at European tables! It never seemed to occur to anyone that that wasn't necessarily every African's goal.

As in Mozambique, when independence came, it was with stunning rapidity and a complete lack of preparation. The Portuguese colonizers looted the country of everything portable, and departed, leaving a political vacuum that was filled by warring factions, which soon became surrogates for great power rivalry. Within a few years Angola had been invaded by Zairian troops (in support of FNLA, an independence movement based in the north), South African regulars (in support of UNITA, a breakaway group of mostly southerners angry at northern dominance), and various gangs of mercenaries in support of whoever would pay them. Most of the remaining white population fled.

The invasions failed, and the MPLA, backed by Cuban troops acting mostly as Russian surrogates, seized control in most of the country by 1976. Jonas Savimbi's UNITA continued its rampages in the south, backed by substantial covert and overt U.S. aid, estimated at better than $50 million a year, as well as South African regulars, angry at what they perceived to be MPLA's continuing support for SWAPO guerrillas in Namibia.[18]

In 1988, as South Africa lost heart for the struggle and began seeking peace in Namibia, the U.S., Angolan, and Cuban governments worked out a settlement— sort of. Finally, in 1991 a cease-fire agreement was signed with Savimbi in Lisbon. Part of the deal was free elections and the integration of the armed factions into a national army. The elections were duly held, and duly disputed, and Savimbi joined the government, unjoined it, joined again, then split, sort of. The integration of the armed forces was still a hot issue in 1996. That Dos Santos and Savimbi were meeting in Gabon to discuss this very issue was one reason the roadblocks were so omnipresent—and one reason why I was so summarily ejected.

Four hundred years of warfare cannot so easily be put aside.

In the morning, two soldiers came for me and took me to the boarding lounge. They sat with me until loading started. I was seated first, at the back of the plane. Everyone treated me with respect. They weren't sure who I was. I might be important.

Thus, I was given the bum's rush out of Angola. The air in the plane smelled stale, but it was better than it had smelled on the ground.

The plane lifted into a thunderstorm, and we bumped and tumbled for the hour-long flight to the Zairian capital. There, I bought a visa from a crooked Immigration official, took a taxi across town to the ferry terminal, and caught the next boat for the Republic of the Congo. An hour later I was in my air-conditioned hotel room in the M'Bamou Palace, staring blindly out the window over Stanley Pool at Kinshasa beyond.

I saw nothing of the river. I saw only the truck of gaily clad corpses, and that terrible smile that was burned into the back of my brain.

THE CONGO RIVER

I had wanted—of course!—to travel down the Congo River. Not just because it was there, or because it has lodged in the Western consciousness as a mythic place, symbol of the unknown, of the primitive, or because it was one of the great rivers on the planet, or because I had heard that barge travel down the river put one in touch with an Africa that had vanished from the cities. All good reasons. But the Congo spoke to a more ancient history.

I'd already spent a morning paddling about in a pirogue, the dugout canoe of Africa, on the great Pool that swirls between Brazzaville and Kinshasa, a place of calm before the Congo plunges down its cataracts in the final 200 kilometres (125 miles) to the sea. As I rocked in the wake of a passing ferry, I stared upriver, towards the heartland, picturing the Bantu as they spread along the river in the Elder Days. I imagined I could hear the distant thunder of the Kanem-Bornu conquests, far to the northeast a millennium and more ago; and the Luba expansions to the east seemed to ring as faint as their rulers' ceremonial double bells through the mists of time. To the north were the Vili kings, of Loango. To the south lay Kongo.

The present mimics the past. The Bakongo are in Brazzaville and along the route to Pointe Noire. The Batéké still live in the plateau area north of the city; they reigned there until their last ruler, King Ilu, ceded his sovereignty to the Frenchman de Brazza in 1880, and even after that they continued their chieftaincy until 1975, when the newly Marxist government of the independent Peoples' Republic of the Congo (now defunct) abolished it altogether.

I had preplanned a river trip, but the arrangements had been a muddle. I had been supposed to join the boat at a place called Mossaka, where the Likouala River flows into the Congo, but, well … maybe "muddle" is understating the case. First, it was the dry season and few boats were running. Then, dry season or no, I had been told at NDjamena, Chad (where through a series of accidents I had briefly found myself), that a flash-flood had washed away Mossaka's airport, and my flight had been cancelled.

The reality turned out to be quite different—Mossaka didn't have an airport, so there had been nothing to wash away, and the flight on which I had been booked had never existed. My ticket had been an elaborate scam. Eventually, I hitched a ride on an "informal" Linea Congo flight via Bangui in the Central African Republic, to Lukolela in the Congo, which did indeed have an airport. To get from Lukolela to Mossaka I had to hire a pirogue.

Mossaka is near the confluence of the Likouala, the Sangha, and the Congo rivers, just after the Congo veers southwards, making a great curve on its run to the coast. Above Mossaka it ceases to be an international border, becoming instead a purely Zairian stream.

The people at Mossaka thought the notion of a flash-flood in the dry season enormously funny, and so was the idea of a Mossaka airport. Everyone was keen to show me the high-water marks set by the catastrophic floods of '82, though.

On its way to Mossaka from Bangui, my barge had come down through the great forests north of Ouesso, among the least tenanted, least explored forests in Africa, where the Central African Republic, Cameroon, and the Congo come together.

There is hardly anyone there except bands of hunting pygmies and fishermen, poling along the lemony rivers, the Ubangi, Sangha, and others, that are the veins of the Congo basin—the only paths through the largest tropical forest on earth outside the Amazon.

This is the jungle of legend, home to the great apes, lowland gorillas, families of chimps, a huge variety of monkeys, lemurs. And other exotica—elephant and buffalo, wild pig, bongo, the "potto," and galago. Bulbuls, herons, cormorants, anhingas, toucans, souimingas. And leopards, the mysterious okapi, pythons thick as thighs, cobras, mambas, vipers, and—worse—the water naja, very venomous. In the steamy heat of a midmorning, my pirogue rounded a bend of the Congo, and a flock of scarlet parrots beat overhead. A fisher plunged into the water, a black bundle of feathers, muscle, talons, and fury. There was nothing to be seen but jungle down to the river's edge; at intervals, massive trees, limbas, okoumes, sapellis, 40 to 60 metres (130 to 200 feet) high, pierced the sky, pushing triumphantly through the surrounding canopy. There were mysterious creeks and inlets, islands of weed drifting slowly by, the eddy of the muddy Congo as it lapped against the boat. From a small village clinging to the water's edge came the beating of a river drum, a subliminal thumping that got under the skin, calling, calling, calling. It was somewhere here that the celebrated German musicologist Dr. von Hornbostel first used scientific notation to delineate the rhythms of the African drums. No one here needed the pedantry. Drums spoke, men listened. Only Outsiders needed to know why, or how.

Away from the river and its tributaries are swamps where only the pygmies go. It's the pygmies who tell stories of the monsters of Lake Télé, many days' march west of Epéna. They call the monster Mokélémbembé, which translates as "the animal who made the rivers flow." This little lake, perfectly round and almost impossible to get to without pygmy help, is about 5 kilometres (3 miles) in diameter. The beast is usually described as a reptile, between 5 and 8 metres (16 to 26 feet) long, brown in colour, with a long neck and a tiny head. It was seen, but not photographed, by an expedition led by Marcellin Agnagna, a biologist with the Congolese Ministry of Water and Forests.

"Ascending the river is like travelling towards the early beginnings of the world," Conrad wrote, "when vegetation covered the earth and the great trees were king. A road of empty water, grand silence, impenetrable forest. The air is hot, humid, heavy, languid..." Great logs float past, with their colonies of parasites. Floating everywhere are islands of hyacinths. Millions and millions of clumps of green leaves, pink flowers, drifting down to the rapids, where they are chopped up and taken to the sea. They were introduced here by a Belgian missionary, who thought naïvely that they would help purify the water in the stream where he was based. Instead, they are choking the Congo basin with flowers. These are no longer European hyacinths. They have become tropical in their sheer size and their furious fecundity.

Few crocodiles live here anymore, just enough to provide a hungry population with baby crocodiles to spit-roast. The rest have been hunted and sent to the European shoemakers. This is not to blame the Europeans, for they would have been killed anyway—crocodiles tend to make for wary bathing, and if you're dependent on the river for your bath water, you too would sweep it of crocodiles from time to time. As well, crocodiles are often thought to have malignant powers, and the short-mouthed crocodile in particular is thought to be the familiar of sorcerers. These drag their victims under water like the others, but to torture them, not eat them. It is said to be common that a fisherman disappears only to reappear several months later, living but not living, because the crocodile kept his soul. The hippos, too, are few. Only on the upper Ubangi can you see them, deceptively still on the sandbanks of the river. The hippos have learned to occupy spaces man does not.

Just outside Mossaka we drifted past one of the "regular" Zairian Kisangani-to-Kinshasa steamers, stuck on a sandbar. It was said to be two weeks late,

At Mossaka, I heard the legend of Maïma: This was a baby, found alive by a young woman in a fish trap at Ebouélé, and adopted by her. He had the power to read the future, and in fact predicted the arrival of white people. His powers aroused jealousies, and the men of the village decided to put him to death. Don't cry, he told his mother, for I will return. If you love me, do not cry. The first day she succeeded, and on the second. On the third day, however, she could bear it no longer and a single tear ran down her cheek. Thus she condemned her beloved child to permanent death. Since that time nothing has ever grown in the spot where he was buried. The locals now invoke his name as a good-luck charm.

which was about normal, particularly seeing it wasn't supposed to be running at all at this time of year. The steamer's crew was taking it easy on the sand, waiting for inspiration; the boat's passengers were swimming, washing, drinking beer, cooking meals, living their lives. No one seemed to be in any hurry.

Since it is entirely dependent on water traffic, Mossaka, inevitably, calls itself the Little Venice of the Congo. It's an exotic town of wood and thatch houses, stopping-place for Congolese steamers going to Bangui, but also for small boats—really not more than motorized pirogues—going up the Likouala River and the poetically named Likouala-avec-Herbes River, which peels off to the north.

The name Mossaka, it turned out, was a mistake. A European traveller passing through last century asked a local fisherman, "Where are we?" The local thought he was asking, "What are you doing?" and replied, "Mossaka," meaning, "I'm making palm oil." These days Mossaka's civic boast is that it's the "sweet-water fishing capital of the Congo."

In the high fishing season about seven thousand of Mossaka's nine thousand inhabitants head off to their fishing camps, along with their families, their fishing gear, and their cooking implements. These camps can be 100 kilometres (60 miles) away; the population virtually disappears into the bush.

I spent a lazy morning with my pirogueier, who seemed in no hurry to return back upriver, and the town's Patron, as the chief called himself. The Patron smoked cigarettes I bought for him, at his insistence—he called it tribute. Most of his villagers seemed to owe him tribute in one form or another. All morning, as commerce proceeded between the boat and the shore, a little pile of gifts was deposited at his feet, until, by the end of the morning, the little pile was substantial, and two of his wives came to take it away.

I had noticed something curious about Mossaka. There were hardly any children. I asked the Patron about this.

"They're all at school," he said.

"Where's the school?"

He waved his hand downriver, in the direction of Brazzaville, four days' journey away. "Down there," he said.

"Is schooling that important?" I asked.

"When the roads come, we want to be ready," he said.

"Ready for what?" I asked, not understanding.

"For the world," he said.

I hoped he wasn't in any hurry; it might take a while for the roads to come to Mossaka. The Congo Republic has thrown off the deadening hand of Marxism, but as everywhere else the prosperity promised by privatization has proved an illusion. There was so much work to be done! I knew that the main road from the Congo into Cameroon, once the spine of commerce for the northern Sangha region, had been effectively closed for twenty years: not by armed bandits, but by neglect and lack of money—it finally got so bad, even for four-wheel-drive vehicles, that it was abandoned altogether and reclaimed by the jungle, leaving the population of the region isolated. The education and social system simply decayed. Now, after a provincial decision to revive the cocoa industry in the north, the bulldozers are back. Or rather, the bulldozer is back, because resources are limited. Nevertheless, the cocoa will have to be taken to Ouesso by truck and floated down the river to Brazzaville. It can't be taken north, because, while there is a road into Cameroon from Sembe in the Congo, you can't go anywhere once you get there, because there are no roads in that part of Cameroon.

None of this seemed to discourage the Patron of Mossaka. He seemed confident his people could outfish and outtrade anyone, given the chance. When I left, he was talking about trading directly with Europe. He had heard they were hungry for fish in Europe.

....

In theory I had arranged a cabin on my Congo River barge, but when I clambered on board I didn't see any. There was a kind of shed for'ard, but nothing that looked like accommodation. The crewman who took my passage money (about $10 for three days' voyage) wasn't much interested either—when I asked him where I was to sleep, he gestured vaguely at the deck, where dozens of bodies were already recumbent in the torpor of the afternoon heat. I looked around; there was hardly any room between the people and their bundles and the cages of squalling and snarling beasts. But a few of the passengers good-naturedly took pity on me and made room in a corner next to a bulkhead, where I was protected from the sun and from being trampled. I decided to make the best of it. I would go in search of the captain when I could. Meanwhile, I would join my confrères in a sensible siesta. Some of the few still awake watched in bemusement as I unrolled my high-tech air mattress and slathered on mosquito repellent (there wouldn't be room for my mosquito net tonight). I lay down, my head on a rolled-up sleeping-bag. It was actually pretty comfortable.

That night I found I did, indeed, have a cabin assigned to me, an airless thing by the forward bulkhead that I was to share with a family of three. There was a small window, a porthole really, but we were downwind of the tugboat, and the cabin filled with diesel fumes when I opened it. With the porthole closed, the temperature was well over 40° Celsius (100° Fahrenheit), and stinking. I retreated to the deck, where I was greeted cheerfully by my erstwhile companions.

The night was not at all peaceful. In the early evening, and again at dawn, I was kept awake by the mournful screeching of the monkeys, imprisoned in bags by the butcher, and the squalling, scratching, yelling, grunting, and mewling of the other wildlife on board. For the rest, there was the cacophony of competing cassette players. Plus much yelling from the humans, almost all of it good-natured but very loud. Most of them preferred to stay awake during the relatively cooler evenings and sleep away the heat of the day—though even at midday it wasn't really oppressive; when the boat was moving, the breeze kept the temperature moderate.

This was a much smaller barge than those used regularly in high season, which were essentially floating villages. But it was big enough. I estimated it carried about three hundred people and was about the size of four large flatbed trucks lashed together. Even here, people found the room to carry on their lives, and their businesses—many of the passengers actually spent a good part of their lives on boats like these, taking commerce to far-flung villages. There was a band on board, "dancings," dormitories, markets, canteens, a hair-cutting salon, and a psychological counsellor. Babies are bathed in plastic tubs provided for the purpose; liboké is grilled on charcoal fires. You can buy kaolin, spices, matches, soap, smoked monkey, baguettes, and baby crocs (live). Everywhere you looked there were piles of mangoes, manioc, and bananas; palm wine; game; dried and smoked fish; sugar cane; kola nuts, yams, and cassava. There were piled bundles of carpets, rolled-up foam-rubber mattresses, and canvas sheets. Beer by the case was stacked everywhere, furniture, piles of clothing— the crew figures around five huge bundles per person is a normal baggage load. On the larger barges, which can carry a thousand people or more, real bazaars are held, where the villagers will buy unmarked vials of drugs, antibiotics, toothpaste (Colgate, made in Cameroon), bug killer, malaria pills, pens, razors, and much more.

Near the stern, animals were slaughtered and roasted over fires. Sometimes, the barge being so slow, villagers paddled out in pirogues filled with smoked fish, avocados, bananas, and small live animals of all kinds, exotic birds, monkeys, baby crocodiles. Even the pygmies occasionally emerged from the forest to trade game for their beloved tobacco.

Monkey is frequently found on Congolese menus, often sardonically called *le cousin*. They sometimes serve it to unsuspecting Europeans with the hands on the plate, which of course look unnervingly human and tend to put people off their feed.

Through the day and night, babies shriek and throw up, people yell and laugh, the beer flows freely—Primus from Zaire the favourite, but also Guinness, Beaufort, and Kronenbourg. My little corner of the deck was friendly, particularly after I was seen to have left them and returned. We became a little clique, and defended "our" territory against possible invaders and thieves. I was both a curiosity and a danger, because I attracted thieves and vendors—I lost count of the times I was asked to buy something because it was the last chance the vendor had of sending a crippled child to school, or getting an aged grandparent emergency medical help. My section of the boat would hoot and jeer as these pathetic stories rolled out. We ate grilled baby crocodile (crisp as Peking duck), boiled monkey, smoked fish, endless numbers of cane rats. We drank beer and fermented ginger juice, something like ginger beer but much more pungent. You could also buy mounds of boiled rice, and if you scraped off the top few centimetres, you'd get rid of most of the fly-borne muck.

Occasionally when we stopped at villages to pick up or discharge goods, I'd get off to wander around. Everyone in town had something to sell. The major item was, of course, food—mostly pineapples and coconuts and roots of various kinds. These were classic jungle villages, a few thatched huts clustered around a chief's compound, a few goats and pigs and chickens, small gardens carved by slash-and-burn from the jungle, a banana grove, some plantains and pawpaws, and a well-trodden track leading into the deep bush. They are as close to being self-sufficient as possible: they produce all their own food, ferment their drink, make their own houses from materials to hand.

The list of what they need to buy from others is small: machetes, tobacco, plastic containers for carrying water, or for laundry, or for bathing babies, and clothing. They are still capable of making their own clothes—the women still make raffia-cloth—but they prefer cheap Western hand-me-downs, especially T-shirts. So it is that I saw a young Téké woman in a T-shirt that proclaimed, in English, "Bomb Me Back to the Stoned Age," which must have been printed in Haight-Ashbury in the sixties.

I asked in one of the villages if there were others living farther inland, away from the river. "No," one of them said. "No one there. Only pygmies."

"Where do the young people find wives and husbands?" I asked.

He pointed to the river. "They come, they go," he said.

"Is there a chiefdom in these parts?" I asked.

He pointed to the chief's hut.

"Yes, but does he have a chief? Is there a bigger chief?"

"Once it was said there was a grand chief, long ago, before there was money."

I remembered that there were fewer than 600 kilometres (370 miles) of paved roads in the entire Republic of the Congo; that three-quarters of all Congolese live within 100 kilometres (60 miles) of the country's only railway line, which runs 500 kilometres (310 miles) from Brazzaville to Pointe Noire. Also, the slavers emptied this part of Africa. With the result, ironically, that the Congo is the most urbanized country in black Africa.

The higher reaches of the Congo, in Shaba where the river begins, is the heartland of the Luba people.

The diligent diggings of the archaeologists can't (yet) tell us when the Luba "began." Their precursors were flourishing around Lake Kisale and the upper Lualaba River in the fifth century of our era. The Luba themselves left the Lake Victoria region between the tenth and twelfth centuries. The assumption is that they simply pushed aside the earlier culture in Shaba. Being close to one of the richest sources of copper in Africa probably helped their development of new kingdoms—there is evidence for the prehistoric workings of local copper all over northern Zambia and the Lubumbashi region in southeast Zaire. Iron-working was also a well-established technique, and they had even discovered how to make steel. Trade goods from the Indian Ocean have been found, dating from the eleventh century.[19]

Perhaps it doesn't matter. The Baluba are now spread all over southeastern Zaire, in Kivu, Shaba, and Kasai Oriental provinces under a bewildering variety of names—the Shankaji and the Hemba, who are renowned wood-carvers, the Songye (whose art uses "great cubist masses with flowing systems of parallel incised and painted lines, which comes to life with dramatic effect when seen in the motion of the dance,"),[20] and many others.

The real story of their origins matters less than the heroic myths, which recount the struggles of the great kings Kongolo (Nkongolo) and Ilunga Mbili. The most popular version has it that the Luba triumph was begun by the four sons of the great king Sendwe Mwalaba.[21] The eldest son, Ilunga Mbili, became the progenitor of the senior royal house of the Luba. According to this version, the previous inhabitants were a copper-skinned race called the Baleya, or Bakalanga, related to the Songye. The population was not large, and the oral tales say that there were no hereditary chiefs, nor a reigning house. However, some time previous to the coming of Ilunga Mbili, there arose a man of exceptionally strong character called Nkongolo, who became, through sheer force of his personality, a ruler or dictator over all the area now occupied by the Luba people. Nkongolo was to become the maternal uncle of the great Ilunga Kalala, son of Mbili and father and architect of the kingdom of the Luba.

Another version says that the local people were the Bena Kalundwe, who built their capital on the Lubilash River. This country was infiltrated by the Songye, under the mighty warrior Kongolo. Kongolo set up his capital near Lake Boya. There he was joined by a hunter, Ilunga Mbili, and his following; but after a period of amity, there was a quarrel, and Ilunga returned whence he came. Shortly afterwards a son, Ilunga Kalala, was born to Kongolo's half-sister (Ilunga Mbili's wife). He grew to be a warrior of great prowess and helped Kongolo to extend his kingdom to the west. When Kongolo became jealous of his nephew and sought to kill him, Ilunga Kalala went to his father's homeland, where he recruited an army with which he defeated Kongolo, bringing the first Luba Empire to an end and establishing the second.

Kongolo's successors formed the Songye dynasty, of whom notable rulers were Kongolo Mukulu, Kongolo Miketo, and Kongolo Mwana. The empire expanded, particularly to the east, and formed new villages and subject states. Eventually, the capital of the empire was moved east to Muibele, beyond the Lomami River. At the height of its power, the Luba-Songye Empire probably spread from the Lubilash to the Lualaba, and perhaps even farther. In the middle of the nineteenth century, dependencies and offshoots stretched 1,500 kilometres (950 miles) from east to west.

When Arabs from Zanzibar, under the slaver Tippu Tip (whose private army numbered more than fifty thousand), conquered eastern Zaire 150 years ago, the towns they found matched in luxury the towns of the East Coast traders—even the common soldiers slept on silk and satin; the notables had European tableware and fine china. Leo Frobenius, the German explorer who came after Tippu Tip, found in the Luba heartland "substantial cities, with the principal streets laid out in geometrical precision and lined neatly with rows of palm trees."

The Songye and the Luba are entangled in the legends. The Luba later mutated into the Lunda, for no apparent reason than that, in the seventeenth century, certain people of Luba origin began to refer to themselves differently, as the BaLunda, under their independent king, the Mwato Yamvo. At some period, three other states—Kaniok, Kalundwe, and Kikonja—became established as Luba kingdoms.

Even here in the Bantu heartland the notion of "tribe" is far from static. Tribes are called "mushyobo," which means "kind," and are not considered as old as clans. The assumption is that tribes arose in comparatively recent times. Thus, while there are no legends about the origins of clans or clan names, there do exist accounts of the origins of tribes and tribal names, known in Luapula terminology as Owners of the Land.

In a story of the Luapula people, the origins were explained this way:[22] The people of Nkuba threw a doll belonging to Chitimukulu's people into the water, and Chitimukulu demanded a human being in recompense. Nkuba refused, and therefore had to leave. He sent two men to look for a piece of country with no people. They reached the Luapula River valley and found people who had no chiefs and who used ivory as hearth-stones. Their leader was Twite, who was an Owner of the Land, and they asked for his blessing in hunting. They killed elephants and took ivory to Twite in tribute. Twite said: "What is this you bring me? If you want to give me a present, give me meat; we do not eat ivory." The two men then collected all the ivory they had hunted, and set off. Later in their travels they found another Owner of the Land, who also refused ivory as tribute. They returned to Nkuba and told him they had found a good country to live in, for the people were Bwilile (a word derived from the verb *kwilila*, to eat on one's own. It implies that when meat was killed there was no chief to eat it and no one who knew the custom of giving tribute of ivory; in other words the people lacked the knowledge of what a chief was, his main attribute being the receiver of tribute. Bwilile were therefore ignorant people who knew no chiefs). Nkuba moved westward into their territory around the Luapula River with a great number of his brothers, sisters, and sisters' children. By means of intermarriage and some battles, he set himself up as chief over the whole of the lower part of the Luapula valley and around Lake Mweru. He sent out relatives to be chiefs over the various territories of the Bwilile, which enabled him to claim tribute from the people.

The ruler of the Luba-Kunda state, the Mulohwe, supposedly made a practice of marrying his sister or niece. Such a practice would have ensured that succession could be carried down both through the male and female line. When the Mulohwe died, he was buried in a dry river-bed, together with a number of wives and slaves. His spirit passed to a woman, who received many lands and honours and was appointed to rule over his capital. She was never allowed to see the new Mulohwe, who had to go and build a new capital elsewhere.

From Birmingham, Trade and Conflict in Angola: The Mbundu and Their Neighbours under the Influence of the Portuguese, 1483–1790

Nkuba's people, who took the name "Luapula," after the river, were now Owners of the Land.

The fluidity continued. Some of the Luba-Lunda expanded southwards and eastwards; this migration resulted in the foundation of the Kazembe tribe, made up of the new migrants and a group of more or less unrelated people whose only commonalty at that point was as refugees from wars between the Luba and the newly named Lunda. Migrants and refugees alike came under the protection of the warrior king, Kazembe, whose people included the descendants of the two previous "Owners of the Land." He set up his kingdom on the continental divide, just inside present-day Zambia, and it became famous for being a great trader in slaves and ivory, and for successfully preventing the Portuguese from creating a bridgehead across the continent between the ports of Sofala and Luanda.

The Kazembe, thus, were "created" by Lunda expansion, caused in its turn by the Lunda's wealth in guns, traded by the Portuguese of Angola. Many other small groups were either conquered by or attracted to the Lunda and their ostentatious displays of wealth; Lunda traditions maintain that the very appearance of the chiefs' regalia and the sound of the royal drums was enough to dazzle lesser peoples into submission.

The Kazembe dynasty reached the height of its power during the reign of Kazembe III from 1760 to 1805. In the second half of the nineteenth century, it went into decline, suffering from the plundering invasions of the Ngoni armies from the south (escapees from Shaka Zulu), a sharp drop in trade with the Portuguese, and the predations of the notorious slave hunter Josedo Rassrio Andrade-Kanyemba, who in 1877 led an army of six hundred men on a raid north of the Zambezi.

Nevertheless, the kingdom continued to exist until late in the nineteenth century, when it was finally colonized by the Belgians, and dismantled.

And as we saw in the first section, their troubles are not over. These people were among the "Luba" persecuted by Zaire's Mobutu; it was their grim convoy I had seen fleeing into Zambia.

Modern Zaire, ex–Belgian Congo, ex–bifurcated lands of the Kongo kings and the Luba-Lunda tributaries, is as chaotic, as fluid, as ever the land was in history. As the long rule of Mobutu Sese Seko reached its unedifying end, beset by corruption, endemic theft, and rebellions, the immense territory seemed to be fissioning once more. No doubt a strongman—or several strongmen in succession—will attempt to govern the almost ungovernable; it was also possible that many would replace the one, and that Zaire will need another century or so to sort itself out. From the perspective of history, that's no great matter. Africa has lots of time.

The Brazzaville terminus for the Congo riverboats is a swaying, creaking wharf close to the French-owned Elf Tower, the closely guarded high-rise that is famous in

Brazzaville for being a high-rise. I hauled my bags onto the land and watched as the crowd seethed ashore, dangerously tilting the barge as they did so. Even the crew had no sooner moored than they vanished. Within minutes there wasn't a human left aboard and I was surrounded by taxi drivers wanting to take me north, south, to the Plateau, to a hotel, to Kinshasa across the Pool, anywhere, immediately, hands clutching at my baggage and clothes, yammering away in rapid-fire French. One of them grabbed my hat. I grabbed it back. The only thing to do under such circumstances is to hire one of them, which I did. The others vanished.

I always felt safe in Brazzaville, "Brazza." I looked around affectionately. The city is a sprawl, running for almost 14 kilometres (10 miles) along the river just below Stanley Pool. It has a somnolent feel to it; behind the shabbiness and the peeling paint there is the beautiful skeleton of an art deco colonial town. Even the main roads are still treed, giant "fromagers," palms, huge mango trees, frangipani with their seductive scent, hibiscus and bougainvillaea in violet, red, and orange. André Gide found the city "indolent" in 1920, and it still is, despite its million inhabitants. Sure, there are bandits, rush hours, hustlers, and hookers, but there is also courtesy, friendliness, and charm. There is music and dancing everywhere, and passers-by are always invited to drop in and take part, and they usually do.

How different from the much larger and angrier city across the Pool, the Zairian capital, Kinshasa. I stared across the Pool. Kinshasa was close enough that you could, when the weather was right, actually see vehicles moving. I couldn't think of another example in the world where the capital cities of two countries stare at each other like that across so small a divide. And yet this is not an accident of colonialism, but an accident of a history far older: the Téké and the Bakongo were bristling at each other long before the first Europeans set foot on this coast.

Kinshasa is a mess. I hadn't been there ten minutes before I saw a man, bleeding profusely from a knife cut, stagger across the six lanes of the main boulevard and collapse, mortally wounded, against the doors of a bank. The customers went in and came out, counting their sheaves of rapidly devaluing money, while he lay there, leaking, and died. Early in 1997, as the city waited for the rebels to come and liberate them, armed bandits patrolled in convoys or waited at intersections. The police were the looters, the thuggish army protected only the governing thugs, every diplomat had an armed escort, foreigners were marked for mugging and murder, what government existed was dedicated only to corruption, civil servants hadn't been paid for more than a year. The luxurious mansions of the rich in the Binza hills were surrounded by private armies. Ironically, about the safest place in the city was the shambles called the Cité, the great slums of the poor. Outside the city's hospitals you could find vendors of stolen drugs, steroids, and anti-inflammatories, antispasmodics, antibiotics, analgesics. It's the only place in Central Africa you're likely to find sterile needles; you can buy syringes still in their sealed packages, looted from the Red Cross, just another shipment of aid that never got where it was intended.

And yet the city somehow, mysteriously, works. Traffic lights change from red to green, the street lights come on in the dark, the trains run more or less on time, the schools hold classes, the Zairian basketball league plays its games as scheduled, banks open on time and hand out money to account holders, albeit ever larger stacks (inflation hovered around 15 per cent a month when I was there). And in Kinshasa I had the only taxi driver in Africa (and perhaps elsewhere) who refused a tip.

I checked in at my hotel, and then hired a pirogue to see how close I could get to the helicopter-equipped yacht that for the past year or so had been the dictator's Zairian bunker—in late 1996 he no longer dared risk a land headquarters. Close wasn't very close at all—my pirogue paddler was nervous, with good reason; there were armed patrol boats circling the yacht at all times, and when we ventured closer than they liked, they peeled off to warn us away. So we never saw Joseph Desiré Mobutu, aka Mobutu Sese Seko, aka Mobutu Sese Seko Koko Ngbendu wa za Banga, the All-Powerful Warrior Who, Because of His Endurance and Inflexible Will to Win, Will Go from Conquest to Conquest Leaving Fire in His Wake. Later I learned he was already in Europe for treatment for prostate cancer.

Mobutu was by then nearing the end of his string. Of course, he had been close before, and had survived, mostly by slaughtering his opponents and making millionaires of his friends. Mobutu had at times been propped up by the Belgians, the French, the British, the Americans, the South Africans, and mercenaries. Indeed, the French would have propped him up again in 1997 had the Americans not quietly but vehemently vetoed intervention. He was also propped up by international bankers, who allowed him to loot his country ($6 billion and counting) and at the same time run up debts of $12 billion, "restructured," every so often. No question: the free-market system made a terrible case far worse. Mobutu, it was said, had taught the Zairians only one thing, how to steal.

In many important ways Zaire no longer existed as a state, any more than Liberia or Somalia did—it was just, as *The Economist* put it, "A Zaire-sized blank on a map."[23] After all, more than four hundred dialects are spoken in Zaire by almost as many ethnic groups. All of eastern Zaire, including its largest cities and its richest resources, were occupied early in 1997 by rebels egged on by Uganda and others, and they were heading straight for the capital. Each of the eight provinces was effectively running its own affairs. One of them, Kasai East, no longer accepted Zairian currency. Kivu had in spirit and in commerce joined East Africa. Shaba, which was importing Boer farmers from South Africa to help feed itself, was reverting to self-rule.

Does it matter whether Zaire is a state? I thought back to the days of the Luba hegemony. What was happening was entirely consistent with the past. The Zairian anarchy was only partly a fault of colonialism, in so far as the Western ethos regards the nation-state as the basic unit of sovereignty. It was not so much the West's alien and artificial boundaries that were the problem, but the notion of boundaries at all. African empires and kingdoms dissolved and reformed in the light of contemporary realities. They have not been able to do so recently, because they are strangled in the far more potent and powerful Western reality, bureaucracy. But the coming realignment would be entirely consistent with what had gone before. Kongolo and Ilunga Kalala would have been comfortable here.

....

The colonial history of Zaire, or the Belgian Congo, is perhaps the most extraordinary, not to say outlandish, story of the scramble for Africa. Henry Stanley had, at least to European eyes, "opened up" the Congo by demonstrating its navigability above the rapids. When Britain paid no attention, regarding the Congo basin as of no value, Stanley hired himself out to the King of the Belgians, the hyper-energetic, maniacal Leopold, who managed to fiddle a geographic conference in Brussels into granting him, as his personal fiefdom, a section of countryside as large as Europe.

He did this by appointing Stanley chief agent of his Association Internationale du Congo and establishing a chain of stations on the river itself. Leopold acquired "recognition" by a series of bilateral agreements conducted on the sidelines of the Berlin West Africa Conference of 1884–85 and emerged as sovereign in his own right of the Congo Free State.

Mobutu Sese Seko had in Leopold a perfect antecedent, a man who thieved and killed on a monumental scale. Truly, Leopold was one of the great villains of African history.

Not long after he took possession of his "little patch of ground," the invention of the motor car led to an insatiable demand for rubber, followed inexorably by the "rubber atrocities," by which was meant Leopold's reinvention of slavery. Damned Africans wouldn't work hard enough or cheaply enough, so he enslaved 'em. Leopold's agents set impossible quotas; the gang bosses, to prove they had been ruthless enough, were obliged to present, along with inventory and invoices, baskets of smoke-cured human hands, cut off for slacking.

Leopold's atrocities become so outrageous that they caused an international scandal. Belgians felt obliged to seize back the territory from their disgraced sovereign, and—in the cant of the time—saw it as a matter of national honour to remedy the evils for which they were responsible. If so, they were lackadaisical in its execution. Private Belgian companies went on looting the Congo with impunity. Belgium didn't concern itself with education, or training Africans to govern. Probably honour didn't demand it.

In 1958 the French (themselves no paragons of colonial virtue) were forced to cede independence to neighbouring Congo Brazzaville, which set off riots in Leopoldville (as modern Kinshasa was predictably called). When Belgian troops failed to quell the riots, the Belgian government lost its nerve. It abruptly announced that, six months hence, the Congo would be independent. As a departing governor put it, "It is very hard for any white man to penetrate the African mind in its primitive state," and he clearly thought it wasn't worth trying, so off he went.

Patrice Lumumba, head of the only party with any notion of a pan-Congolese program, won the ensuing election. The army promptly mutinied, Moise Tshombe took Katanga (Shaba) independent, the U.N. intervened (not the first and far from the last futile intervention in African affairs), went bankrupt, and withdrew. Lumumba asked the Russians for help, which was too much for an unholy alliance of Western forces (South Africa, the CIA, and the Belgians once more). Lumumba was overthrown by the army and handed over to Tshombe, who promptly had him murdered. With U.S. and Belgian help, Mobutu conquered the rest of the country and, less than a year later, staged a coup.

Over the years there were many uprisings against his rule, most notably in Kinshasa in 1992, which pushed Mobutu onto his yacht in the Congo and turned Kinshasa into one of the most violent cities on the planet.

In the end, Laurent Kabila's Rebel Alliance got to Mobutu before the cancer did, and the ageing dictator fled. By the middle of 1997 Kabila and his meddlesome Rwandan and Ugandan allies were confronting this "Zaire-sized blank" and were already making strongman noises. Zaire has been there before.

LOANGO

A day or so later I went back to the Congo rapids. I sat on the bank with a couple of Zairian fishermen and again watched the hyacinths dashing themselves to pieces on the rocks. The water was the same muddy lemon it had been when I first saw it, up in the north near Mossaka. The Zairians, of course, had changed its name to the Zaire, but no one else called it that, least of all the residents of the Republic of the Congo. Every second, I had read somewhere, between 30,000 cubic metres (1,059,400 cubic feet) (July) and 55,000 cubic metres (1,942,300 cubic feet) (December) per second pass by any one spot. If these Congo rapids were channelled and electrified, someone had calculated, they could supply about a sixth of the world's hydro-electric power. Mobutu had had, in fact, a typically grandiose scheme to provide power for most of Africa by doing precisely that, a plan that I had heard about on the Zambezi, where it had been greeted with much-justified scepticism.

Stanley had had a notion to open the Congo to international traffic. He'd built a series of staging-posts and marked out a portage route, but had apparently never contemplated a real road. Instead, the Germans began, and the French completed, a railway from Brazzaville to Pointe Noire.

I went down to the railway yards and hitched a ride on a cargo train hauling immense logs of virgin rain forest to the veneer-houses of Europe, eco-protesters be damned. Each log was 2 or 3 metres (6.5 to 10 feet) thick and the full length of a railway car—what a wound they must have left in the forest!

The Congo Ocean Railway, one of the most notorious projects of the colonial era, resulting in thousands of deaths, was opened in 1934. Officially, Congo is now silent on the toll it took to build, for it is vital to the country's economy and gives Brazzaville its only link to the sea. When Brazzaville was the capital of the much larger French Equatorial Africa (Central African Republic, Cameroon, Gabon, Congo), Pointe Noire was the main port of the whole region. But at what cost! It was built with forced labour brought down on barges from as far away as southern Chad. This was slave labour, pure and simple, seventy years after slavery was supposedly abolished. The atrocities and abuses were as bad as Leopold's—men who refused to do (forced) labour for the French were simply chained to trees and left to die. In some parts more than half the population was killed, either by physical abuse or through starvation caused by agricultural collapse because the men were removed.

And now the Congo railway has become a beloved thing, a way of life for thousands and an economic lifeline for millions. There is even a Congo Ocean Railway Preservation Society—as modern engineers punched a straighter railroad through the Mayombe Forest, avoiding the rugged hills around Mount Bolo, those nostalgic for the old ways raised money to keep the older track in repair.

Pointe Noire, the terminus of the Congo railway, is a curiosity. Its station sets the tone: a replica of the train station at Deauville, it has the prim air of a bourgeois French village, set among the lush palm trees and the golden beaches of the Atlantic. Through the turmoil of African independence it became the haunt of mercenaries from a score of countries. Mad Mike Hoare of Katanga used to hold court here, and so did the discards of a dozen armies and veterans of half a hundred wars, most of them tropical, small, and ferocious. The "vets" would hang out in the bars with the Loango whores, just as they do now in Luanda.

Now, Pointe Noire is an oil town, a freight terminal, and a resort for diplomats and tourists and the Congolese élite. There are bars and cafés where the food is metropolitan and expensive; I had an early lunch of grilled prawns and avocados, with a bottle of chilled Muscadet, and it cost me more than a three-star meal on the Île St. Louis. There are beaches just outside town on which it is safe to sleep. I rented a hammock for a day, sipped freshly squeezed guava juice, and then snoozed, dreaming of the Loango kings.

I'd spent a melancholy morning poking through the Museé Ma Loango, housed in a fading colonial mansion in Loango itself, just beyond the lovely little resort town of Point Indienne. The curator later took me to see the mausoleums of the Loango kings at Diosso, just up the coast. Once he saw I was interested, he wouldn't let me go. I was his only visitor that day, or that week, and he wanted to make sure I understood the context of the kingdom I was visiting. There is nothing left of the Loango kingdom at all, he said. It is gone, demolished, dispersed, obliterated, rolling the verbs off his tongue, oddly gleeful at this litany of woe. He took me over to one of the cases, a head-dress of one of the great kings. "It is soaked in blood," he said.

I peered at it. It was an embroidered cap, in white, set with shells, with a white tassel. There was no sign of blood. "I don't see any blood," I said.

I had missed the point. "I mean infused with the blood of the people," he said. "The kingdom of Loango grew wealthy on the back of the slaves."

"Oh! Slaves were shipped from here?"

"In the days before the railway, caravans of slaves would be driven down from Brazzaville," he said. "And through the Batéké lands. From Gabon, Cameroon, everywhere."

No one really knows, he said, when the kingdom was founded. It was certainly there earlier than Kongo. The Vili tribe, the people of Loango, speak a curious language, oddly unrelated to the other languages of West Central Africa. There's a theory that the Loango coast state was founded by refugees from the Songye–Luba expansions, which might explain why the language is closer to East Africa than to West. This means the Loango dynasty was already in place by the thirteenth century. The curator at Point Indienne thought this probable; it was in line with the oral tradition.

He took me over to see a plan of Diosso, then called Loango, in its glory days. The sketch was by Olfert Dapper, the seventeenth-century Dutch explorer. I was somewhat sceptical of Dapper, having seen first-hand his exaggerations at M'banza Congo, but still, he was clearly impressed with what he'd seen. In the foreground are groups of figures. Some are playing musical instruments. Bearers are carrying a dignitary in what looks like a hammock. Off to the right a group of soldiers are dragging away captives, bound to poles. The city appears to be more than a kilometre wide, palisaded and barricaded with ramparts, pierced by a dozen gates guarded by detachments of soldiers. Neat thatched houses line wide boulevards, interspersed with gardens and plantations. A series of terraces at the far end lead up to the royal palace, a compound of buildings surrounded by its own walls, arranged in a series of enclosed courtyards. In case you missed the point of the richness of it all, Dapper also appended a sketch of the king himself, dressed in embroidered brocades and seated on his throne, surrounded by musicians and courtiers. He wears a heavy bonnet and carries an immense sceptre. The totem of his house is on a pole next to him. Children are crawling into his lap. In front, a supplicant offering ivory and leopard skins is on his knees. The whole sketch is one of barbaric splendour. I asked the curator if he knew how much of it was the Dutchman's fevered imagination. He had no way of knowing, he said, but it was probably not much exaggerated.

"Loango was rich and powerful," he said. "When Diogo Cão landed in 1492, it was very prosperous, with a hundred thousand inhabitants."

After it became independent of the Kongo in the sixteenth century its reach was as far as Cabinda, Southern Congo, and Gabon. All accounts say the capital was astonishing, full of prodigies and miracles.

Later, in my hammock, I thought back to the sketch of the king, staring expressionlessly over the supplicant kneeling before him, down the hill over the city to the palisades beyond, to where his armies exercised and his traders brought their caravans. His men knew their way up the Congo River and the Sangha and all the way across country to the Kanem-Bornu trading stations near Lake Chad, which in turn traded with Cairo and the Mediterranean. Slaves and ivory, ivory and slaves, the engines of his economy.

The Loango kings were venerated as gods. This was not surprising when you consider what they had to go through to become king. A king could be crowned only after an arduous seven-year probation, during which time his reign had to be "exemplary." After that he had to make a one-year voyage of celebration to every part of the kingdom. During this year-long pre-coronation voyage, a "delicious young virgin" shared his bed, but he was not allowed to touch her, his abstinence being a symbol of his will and force of character. On return, he still had to demonstrate his physical prowess: he was obliged to tour the Forest of Tchebila on one foot, and to climb a tall palm tree using only his hands and one leg. If he failed any of these tasks, he could not be crowned.

After coronation, everything changed. The king was confined to the royal compound, and could venture out only for the reception of notables "from away," or to hunt leopards, the royal animal. It was at his investiture that he took on the real power and responsibility of kingship: to control the rhythms of the seasons, and to decide on the abundance of the harvest and of the fishery. He was the intermediary on earth for Nzambi, the supreme god, the ancestors, and the spirits. Obviously, he couldn't be allowed to wander at will around the countryside. His responsibility was too great. And so was the terror of meeting him: coming face to face with God's representative was more than people could bear.[24]

I watched the sun going down over the ocean. A troop of soldiers went by on a training run, lifting their knees high, like trotting horses. A group of women were soaping themselves in the surf, black skin a gleaming ebony in the fading light; they looked like a sculptural frieze against the flaring sky. At dusk the bats came out, flitting across the crimson sun. I thought regretfully of the seven-year probation the Loango kings were forced to undergo, a wonderful precedent for politicians everywhere. But that god business was a problem. Too many of our leaders already believe themselves divinely inspired.

....

After independence in 1960, the Congo, perhaps in retaliation for the uncaring brutality of French rule, became a client state of the Russians. Pascal Lissouba, later the president, was then a minor functionary in the Agriculture Department of what became the Peoples' Republic of Congo, a hard-line Marxist regime that quickly destroyed what little remained of the traditional kingdoms—*sic transit Loango* ...

But the Marxist rhetoric began to collapse even before the Berlin Wall came down, and after that the transformation to a multiparty democracy was swift. In the early nineties, before Lissouba's election, the government of Denis Sassou-Nguesso decided that the quarrelsome politics called democracy was "un-African" and should be discarded in favour of something more decently hierarchical, but the furious reaction of the population caused them to back down. By the late nineties, the politics of Congo were fractious, energetic, optimistic, fragile. Lissouba was still president, but after a motion of censure by the opposition, he created a government of national unity under premier General J.J. Yhomby-Opango, in which the various opposition parties held 60 per cent of the votes and the presidential majority party 40 per cent. New elections were scheduled for 1997; meanwhile, rapid decentralization and privatization, the clichés of the day, were being undertaken in the middle of a prolonged recession, largely caused by plunging oil prices.

Generally, the press had taken on itself the role of national nag; they were not going to let the politicians forget that the people were watching. But the press was also filled with discussions of political morality. In an essay published in the *Temps* of Brazzaville early in 1996, Henri Boukoulou argued strongly that the oral culture of Africa was damaging and helping to keep the continent backward. "Oral culture, still dominant in our society, does at least have significance and a certain nobility in the traditional society. The elderly, masters of the word, knew how to steer information in the breast of society to keep its equilibrium and its cohesion. In traditional society, the word was the property of the wise. These knew that the word is, by its nature, ambivalent. It has the power to unify and disunify, to build or to destroy, to create love or hate. Today we are a long way from these traditions and our wise have disappeared along with their wisdom. Integrated into the modern world without our own internal order of conduct rooted in our past, we live in a universe in total rupture with the constraints of development. Without written communication, we are left in a weakened situation, in which rumour becomes our principal mode of communication. And in the context of the profound changes we are undergoing, rumour only causes moral and psychological crises. And the worst of it is that the politicians and the media, forgetting grandeur and ignoring the need for wisdom, have chosen to make rumour a weapon in political combat."

BANGUI

T he Central African Republic and Gabon (once part of French Equatorial
        Africa), Equatorial Guinea (once part of Spain's attenuated African empire),
        São Tomé and Príncipe (Portuguese), and Cameroon (German first, then
French and British) were all, once, on the periphery of Great Doings. By the standards
even of Loango, though, they were small fry. The CAR was depopulated by slavery;
Gabon was ignored even by Loango (which didn't prevent the Fang and others producing some of Africa's great art); São Tomé was developed, at least in part, by the slavers
who emptied the CAR; Equatorial Guinea was coveted by no one and so left alone;
and Cameroon ... Cameroon was swept by currents from beyond its borders, hearing
echoes of the Kanem-Bornu conquests, of the Fulani jihads (which set in motion the
spread of the Fang), of great wars in places far away, while its own small kingdoms
prospered, secure, alert for wars that never came. In all these places, there were no great
ruined capitals to seek. But of course, like every corner in Africa, they were not without their interest. In Cameroon, at least, I would get a chance to visit the pygmies, and
to make contact with the Fulani and the Fang.

Many of the Congo riverboats begin their journey to Brazzaville in Bangui, the
besotted and deadly little capital of the Central African Republic. I had found myself
there inadvertently, and found its reputation fully justified: the police were surly and
aggressive, and the population filled with drunks and muggers. Bangui also has a
substantial resident French population, many of them either in mineral exploitation
or hunting; the capital, a sleepy little city on the banks of the Ubangi, is still thor-
oughly segregated, with little white–black mixing.

It's hard to blame the people for their unfriendliness. First of all, there are fewer of
them than there might be—this is perhaps the most underpopulated country in
Africa. The reason was simple enough: the Central African Republic was too far north
for the Kongo and Luba emperors, and too far south for the Kanem-Bornu governors.
There was, therefore, no central government in the region, and the isolated villagers
were easy prey for slave traders, first the Arabs from the north, and then the
Portuguese agents from the coastal Loango states. Slavery emptied the countryside.

The colonial period wasn't much better. The French, who owned it for a while, called
it Oubangui-Chari, hacked it up into seventeen "concessions," and handed them over
to private companies to do with as they wished, in return for a 15 per cent royalty. It
was the rich diamond fields that really attracted them, though the country is relatively
wealthy in other minerals too. The companies were permitted—even encouraged—to
conscript local labour. Labourers who refused conscription were tortured or killed. A
series of unsuccessful rebellions followed, put down with French troops. At the same
time, the country turned into a hunting preserve for army officers and the rich.

In 1958, the CAR became a self-governing republic. The president elect, Bathelemy Boganda, was killed in a plane crash before the elections, and David Dacko, an inept and corrupt French puppet, was elected. He was overthrown a year later by his cousin, the commander-in-chief of the army, Jean Bédel Bokassa. From 1965 to 1981, when the French had finally had enough, Bokassa ruled the country through murder, torture, and acts of savage cruelty—killing schoolchildren, for example, when they refused to buy clothing from his wife's factory. You can still see the lion and crocodile pens at Bokassa's home in Bangui into which he tossed his political opponents for his after-dinner enjoyment. (He was also widely reputed to have eaten some of them.) Bokassa attracted international ridicule when he had himself crowned Emperor for Life in a ceremony that cost the country $20 million, paid for by the French. Fair's fair: Bokassa gave the French president, Giscard d'Estaing, hundreds of diamonds as gifts whenever he visited the country to kill another elephant or two.

In a French-led coup, General André Konlingba became president in 1981.

Bokassa was granted exile in the Côte d'Ivoire, but three years later he transported himself and his family to Paris, where the French loaned him a nice little château. After another three years, secure in the knowledge of his own invincibility, he returned home to Bangui and dared Konlingba to try him, which the president duly did. Bokassa was still there in 1997, doing hard labour in a hard prison, and (if there is any justice) facing the ridicule and humiliations of his captors.

By late 1996, Konlingba's days were clearly numbered. The "democracy movement" that had shaken the Congo had infected the CAR too, and Konlingba was driven to promising a national political conference, to be followed by elections. No one believed he would fulfil this promise voluntarily, for if he did he'd almost certainly be thrown out. There were riots in the streets, put down with the help, again, of French paratroopers.

....

Well, there was Bokassa and then there is . . . Marie Rose. Marie Rose lives in a small village far from any centre of power, and she is of absolutely no consequence in the grand political scheme of things, but I put her in my notebook as an antidote to the appalling history recounted above, as a reminder, should it ever be necessary, of how Africans have so often mined joy and pleasure in the midst of adversity—a reminder of the gentler virtues.

"The young woman came out of her house"—I'm transcribing notes, written as I sat under a tree in the shade, waiting for a bus—"and made her way across the yard to the bathing stream. Beyond her followed her young child, who had just learned to walk. There were a couple of crumbly steps halfway across the yard, but she swung down them gracefully. This was not as easy as it sounds, since she has no legs, and both arms ended at her wrists, in callused stumps."

Marie Rose, for it turned out that was her name, was proudly described by her village neighbours as a housewife, and indeed it was something of an achievement, for she lived alone and tended her child and cooked and cleaned house, and did all the other things African women must do, which is to produce much of her own food and have enough left over to sell, and fetch her water from the stream. She raised chickens, and manioc and bananas. Of course, she couldn't pick the bananas—the local kids did that for her—but she could peel and cook them on the fire she made from the wood she gathered and brought home—for Marie Rose, housewifery was a twenty-hour-a-day task. Her husband was in Cameroon, and sent her money sometimes, when he had any. Her neighbours marvelled, because she was good-natured and laughed a lot. Marie Rose didn't want help. Help offended her.

"She swung down to the stream on the stumps of her arms, and slid down the bank, clutching her son to her. There, she peeled off his clothes and then hers, using the apparently clumsy stumps with great dexterity to slip her dress over her head. Her figure was full, heavy-breasted, maternal. 'Seated' in the water she was beautiful despite her height, which was less than a metre. She lovingly washed her baby, making it chuckle, then she started to sing, a sweet *fais-do-do* that caressed the child anew and she drew him up on the grassy bank and they went to sleep there, peaceful for a while, until she had to wake and face her world and haul herself on her stumps across the gravel yard and into the house, where there was work to do."

The bus came, eventually, and took me back to town. In the late afternoon, on the outskirts of Bangui I came upon a group of men setting fire to a car, for no apparent reason than that it was in the way. Two of them were naked to the waist, and their torsos were carved with intricate scars in abstract patterns; elsewhere in town I saw a young woman with her head unnaturally elongated into the shape of a gourd, her skull vanishing to a point, her cheeks drawn back into a perpetual snarl; and the baggage handler at the airport, a young woman of almost ethereal beauty, had two lines of deep scars down each cheek, badges of belonging to a culture far older than ours. "Have a nice flight," she said mechanically, as she shoved my bag onto a cart.

GABON

There was an outbreak of Ebola in Gabon while I was in neighbouring Congo, not more than 200 kilometres (125 miles) or so from Albert Schweitzer's celebrated hospital at Lambaréné, but it was swiftly suppressed by Gabonese and American medical teams, and so was any news of it—no international press coverage followed, as it did after the outbreak at Kitwit in Zaire two years earlier. Nothing must be allowed to disrupt the flow of oil.

In a curious way, Gabon is a country without recorded history. The Fang dominated—and still do—and the Fang were artists and mystics and warriors, but not king-makers. Life went on in the villages as it did all over Africa: the clans and lineages fused and fissioned, warfare broke out, and peace. But of great kings there were none. Or, at least, the folk-tales do not tell of them.

Gabon's cities are without character, in the modernist way. Except for the oppressive humidity and the occasional violent outbreak of frangipani blossoms, they could be anywhere. Commerce dominates. Oil is king.

Who is to say this is a bad thing? Gabon has the highest per capita income of any country in Africa, and there's less obvious poverty here than elsewhere. There are no beggars. The literacy rate is high. The health care at Lambaréné is better now than when the eccentric Swiss doctor was there—Schweitzer ran his place in a tyrannical if benevolent way, his methods now rejected by Gabonese physicians as the sheerest paternalism. The Gabonese physicians are well respected, for, as a Gabonese diplomat put it, "they have plenty to practise on." Yellow fever is endemic. Cholera is frequent. Leprosy still infects thousands. More than a quarter of Gabonese women are said to have one sexually transmitted disease or another. AIDS is a huge problem. Gabonese mosquitoes are increasingly resistant to drugs, and debilitating malaria is a major killer.

Most of the tales told about Gabon's history involve one or other of the Western flotsam who washed up on these shores. Trader Horn, aka Aloysius Smith, that much-celebrated and larger-than-life hero, had his headquarters at Cape Lopez, near where the modern city of Port Gentil is now. He was preceded by Cap'n Dick of Noo Yawk, one Richard E. Lawlin, who bought the Island of Mandji at the mouth of the Ogooué River from a local chieftain and called it Brooklyn. After a while he moved up in life and renamed his newly constructed bamboo village New York. He helped start the lumber trade, and you can still see immense rafts of exotic logs—mahogany, rosewood, ironwood, okoume—floating down the river to Port Gentil. The Frenchman De Brazza, departing from Cape Lopez, poled up the Ogooué for 1,000 kilometres (620 miles) before haring off to Stanley Pool and claiming it for France.

Now Port Gentil is an oil town, and charmless, despite its frangipani and hibiscus hedges. It's expensive, with lots of foreign white folk eating in pretentious restaurants.

....

No one outside Gabon paid much attention to it before the middle of the last century. The Portuguese, though they helped name it (*gabao* means cloak in Portuguese, so named for the forests that cloaked the shores) passed it by. In the centuries that followed, various Dutch, French, and British ships arrived, searching for slaves. From early in the eighteenth century the Fang showed up from the northeast in successive waves, and took over the weak and leaderless villages of the coast. In 1849 the French captured a slave ship bound for the Indies and released the captives on a sandy promontory in the Komo River estuary. The slaves promptly dug in and built themselves a town, calling it Libreville. This is now the country's capital.

Gabon was finally captured by a colonial power when France did a deal with one of the coastal leaders, King Denis, otherwise known as Chief Kowe Rapontchombe, becoming, in the euphemism of the time, his Protector. Which of course meant the usual colonial foofaraw. The place was turned over to private concessionaires, who reintroduced slavery (aka "forced labour") and stripped the forests around the coast.

....

In the first presidential election after independence in 1960, the former mayor of Libreville, Leon M'Ba, was elected. A few years later he abolished political parties and banned his prime minister, a fellow Fang called Jean-Hilaire Aubame, who retaliated by staging a successful coup.

Short-lived success, however. The next day French paratroopers reinstalled M'Ba, and he ruled until his death (of natural causes) in 1967. He was succeeded by the present incumbent, Albert-Bernard Bongo.

Bongo, who has since renamed himself El Hadj Omar Bongo, props himself up with French and Moroccan troops, but there were serious riots in Libreville and Port Gentil in the early 1990s. Bongo, under French pressure, promised multiparty elections in 1993. These were duly held, and Bongo squeaked back in, though by a mere 51 per cent of the vote.

By the mid-1990s there were dozens of opposition parties, including the Lumberjacks, and Bongo's days appeared to be numbered. Democracy was well installed. The French were insisting on it. Once more: Nothing must interfere with the flow of oil.

....

One of the great excursions from the capital is the Transgabonnaise, the newly built, highly efficient, and ridiculously overcrowded cross-country railway, which ends up, not surprisingly, in Franceville, which is near Bongoville, which is, of course, where M. Bongo, a member of the Téké tribe, was born. There's nothing very much to do when you get there, but the journey itself is worth it, passing as it does through some beautiful hills thickly covered with equatorial jungle. Or, if you want something a little more rugged, take an Air Gabon flight to the northeastern city of Makoukou, and see if you can hire guides to take you deep into Gabonese pygmy country. In Libreville the advice is to hire a pirogueier to take you into the pristine northern wilderness, filled with gorillas, elephant, bongo, and other game. But there is rugged and rugged—you'd have to take all your supplies with you into the bush. It's easier to do what I did, and drive from Ebolowa in Cameroon, over not quite terrible roads passable with a four-wheel-drive vehicle, to the border village of Yen. It is, after all, the same forest.

A Cameroonian gendarme who served a not exactly thrilling watch at the Cameroon–Gabon border post, volunteered to take me on a hike into the bush, crossing as we did so the national frontiers, which seemed to me sloppy of him. He promised to show me gorillas, but we saw none, though we did see their tracks and the plants they'd ruined in their foraging. The gendarme, a Fang named Jean-Bernard, was convinced that gorillas were savage creatures just waiting to rend humans limb from limb. Of course, his stories of their savagery might just have been told to puff up his own bravery, but he seemed convinced enough, and started at every noise, of which there were plenty, and carried his carbine at the ready.

Naturally, I was sceptical, having been reared on *National Geographic*'s misty sentimentality about the great apes and their gentle ways (and having seen the movie, in which the villains were always human poachers). This irked Jean-Bernard, who insisted I didn't know what I was talking about—typical white attitude. Not only did they kill humans, he said, but they ambush them, and drag their victims off into the forest.

"And there eat them?" I asked, even more sceptical.

"No, they eat fruit," he said impatiently. "They just torment the people."

I said I'd heard some Fang women smoke tobacco in the forest to ward off gorillas, who were thought to hate the smell, but Jean-Bernard thought this was nonsense. "Women smoke all the time here," he said, "whenever they can steal money to buy it."

There were elephants everywhere, and we occasionally caught sight of them swaying through the jungle, as wrinkled and ridiculous as pantomime horses. A large python was furled around a tree limb in the sun, its head hanging down, peering at us beadily, for all the world as though it was about to say boo. A family of buffalo splashed through a creek.

Jean-Bernard and I stood on a small hill, peering southwards, where there would have been a view if the jungle hadn't been so dense. Not far away—an hour's drive on a good road, a day or two bashing through the bush here—had been the most recent Ebola outbreak. I asked Jean-Bernard about it.

He shrugged. "Not a problem in Cameroon," he said.

We were then standing in what he thought was Gabon.

"It doesn't spread?"

"No," he said. "You have to touch the dead to catch it."

He was a gendarme. "In your job, don't you occasionally have to touch the dead?" I asked. I was mindful of the Fang reputation.

He was horrified. "Never!" he said, and led the way back to the pathway.

EQUATORIAL GUINEA

The first time I went to Equatorial Guinea, I went in a dugout canoe. But there was no one there, so I left.

After a while, I tried again. Again, there was no one there—not a border guard, not a Customs official, no state presence at all. On the Rio Muni side (as the mainland portion of this curious little country is called), I phoned for a border guard so I could get a visa and be legal on my entry, but when he arrived he'd left his stamps at home, so he told me to just go ahead and forget this troublesome visa business. "No one will care," he said. I thought this unlikely, but had no real option. In any case, he clearly didn't want to be bothered. Later, getting back out was just as easy. As far as the authorities were concerned, I could have spent a week lounging on the white sands of the riverbank, staring across at Cameroon, dreaming of . . . whatever loungers on the Campo River dream about.

It was Clement, a Fang I'd met near the Campo River, who'd persuaded me to go. He was from Cameroon himself, from the village of Bipindi, inland from the coastal resort town of Kribi, but all his family were south of the border, in Rio Muni, and south of that, in Gabon. He went frequently, never bothering with papers. He just took a canoe across the river, and walked to the city of Bata, a few hundred kilometres down the beach. There is in theory a border post, but since most people, like Clement, simply cross the river and then walk down the shore a day or so, it hardly seems worthwhile. There aren't any roads up in that part of Guinea anyway. My pirogueier volunteered that he was Fang too, as were the fishermen I photographed. There are Fang on both sides of the border. Those in Equatorial Guinea speak Spanish and Fang, those in Cameroon French and Fang. The Cameroonian Fang spoke to each other mostly in French. Nobody seemed to care what country they were in. It was all very refreshing—particularly given the region's turbulent recent history.

Most of Equatorial Guinea is offshore, on the island of Bioko (formerly Fernando Pó, named after the Portuguese explorer who came across the place twenty years before Columbus reached the Americas; and for a while renamed Formosa, for reasons now obscure). This is where the capital, Malabo, is located. The people who live there are of the Bubi tribe. For years Bioko was regarded as the hellhole of colonial postings, the most deadly of many disease-ridden African outposts—at one point fully three-quarters of the population were said to be suffering from syphilis. The British consular authorities, finally fed up with Richard Burton's high-handedness and arrogance, once posted him there, perhaps hoping he would catch one of its many diseases. Alas, the tough old explorer survived, as usual.

Rio Muni, the mainland, is a rectangle of land, flat and featureless, whose only advantage is its fertile soil and (more recently) its offshore oil.

The contemporary relaxed attitude towards outsiders and regulations is even more remarkable when you consider that less than two decades ago the country was run by a megalomaniacal tyrant every bit as nasty and brutish as Jean Bedél Bokassa or Idi Amin. Macias Nguema, a Fang from the mainland, won the first post-independence election in 1968 and embarked on a reign of terror, torturing and killing his opponents; fully a third of the country's 300,000 population fled, and one out of ten of the rest was in a forced-labour camp. The economy collapsed and, in an attempt to keep the cocoa plantations open, Nguema reintroduced slavery, under the same euphemism used by the French and Spanish colonialists before him, "forced labour." Things got better when his nephew, Théodore Obiang Nguema Mbasogo, overthrew the tyrant in 1979 and had him executed. Obiang has been running the place ever since. He's no natural democrat, and so far has ignored the 1991 referendum on the conversion to a multiparty democracy (146,000 for, 1,800 against), but his rule is not particularly severe by African standards, and several attempts at comic-opera coups against him—one by fewer than thirty people—were suppressed with a minimum of rancour. There is virtually no violent crime in the country, and even petty thievery is surpassingly rare.

My Fang friend Clement wanted me to visit his cousins, who lived a mere 30 kilometres (18 miles) down the beach at the town of Mary, but it was farther than I wanted to walk. He was disappointed. They would have shown me, he said, their version of the *ibanga*, the famous Fang national dance, in which the men and women cover themselves with white powder and dance themselves into a sexual frenzy. I didn't mention that earlier that morning I had stopped for a drink of pineapple juice at a small "bar-dancing" on the beach where a couple of drummers were playing. The patrons and the staff were all dancing, in a dreamy and relaxed kind of way, perhaps having to do with the idyllic setting of the thatched bar itself, nestled under palm trees with a view across the milk-white sand to the rolling breakers of the South Atlantic. The waitress was dancing as she took my order. She, too, was a Fang. Her face was a gleaming ebony, filmed with sweat until it looked polished, the shape of a stretched heart, like a Modigliani painting; scars had been picked out on both cheeks in diagonal slashes. She was wearing a lime-green blouse open to her waist, and voluminous pantaloons, in scarlet and yellow. Her feet were bare. Her upper body was utterly motionless as she danced, but she moved her hips in a gentle, insinuating roll, terminating each chord with a sudden bump, as though a spring had been winding up inside her pelvis and had suddenly released, with a startlingly sexual effect. I was riveted. The xylophone players started to laugh, and picked up the beat, each one breaking into song half a note behind the others, and the complicated rhythms of Africa went sweeping across the beach, to be lost, first in the sylvan breezes, and then in the crashing of the waves rolling in from Brazil.

"Pineapple juice, please," I said. "Pineapple juice. I'm very thirsty." I probably sounded as though I was begging.

The waitress stared at me with enormous almond eyes, her hips still moving in that delicate sexual swirl. Then she opened her mouth and smiled, and swayed away towards the bar. One of the drummers caught my eye. I thought he looked sympathetic, though in my confusion I couldn't be sure.

SÃO TOMÉ AND PRÍNCIPE

J ust before I was to leave for the two little volcanic isles that form the sovereign and altogether splendid country of São Tomé and Príncipe (the second-smallest state in Africa, with only 120,000 inhabitants), there was a coup. A bulletin went out over the Internet that said, rather blandly I thought, that the "president and his cabinet have been taken into custody." Redundantly, calm was urged. Few other details were available, there being hardly any diplomatic representation on the islands from abroad— even the United States watches São Tomé from neighbouring Gabon. It was a shame, I thought, for little São Tomé had recently developed the reputation for being the most democratic and easygoing country in West Africa. And in fact the coup reports seemed to have been overblown; even afterwards the planes that swept around the forested peaks into the dangerous little airport landed as usual, and were met as usual with the indolent disinterest habitual to an island where watching other people snorkel seemed to be a major industry. Everything, in fact, seemed—and was—absolutely normal. It was just that someone else was in charge.

These little islands were uninhabited in pre-colonial times, but their history is nevertheless a curious though not altogether melancholy one. The Phoenicians are supposed to have called here, in their voyage around Africa in six hundred and change, but of course no one knows for sure. The Portuguese explorers called the island the Pearls of the Ocean. Sailors, though, had a grimmer name, Home of the Sharks. Still, this was nothing to what the Angolan slaves shipped here, never to return, called it—*Islas Dolorosas*, Misery Islands. Other slaves called it the Inn, in bitter and sarcastic anger.

The first wretched inhabitants, though, were not slaves, but persecuted Jews from Iberia. In 1473 the navigator Ruy de Sequeira first caught sight of the forested peaks of the island he was to name after Saint Thomas; twenty years or so later, the king ordered that the island be populated, and it was done in a way that cruelly satisfied the demands of Lusitanian politics. Nearly a hundred thousand Sephardic Jews had recently sought asylum in Portugal from the Church Militant in Spain, but they were ordered to quit forthwith or convert. Given a mere eight months to leave, most of them stayed but refused baptism. The royal household then decided that examples had to be made. The children of those who stubbornly refused the manifest benefits of Christian blessing were shipped out "to become Christians as they may," and deposited on the Guinea coast, along with the seditious, the criminal, and the heretic. Several hundred Jews—boys all—were dumped on the forgiving shores of São Tomé. And there they remained.

Of course, as Jews they vanished, there being no Jewish women. Within a generation they were gone, slipping into the ever-accepting gene pools of Africa, leaving researchers for centuries thereafter to imagine a Semitic cast to islander features, and to come across in unlikely places tales that were vaguely Talmudic in flavour.

The early Portuguese settlers on the islands prospered, planting sugar on the small plains near the coast and building themselves improbable castles of tropical woods high up in the hills, where the breezes were cool. One of them built an edifice modelled after the Donjon at Vincennes, in Paris, where he had apparently been imprisoned for a time. He would patrol the ramparts with his musket, taking potshots at the giant butterflies fluttering about below—the island was famous for its exotic butterflies, and in a later century a contemporary of Charles Darwin's plunged to his death down a São Tomé ravine, grasping after the *Charaxes odysseus*, whose purple wings were much prized by Victorian collectors. Several of the planters kept private armies, and their idle days were spent in mini-wars against other planters. If you poke about the hillsides you can still see traces of their mansions, and every now and then a piece of crystal or a ceramic plate will turn up, exposed by a tropical downpour (or by the uneasy shifting of the soil—these are, after all, active volcanoes).

The planters grew rich on sugar and on slaves they imported from the stinking, fetid Niger delta, near where Lagos is now. These slaves were never fed by their masters. They were given gardens and were obliged to feed themselves. Ironically, the white masters seldom lived beyond fifty, succumbing to indolence and pestilence, whereas hundred-year-old Toméan slaves were not at all uncommon. The lushness of the island defeated the cruelty. The slaves lived on goat's milk, tortoise, palm wine, and millet, and their bodies prospered while their souls withered.

Around 1530 the slaves staged a successful revolt, and the planters fled to Brazil. Of course, they soon returned, the anarchic "government" of the slaves was put down by musketry, and the former life resumed.

In 1540 the slave ship *Amador*, bound from Luanda to Brazil with a load of slaves from the Mbundu kings, was wrecked on São Tomé. Hundreds of slaves—those who could break their chains—swarmed through the shark-infested waters and headed for the hills. The island was (and still is) largely covered with dense tropical forest, and cut with deep gorges, perfect hiding-places. After a while they built fortified villages, and spent the next century raiding the plantations and terrorizing those who would have been their masters.

The descendants of these Angolares, as they came to be called, are still there, still living apart, often in their own fishing villages, still with an insolent culture of dissidence. "Angolares never work" is one of their catch phrases, and the one that most irritates the rest of the islanders.

The Dutch invaded shortly after the wreck of the *Amador* and occupied part of the island. Most of them died of tropical diseases and they soon left for more salubrious climes. A hundred years later the French took their turn, with similar results, but before they departed they burned the capital to the ground in a fit of Gallic pique. Soon the slaves revolted again. Then pirates plundered the shore villages and sank visiting vessels. The islands declined into genteel and decadent decay.

The decay didn't last. The volcanic soil is so rich that crops virtually plant themselves. Rubber, coffee, and cocoa brought wealth to a new generation of planters; by 1875, when the Portuguese finally abolished slavery, the little island was producing more than a sixth of the world's supply of cocoa.

On Liberation Day the planters at last freed their slaves. They also cut off their food supply by seizing their gardens. Within weeks, most were starving. The masters ignored them and imported new ones, Kru tribesmen from Liberia. They called them "contract labourers." The Kru ungratefully regarded a contract as binding and, when their contracts expired, insisted on being repatriated. The planters refused, so the Kru secretly built a fleet of pirogues in the forests, and one amazing day three thousand of them set out in these fragile craft for the mainland, 350 kilometres (220 miles) away. Thirst and sharks accounted for two-thirds accidents got most of the rest. A few were picked up by passing ships and taken back to São Tomé. As far as history records, not one made it home.

The planters continued to send agents to Angola, to Zaire, and to the headwaters of the Zambezi. Year after year, five thousand and more unwilling "employees" left Luanda for the Islas Dolorosas. Not one returned. Their contracts were torn up.

By a curiosity of history, most of the cocoa trade was funnelled through England, and the English trade was controlled by the Quakers, led by William Cadbury. In 1908 Cadbury heard rumours that the Portuguese had reintroduced slavery to São Tomé, and sent agents of his own to investigate. Of course, the planters denied everything. These people were savages, *stupidos*, lucky to have a civilizing job. Cadbury's people weren't fooled. They watched the overseers beating their slaves with the bat-like paddles called *palmatoria*, and it was enough. The Quakers ordered a boycott of São Tomé cocoa that ruined the planters and freed, finally and for good, all the slaves.

....

The English writer Winwood Reade visited Príncipe in the middle of last century on a botanical expedition. He was so beguiled he nearly stayed. "There were no vices, since there were no restrictions," he wrote longingly, years afterwards. "No crimes, since there were no incentives; no paupers, since there were no wealthy men. I have certainly never seen so many happy people in Africa as I saw on Prince's Island, nor so many pretty girls."

Of course, he didn't notice the slaves. No one did, then.

On the other hand, he wasn't altogether wrong. Príncipians still lack many of the vices of the outside world. Theft is virtually unknown. Even the coup that briefly ruffled Government House left them unmoved, of little more consequence than a tropical storm. Take shelter, then come out into the sunlight. As a political credo, it's hard to beat.

CAMEROON

C ameroon is whimsically named after the Rio dos Camaroês, or River of Prawns, the name given to the Wouri River estuary by the Portuguese in the fifteenth century. As the South African traveller Lawrence Green once put it, at least "the natives knew better [than the Europeans] to name an enormous colony and a 13,000 ft [3,960-metre] active volcano after a shrimp. They called [Mount Cameroon] Mungomalobeh, the Throne of Thunder."

I asked dozens of Cameroonians what the country had been called before the whites arrived. None of them knew. Most of them thought it hadn't been named anything, and I came to understand that the naming of places is a European fetish. In Old Africa, a place is named after the tribe, and the tribe is named after either the domi-nant clan or the current ruler or a ruler eminent in the past. Thus, like tribes, the names of countries are mutable—just as countries are. To think otherwise is to freeze culture in an unnatural way. Names go against nature.

Cameroon is also a country on the cusp, between the deep forest and the endless desert; it ranges from the dense rain forests of the southwest to Lake Chad in the north, on the fringes of the Sahara. In the south are the pygmies, the Fang, the Bamiléké, the Douala, and the Bafo. In the south, too, are the rain forests, and the volcanic massif of Mount Cameroon, one of the wettest places on earth (1,000 centimetres/400 inches of rainfall each year). This part of Cameroon is, in a way, an extension of the great Congo rain forests, and thus belongs in this section.

In the centre of the country, past the beautiful hills of the Côte Bati, in the open country in the mountainous heart of Bamenda, was the old kingdom of Kom, one of some seventy small states and village chiefdoms, including the Bamiléké, the kingdom of Bamum, and the Tikar. And in the north, where the lushness flattens into savannah and then into desert, are the Fulani and the Kanemri, and their historic enemies, the Kirdi ("unbelievers"). We will see this part of the country when we reach the kingdoms of the Sahel, in Part VI.

I went looking for the pygmies in the deep rain forest of Cameroon. To find them, I had hired Clement the Fang as my guide, for he had told me he spoke fluent pygmy. After a while, when we had become more comfortable with each other, I told Clement how much his tribe's sculpture was admired by collectors in the West (at its best, Fang art is highly abstract; it was "conceptual" centuries before its Western time); then, having softened him up, I asked him about the Fang's cannibal reputation. Cannabalism was, as I perfectly well knew, surpassingly rare in Africa, and even then "cannibals" only ate human flesh for ritual or religious purposes, not as a casual part of their diet. The Fang, however, had this reputation ....

"In Gabon," I said, safely distancing ourselves from the story, "it was said the Fang had no slaves, no prisoners of war, and no cemeteries."

"Is that right?" he said, grinning at me.

"You mean it isn't true?"

"How would I know?" he asked, when he had stopped laughing. "We never had human for lunch."

The Fang, aka Pangwe, Fanwe, Pahouin, Paanway, were also supposed to be among the fiercest tribes in Africa. To disconcert the enemy, they used to bevel their lower incisors and file their uppers to a point, imitating "our father, the crocodile."

I showed Clement a quote from the British explorer Mary Kingsley, who had once ascended Mount Cameroon in a day, Victorian petticoats notwithstanding. (Kingsley finally died of typhoid in South Africa while she was administering to Boer prisoners of war, but she made many an expedition among the Fang of Gabon and, as she put it, "danced many a wild dance with the wild river"). "To be short of money in a Fang village is extremely bad," she'd written, "because when a trader has no more goods to sell them, these Fang are liable to start trade all over again by killing him and taking back their ivory and rubber and keeping it until another trader comes along."

Clement started laughing again.

Was their reputation for fierceness true?

"Not a bad reputation to have" was all Clement said, before he lost interest in the subject.

The books say the Fang had been driven from northern Cameroon, near Lake Chad, by the invasions of the Peul, aka Fulani, who had rampaged across the Sahel for several centuries before finally running out of ethnic steam. The Fang arrived in the Gabon estuary in the second half of the eighteenth century. Most of their legends speak of their homeland as being "far away to the north-east, a country with very different animals and inhabited by white men who rode horses and were skilled in the working of iron," presumably the Fulani or Arab invaders. They still associate themselves with the Upper Nile, and recall a time when their ancestors dressed like the Hausa, in an adaptation of desert garb. Their arrival in the forest is symbolized by a folk-tale which spoke of "passing through the hole in the adzap tree," the Eye of the Forest.

Clement had no idea what an adzap tree looked like.

No one, he said, makes much art any more, confirming what I already knew.

Clement said if we took the Lobé River inland, we would come to pygmy villages. He knew where to find them.

....

There are pygmies throughout the Central African rain forests, in Cameroon, Congo, Zaire, Central African Republic, and Gabon. There are perhaps forty thousand of them in Cameroon. They have fascinated travellers for centuries, not just because they are so small (a substantial male reaches little more than 150 centimetres [4 feet 11 inches]), and not just because they were here first (all the Bantu tribes concede this), but because their culture is so ... particular, and because they have adhered to it with a stubbornness that is a marvel. They adopted virtually nothing from the Bantu invaders, and when the white men came the pygmies refused to have anything to do with their culture either. Instead, they continued their inturned, early Iron Age existence, rejecting not just technology (an achievement in itself), but the entire Western cosmology. Everyone who met them commented on the purity of their beliefs. Despite their having lived for centuries among the Bantu, a race and a culture as addicted to violence and warfare as any on the planet, the pygmy language still didn't have a word for war, and violence was virtually unknown among them.

The Bushmen of the south are similarly pacifist. The popular explanation for the absence of the baser emotions like anger and jealousy in Bushman culture is that their existence is so precarious that no thought can be spared for killing or wounding each other. What, then, to make of the pygmies, who live in what is as close to Eden as any human society? The pygmies don't have to go for water—it falls on their heads each day. They don't have to farm—wild fruits and roots grow in fantastic abundance. They barely have to hunt—the game passes them by, if they wait long enough. Theirs is a pretty soft life. So how to explain their absence of rancour?

In any case, only their fierce adherence to their own ways has saved them from cultural extinction. As with the Bushmen, the greatest threat to their existence are the do-gooders who want to "empower" them, to enable them to develop. The pygmies know this: the gravest danger to their way of life, I was told more than once, is the school.

Clement and I had spent the morning on the Sanaga River, which curves away from the coast to the east. Just after dawn we had poled up a tributary. It was a typical jungle river. Lush vegetation overhung the banks on both sides, mangroves and swamp grasses grew elephant high, giant trees thrust up through the canopy on both sides, islands in the sky. The only sound was the harsh cry of a raptor and the swirling eddy of the paddles; it was easy to imagine the jungle as secretive, sinister, a hiding-place of cruelty. (Appearances were deceptive, though—not far from the riverbanks the jungle had been cleared for hectares of palm-oil plantations.)

On the Lobé, too, the river was silent for kilometres. Occasionally, pygmy families could be seen by the riverside, washing themselves or their children or their meagre stock of clothing. At a distance, it was impossible to tell how small they were. Their skin glinted in the river water, the colour of chocolate milk. There seemed to be dozens of children.

We banked our pirogue in a small cove. It looked like hundreds of others, a small clearing in the blank face of the jungle, but Clement said the pygmies he knew were close by. We slipped into the jungle. After a few metres we came to a dense thicket of bamboo. "Don't worry!" Clement yelled, as he plunged in. "It gets better." For a hundred metres or so, it didn't get better. It was a dense tangle of vines, ferns, bamboo, creepers, fallen trees, bushes. "When do we get to a path?" I yelled ahead. "This is the path," he yelled back. I could hear hacking sounds as he tore his way through. Farther in, the forest opened up, as the overhead canopy became more dense. It closed over us with an oddly familiar feel, like a Kew Gardens greenhouse—the same fetid humidity, the same thicket of ferns and bamboos, only much, much bigger. We walked for half a day after that and saw nothing but giant slugs and the odd centipede 50 centimetres (20 inches) long. Everything was oversized. There were flowers something like lilies, only immense, the size of a mature tree. Vines like trapezes. The smell of damp and decaying wood was overlaid with the acrid odour of termites, busy transforming cellulose back to earth.

Near noon Clement held up a hand and brought us to a halt. Silently, like a ghost from the distant past, a small figure glided out of the bush, intent on a spot about 20 metres (20 yards) from where we had stopped and, judging from the angle of his head and the tilt of the arrow already notched in his bowstring, a good deal over our heads. Here was truly an atavistic figure. Small, tense, naked, bow at the ready, the very picture of a deadly hunter. He looked as though he belonged here, which of course he did, by more generations than it was possible to count. The legends say they and their distant cousins, the Bushmen, were the First Men in Africa, and here it was easy to believe. He was small, but not tiny, wizened but muscular. Just then the pygmy hunter loosed his arrow, and it flew true: there was a solid thunk and a tough old porcupine fell to the earth.

"Hola!" said Clement approvingly.

The little hunter whirled around, quick as a crab on a beach, and backed into a thicket so that only his eyes and the tip of an arrow could be seen. He had already notched another arrow to his bow. God, he was fast! But if he was the hunter the pygmies were supposed to be, shouldn't he have heard us coming? I mean, we weren't exactly creeping. We were *trying* to be heard. For a long moment I suspected a put-up job, and looked over at Clement suspiciously. But he was motionless, staring at the pygmy, hands at his sides, palms up, empty. He had dropped his machete. The pygmy had, apparently, indeed heard nothing—we had come as an unpleasant surprise to him. I hoped he wasn't going to take it out on us in a fit of wounded pygmy pique, but he didn't. In some ways they are definitely more civilized than we are.

The jungle wasn't exactly trackless—it was full of game paths—only roadless. But for those who knew what to look for, the signs of human passing were there to be seen—blazes on bark, a banana tree stripped of its leaves, cut bamboo, old camp-fires. In a clearing kilometres from anywhere we heard the sound of machetes, and came across a small group of chattering pygmies cutting broad leaves. They looked like thatching leaves to me, but Clement said they were "for the dances." They were also cutting the lianas, those tough parasitic vines. He made his way along a network of game trails, at every fork and at regular intervals making a baboon-like barking sound, a deep sound that seemed to carry well under the canopy. (Later I was told that the sounds that carried best in the forest were the deep barking of the great apes and the treble of the human female. Women, therefore, yelled to orient themselves; men barked and boomed.) Periodically, the barking was answered.

We arrived at the pygmy encampment—five huts arranged in a semicircle around a clearing in which one large tree had been left standing, for shade. The huts were lean-tos made by driving bamboo poles into the ground, tying bamboo cross-pieces to them, and "thatching" with broad palm leaves. The thatch was rudimentary, but then they had no need to make it watertight—the rains were pleasant in the steamy air, and they had no possessions to be ruined. The beds, bamboo poles lashed together, and the bedding, freshly cut fronds, dried off quickly. The beds and sim-ilarly built benches were the only furniture. Inside one hut was the remains of a cook-ing fire. In another, two young men were asleep, one with his arm around a drum. The rest of the village was sitting on benches. One of the men was holding a small child with a puffy abscess on its knee. Most of the women sat in a row outside the largest of the buildings. One of them was nursing a baby. There were no old men in the village, and only one old woman, who looked a little crazy. Mangy dogs crawled and scratched and bit at themselves and barked. I was warned not to touch them. The people all wore hand-me-down Western clothes, well washed but tattered. They washed their clothes every second day, and put them on wet. The women wore volu-minous dresses, the men generally shorts without tops. Beach flip-flops, the more colourful the better, were the preferred footwear, though a few still wore the tradi-tional leather thongs.

Apart from the slit drums, there was no sign of crafts, in the sense of clothing or artefacts, but I supposed they could still do those things when called upon. Aside from their clothing I saw only one manufactured article in the village—a prized blue plas-tic bucket that doubled in emergencies as an extra drum. They obviously made their own bows and arrows and spears. The bows looked small and powerless, but since they used poison, a light puncture was enough to do the killing for them. They lived by hunting, foraging, and trapping—that evening we ate braised porcupine, sweet palm wine in gourds, and wild pineapples, an utterly delicious meal punctuated with pygmy singing and wild monkey cries from the canopy overhead. Plates were banana or other broad leaves, cooking utensils bamboo skewers. They hunted with snares, spears with 15-centimetre (6-inch) steel blades, honed to a fine edge, and the bows. I gingerly felt the tip of a spear, having asked whether it was poisoned, but they said no, only the arrows. They showed me the leaves from which the poison was made—it looked like ivy and oozed a black sap when crushed. They subsisted on porcupine, antelope, wild pig, various rodents, of which the hardest to take for the squeamish outsider was the common rat. Large centipedes made a delicious first course. Monkey was prized, possibly because it was so hard to catch. Generally they smoked the meat and kept it hanging in the camp. They also ate manioc and maize made into a paste and steamed in leaves, but these they had adapted from the Bantu, not being culti-vators themselves. They tended to harvest these things wherever they could and from whatever field they came across, but I found no one who minded this poaching. There weren't very many of them, and this wasn't hard-scrabble territory. The Bantu seemed to treat the pygmies rather as the Irish do the leprechauns—it was good luck to have a few around.

I was thirsty. I asked where they got water, and they looked at me as though I was crazy. Water? It rained every day! Later one of the pygmies showed me a trick. He snapped a vine—one that looked just like all the others—and a litre or more of fresh perfumed water cascaded out. Mostly, he said, they got their water from springs; I guessed these vines were the equivalent of roadside vending machines.

That night, after supper, I tried as politely as I could to answer their questions and to interrogate them in turn. How long had this little village existed? They were vague. Time-keeping wasn't on their skills list. "Since the old man died" seemed to be the marker, but no one could say "when" that was. They moved the village whenever someone died, they said. It was good insurance. The dead person's spirit may well be benign—but why take chances? Spirits, apparently, were stuck where they died. Moving was easy: you just picked up the kids and the drums and the weapons and off you went. Where to build a new village? Wherever you liked. Who was to stop you? Find a likely clearing, drop your bundles, cut a few poles—home! The world was full of stuff. Food was everywhere. I marvelled at the innocence of it.

Hunting was not always successful, and there were accidents occasionally, but game was plentiful. There was little to break, and therefore little to fix. Cooking and firewood-gathering took some time, but not much. I tried to work out a typical day, a typical workload. Compared with Western farmers, these guys had it easy. Three, four hours a day and you were done. You had brought home the bacon and it was time to relax. For the rest, it was gossip, storytelling, dancing, and music.

Music was not necessarily a night-time thing. The urge could come upon any of them at any time, a drum would sound, someone would take up the counterpoint with a voice, other drums would appear, and soon they were dancing. Music and movement seemed inseparable. The music was rhythmic and regular, but not simple, as complex and polyrhythmic as the Bushmen's. Other than the drum and the human voice, there was only one other instrument in the village, a one-stringed lyre that used the human voice-box as a resonator. I was told that in other villages other kinds of stringed instruments were occasionally heard, and hand-pianos. Elsewhere, too, they now occasionally build their houses in the Bantu way, with wattle and daub—much harder work, making for more permanent settlements, an erosion of their traditions.

What I could follow, through Clement, of the after-dinner conversation seemed to me to concern the universal human vanities, and a good deal of it was frankly low-grade gossip, along the lines of who had done what to whom, and who had it coming. The young men talked about women and hunting. What the women talked about among themselves they wouldn't say. And of course the men didn't know.

The rest of the conversation, though, was in some ways didactic. They discussed water sources, and likely thickets where game might be found. They discussed the various available remedies for the abscess, and for a sore tooth one of them had—illness and disease were grave matters. Indeed, these were all important community affairs—and the children were always there, listening and being instructed. Everything was made transparent to the children, including how they themselves were made and came into the world. I wondered if this didn't account for the famous mental health of the pygmies, and their friendliness and pacifistic nature.

I asked them about their history, but drew a blank—they hadn't a clue where they had come from, or when they had arrived in this country. Clearly they thought I was obsessed with this thing about time. As to the origin of the tribe, I got no further than who was married to whom. I had better luck with the origin of the species, at least in the sense that they understood the question. The answer was simple enough. Man had always existed; it was the world that was new. I tried to find out whether man and god (the spirits) were the same thing, but was instead treated to a disparaging lecture by Clement, my Fang translator, who thought the whole line of inquiry completely improper. So I tried a trick I had used successfully elsewhere, to get the old people to recite the lineages of the clan. But when no one could or would go beyond his own grandfather, I desisted. I thought the old woman, the mother of the lad who seemed to be headman of the village, was more interested in all this than the others were. But she said nothing, only fixing me with a stare so intense it burned. In fact, that stare made me very uneasy. I didn't want to make a crazy pygmy lady cross, not if I was spending a vulnerable night in the village. So I stopped, and listened to the singing and to Clement's occasional translations of the conversation.

Bands like this are scattered all through the jungles. This village was part of the Baka group that inhabited Cameroon, Equatorial Guinea, and parts of Gabon.

Many other bands live in the Central African Republic, and in the dense and relatively impenetrable jungles of Zaire and Congo. But their numbers are diminishing. Despite their millennia-long survival, their culture is fragile and almost certainly doomed.

The next morning I went hunting with two of the young men and their dogs. A hundred metres or so from camp they took diverging paths, entirely without explanation, not that I would have understood had one been offered, Clement having stayed in camp to have a leisurely smoke. I followed the one closest to me. For a while, they kept track of each other by their baboon-like barking. The dogs ranged on ahead, and I brought up the rear, comfortable in the knowledge that I was in competent hands. May the gods punish such confidence! An hour later, the dogs set up a howling, and my guy, whose barking companion had long since faded, pounced triumphantly on a hapless porcupine and killed it with a thrust into the brain through the eye. When he had fixed the animal on a carrying stick, we turned for home. He barked for his companion. There was silence. He barked again. Nothing. For several minutes this went on. He turned in all directions to issue his bark. I might have been imagining it, but the barks sounded to me more anxious than I thought they should. He stood for a moment, looking irresolute, then strode into the bush. I hurried after him. I thought it was altogether the wrong direction, but I was obliged to trust him. What did bother me was bumping into him coming back and hurrying off in quite another direction, apparently trackless. Great! I thought. I'm in the goddam jungle with the only pygmy in Africa who can get lost! I looked gloomily at the underbrush.

Of course, it was all a false alarm, a misunderstanding. After some minutes of this casting about, he swivelled on his heel and set off at a headlong pace, once more in what I was convinced was entirely the wrong direction. Within minutes we could hear the women chattering and had reached camp.

Part V

The Gulf of Guinea

THE RAIN FORESTS OF
CAMEROON

I sat for a while on the beach near Ouidah, in Togo, staring out into the Gulf of
Guinea, trying to fix the coast and its old kingdoms in my mind. Guinea *is a
version of the Berber* aguinaw, *or* aguignawa, *meaning black man, and that was
appropriate enough, for the Bantu had come down from their ancient heartland, somewhere in the south of Nigeria, and in the tropical forests and near the mangrove swamps
of the coast they had exploded into an astonishing diversity of cultures, rich in exotic
religions, fecund in the plastic arts, inventive in politics. And also restless, quarrelsome,
and aggressive, traits further selected for in the forcing-grounds of the slave trade. The
Ivory Coast was along there, to my right as I sat on the beach staring out to sea. The
Gold Coast too. The Slave Coast to my left, and right here where I sat. All three of these
commodities—ivory, gold, and slaves—brought traders: first the merchants of Old
Mali and their Berber cousins, then the Portuguese and the other Europeans.*

*The Guinea Coast of Africa stretches from—logically enough—Guinea and
Guinea Bissau in the northwest to Equatorial Guinea in the south. But we're defining
it a little differently, to better fit the ancient patterns—as the homelands of the old
kingdoms that arose in the Middle Ages, from Nigeria and Cameroon in the east, to
Sierra Leone in the west.*

*The places I wanted most to visit were the Yoruba city-states of Ife and Oyo, and the
powerful pagan kingdom of Benin, all three in Nigeria. In Benin itself and in Togo,
the important presence had been the aggressive, militaristic kingdom of Dahomey. In
Ghana, the Akan peoples had been dominated by the Ashanti in the interior, and by
the Fante and Akwamu on the coast. Beyond Ghana, there had been no kingdoms of
significance along the coast. The original culture of Sierra Leone, the richly artistic
Sapi, disappeared early, probably through Malian imperialism.*

*Most of these kingdoms were small and short-lived. This is not easy country in which
to organize an empire. The coast is swampy, with few natural harbours, separated from
the interior by a belt of muddy, mangrove-tangled creeks and lagoons, rank, fetid, and
home to countless noxious pests and ghastly diseases. João de Barros, an early Portuguese
explorer of the Guinea Coast, blamed God for placing apparently limitless wealth there,
and then guarding it "with a striking angel with a flaming sword of deadly fever who
prevents us from penetrating into the interior to reach the springs of the garden."*

The cities of West Africa are still rife with disease—almost everyone has some form of malaria. Too many of the countries are either dictatorships or ungovernable, even though the number is diminishing. The ridiculous colonial boundaries are still holding. They can't possibly last—nor should they. Nevertheless, cynicism and despair are themselves diseases. Think of the heroism of the Sierra Leonans, standing in line to vote, braving the beatings of army thugs. Think of the lively, quarrelsome Ghanaian press. Think of the way Benin shrugged off its dictator. Hope is in short supply, but there is still stock on the shelves.

I started this section of the coast, however, still in Cameroon, when Abel, a Bamiléké from Yaoundé, took me to the Korup National Forest Park on the Nigerian border to look for lowland gorillas.

We picked up a park guide in the village of Mundemba, close to the entrance, and in half an hour were in a "primary rain forest," deeper, older, and more exotic than the jungles through which the pygmies move so easily. It was steamy hot, and everything dripped with moisture. There were butterflies overhead as large as kites, cobalt, turquoise, scarlet, and garish green, dipping and swooping. A flock of bright-red parrots squawked past. Skimmers patrolled the streams, greedy red beaks open. More butterflies, the size of umbrellas. Overhead a troop of screeching monkeys flashed by, so far up that they were entirely hidden in the canopy; only the movement of vines could be seen, jerking against the boles. The vines were roots up, fronds down, sucking their nourishment from somewhere up high, hanging down like drunken sloths. About 9 metres (30 feet) overhead they were choked into a thick mat of vegetation, debris, muck—it was like looking at the earth from a root's view, where the worms and the creeping things are. The forest floor itself was relatively clear and easily traversable, but still thick with underbrush and loud with the buzzing, hissing, and crackling of fecund life that crept and crawled and stung. I wore thick socks, but the ants stung anyway—you don't dare sit down, you'd be swarmed in seconds. Huge black ants eat the living trees, and every now and then there was a massive crashing in the forest. The red driver ants we used to call "army ants" in South Africa were constantly on the move, choking the pathways, such as they are. There are pygmies who seem to share their villages with these predators and never get bitten.

Deep in the forest we crossed a wildly swaying rope bridge our guide said was "very secure," but he panicked halfway across, which was not at all reassuring. The bridge was 120 metres (130 yards) long and crossed the evil-looking Mana River, riven with black rocks that looked depressingly sharp. It was okay if you fell in, I was told. Nothing bad lived in that stream. Nothing except bilharzia, hookworm, leeches, and a particularly virulent black fly that causes liparia disease, whatever that is. The bridge consisted of three sets of twisted vines, one for the feet and one for each hand.

Some of the trees were immense. Hollow one out and you could easily park a compact car in there, with room left over for a baby-carriage, a mower, and a dog-house. They towered overhead, creeping with parasite vines, stretching through the junk of the underlayer—ur-trees, as they were at the Beginning.

In fact, this may well be true—this may be the oldest forest on earth, having mysteriously missed all the ice ages and extinctions. It has existed here, in much the same form, for 65 million years. Of course, before we get too reverent about this, so has the mosquito. Still, there is no doubt that it would be in the planet's interest to somehow preserve this marvellous relic, but it didn't look hopeful—the previous day we had seen immense trucks heading up the highway to Douala, each one hauling a gigantic log.

Korup Forest, designated a National Park of Cameroon in 1986, is contiguous with the Nigerian Cross River National Park, and thus protects a significant portion of West African rain forest. Because it is so ancient, it has a huge diversity of plant and animal species—almost a quarter of every living thing in Africa exists in this small place, more than 400 species of trees and as many birds. So far they have counted 190 species of reptiles and amphibians, as well as many of the larger mammals—elephant, leopard, buffalo, sitatunga (spiral-horned antelope), drill, and chimpanzee.

Alas, I saw no more gorillas than I'd seen in Gabon, but my guide did point out fresh knuckle prints pressed into the mud, as clear as fingerprints. We heard a troop browsing a short distance away, but the underbrush was too dense and we saw nothing. Nevertheless, it was a thrill. The great apes still walk here, in these days of their perilous dispersal, and that counted for something.

At a roadside stall outside Mundemba, near Korup, vendors were selling pins made of exotic tropical butterflies, in all their improbable colours and patterns. I bought one, in a deep indigo, colour of the midnight sky, but it shattered before I could get it home. The sale of butterflies is the brainchild of the Korup Forest Project, which is always casting about for ways to involve the local population in conservation. The idea was that, if local villagers could be persuaded to breed exotic butterflies for export to collectors and scientists worldwide, they would develop an appreciation for wildlife and an intention to keep breeding populations active. It's the same approach as the Crossfire Program in Zimbabwe.

Later, in Mundemba itself, we were sitting outdoors in the dusk when hundreds of kites descended, whistling their harsh but melancholy cries; they wheeled overhead for a while, then settled into a giant tree near the park entrance. There were so many that the sultry air was disturbed 40 metres (45 yards) away, and the sound of their wings was like a rushing waterfall.

In the south of Cameroon, along the coast, I picked up a hitchhiker at a police road-block. His car was *en panne*, and he needed a lift back to Campo, near the Equatorial Guinea border. I was never absolutely sure that he wasn't a police stooge, particu-larly since he soon steered the conversation around to politics. He was, as he put it, *anglophone*, and within two minutes had launched into a separatist riff. The English Cameroonians were being deprived of their civil rights. They were a despised minor-ity in their own country. The unified government had no place for them at the cab-inet table. The new constitution wouldn't help, cobbled together as promised after riots in the Bamenda area by disgruntled anglophones a few years earlier. The Western Cameroonians, who had been British once, had been bamboozled into join-ing with French Cameroon. They had thought it would be a loose federation; instead, the country was dominated by French-speaking Muslims from the North, and ... He rattled on.

"Perhaps," he said hopefully, "joining the British Commonwealth will help. You know Cameroon just joined? Do you think this will help?"

I said I doubted it. Canada, the other country in the Commonwealth with a bilin-gualism problem, was too busy assuring its own francophones of their rights and hoping separatism would go away to be of any help. My hitchhiker, it turned out, desperately hoped Quebec would secede peacefully from Canada, thereby giving the two western anglophone provinces of Cameroon an opening.

"Even though you'd be like Pakistan, a country severed in the middle? Why not join Nigeria instead?"

"Never! You see what those people are like, what's going on there ..." He was referring to the then-current military crackdown in the Nigerian hinterlands. Ever cautious about what part of this conversation might get back to the authorities, who were wildly unkeen on separatists, I promised to tell people in Canada about the notion of Anglo-Cameroonian independence. This seemed to satisfy him. It also seemed to me a fragile political hope.

I was fascinated that, in a country with 247 dialects, identity was derived from a colonial linguistic heritage. French-speaking Bamiléké were oppressing (at least in the view of the English-speaking Bamiléké) their own people. In Cameroon, perhaps uniquely in Africa outside South Africa, language easily transcends tribe, clan, or ide-ology as a political force.

Later, I spent a morning with the hitchhiker's family in a small village, tradi-tionally built of mud and wattle, most of the houses with corrugated-iron roofs, many with gardens. There was a public school, and two churches. The school bell was recycled auto-wheel rims suspended from a chain. Everyone, I saw, was poor, but no one was destitute. (This was true of much of the country. There are no beggars in southern Cameroon.) We ate stewed goat and drank Guinness, and talked, in a mixture of French and English. In the afternoon I had a toothache, and the family took me to the village's "traditional" doctor, a dispenser of herbs and local pharmaceuticals, a creature different from a witch-doctor or sorcerer. He gave me a leaf to chew, which stopped the gum bleeding and muted the pain. I asked him what it was, and he laboriously translated it as "toothache leaf," which wasn't really helpful.

Cameroon is, unusually for Africa, a net exporter of food. It has oil—you can see the oil derricks offshore from the resort beaches around Kribi; and, on many roadsides, vendors sell *essence* from rusty barrels and plastic containers. Many Cameroonians scorn the lower-octane fuels at the pumps, because petrol is very cheap, a few cents a litre. The country has mineral wealth. It has great forests. It has one of the safest deep-water ports in Africa, on the Wouri River in Douala. It has a stable government. Why, then, do virtually all Cameroonians assume the country is a mess, and are they gloomily happy to talk to strangers about it? Why does the Cameroonian oil company actually manage to lose money? Despite the low worldwide oil prices, no one I talked to attributed it to business, only to politics.

Every second Cameroonian moaned about "our constitutional problems." Everyone mentioned the "economic crisis," but no one would say what causes it— people talked of politics, but never of the president, Paul Biya, another African ruler with billions in Swiss banks.

Biya certainly has something to do with the mess. But Cameroon's colonial history didn't help.

One of the Douala chiefs had signed a commercial treaty with the English in the middle of the nineteenth century and, seeing which way the colonial wind was blowing, sent an urgent missive to the queen, inviting a British protectorate. The British ignored the letter, and the Germans got there first; the explorer Gustav Nachtigal initialled a treaty with the Douala in 1884.

Signs of the German occupation are still found everywhere in Cameroon. They built railways and wharves, imported pineapples and mangoes, and set up massive plantations of palm oil and rubber. But their rule was harsh: the annual death rate at some of their enterprises was as high as 20 per cent. Still, the modern Cameroonians remember them fondly. See a bridge over some jungle river—"Oh, the Germans built that." Rattle along on the Douala–Bamenda narrow-gauge railway—"Oh, the Germans built that." Stop to pick bananas at a plantation—"Oh, the Germans planted those." But after the First World War, the League of Nations gave most of Cameroon to the French and two non-contiguous segments to the English, thereby carelessly dividing one country into three. The British ran their sections as part of Nigeria, paying them scant attention.

In the fifties, two independence movements arose, one supported by Christian southerners, mostly the wealthy Bamiléké, and the other supported by the Muslim

North. The northerners, under Ahmadou Ahidjo, won the first post-independence election in 1960, which set off a rebellion in the anglophone and Christian West, around Bafoussam. It was ruthlessly put down by Ahidjo, who borrowed French troops to do so. It took nearly a year. Tens of thousands were killed. A year later the two parts of British Cameroon held a referendum. The northernmost segment voted to join Nigeria, which they did; the southerly segment voted to join what they thought would be a loose federation with French Cameroon. In 1972 this loose federation merged into a unitary state. There was no further rebellion. But the grumbling didn't cease.

Ahidjo was an interesting figure. Ruthless, secretive, and arrogant, he tolerated no dissent, and at one point had 25,000 political prisoners in jail—the population was only 6 million. Nevertheless, in other ways he governed relatively well, and his economic policies helped the country to prosper. He managed to avoid the excessive borrowing and massive "prestige" projects so beloved of other African leaders. Instead, he concentrated on education, roads, health care, and farming. In 1982, satisfied with his work, he abruptly resigned, and picked Paul Biya as his successor.

Bad move. Biya was to be no one's protégé. Within weeks he was moving against Ahidjo loyalists. A year later the former strongman, no doubt regretting his hasty departure, attempted a coup. It failed, and he was driven into exile and sentenced to death *in absentia*. Biya has been president ever since.

In the early 1990s the infection of democratic thought that had taken hold elsewhere in Central Africa, most notably the Congo, spread to Cameroon. Biya suppressed the first attempt at multiparty politics by refusing to call new elections. In retaliation, the Cameroonian people launched a massive campaign of civil disobedience. Bafoussam began it. The whole town went on strike, and their strategy, to create so-called *villes mortes* by forcing the population, under threat, to stay home, was widely copied in western Cameroon. Finally, in 1992, Biya had no choice but to call for multiparty elections. The opposition won, despite heavy-handed pressure from government goons, and Simon Achidi Achue formed an anti-Biya coalition government.

That, in early 1997, was where it remained: legislature and president at loggerheads, the president still diligently looting the treasury, the economy slowly sinking, the crime rate rising, the population sardonic and angry. French sources have estimated Biya's fortune at more than $5 billion, a substantial percentage of the national debt—perhaps only Mobutu has done better for himself.

If Biya were to vanish, and the democracy movement to take hold, Cameroon could yet be a model for Africa.

I put this (carefully phrased, just in case he was a "political") to my hitchhiker before I took my leave. He didn't want to talk about Biya. Finally he said this: "If. A very heavy word, the biggest word of all. We have learned never to trust this word, if."

....

Douala, the most industrialized city in Cameroon, has been described as the armpit of Africa, but I felt comfortable there anyway.

Like the other cities of Cameroon—indeed, like so many cities in Africa—Douala is, on the surface, heart-breakingly dismal, with overcrowded slums and disgusting refuse dumps along the roadways. Car wrecks are abandoned on the sidewalks. The markets themselves are dusty, dirty. Merchandise is spread out higgledy-piggledy. Walls are cracking, tiles peeling off, buildings never finished, autos and buses belching noxious fumes, everything a hateful mess.

Much has been written about these great slums of West Africa, which only grow worse as the cash economy drives millions of peasants into the ever-expanding cities, spreading far faster than the capability of governments to service them, with the inevitable result of poverty, disease, and escalating violence as the people turn to crime to make their way in the modern world. I'd seen many of these cities myself, and agreed they were ghastly, but found it hard to share the almost pornographic eagerness for apocalypse expressed by some of the outside observers. There is nothing here that good government and a little money can't fix (as Accra has proved); and there is a fierce desire for betterment almost universal among ordinary people.

Douala might be an armpit, and armed robbery might be endemic outside the tourist hotels and banks and embassies, but if you take the trouble to plunge into the markets, the people are friendly, concerned for the welfare of tourists, and sardonic about their own shortcomings. Sure, Douala's slums are ghastly. But one afternoon I stopped at a roadside stall to buy a few music cassettes and, when I asked a few passers-by for their recommendations of the best in Cameroonian pop, set off a happy riot. They drew in more passers-by, who drew in their friends, who drew in nearby shopkeepers, until the road was jammed with people, all wanting to give me advice. It was friendly, but by the time I escaped with a couple of cassettes, there were more than a hundred people arguing in the streets, and it could easily have gotten out of hand had the cops not arrived to break it up. I left with recordings by Manu Dibango, Sam Fan Thomas, Moni Bile, Toto Guillaume, and Francis Bebey. Cameroonians regard Cameroonian music as being the best in Africa, with some justification, since it's a more complex amalgam of traditional Western pop and jazz rhythms than the much more widely played music of Zaire; Doualan nightclubs (which is where groups like the internationally known Les Têtes Brûlées got their start) are famous throughout the continent. Besides, I like puns, and the Doubloons are inordinately fond of them, using a witty French whenever they can (I had some cleaning done at Le Pressing Savoir Fer, and did some shopping at Afritude).

I was also predisposed to like Douala because a Cameroonian diplomat at the embassy where I got my visa invited me to call him when I arrived in Douala. He gave me his mother's telephone number, which I thought was well beyond the call of diplomatic duty.

Of course, I called, and his mother immediately took me to see the fetishes for sale in the Douala market. She was impatient at first, because the vendors wanted to show me only the tourist stuff, second-grade fetishes empty of meaning, like the "Fang" and "Luba" masks sold all over Central Africa.

I'd had a conversation the previous night with the diplomat about African art, wondering where it had gone, this wonderfully fecund sculpture of the Cameroon. The carved doorways of the Bamum were highly sought after by collectors; elsewhere in the country, and in Gabon, there had been produced, in centuries past, sculpture at a level of abstraction not seen until hundreds of years later, when the European Cubists mimicked their technique.

At first, he was defensive. "Have you ever been in Tokyo?" he asked. "It's a city of impermanence; there is nothing there but neon and business and grey concrete and high prices—where are the Zen masters? It is a question of the worldwide barrenness of modern art." For my part, I thought of the soullessness of North American tract housing, every bit as dismal as the buildings of modern Africa—richer, yes, but no more soulful—and of the degeneration of Western art from creativity into sensation, from evocation into the desire to shock. "Most sculpture done in our country now is poor stuff," he admitted. "I won't blame it on missionaries, that's too easy and too long ago. But I do blame it on Christianity, which emptied our sculpture of its meaning." He explained that the great artists of earlier times believed they were connecting the living with the endless chain of the dead, which was a task worthy of reverence. "The Christians don't allow this. They have only one gateway to the dead. Only one voice speaks for the dead. It is a culture that disapproves of creativity." I thought of the great *pietàs* of the Renaissance, but said nothing; it was certainly true that they were executed within the tight conventions of their form—no Cubist experiments there! He went on: "In the old days a sculpture was more than art, it was a way of reaching the forces that governed the universe—no wonder the people took it seriously. But in modern times a carved head is just a head, great man though the model may have been, and it no longer has any great meaning, or any meaning at all. That's modern life: people don't really believe it has any meaning. And so art just becomes politics, like in the West, or, at best, a commodity to be bought and sold."

That was certainly true of the "above table" fetishes on sale at the Douala market. But hidden in tin boxes and old sacks was another kind of fetish: those that have, or have had, or will have, a meaning that altogether evades the Christians, no matter how well intentioned. This is a meaning that connects its user to all the tribe who have gone before, and to the lesser spirits among whom they dwell. This isn't to say that these connections are always benign. They are in fact as diverse as human motivation. That was another thing the diplomat had to say about the Christians, that they are "a one-stringed lyre. They pretend humankind and its god are suffused with love. They have forgotten the dark impulses." Again I said nothing. It seemed to me humankind had enough dark impulses without having to invoke the supernatural. But it didn't seem the occasion for extended theological discussion, so I forbore (and in any case the Christian God, so pitiless in his wrath, had always seemed to me dark enough).

After poking about for some time, the diplomat's mother hauled up from under a table a small, rank, grubby statuette crudely carved and wrapped in dusty sacking. A hole bored into its stomach was filled with some noisome paste. It was, she assured me, made from snake's liver and the blood of a goat, and I certainly wasn't going to dispute it. Its purposes were many, she said, but they weren't evil, unless it was evil to harm an enemy. In other parts of Africa, I said, I had found people reluctant to talk about fetishes, particularly the noxious ones, to outsiders. She was contemptuous. "It's part of what we are," she said.

THE LITTLE KINGDOMS

T*he highlands of Cameroon had been on the fringes of empire. Before I returned to the coast, I'd go north for a bit. I wanted to see little kingdoms like the Bamum's, now in the nineteenth generation of the present lineage, a succession unbroken since 1398. Without colonialism this little kingdom would have been absorbed by others, or through wars and alliances absorbed others in its turn, perhaps to disappear at last in some grander alliance.*

Somewhere between Douala and Bamenda, in the central highlands, I stopped for a meal at a roadside place with an irresistible name, the Bar St. Narcise. I ate game stew in a lusty chili sauce, and baton de manioc, *along with the inevitable Guinness. Manioc is steamed in huge leaves; you unwrap it as you eat. The baton looks rather like a corn cob without the kernels, and tastes bland, like unsalted rice, with the texture of boiled potato. The meal was served by a very tall, striking young woman in a gendarme's cap, with big doe eyes and strong body odour.*

Afterwards the men in the bar fell to talking. Mostly it had to do with men and women and their places in the universe, and why polygamy is a natural African thing. Unsurprisingly, woman's role was to fetch and carry. There was a considerable body of opinion among these male barflies that a man's lot is much more stressful than a woman's, and that's why he deserves the recompense of as many wives as possible, and why they should serve him as best they can without complaining.

The young woman looked wrathful. No one noticed.

The countryside changes rapidly as you recede from the rain forests along the coast. It becomes hilly, with large plantations of bananas and pawpaws. As the road ascends, the air begins to cool off and becomes much less humid, rather like California only with more rain. That's where the coffee is grown. South of Bafoussam, every house had a fruit stall piled high with mangoes, pineapples, guavas, avocados, sugar cane, bananas, and roots of all kinds. At Bafoussam the land begins to flatten out into plains. Cattle started to appear for the first time, and became more common as we moved northwards. By Foumban the countryside is still very fertile, but very dry, and begins to resemble the Africa I know best, the Africa of the savannah. Every little house had a banana grove, and many a coffee tree or two.

The landscape is stunningly beautiful. The road runs along the Côte Batié, high on a ridge between two verdant valleys. The traditional Bamiléké architecture is distinctive, with sharply conical roofs in thatch; the new bourgeoisie are all building themselves villas in the high hills, roofed with aluminium, and the effect is unexpectedly alluring, green valleys lit up by flashes of silver.

On the way to Foumban I photographed the Bamiléké chief's compound at Bandjoun, a wonderful and harmonious collection of traditional buildings, with intricately carved doorways and patterned bamboo ceilings, massive and impressive, as befits a wealthy monarch. My guide was an old man who had helped reconstruct the buildings in the sixties (the ceilings were his work, and I made sure to photograph those). Nearby stood a small museum in which they have preserved the thrones of all the fourteen Fons (chiefs) in the lineage. The current Fon's throne is covered entirely in cowry shells. He is Ngnie Kamga, and has eleven wives, but so far only

---

Most of the Central African governments have launched a campaign to increase national food supplies and food self-sufficiency. One of the efforts, in Cameroon, is the encouragement of "mini livestock," designed, among other things, to bring productive agriculture into the cities. Suggested species: snails ("very economical in space, and as nutritious as chicken"); the grass-cutter or cane-cutter rat; the Gambian or giant rat; ground squirrel; hedgehog; porcupine; guinea pigs; frogs; worms; termites and maggots (these latter for animal feed).

La Voix du Paysan interviewed one young farmer, Valentine Munga Suh. He was rearing rat moles and guinea pigs:

"Are you aware that some people also rear worms, frogs, etc.?"

"I know only of ants, which some people rear around our area here."

"Why do they rear them?"

"Well, they say they rear them for some whites, who always come to buy."

22 children, pretty pathetic next to his predecessor's 250. I asked at the museum when the Bamiléké had arrived in the area, and from where, but they didn't know. In Bamiléké society, history is a matter for the secret societies and the king, not for ordinary people. Their origin, I was told, lay 100 kilometres (60 miles) to the north, which would put them in the middle of Bamum territory, so that was almost certainly wrong—unless the Bamum were newcomers, which they weren't.

Foumban, an hour or so north of Bafoussam, is the seat of the Bamum dynasty, one of the few kingdoms left over in Old Africa from pre-colonial times. Until recently the kingdom was governed as it always had been, by the sultan and his council, who made wars and alliances and kept their little kingdom going long after the great empires had collapsed in the face of European attrition. Until 1917, when it was pulled down, the sultan's palace was one of the grandest buildings in the traditional African style on the continent; there are still faded photographs of the sultan of the time, the great Ibrahim Njoya, receiving a delegation of German diplomats, seated on his throne in front of the palace façade. It's fully 200 metres (220 yards) wide, lined with carved pillars that told the history of the Bamum in pictographs; the doorways were guarded by elephant tusks; the doorways themselves were large enough for an elephant, fully tusked, to stroll through without hindrance. Alas, in 1917 Njoya, envious of the German governor's residence, tore it down and built the current palace, a bizarre copy in brick of a Renaissance château. It is less alien than I had at first feared, and has an impressive "baronial" hall on the first floor and a pleasing museum on the second. Nevertheless, Italian Renaissance may suit the sultan, but the old palace, with its thatched roofline and carved pillars, would have been a touch more . . . authentic.

Njoya, the sixteenth sultan in line, is widely regarded as the greatest of the Bamum kings. Njoya created, among other things, his own alphabet, still taught to the kids here in the equivalent of Sunday school. He started his own syncretic religion, a blend of Islam, Christianity, and native beliefs, which is also drummed into the present generation, but has hardly caught fire. He also wrote a history of the Bamum people.

I arrived at Foumban just as Ramadan was ending. The timing couldn't have been better, for, as I pulled up, the present sultan, Ibrahim Mbombo Njoya, the nineteenth in line, was just emerging for a celebratory march to the throne of his palace, set up in the doorway to the courtyard under a large umbrella. He was accompanied by his *griots* and court musicians. Once he was ensconced on his throne, the notables of the kingdom went up, doffed their caps, and paid their respects on bended knee. The sultan, spotting me lurking in a corner with my camera, encouraged me to do the same, and I did, taking off my cap and creaking down on one knee, to great cheers from the crowd—I was the only non-Bamum in town that day.

After the ceremonial was over, the crowd drifted across the square to the market, and I followed. At one end of the market square stood the palace, and at the other an imposing mosque. The food market was to the left, the medicinal market to the right.

Also on the right is Njoya's original hanging tree—apparently he disapproved of jails, so he either freed criminals or hanged them. Next to the hanging tree is a small building containing a very old throne and the royal war drum, a massive thing, about 4 metres (13 feet) long, made from a single forest giant. It was sounded only when summoning people to war, its voice supposedly carrying 60 kilometres (35 miles).

Later, in a vacant lot, horse-races were held, some of the horses draped with what looked like medieval quilting. There was racing, jousting, music making, lots of spontaneous partying and dancing, demonstrations, kids' races, a whole festival. Vendors of food were everywhere. Many of the men were armed with venerable (but well-maintained) carbines. The police were conspicuous by their absence, as was any government presence.

IFE, OYO, AND BENIN

At Foumban I turned back to the coast. North of Foumban, the countryside and the people are more attuned to the old kingdoms of the Sahel, the arid plains fringing the Sahara, than they are to the tropical forests of the Gulf of Guinea. Instead of going there now, I'd visit when I dealt with the Sahelian Empire of antiquity (Old Ghana, Mali, Songhai, Kanem-Bornu, and the Hausa), in the modern countries of Chad, Niger, Mali, and Mauritania. So I headed towards Nigeria.

I hadn't much looked forward to going to southern Nigeria, and especially dreaded Lagos, which I knew was another world from the more orderly Islamic Hausa homeland to the north, but I particularly wanted to see Old Benin, home to some of the greatest art ever produced on the continent. Then, just as I was to leave Douala, the Nigerians cancelled my visa anyway—the Canadians were threatening economic sanctions after the execution of a dissident leader, and the Nigerian military dictators retaliated by cutting off traffic between the two countries. Then, in another reversal of fate, my Air Afrique flight to Ghana, for some reason never explained, landed instead in Lagos. The plane was promptly impounded, again for reasons never explained (except for rumours of a mysterious "criminal conspiracy." Probably someone hadn't paid enough squeeze. In the end, the authorities contented themselves with stealing a container of luggage). So there I was. In the end, no one seemed to care.

Lagos contains almost ten million people, and the population will double within ten years. Half of all residents are under sixteen. There are no jobs. It's said to be the most violent city in Africa (residents band together for defence, taking turns mounting armed guard on their homes). It is more dangerous by far than chaotic Kinshasa. The police are thugs. Most taxi drivers seem to be robbers. It is, for the most part, a huge, sprawling, stinking, unsanitary slum, with pockets of exceptional affluence.

The Nok were the first people of Nigeria to leave traces of their passing, but still almost nothing is known of them except that they worked iron sometime in the first century B.C., and that they left behind large numbers of enigmatic terracotta heads. They were followed by the quarrelsome Yoruba kingdoms of Ife and its successor Oyo, and by the Empire of Benin, whose rise was contemporaneous with Great Zimbabwe, around 1400.

Ife, or more properly Ile-Ife, as far as anyone knows, was the first of the medieval Yoruba cities. In Yoruba legend it is sacred as the place where the world—and humanity—were created, *where the gods climbed down from heaven*, and where some of the great works of African sculpture have been found.

Ife was a going concern at least by the eleventh century, when they were already casting sophisticated bronzes in the region; it seems also to have been a centre of cultural ferment—they were said to worship 401 gods in Ife. Still, the origins are obscure: Oranmiyan is the legendary founder of the Yoruba peoples, and therefore of Ife and Oyo, but he didn't live until the fourteenth century, and was just as responsible for the founding of the rival city and empire-to-be of Benin as he was of the Yoruba kingdoms. There is an accompanying legend: an Ife artist is said to have taught bronze casting to the Edo of Benin, and soon thereafter Ife bronze art lost its vigour.[1] An alternative legend is that Ife bronze casting was stopped by a king irritated at the veneration given the life-size bronze statue of his predecessor.

Whatever the truth, there is nothing much left of Ife. It has become a modern African town, home to one of the largest and most energetic universities in Nigeria, but otherwise a place of few distinctions—there is a museum, poorly run, and, for those who are interested in these things, Oranmiyan's Staff, a massive monolith in stone spiked with iron and carved by unknown artisans. Although archaeological digs have been conducted in the area for several decades, little has been published. Where the present city peters out—just beyond the ancient city walls (of which only traces remain)—substantial compounds were built in the thirteenth century, and archaeologists have patiently picked out their outlines. "They're all precisely oriented north and south, the walls and columns decorated with mosaics of pottery discs and paved in geometric patterns which draw attention to semi-circular altars and the neck of a pot buried in the centre of the yard. An art historian has been able to interpret the altars as Yoruba *ijoko orisa*, the god's seat, and the central pot as *ojubu*, the face of worship. The sculpted reliefs on at least one of these pots can be shown to illustrate the apparatus and insignia of extant Yoruba secret societies ... once concerned with law and order and with executions ... Outside the compounds, a small wooden shrine once contained dismembered human heads mixed with sculpted heads broken from their bodies and depicting men deformed and distorted."[2]

Oyo eventually succeeded Ife as the centre of Yoruba life. It was founded at about the same time as Benin, around 1400, reputedly by a great Yoruba ancestor and hero, Oduduwa, whose son became the first significant ruler of Oyo.

....

Oyo is today a small town, dusty and impoverished, with an unimpressive market and an equally unimpressive Alafin of Oyo's Palace. There are generally old men lounging outside, who, if encouraged, will give a performance on the "talking drums," along with as much of an explanation of the vocabulary and syntax of the drumming "language" as you have the time for. But at its height, which was around 1650 to 1750, Oyo controlled much of the territory between the Niger and the Volta, all the way to modern Ghana; it succeeded, at least according to old Oyo traditions, because of its favourable trading position, its natural resources, and—they insist on pointing out—the industry of its inhabitants. At some point the Yoruba kings made a significant political change: they did away with the ancient kinship links and replaced them with a mercantile system in which freemen and slaves were bound together by common economic interests into "corporations" headed by the leading merchants.

Oyo's kings had a reputation for being formidable leaders with a talent for manipulative politics. Perhaps such a talent was necessary, for, as tradition had it, they were isolated figures whose influence was shadowy and secretive. Part of the coronation ritual was for the king to eat the heart of his predecessor, being thereby transformed into a deity, the very personification of his ancestors. After that, like the Vili kings of Loango, he retired from public view, appearing in public only on ritual occasions, three times a year, and always heavily veiled—it would not do for the ordinary populace to look on the Son of Heaven. He used slave eunuchs to represent him in ordinary governance, and spent most of the rest of his time playing one group of hereditary chiefs off against another and trying to avoid the great personal danger that would ensue if both groups were to unite against him.

Occasionally, this happened. In the 1750s the town chiefs who commanded the kingdom's by then formidable army, converted the kings into puppets, but in 1774 they made a mistake, giving the throne to Abiodun, who brought in rival provincial forces to re-establish royal authority over the capital. When the town chiefs rose in rebellion, the northern provinces called in Fulani troops from the Hausa kingdoms. As a consequence, the kingdom lost control over its northern trade routes, on which the provinces had depended for their supplies of horses and slaves. In 1836 they had to evacuate their capital to the south, by which time there was no central authority at all, and grasping provincial barons were everywhere competing for personal commercial empires.[3]

Oyo's rival kingdom to the west, Benin, owes a good deal to the Yoruba states, even its founder, as we have seen. But not everything.

Eweka, the first Oba, or king, of Benin, built his palace in 1350, and for a hundred years the kingdom slumbered. When it wakened, it did so abruptly, for in 1440 a king called Ewuare the Great came to power, reigning for the next forty years.

During this time he completely rebuilt the city, conquered most of his neighbours, and, between these bouts of empire-building, spent his time exploring—he was said to have travelled down the coast as far as the Congo. His successor, Ozolua, extended the state's boundaries even more, trespassing on Oyo territory, and is remembered in the legends as Ozolua the Conqueror. It was Ozolua who welcomed the first Portuguese explorers—he was the first king in sub-Saharan Africa to exchange ambassadors with a European power.[4]

The Portuguese, as they would try to do farther south, in Kongo, hoped to control the trade in the Bight of Benin by converting the kingdom to Christianity. But the Benin monarchs would have none of it, and they were powerful enough to reject every overture (even those backed up by regiments of arquebuses). Around 1520 the Portuguese were pushed out of Benin altogether, and were forced to conduct what trade they could from São Tomé.

Ewuare's capital was no savage village in the equatorial jungle. Between 1490 and 1590 the arts flowered, and the monarchs of Benin commissioned hundreds of copper and bronze sculptures. A seventeenth-century European report described it thus: "The king's court is square, and stands at the right hand side when entering the town by the gate of Gotton [Ughoton] and is certainly as large as the town of Haarlem, and entirely surrounded by a special wall. It is divided into many magnificent palaces, houses and apartments of the courtiers, and comprises beautiful and long square galleries, about as large as the exchange in Amsterdam, but one larger than another, resting on wooden pillars, from top to bottom covered with cast copper, on which are engraved the pictures of their war exploits and battles, and are kept very clean. Most palaces and the houses of the king are covered with palm leaves instead of square pieces of wood, and every roof is decorated with a small turret ending in a point, on which birds are standing, birds cast in copper with outspread wings, cleverly made after living models."[5] The royal court took up almost a fifth of the city; artists belonged to the king, did their work on commission, and their work became royal property. Much of it was magnificent. The Obas (kings) wore extravagant amounts of ivory; vassal chiefs were decked out in kilos of bronze.

Benin bronzes were the first of the African arts to win widespread acceptance in Europe, and Benin's artists produced carved ivories for the European market.

The kingdom remained powerful, the Oba controlling trade from his palace, the chiefs becoming wealthy through slaves and ivory. There was warfare with Dahomey, to the west, and for periods of time Benin controlled Dahoman territory. And so it went, until the British put a stop to the slave trade, after which both kingdoms declined, their main source of wealth taken from them.

The grand palace of the Benin kings has gone now, burned to the ground by the British amidst mutual accusations of savagery, and never rebuilt. Its end was a pathetic example of colonial misapprehension and confusion. A British expeditionary force moved into Benin territory in 1897, bent on conquest. The Benin kings, naturally, prepared for the invasion by sharpening their weapons, but also by invoking the proper rituals—which in their case, at that time, involved human sacrifices to the gods. The British, entering the courtyard and finding a row of decapitated corpses, burned the place to the ground in an orgy of righteous indignation. But not before they had looted more than two thousand magnificent bronzes and packed them off to Europe, where they made their way into museums and private collections, to the great profit of the conquerors.

Today, there is very little sign that Benin ever existed. The town is sprawling, dusty, utterly unmemorable. Benin now lives only in memory and in the inventories of European museums.

....

At the height of the slave trade, life on the coast was even more chaotic and violent than it is now. This is not exactly surprising: nearly half the total number of slaves exported from Africa came from the Niger delta. Every traveller who passed through in the eighteenth and early nineteenth centuries commented on the restless anger of the coastal tribes, and how their way of life had been fatally disrupted, bringing polit ical chaos in disruption's train. In 1830 the British traveller Richard Lander watched while two women had their throats cut in his sight—no one else paid much atten tion. Suspicious of British attempts at the time to shut down the trade, the local chiefs reacted to his presence by accusing him of spying. He was marched before the king and forced to drink a quart of some noxious liquid he was assured would kill him. According to his own account, he swallowed the lot and, before an astonished throng, marched out and back to the privacy of his hut, where he took a powerful emetic that emptied his stomach. This did his popularity no end of good, and though the slavers made no secret of their continued hatred, the now-friendly king let him go, warning him not to travel unarmed.[6]

Sometime later he was heading down the Niger, and arrived at the town of Badagri. "[It] was as beastly [a place] as ever ..." and he got away just in time to avoid watching the sacrifice of three hundred men and women that the king, with some relish, was planning. There was a confusing variety of peoples, he reported, most of them on bad terms with their neighbours and not interested in the river beyond their particular stretch. In the delta, his party was attacked by Ibo river pirates, their possessions plundered, and they were captured, in effect enslaved. They were extricated from their predicament by a minor chieftain who ransomed them from the king and transported them down river, where he hoped to make a reasonable profit by turning them over to an English ship anchored there.[7]

Nigeria's already fractious politics were polluted by slavery and the uncaring rule of the colonists, and have yet to recover. The evil effects of slavery are the easiest to track, governed, as the trade was, by fear and driven by greed—only the venal and the corrupt escaped and prospered. The effects of colonialism are harder to see, but from the perspective of a hundred years the outlines can be made out. On the economy: the colonists destroyed subsistence farming by substituting cash and commodity crops for small-scale husbandry; they destroyed industry by expropriating (for example) twenty thousand small-scale tin producers and turning their property over to European companies—who hired them back as wage labourers with no rights. On politics: the British callously destroyed the indigenous kingdoms, and replaced them with ... nothing. They left the chiefs in charge of the villages, shamelessly using them as puppet governors, and where there were no indigenous chiefs (for instance, among the Ibo) they simply appointed them. Worse, they "solved" the question of Nigeria's complicated ethnic make-up by dividing the country into three regions, each governed by a different tribal coalition: the Ibo in the southeast, the Yoruba in the southwest, and the Hausa–Fulani in the north.

The first government after independence was such a coalition, led by Abubakar Balewa, a northerner, and it was a mess, all regions squabbling for position and privilege. In 1966 the army staged the first of many coups, assassinating Balewa, most of the regional governors, and dozens of loyal army officers. An Ibo general took over. There were anti-Ibo riots, and thousands more were killed. There was a counter-coup. In 1967, after almost thirty thousand Ibos had been massacred, the Ibos declared the independent state of Biafra. In the civil war that ensued, more than a million people died. Starving Biafran children with their hopeless eyes and distended stomachs became a staple of world television screens. Nigeria won.

A decade later there was an oil boom, and Nigeria, finding itself with a $5-billion annual surplus, went on a spending spree. The three Cs followed: crime, corruption, and chaos. There was another coup. It failed. Another. It succeeded. The military said they'd hold elections and they did. The oil boom collapsed in the world recession of the eighties. The military took over again, under General Ibrahim Babangida, who started building dozens of grandiose projects—the world's largest this, the world's best that—and

> "**A**mong the Ibo the art of conversation is regarded very highly, and proverbs are the palm-oil with which words are eaten."
>
> Nigerian novelist Chinua Achebe

within a few years the country was bankrupt, with an annual deficit exceeding $4 billion. Keeping to a promise, Babangida held elections in 1992, but voided the results when Moshood Abiola, a Yoruba from the south, won. He scheduled new elections, appointed a puppet to lead the transition, and resigned. Within months the new vice-president, General Sani Abacha, had kicked out his boss and taken over.

By early 1997 Abacha was facing a fire-storm of protest, much of it from within. There were crippling strikes among the Ibo in the oil fields. The Ogoni tribal home-land, where much of Nigeria's oil is to be found, has been polluted almost beyond repair, and when one of the Ogoni leaders, Kenule Saro-Wiwa, objected publicly, he was arrested and hanged. Nigeria's intellectuals, including the writers Wole Soyinka and Ben Okri, protested vigorously. Factional and tribal warfare loomed.

On the other hand, the economic news was not all catastrophic. The tax-free export zone the regime had set up in Calabar was attracting foreign business, and economic activity in other parts of the country started to pick up—so rich is the countryside, and so fertile the entrepreneurial skills of the canny Nigerians, that they were threatening to overcome even the bull-headedness of the generals.

In 1997 no one knew whether Nigeria, Africa's most populous country, would sur-vive. If in time it splits into three or more smaller countries, if the boundaries shift along with allegiances, and new polities take shape—well, this has happened before in Africa.

DAHOMEY

B y contrast with Nigeria, Benin—the country, not the old kingdom—has the friendliest Customs and Immigration people in Africa. They weren't much interested in my passport, couldn't have cared less about health certificates, money, or my destination or purpose. They only wanted me to "have a good day, have a good stay," and they seemed to mean it. I was suspicious, of course, having recently dealt with bureaucracies whose definitions of "salary" and "theft" seemed to overlap, and as I drove into their country I thought they must either have been chewing too many kola nuts or wanted something devious. My suspicions turned out to be groundless.

Late in the day, just before closing, I bought a ticket to the royal palace in Abomey from a large glum guy in a rumpled suit, with teeth that stuck out of his head like quills from a frightened porcupine. With him in the office were three more men, also rumpled, and behind them, at a desk, a small woman almost buried by a pile of files. It struck me as ironic that this rump palace, only a small portion of the magnificence of the past, was now guarded by male bureaucrats and petty functionaries—what had happened to the legendary Amazons of the Fon kings?

I'd been thinking about the women of the coast that morning as I headed for Cotonou before making my way upcountry to Abomey, which is about 150 kilometres

(95 miles) north of the sea. Somewhere between the border and the capital we had overtaken the strung-out field of a marathon. In the lead, running with the effortlessness of the natural long-distance athlete, was a tall, slender woman with a white headscarf. For a while we had to idle along behind her, because there was too much traffic coming in the other direction to pass. The rhythm of her legs was hypnotic, the tendons as defined as the fetlocks of a horse, the powerful muscles of the buttocks bunching with every stride, and I remembered a fragment I'd read from the Scottish explorer Hugh Clapperton, who'd been wandering about the Hausa lands in the previous century. Clapperton and his party arrived at Kaiama, an important market town, "the ruler of which was attended by an unusually attractive bodyguard of six young female slaves, naked as they were born, except a strip of narrow white cloth tied around their heads, each carrying a light spear in their right hands." The ease with which they appeared to fly over the ground as they ran alongside his horse when he was galloping made them appear something more than mortal, he reported, clearly envious.[8]

The local rulers of Kaiama had nothing on the kings of Dahomey, that savagely expansionist (if rather short-lived) kingdom. There were dry references in all the encyclopaedias to Dahomey: "... it was this kingdom, which had its capital at Abomey, that was renowned for its Amazon warriors, an elite corps of women soldiers who fought in the armies of the king."[9] Titillated (male) European travellers had reported that, well into the nineteenth century, the king's bodyguard was composed of female soldiers, more than two thousand strong, and armed with a variety of weapons, including knives like razors 45 centimetres (18 inches) long, muskets and antique blunderbusses, traded or stolen from slavers up and down the coast. They also had a reputation for ferocity, and a habit of taking the heads or jawbones of their opponents as battle trophies. In theory they were celibate and virgin (though the king was allowed to take any of them he wished). Richard Burton, who of course could be counted on to have inquired into the matter, took a more cynical view, commenting that they were "mostly remarkable for a stupendous steatopygy, and for a development of adipose tissue which suggested anything but ancient virginity."[10]

Before going into the palace itself, I'd wandered around the perimeter to look at the carved reliefs, which, along with the royal tapestries inside, represent a pictorial history of the kingdom. And what a bloody history it was! Everywhere you looked, armies were overrunning their foes, spearing, stabbing, shooting, or just beating the hell out of them—one of the tapestries inside shows the Dahoman king beating an enemy insensible, using as a club a leg he'd torn off another vanquished soldier.

This was clearly not a place for the weak of spirit.

There couldn't have been weaklings among the kings, either: it was an iron law of Dahoman statecraft that each king had to leave behind a kingdom larger than the one he inherited, which he mostly did by warring on the inoffensive Ibo, and by nibbling away at Benin and the Yoruba kingdoms. The same mine-is-bigger-than-yours attitude was brought to the royal residences: each successive king built his own palace, tacked on to but more imposing than the one that went before. This competition was begun by the third king in 1645, and by the nineteenth century the palace complex was immense, with a perimeter wall 5 kilometres (3 miles) long, enclosing an area of 40 hectares (100 acres). By this time more than ten thousand people lived inside the palace walls.

Considering what had been there, not much is left. The last of the independent kings, Béhanzin, ordered the palace burned when he fled the French in 1892. Fortunately, not all was destroyed, and the Getty people from America have spent millions helping restore what was left. So well have they done that the complex has been declared a World Heritage Site by UNESCO. The thrones of eleven of the twelve Dahoman kings are preserved; like the kingdom and the palace itself, each one outdoes the others in magnificence. Only the last is missing, destroyed in contempt by the people when its owner opted for subservience to the colonizers.

....

On my way to Ghana from Abomey, I stopped in Ouidah, Togo, the chief voodoo town in West Africa. Here voodoo is more than a curiosity—it's a religion for every day. From the town, I walked down the Route of Slaves to the old port, about 4 kilometres (2.5 miles) away, passing a few curious houses built on stilts in a lagoon, a copy of the more famous stilt village of Ganvié, some way to the east. This road is one of great supernatural power, and there are many legends associated with it, and fetishes along the way to honour the dead and protect the living from evil. Down this road the slaves came, chained in gangs, from Ouidah's old Portuguese fort (now a voodoo museum) to the ships, where they were taken to Brazil, and Haiti, and Cuba, and America. The many statues along the short walk are not very well executed and not very old, but pregnant with meaning none the less. At the port there is nothing very much left to see, no sign of the Portuguese barques into which the slaves were jammed for their hazardous journey across the unknowable ocean. But on a scruffy piece of beach, I found a young American girl squatting on her heels and weeping silently into the sand. I guessed she was in touch with the ghosts of her own past, not needing a fetish to do so, and I had not the heart to interrupt, so I turned and left, and went back to town.

....

Vodun (voodoo in its Haitian incarnation) grew out of the complex beliefs of the coastal tribes, driven by centuries of political uncertainty, rampant disease, and sundry natural and human disasters. It is to animism what mystical Catholicism is to mainstream Protestantism, a web of secret ties and hidden influences, priest-ridden, sacrificial, superstitious. Vodun, which means god or spirit in the local language called Fon, is the belief that a fetish object is the embodiment of a powerful spirit. Gods or spirits attach themselves to individuals or families and often demand ritual service; rather like capricious guardian angels, they help, protect, guide, and chastise, communicating through fetish priests or through dreams and trance states brought on by drumming and ritual dancing. The kings of Dahomey and of Benin practised voodoo in some form. The Fon still do. So do the Ewe of Togo and Ghana.

In vodun belief, each individual has an associated fetish object for its attached spirit. So does each family and each village and each people. The fetishes of the Dahomey kings are still kept in the palace museum at Abomey, there among the skulls of defeated enemies, and a grisly and gloomy lot they are. Outside town, at Djima and other places in the country, many fetish shrines can still be seen. I passed a small group singing at one for what they called "denny sickness" (which may or may not be dengue fever); a chicken had been killed to cure a family member, who had offended in some obscure way.

In its original, African incarnation, there were no zombies, dolls stuck with pins, or human sacrifices ordered by malevolent gods. Those are New World inventions, revenge fantasies of Dahoman slaves, devised as a way of making sure their masters paid, if not here, then in eternal torment in the afterlife—it was why they adopted, of all the Christian creeds, the ones that most believed in hell-fire. But even in Africa, the gods are dangerous if crossed. And the social damage they can still do is considerable. At Adidome, on the Ghanaian coast near the Togo border, there is a missionary-run refuge for *trakosi*, young virgins sent to fetish shrines as penance for crimes committed by members of their families, usually male, and sometimes as much as three hundred years earlier. These girls, who are deprived of education, and even the possibility of marriage, usually don't stay virgins long, but are used as sex objects by the priests.

Togo and Benin are both pocket-sized countries of more or less the same hectarage, are both truncated parts of the old empires (Benin and Dahomey), are both dominated by the Ewe tribe, and both came to independence more or less at the same time. But they have diverged radically since then, Benin after a rocky start becoming something of a model for African democrats, and Togo, after a brief flirtation with multiparty democracy, falling back into the hands of a dictator with a dismal human-rights record.

In Benin in the early years of colonialism, the Dahoman élites segued from their now-futile rivalries in war and went after education with the same intensely focused drive. In the twenties and thirties, Porto Novo, the capital, and Cotonou were known as the Latin Quarter of Africa. Ungratefully, the newly educated Dahomans used their education to agitate for independence, which they were duly granted in 1960. Three years later the small army staged a coup.

After that, "Benin became the Bolivia of Africa, with four more successful military coups, nine more changes of government and five changes of constitution—what the Dahomans called in jest *le folklore*. However, reflecting the civil manners of the Fon, not a single president was ever killed. When the army deposed General Soglo in 1967, they politely knocked on his door and told him, 'You're through.'"[11]

From 1972, under the control of Colonel Ahmed Kérékou, the country, renamed Benin, went through its inevitable flirtation with radical Marxism, attempting to mobilize the mutinous peasants into revolutionary cadres. During the late seventies and early eighties, there were more than twenty attempted coups, and finally, under strong French pressure, Kérékou agreed to hold a national conference to discuss constitutional changes. To his evident astonishment and chagrin, one of the changes the conference made was to strip him of all his powers. A new cabinet was formed, and elections duly followed in 1991. Kérékou was defeated, and Nicéphore Soglo became prime minister of newly democratic Benin. Since then Benin has suffered virtually no civil unrest, the economy has improved, and it has become one of the most democratic countries in the continent. It's hard to say what the Dahoman kings would have made of all this.

In Togo, by contrast, the road has been much more difficult. It started when, to the dismay of both the French and the British, the Germans abruptly took over "Togoland" in 1884. Within a few years the colony was paying for itself, and by the First World War three-quarters of its children were at school. But the German-imposed system of forced labour made them as unpopular in Togo as it made the French in Congo and the Belgians in what is now Zaire, and when war broke out the Togolese eagerly helped the French and English colonists defeat a German force (one of the first victories of the war for the Allies). In the postwar era a slice of "English Togoland" was joined to Ghana through a neat piece of electoral chicanery; independence duly came to the French part in 1960. In less than three years there was a coup—an African record for post-independence speed. After another coup four years later, Etienne Eyadéma took over. He was still there in 1997.

As in Benin, Eyadéma did agree to a national convention in 1991, and was stripped of office. But, unlike Kérékou, he used the army to regain power, and has never let it go, winning the "elections" in 1994 through intimidation and murder.

At the same time, he cracked down on what he called "obstinate tribalism," by which he apparently meant any ethnic group not in tune with his objectives of the moment. One of the targets of his hatred, sadly, were the Somba people, who spill over into Benin from the savannah country of northern Togo. Like the Kirdi in northern Cameroon, the Dogon in Mali, and the Lobi of the Ghana–Ivory Coast border country, the Somba are a hold-out people. They have almost literally closed themselves off by building windowless castles in the savannah, claustrophobic compounds that are designed to look like fortresses—and in some ways are, at least fortresses of the mind. A farming people, they are almost completely harmless. But they somehow came to offend the president's sense of Togolese nationhood. The government has banned the construction of any more castles and is forcing the Somba to integrate by driving them into the cities, where there is no work for them. I couldn't help comparing their treatment with the solicitude the Botswana government, say, showed to their San minority.

THE ASHANTI

I crossed from Togo into Ghana with some trepidation. Another of Eyadéma's targets has been rebellious groups of Ewe, and President Jerry Rawlings of Ghana, the antithesis of everything Eyadéma stands for, has an Ewe mother. As a consequence, the Ghanaian border often closes abruptly, and relations between the two countries are often surly. But the Togolese seemed glad to see me go, and as a consequence the Ghanaians were sunniness itself.

A few days later I was in Kumasi, once the capital city of the aggressive and warlike kingdom of the Ashanti. I went down to breakfast in my hotel, a little bleary from too much Ashanti good cheer, and—big mistake this—ordered an "English breakfast." I tucked in, but found the bleeding body of a very white and anorexic Christ staring up at me from behind a fried egg, where he'd been painted into the ceramic. This was a bit much at seven in the morning, and I hastily covered him over with a piece of bacon. Despite the fetish priests and the persistence of vodun (or perhaps because of it), Christianity is more obvious and more omnipresent in Ghana than in any other country I'd seen in Africa. There are Christian slogans everywhere—on buses, trucks, shops, on the radio, on factory walls. Small churches can be found tucked in between shops on every street. The Ashanti king is a devout Anglican. Everywhere, people are surprised at the foreign idea that there should be any divorce between Church and State.

As I travelled around Kumasi that morning, I jotted in my notebook the names of some of the small businesses I passed. Many of them were unselfconsciously Christian in tone. I liked, for instance, the Lord's Way Plumbing and Heating Service, the Last Respects Engineering Works, and, my favourite, the Lord Is Able Spare Parts Service. Angela Fisher and Carol Beckwith have documented the Ghanaian flamboyance with funerary ritual, and have photographed some of the coffins the Ga people of the coast have devised to take them into the Hereafter: a coffin-sized green onion for a farmer; a tséle fish for a fisherman, complete with scales and satin interior; a truck for a coal-heaver (with lumps of wooden "coal" and the motto that the deceased had used to guide him in the material world: God's Time Is the Best).

I asked Monica, a guide from the woman-owned and -operated Fredina Tours, about this, and she sounded surprised that I was surprised. Christianity, clearly, has made a kind of clean sweep of the cities. Only in the far north are there small communities of Islam. And only in the countryside do the priests of vodun still practise their trade.

Later that day there was a mix-up at the Ashanti king's palace, and I found myself admiring the flower-beds in a formal garden, thinking I was in a public park—it never occurred to me I was in the private royal enclave. The king, when I bumped into him, looked a little bemused at being confronted by a camera-wielding stranger in the grounds of his own palace, as well he might, for his universe is usually better regulated than that. However, the guard at the gate, thinking me a misplaced member of a delegation that had been promised an audience with the king earlier that morning, had shooed me into the palace just as the others were being shooed out the other side, and the king was already unwinding from his duties with a stroll in the garden. But His

> **Some names of Ghanaian "chop bars" (fast-food eateries):**
> Very Nice Too Spot
> Mama I'm Here Chop Quick Food
> Lord Is Everywhere Bar
> God Is Seven Chop Bar

Majesty Otumfuo Opuku Ware II, *asantehene* (Ashanti King), for twenty-six years the spiritual and political leader of all the Ashanti, quickly recovered his royal aplomb and was graciousness itself as I, not having a clue whom I was talking to, asked my way to the royal museum. What I saw was a rather portly old gentleman with a benign face, wearing scuffed shoes and a worn suit; what I couldn't, of course, see was that this portly old gentleman was the Possessor of the Golden Stool, about whom the praise singers had sung:

The Lion is on the move,
The possessor of the land . . .
The great warrior who executes the malefactors
Who possesses the power of life and death,
Hail thou art excellent and noble . . .

And so on and so on.

His Excellency is also a barrister-at-law, trained at the Inner Temple, London. It doesn't do to judge by appearances.

In any case, I think it rather tickled his royal fancy to be mistaken for a guide in his own home, and after clearing up the confusion he pointed out the way, telling me not to miss the statue of his great-grandmother, the old dame who had warred contemptuously on the mighty British Empire in 1900. Of course the British were somewhat distracted at the time by their other war in Africa, that against my own grandfather and his fellow Boers. I was thinking of telling the king about this happy coincidence in our lives, but just then a courtier came by and hustled him protectively out of sight, yelling for a guard as he did so.

The British had brought the Ashanti war on themselves. A boorish officer, determined to teach the bally wogs a lesson, demanded that the Ashanti bring out for his use the Golden Stool, emblem of kings, so he could put his British arse on the thing and show them who was who. He either didn't understand (or didn't care) that this wasn't just a throne, but had been spirited down from heaven itself, making a miraculous appearance that permitted the unity of the Ashanti kingdom—it was, in effect, an object both temporal and divine; nobody, in fact, ever sits on the Golden Stool, not even the Asantehene. When I learned all this from an earnest young guide in the palace museum, I expressed the hope that the British idiot had got himself shot in the subsequent uproar. The guard was too well schooled to agree openly, but I did notice that afterwards he addressed his museum patter directly to me, ignoring the gaggle of other visitors poking about the exhibits.

I spent some time in the museum, because I had become fascinated with the Ashantis' own self-image, which was one of warfare and aggression. The songs of the Ashanti celebrate heroism and are full of scorn for cowardice; Ashanti proverbs are full of sly advice about manipulation and trickery. They are both wise and cynical. My favourite proverb, told to me approvingly by a curator at the national museum in Accra, had to do with power: "To get power," the saying went, "sell your mother. Once you have power, there are many ways of getting her back."

The museum is small but revealing. It used to be the palace itself, and there are rooms inside that are furnished with the original desks and chairs and other artefacts of royalty. There are also rooms full of gold. The sheer amount of gold worn by the Ashanti kings was reported incredulously by early travellers—gold sandals, gold anklets, gold tunics, gold amulets, gold head-dresses, gold swords, gold staffs—everything in gold, including the emblem of royal power itself, the Golden Stool. Also on display is the Mponponsua Sword, symbol of Ashanti peace. There is also a large brass container that had been looted from the Ashanti by Lord Baden-Powell, founder of the scouting movement. It had been full of gold dust when he took it. His widow eventually returned it, though empty of the gold. But, after a while, so much gold brings only ennui. What interested me more were the wonderfully lifelike effigies of the royal family, going back several generations. The old Queen Mum sits on a chair, staring across history at what her ancestors had wrought. And you can see at once why she wasn't going to put up with British bullshit, why she took her country to war against the mightiest empire on earth, despite the fact that her son, the king, and his family had already been exiled to some remote Indian Ocean island. And there she sits, this stern and purposeful old woman, glaring out at the world, a rifle across her knees, cocked and ready to fire.

I knew that the Ashanti had parlayed their gold and their complicity in the slave trade into an extensive trading empire. And yet, and yet ... it's impossible not to like the Ashanti. Years before I had written of my own people, the Afrikaners, that "there are no people with a greater dislocation between their political and private actions than the Afrikaners; their tribal reality is in conflict with their dimly remembered European past. Politically, they're intolerant, arrogant, determined to get their own way. Privately they are hospitable and want badly to be loved." I see now that I was naïve. There are many peoples like that, in Africa and elsewhere. The Ashanti are among them. Their history, as an Ashanti historian has himself written, is one of "cruelty, desolation and despondency."[12] But in their social lives, the Ashanti are easygoing, fun-loving, generous, and hospitable. So power is not everything. There is another Ashanti proverb: "He is a man who can sew stones." Which means, "he is a man who can make peace with everyone."

....

The Akan people, some of whom were to become the Ashanti, drifted into the area in successive waves between the eleventh and eighteenth centuries; they spilled over into what today are the states of the Ivory Coast, to the west, and Togo, to the east. There they grouped themselves loosely into matrilineal clans tracing their origins to a common ancestress. Already by the fourteenth century Mande traders of the Dyula tribe, pushing southwards from Djenne, were opening up new trading routes to the gold fields being developed along the Upper Volta and to the south, in modern Ghana. Kola nuts joined gold as trade goods—they were in high demand among Muslim societies to the north, where other stimulants were banned by religious decree. Local Akan chiefs began to exploit the power that being astride the trade routes gave them, and larger kingdoms began to develop—the kingdoms of Bono and Banda were probably in existence by about 1400.

Seemingly inevitably, tensions between the Dyula traders and the increasingly powerful pagan Banda monarchy erupted into a civil war in the seventeenth century, which destroyed the kingdom and led its Dyula merchants to establish a new trading base of their own farther to the west, at Bonduku.[13] At the same time the Bono became more important in the gold trade; the kings of Bono brought in new mining techniques they had learned from the western Sudan. They are also believed to be the originators of the figurative style of gold weights used by the Akan peoples.[14]

There were other kingdoms, short-lived, which came and went. The Akwamu state lasted only a hundred years, but in the early eighteenth century stretched more than 300 kilometres (185 miles) along the coast and for some way inland. It was hemmed in on the north and northwest by the state of Akim and others, in a loose alliance with or subject to the powerful confederacy called the Denkyera.

Meanwhile, a small and otherwise unimportant satellite state of Akim called the Ashanti was growing rich and powerful.

....

The founders of the Ashanti nation were a prince of the royal clan, Osei Tutu, and his friend and Svengali, Okomfo Anokye, an Akwamu chief.

It was Anokye, as high priest of the new state, who caused to be conjured from the heavens the Golden Stool, whose mysterious power came to symbolize the inner spirit of the Ashanti people. It appeared one day in the royal compound, an object of veneration and power, brought there, it is said, by the intervention of the Priest with the High Powers in Heaven. Anokye, whatever else he was, whether charlatan, true believer, or some early Ashanti version of a spin doctor, understood perfectly the power of symbols on a credulous population. A palm tree still grows in a grove near the museum at Awukagoa that bears the marks of Anokye's sandals. He climbed the tree—sandals and all—over three hundred years ago to convey a message from the gods, and it's an eerie thing running your hands over those slight scuff marks today, as though one is touching a tree Moses had used to haul himself up the mountain, where he was given the Tablets of Stone.

At the same time the two leaders had made another, more practical discovery— they came to understand where the real power of the Denkyera came from: European firearms. So they set about to acquire some for themselves, and soon found traders eager to change gunpowder for gold.

In the late 1670s, the Denkyera, under an inexperienced and ineffective leader, were crushed, and the Ashanti became the dominant power in the region. Osei Tutu was installed as *asantehene*, king of all Ashanti.

....

Under the Ashanti kings, a state of "peaceful warfare" persisted (by which the Ashanti mean, essentially, that they kept on winning). There was more or less constant fighting. "The Asante ravaged towns and villages, burnt farms, murdered, raped and brutalised the inhabitants, [from whom] they made considerable profits. The evil effects of these wars ... also took the form of widespread unstable social structures, lawlessness, slavery, and frightening famines and plagues."[15] While the court grew rich (the *asantehene* dined off European silverware under an English chandelier) and trade progressed (the sophisticated Gold Coast banking system was then already under study by European businessmen, who used it as a model in colonial development), the ordinary people suffered.

By 1860, the population of Kumasi was around fifty thousand. Kofi Karikari was *asantehene*. The Ghanaian writer A.A. Anti has reconstructed what it was like. The king's palace was at the centre of town, protected by a high wall, and almost sur-

rounded by marshes. The main entrance was arched, with enormous wooden doors.
Nearby were the houses of the wealthy, each with a wooden stake in front, on which
was a pan of sacred water. At the foot of the stake was an image of the family god and
the necessary charms to ensure the family's health and wealth. The market was
to the east. To the west, the melancholy *asaman*, the quarter of ghosts, where the
bodies of the executed were thrown, unburied, to rot. Kumasi had three places
of execution: one where criminals were put to death; one in the palace for enemies of the king; and the sacred grove at Bantama, where human sacrifices were
made to ensure the eternal peace for the bones of the royal ancestors.[16]

I visited Bantama early in my stay at Kumasi. It's now an industrial suburb,
but the royal mausoleum is still there, housing the mortal remains of the
Ashanti kings. In the Stool House are the so-called Black Stools, which contain the
spirits of the departed chiefs, "who have gone elsewhere," but are brought back to
life when the *asantehene*, on ritual occa-sions, "feeds the ancestors" through the
slaughter of a sheep. I never saw these stools. Outsiders are not permitted in
the building.

Thomas Bowditch, sent on a diplo-matic mission from England to Ghana
to increase the gold trade, was in Kumasi in 1817, during the reign of King Osei
Kwame. He found the royal court a scene of unbelievable wealth, "a colourful and orgiastic display. Gold covered the thrones and stools, and gold threads
embroidered the robes of royalty. It was cast into every conceivable form of ornament, from the King's crown to courtiers'
talismans, and the gold leaf applied to ceremonial staffs was even used to cover the
collars of dogs at court. At festivals thousands of courtiers, extravagantly adorned,

Kente cloth, the colourful Ashanti and Ewe weavings that, like tartans for the Scots, have travelled beyond Ghana's borders and become
symbols in the African diaspora of a rich and royal African past, were traditionally produced in villages like Domwire, near Kumasi—and indeed
they still are. Now, they can be found as hatbands, bookmarks, handbags,
even bowties. Traditionally, kente pat-terns and weavings contained a rich
iconography. Certain patterns were reserved for royalty, others for
chiefs, and couldn't be purchased by men without standing, or young men.
Occasionally, in an embarrassing *faux pas*, a junior chief would show up at
a conclave in the same pattern as worn by a senior chief—if this happened, the junior scuttled off to change, while everybody else pretended they hadn't noticed.

Kente patterns are not clan-based, like tartans, but are regional
and tied to status.

Only one pattern is tied to lin-eage: the "Asasia" can be worn only
with the explicit permission of the *asantehene* or by inheritors of such a
permission.

paraded under silk-tasselled umbrellas, their ornaments proclaiming the prosperity of the Asante kingdom."[17]

There were festivities all night, and the next morning the king ordered a barrel or two of rum to be poured into brass pans and left around town to be drunk by whoever felt the need. "In less than an hour, excepting the principal men, not a sober person was to be seen, parties of four reeling and rolling ... strings of women covered in red paint, hand in hand, falling down like rows of cards ..."

The king's duty was generosity. In the Ashanti saying, "the king has the largest breasts of all."

Still, when the king lay dying, the people had to be generous in return, and send envoys to accompany him to heaven. He and his wives would select whom they wanted to die with him, and at the funeral the chosen women, dressed in white and wearing all their gold jewellery, would drink themselves into oblivion before being strangled and buried with the dead monarch.[18]

....

Europe has had a long history in this part of the world. In 1481 the mariner Diago d'Azambuja, acting on orders from King João II, built a fort on land seized by force from the local king. The fort of São Jorge de Mina (Elmina Castle) is still in Elmina, a heavy and brooding presence, its face to the Atlantic, its back to the interior from which its wealth was derived. A few years later the Portuguese built three more, at Aiyim, Shama, and Accra—in the sixteenth century one in ten ounces of gold mined in the world was making its way to the Ghana coast and to Europe in Portuguese vessels.

Through the centuries that followed, more Europeans arrived and built more forts—the Danish, the French, the British, and the Dutch. All of which presented the kingdoms of the interior with something of a political dilemma: how to deal profitably with this new presence in the land and at the same time prevent the newcomers from tampering with their native sovereignty. One way was to lease the land for the forts, though of course the Europeans overrode leases whenever they felt like it. Every now and then the Akan believed that stronger control measures were needed; for example, they destroyed the Portuguese fort at Accra in the 1570s.

....

And all through the ebb and flow of politics and the gold trade, the coast was leaking slaves.

If you travel along the coast today, from Accra in the east to Elmina and Cape Coast in the west and to all the dozens of forts in between, you can see the pilgrims there, from Brazil, and Jamaica, and the Carolinas, and Chicago—descendants of the men and women who spent their last days on African soil bound and shackled in dank and gloomy dungeons. I thought back to the young woman at the end of the Slave Route in Togo: she was a pilgrim too. And here they were again, these Americans come back home, feeling the weight of their ancestors' sorry history. Even the kids, rumpled in baggy shorts and overlarge Nikes, are struck dumb. I watched a young boy, in horn-rims and braces, and blacker than the Ghanaians around him, stroke a ring-bolt set into the stone walls of the cell, buried deep under the castle; other young boys had been chained to that bolt, in years past, and some of them had died there, standing, for there was no room to fall. And then overhead a foghorn moaned, up there in the sunlight, where there was no fog, and the young boy snatched his hand away as though he'd been burned, and maybe he'd heard in the low groaning of the horn something that touched some ancestral legend, some long and oft-told family story, and he went to his mother and she took his hand, and turned away.

I talked to a castle tour guide later, after the Americans had gone, and told him I'd overheard an American woman complaining about her guide, how his patter had been too light, full of anecdotes and stories of heroism, but not nearly full enough of anger. He was compassionate. "They don't know how to deal with their grief when they come here," he said. "We try to help them. But it is different. For us, we threw the slavery away, and got our country back. It is over. Despite," he added without prompting, "the morality of it, that some of us grew rich on the backs of slaves, owned slaves ourselves. But for us it is gone. For them . . ." His voice trailed off. "For them, they're still living in their history."

This was called the Gold Coast, not the Slave Coast—that title was reserved for the Bight of Benin and the Niger Delta, down there towards Nigeria. He gestured vaguely oceanwards, towards Togo. The Togolese port of Little Popo had been one of the main slaving ports. So had Ardrah, or Porto Novo, in Benin; and in Nigeria, in the lagoons west of the delta, the ports of Badagri, Lagos, and Gwato.

Along the Gold Coast the Dutch became the chief actors in the trade in human beings. Newly triumphant in the Caribbean and western Atlantic, where they had trounced the waning Spanish Empire, they found themselves in possession of huge plantations and needed slaves to work them. But like the rest of mercantile Europe, the Dutch soon realized that the trade itself was more profitable than the plantations; for inspiration and example they looked to the south, where the Portuguese had been "harvesting" from Angola to Gabon for centuries. The huge profits the Dutch West India Company began to make attracted yet more merchants from France, Britain, Germany, and Scandinavia.

The French took control north of the Gambia River and the British down to Lagos, leaving the south to the Portuguese. The peak of the Atlantic slave trade was probably reached in the 1780s, when something like seventy thousand slaves were being landed in the Americas each year, about half of them transported in British ships.

I thought back to the American woman who'd complained of her guide. She'd said something else. "How very dangerous it was," she'd told her husband, "to be an African in Africa."

By which she meant, she explained, that there had been nowhere safe for a person to be. The continent was besieged. Anyone could be taken at any time from his village or her field; disaster could strike at any time; and they could be plucked away, to stumble down to the coast in a chain gang and be spirited off ... where, no one knew. Did it matter that many of the available slaves shipped from the interior were unfortunates in their own societies—debtors, criminals, the handicapped? Did it matter here, any more than it had in Angola and the Congo, how complicit the Bantu kings and chiefs were in the trade, how some of them thrived and became rich? Did it matter that there had always been slavery in Africa, long before Europe smelled profit in it, and long before Arab raiders came down from Arabia Felix in search of who knew what treasure?

No, what mattered was the industrial efficiency the Europeans brought to the trade, how they turned it into *business*, a kind of insane production line. That changed everything, and left a bloodied continent in its wake.

There'd been a flickering video in a back hall of the castle's museum that made the point in a simple yet frightening way. It was a map of Africa, and red was leaking off its coasts into the ocean, emblem of humans lost forever to their homeland. I squinted at the grainy screen, surrounded by rapt kids from the cities of America, all of them absolutely silent. The red that seeped off the land covered almost all the perimeter of the great land mass of Africa: the only places where slaves were not seized were places with no harbours. From Somalia to Sofala, slavers were active. From Angola to the Congo, from the Congo to the Gambia, slavers were active. From the Sahel to the Barbary shore and all across the great desert, slavers were active. In the very heart of the continent, in what is now the Central African Republic, in Uganda and the Great Lakes, weary slaves stumbled on in their dreadful queues.

Well, there was one gap in this red seepage, way down there in the south of the continent. There, slaves were brought in by the Dutch, not shipped out, some of them coming from the Indies, from Java, and from India. To the enslaved, it made little difference. They were simply assets on the balance sheet of this grisly business of import–export.

In the end, it was the British who put a stop to slavery—in part because of churchly revulsion against the trade, and in part because of the secular humanism that was a consequence of the ferment in France. And substantially because British commercial interests had changed—by this time the captains of industry needed the raw materials that the tropics produced (especially palm oil to grease the wheels of their industrial revolution) more than they needed slaves abroad. If they depopulated the African countryside, who would produce the palm oil?

Thus, as so often, morality was harnessed in the cause of commerce.

The British navy maintained a fleet of 20 warships in the waters off West Africa between the years 1825 and 1865, arresting 1,287 other vessels and liberating 130,000 captives (a nice number, but in the same period about 1,436,000 are believed to have been landed in America).

Another consequence of the effort to end slavery was increasing interference in the affairs of the African states: We don't deal in slaves, nor should you. This caused the inevitable cycle: the interference caused instability, which caused local traders to call for more security, which brought more interference, which ... often led to warfare.

There was a bout of foot-shuffling as the European powers jostled for influence. Of the thirty or so major forts along the 400-kilometre (250-mile) stretch of coast, the Dutch, British, and Danes held the most. In 1850 the British pushed the Danes out. But the presence of the Dutch prevented them from imposing what they considered proper levels of customs and excise taxes, and squabbles continued. The Ashanti of the interior, irritated beyond bearing at the interference, began to take over vassal statelets on the coast. The British shuffled into the Dutch forts when the Dutch withdrew altogether. This left the British and the Ashanti as the only legitimate powers left in the Gold Coast.

There was warfare in the 1820s. In 1863, under Kwaku Dua, the Ashanti again challenged the British by sending forces to occupy the coastal provinces. In 1869 the British took possession of Elmina (over which the Ashanti claimed jurisdiction), and in 1874 an expeditionary force marched on Kumasi.

For more than twenty years, there was vigorous resistance. In the end, though, the war launched by the current king's great-grandmother came to nought. The Ashanti were, at last, overmatched, and the Ashanti lands became a Crown colony in 1901.

An Ashanti Confederacy Council was established under British rule in the 1930s, and the *asantehene* was installed as a figurehead sovereign.

....

Sometime later I returned to Ghana from Abidjan, in the Ivory Coast, arriving in Accra around midnight. My seat mate, a young Ghanaian from the eastern part of the country, had been travelling since seven that morning, from Jedda in Saudi Arabia, via NDjamena, Niamey, and Abidjan. He was a member of the Muslim minority in Ghana, and was returning from his hajj to Mecca.

The young man, bubbling over with enthusiasm at returning home after so many months abroad, poured out his story. It was a common-enough story, and yet how much it expressed the many dilemmas of modern Africa. He came from a poor family.

His father was already sixty when he was born, twenty-six years ago, and when he was still a child his father was already too old and too ill to work. His elder brother simply disappeared, they thought to the West.

"My mother wanted me to get as much education as I could, but I had to start work to support the family."

"How old were you then?"

"I was sixteen. Oh, and I had so many jobs! I worked for whoever would have me. I worked as a farm labourer, then in a factory, then as an assistant in a foreign exchange bureau ... And then ... so many more ..."

Still, he put himself through primary school and two more grades before the workload overwhelmed him, and he had to stop. Eventually he scraped together enough money to make his hajj. How, he wondered, to parlay all this into a better education? How to save some capital so he could make something of himself? "With education," he said, "I can get somewhere."

"Are you married?"

"I'm already twenty-six, but I can't afford it now. I want to make something of myself first." Did I have any ideas?

Of course, I had none, beyond platitudes and banal assurances. From our position of impossible privilege, how dare to offer advice? There are millions like him, young men and women, all over Africa. Whenever I feel discouraged about Africa, I think of him, how bright and eager he was, how willing to learn, how fierce his desire to make a better life. What a resource for a statesman to tap! What an engine of industry he would be! But if politics poisons his hope, turns it to disillusion ... well, it was not hard to see what would happen. Nigeria and Zaire and Sierra Leone and Liberia are examples grim enough for all.

....

It was election year in Ghana, and every few days there was another rally, almost always preceded by hours of feasting and dancing to attract the partisans. My young seat mate had approved of Jerry Rawlings, the president.

"What's good about him?" I asked, curious.

"He's done what he said he'd do, and is not afraid to admit when he is wrong." Rawlings had taken power in a coup to get rid of a corrupt administration, and then resigned when he said he would. After several more years of even more corrupt politics, he led a second coup. This time, he said, he'd stay long enough to fix the economy, and then he'd hold elections. To everybody's surprise, he did just that. And he won the elections handily, despite raucous opposition.

The young man also liked the fact that Rawlings had forbidden his picture to be hung in public buildings, and resisted any signs of a cult of personality. He thought, probably correctly, that this must be unique. Instead, Rawlings has "rehabilitated" the Founding Father of independent Ghana, Kwame Nkrumah, who led his country so successfully to independence and became a world statesman before falling into grandiosity and messing up the economy. Instead of using himself as a symbol of national unity, Rawlings is using the safely dead Nkrumah, and has built him a suitably pretentious monument which dominates an overly solemn theme park near the ocean in central Accra.

The opposition has been sniping at Rawlings for his stated intention of raising taxes. The young man was contemptuous. "You can't build anything without money, and people must learn to pay their share. The people don't understand if they want roads they must pay for them."

Curiously, the Ashanti, despite their self-professed penchant for power, have never provided a national leader. All Ghana's national leaders have been from minority tribes. This is usually taken as one of the country's strengths. Nkrumah was from a small tribe in eastern Ghana, and so is Rawlings. The Ashanti, and the opposition, have not been above making political capital of Rawlings's non-Ghanaian origins (his father is Scottish), but it hasn't got them anywhere. Nkrumah had himself married an Egyptian, and his widow is still living in Accra.

THE IVORY COAST

T*he Ivory Coast had no important kingdoms, but it was not without its interest. The Dyula were a Mande people from the north who settled in what is now the Ivory Coast, Upper Volta, and Mali. They traded in gold with ancient Ghana, and flourished under the Malian emperors, as part of the Mansas' trading links between the western Sudan and the Gulf of Guinea. The Dyula were often remembered as skilled craftsmen, and their cities described as among the most harmonious and beautiful in Africa. Alas, they attracted the jealous attention of the growing Akan to the south, and by the seventeenth century the increasingly powerful pagan monarchy of Banda (an Akan people) launched a war that destroyed the kingdom.*

After the Dyula disappeared, nothing much happened in what was to become the Ivory Coast until the colonial period. The Portuguese arrived in the fifteenth century, but didn't stay: low population densities and poor harbours meant that the region suffered less from slavery than almost any other part of western Africa.

French traders arrived in the mid-nineteenth century, after which the colony followed some of the usual patterns: local chiefs signed agreements to "cede" the land, the French organized agriculture into large plantations, and introduced their by now customary notion that the locals should be obliged to work without pay, and could be shot or tortured if they refused. There was only one significant difference between the Ivory Coast and other French colonies: the French arrived as settlers and not just administrators, and by independence there were more than twenty thousand white French who called the Côte d'Ivoire their home.

Twentieth-century politics has been dominated by the man who came to be called *le vieux*, the old chap, Félix Houphouët-Boigny. Houphouët-Boigny was the son of a wealthy chief, and he started in politics as a radical, organizing African planters (not labourers) to hire their own migrant labour in competition with the French. He rose to become a deputy in the French parliament (where he was influential in persuading France to abolish the hated forced-labour system in 1948), and was the first African to be elevated to the French cabinet.

After independence he naturally became the new country's first president, and chose a course that put him at odds with black Africa's other new leaders: he continued the country's reliance on the French, and even encouraged French settlers, until there were almost fifty thousand of them. There were complaints, not without cause—two-thirds of all management positions were occupied by Europeans. But the economy boomed, growing at an average of 9 per cent a year. Abidjan, a sleepy little town of fifty thousand just after the Second World War, reached two and a half million in the early nineties, after the French cut a channel from the lagoons on which the city is situated to the sea, giving it a reasonable harbour for the first time.

Houphouët-Boigny's rule was authoritarian; like Nyerere in Tanzania, he was strongly opposed to tribalism and refused to allow tribal symbols in any state institution. He himself wore European suits, and his government banned scarification and tattoos as injurious to the unity of the country. Yet he was never brutal: he solved opposition by co-option rather than coercion, and his favourite way of dealing with an opponent was to give him a well-paying job.

Unfortunately, he was inordinately fond of grandiosity, and his "show projects" were notorious. The worst of these took place in his native village of Yamoussoukro, which he turned from a town of fewer than ten thousand people to a bizarre "national capital" of a hundred thousand or so, mostly by bulldozing all the housing and rebuilding it in the European style, with major expressways going in all directions but terminating abruptly in the jungle. It was here that he built the extraordinary Basilica de Notre Dame de la Paix, the tallest church in Christendom (slightly lower, by papal request, than St. Peter's, after which it was modelled, but trumped with a giant gold cross that puts it, in all senses of the phrase, over the top). The basilica is an embarrassment. Among its many excesses are the figures depicted in its thirty-six gigantic stained-glass windows: they're all white, except for one black

---

CICATRIZATION (aka "scarification")

Scarification and tattooing, whether on the face or on some other part of the body (round the navel in the case of women), are usually tribal marks or indications of social rank. Generally they're inscribed at various crucial moments in an individual's life: on initiation into adulthood, on marriage, on promotion to elder. Scarifications, which are much more common that actual tattooing, can either cause indentation of the skin, as among the Mossi of Burkina Faso, or stand out in relief, as among the Sara of Chad or the Bamiléké of Cameroon, or appear as evenly raised beads, like the group of dots which cover the faces of the Ngala of Zaire. The marks may be very slight, or very elaborate as in central Congo. They may consist of merely a few lines or of an arrangement of highly stylised geometric patterns.

From Leiris, African Art, p 120

---

pilgrim, *le vieux* himself, kneeling at the feet of Christ. The air-conditioned basilica seats 2,000, and another 300,000 can fit comfortably into the piazza outside, but there are fewer than a million Catholics in the whole country. The cost of all this extravagance was reputed to be around $400 million (U.S.).

Yet the country tolerated him. The economy was robust, and because he emphasized small-holder farming and paid farmers decent prices (unlike the commodity-based plantations in other West African countries) the prosperity was, by African standards, very widespread, and it wasn't until the recession of the eighties and a falling standard of living that serious opposition formed, and Houphouët-Boigny was forced into accepting multiparty democracy. In the 1990 elections, he was opposed for the first time in thirty years, and won only 85 per cent of the votes instead of the usual 99 per cent.

Houphouët-Boigny died in 1993, at the age of ninety, and his personally chosen successor, Henri Konan-Bédié, became president. The transition, despite fears that the country would implode into ethnic war, went well. The slippage in the economy seemed to have been arrested, Konan-Bédié was reasonably popular, and crime in Abidjan, rampant through the eighties, was beginning to decline. In 1995 genuinely open elections were held for the first time. Turnout was high, there was no violence, and the results were accepted by all. By early 1997 the country was peaceful. A fragile, fragile peace, but holding.

SLAVERY'S STEPCHILDREN: LIBERIA AND SIERRA LEONE

N*orth of the Ivory Coast is everybody's African nightmare, Liberia, and night-mare's stepchild, Sierra Leone. It is these two, together with Zaire and Nigeria in the west and Rwanda and Burundi in the centre, that have given rise to gloomy prognostications that much of Africa is sliding inexorably into chaos and anarchy. As we have seen, this is a canard: to the north, the Guinea states are doing well, and, to the south, Ghana's democracy is looking more and more robust. Even in Sierra Leone the lessons are not all gloomy. Still, looking at Liberia, I found it hard not to despair.*

In Abidjan I met a missionary from a station on the Liberian border, at Toulépleu. He was depressed, but resolute, as such people usually are. He'd been in the capital looking for supplies, and was returning west the next day. He was dealing, he said, with an outpouring of refuges from poor distressed Liberia. Every few weeks the station was evacuated as the rumours swirled of Liberian excursions, of some ragged boy army straggling across the bridge to shoot down the fleeing refugees, but so far it hadn't happened. "You can stand on the bridge and watch them come, the refugees," he said. "They have the same shell-shocked look common to refugees everywhere. Always the same. Always the killing of God's children by God's children ..."

"What do you do with them?" I asked.

"Feed them and patch them up and send them on," he said. "It's all we can do now."

He was waiting, he said, to get inside Liberia, to begin the healing of that torn country's soul.

....

The land that is now Liberia was outside the pale of Old Ghana, and the Mali traders never made it through the dense forests to the sparse populations of the coast. Many would say it is outside the pale of civilized life even now. The country collapsed into savagery with the coming to power of the illiterate Samuel Doe and the subsequent disintegration of the country into a civil war orchestrated in part by a Boston-educated dandy in Armani suits called Charles McArthur Taylor, and in part by armies of boy soldiers "protected" by fetishes made from the severed heads of their enemies.

There has long been a notion that Liberia was one of only two African countries never to have been subjected to colonial rule (the other being Ethiopia), but this is only technically true: for most of Liberia's modern history they were ruled by a small élite of American Liberians, "freed" (and sometimes deported) slaves from America sent "home" to Liberia. As was common in other such colonies, albeit ones without such a dramatic origin, the new élite ruled the country without consulting the natives—in fact, the natives weren't even considered citizens until this century, and every president until 1980 was of American descent.

The first Americans to arrive were under the sponsorship of the American Colonization Society, which had the patronage of Thomas Jefferson and James Madison. They settled in what is now Sierra Leone, but disease killed them off there, and the colony didn't survive. The society then bought the Liberian coast for the equivalent of $300 in beads and booze. To their dismay, only 17,000 out of a possible 250,000 freed American blacks were willing to go to Liberia in the first quarter-century of its existence; the U.S. Navy brought in 5,722 of them, known to history as "the Congoes." In 1846 the colonists promulgated a constitution, modelled after the American one, and declared independence.

For a hundred years the colony continued on its somnolent way, the "Congoes" forming a somewhat old-fashioned élite. In the 1930s the descendants of the freed slaves were caught sending forced labourers to the Spanish plantations in Equatorial Guinea, causing a scandal; the president and his cabinet were obliged to resign.

For the next twenty-seven years, under Liberia's most eminent president, William Tubman, the country flourished. Firestone, the tire company, set up what is still the world's largest rubber plantation, and many other American companies poured investment money into the country. In the 1970s, however, the corrupt Tolbert family took over from Tubman, and Liberia began its slide into decline. The economy collapsed, there were food riots, and a master sergeant, Samuel Doe, a member of the despised Krahn tribe, took over as the first native-descended president.

Nothing went right. The economy kept on its free-fall, corruption continued, the president got fat and the country began to starve, most foreign companies fled, and aid stopped. Or it stopped but for the Americans, who, mindful of the country's origins and also of their substantial investment in Liberia, poured in about half a billion dollars, most of which promptly vanished. President Ronald Reagan even invited Doe to the White House as an honoured ally (though he annoyed the prickly soldier by referring to him as Chairman Moe), and invited him to stage elections back home. This Doe did, after banning the opposition parties and killing their leaders. Nevertheless, the Reagan Administration cheerfully issued a bulletin praising this one small step for democracy. The following year Doe's soldiers paraded around Monrovia with the testicles of a failed coup leader; the Americans looked the other way.

There were massacres: seven hundred people in a church, the bodies left draped over the pews; six hundred in a refugee camp ...

Enter Charles Taylor, who had fled Liberia after allegedly looting nearly a million dollars from its treasury as a member of Doe's early cabinet. Back in the United States he was arrested on an extradition warrant, but escaped, sawing through the bars of his prison in classic style, and ending up in the Ivory Coast under the patronage of *le vieux*, whose son-in-law had been killed by Doe in one of his periodic attacks of violent paranoia.

When Taylor's ragtag army actually threatened Monrovia, the capital, Doe appealed for help from international peacemakers. His old chums in Nigeria, who understood military rule, responded, and an undisciplined force from six African countries headed for Liberia. Prince Johnson, a rebel who had broken with Taylor over strategy, led the convoy into port.

Shortly thereafter American spies advised Doe it was time to get out of town, and so, in September 1990, he hustled down to the harbour with fifty of his soldiers. Someone had tipped off Johnson, who had by this time broken with Doe too. He was waiting. Doe was bound and taken to a warehouse for "questioning." Johnson, as much a showman as Taylor, phoned the U.S. embassy to see if they wanted to participate, but they politely declined. Johnson thereupon scraped the jagged edge of a broken Coke bottle across Doe's head, sliced off his ears, and left him to bleed to death. Bits of his body were later paraded through the streets.

A cease-fire agreement was signed in 1993, after nearly 200,000 Liberians had been killed and more than that had fled into neighbouring Ivory Coast. Taylor refused to disarm, and a few months later his troops killed several hundred more refugees. In 1994 there was yet another agreement. That one was as futile as the first. A Council of State, which is what the warlords called the joint committee running things in the absence of a functioning government, was precariously in charge, ostensibly preparing for "elections." The factions appointed Ruth Perry, a former senator and a widowed mother of seven, as Council "president," thereby making her Africa's first woman president. They thought she'd be easy to manipulate. Outsiders were reduced to hoping they'd be wrong.

One day in 1996 a small convoy of trucks crossed the border at Toulépleu and headed for Abidjan, to stock up on supplies. The truck in the lead had been seconded from its more normal duties in Monrovia. It had stencilled on its side, in metre-high characters: *Skeleton Team*. Its job was to pick bones off the streets of the capital and take them to the dump to be burned.

Sierra Leone is another country whose sorry history has shaped its present. Wars and invasions swept through the territory in the mid-sixteenth century, leaving almost no trace of the indigenous Sapi civilizations. These folk had the misfortune to be among the greatest ivory carvers on the continent, and the emperors of Mali coveted—and kidnapped—many of them. The Portuguese merchant Manuel Alveres, writing in 1611, noted that "it is the fault of the foreign kings [of the Mani] that the country is so poor, because they have captured so many master craftsmen, and ... have committed so many vexations on the indigenous people that these later have become less and less concerned and have given up the exercise of their arts."[19]

For most of the nineteenth century, Sierra Leone was of small importance to the rest of the world, except that the British, emulating the American experiment, set up colonies of freed slaves there. Many of these were blacks who had fought on the losing side in the American Revolution. They first arrived in Freetown in 1787. Hardly any survived, but the British persisted, and another batch were sent, this time from Nova Scotia. By 1811 there were two thousand Freetowners. Since slaving was the only lucrative profession in the region, the colony remained dependent on British grants. (Not that some of the returned slaves were above profiting from the industry: all up and down the coast, slaves back from Brazil made a good living trading slaves for Manchester cottons. A liberated slave, Francisco Felix Da Souze, acted as a slave broker for inland kings: "His riches and hospitality became the legend ... and he charmed even missionary opponents with manners which were easy and graceful and exhibited the finished gentleman.")[20] During the next sixty years the population swelled to about sixty thousand, "recaptured" from all over West Africa, giving Sierra Leone a uniquely cosmopolitan air. Alas, the "returnee" Africans, called Krios, began to dominate Sierra Leonan society, looking down on the indigenous Mendes in the south and Temnes in the north.

And so it went. The Krios opposed independence, but it came anyway. Instability followed. At one point there were three coups within thirteen months. In 1968 a charismatic trade-unionist, Siaka Stevens, took over and dominated a one-party state until 1985, when he stepped down and turned over a dispirited country and ravaged economy to his chief of army, Joseph Momoh. Under Momoh (known in the country as Dandogo, the Imbecile) the treasury went bankrupt. Matters got even worse when the Liberian civil war spilled over the border under one of Charles Taylor's protégés. After Western prodding, Momoh promulgated a new constitution permitting multiparty democracy, and elections were called. A month later a twenty-seven-year-old army captain, Valentine Strasser, took over in yet another coup. It was Strasser who called into play the Pretoria-based mercenary corporation, Executive Outcomes, who set up a command post offshore (mooring next to a ship owned by the diamond cartel De Beers) and within a few months had secured the country's diamond fields for the government and for its own corporate coffers: it was war as business, a venerable colonial attitude, familiar enough to King Leopold of the Belgians. Strasser, however, didn't last. After ruling for three years, spending much of it looting the economy (his government was described as a "kleptocracy"), he was said to be "exhausted, and looking for a way out." He promised elections, but before they could be held, his chief of staff, Brigadier Julius Amaado Bio, gave him a much faster way out than he had anticipated, taking him in handcuffs to Guinea. By that time the civil war had already killed ten thousand and had displaced a fifth of the country's four and a half million people. As a British newspaper headline glumly put it early in 1996, "Liberia is Sierra Leone a couple of years and maybe 150,000 deaths further down the track."[21] Bio, in turn, promised elections, and they were duly held, but against a background of threats and intimidation.

"In the little [diamond mining] town of Bo," a British reporter said in a dispatch, "I met a man who had had his right ear and his lips cut off. Someone had carved on his chest the word *terror*, and on his back *Against the election Feb. 26.*"[22] A Médecins sans Frontières field hospital reported what it called dozens of "involuntary amputations." Some of the amputees said the "rebels" who assaulted them asked for whom they had voted. If they gave the "wrong" names, they had their hands cut off. Everyone commented on the almost incredible bravery of the Sierra Leonans in exercising their precious right to vote.

The elections were said by international observers to be "fair." In a second round a month later, there was more violence.

By the middle of 1996, the country had apparently deteriorated, once again, into apparently senseless factional fighting. But late in the year, the foreign minister of the Ivory Coast, Amara Essy, brokered a cease-fire, after having been secretly dropped off in the Sierra Leone wilderness for a clandestine meeting with the leader of the shadowy Revolutionary United Front, Foday Sankor, another of Charles Taylor's chums.

Executive Outcomes, naturally, took credit for the cease-fire, an improbable boast largely adopted by the Western media.

The ceasefire was—of course—precarious and didn't hold. There was another coup. Sierra Leone has much unfinished business.

Part VI

The Sahel: The Golden Empires of the Sun

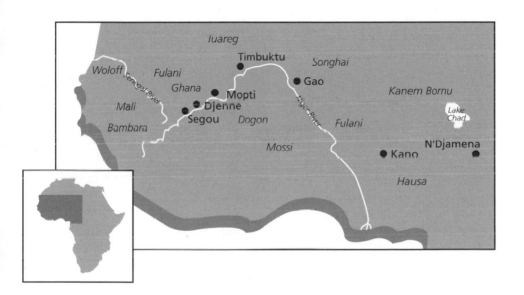

OLD GHANA

The great empires of the Sahel were among the glories of Africa. In the beginning, still obscured by the swirling mists of time, were the pastoralists of the then-verdant Sahara. The first organized state to emerge was the kingdom of Ghana, which was several centuries old when Muslim traders arrived in the Sahel in the early part of the ninth century. After perhaps eight hundred years of ordered prosperity, Ghana slipped into senescence around the beginning of the second millennium, and was succeeded by Mali, the greatest empire of sub-Saharan antiquity. Mali was governed for nearly four hundred years from its capital of Niani, in modern Guinea, and Malians controlled the greatest trade routes of Africa: from the Niger River cities of Djenne, Mopti, Timbuktu, and Gao, and from the desert terminus of Agadez, Tuareg camel trains came and went via the oases of the Great Desert, carrying the gold of Ghana to Tripoli and Alexandria and salt back from the desert. The coins of the Venetian traders were made of gold from Ghana, come by pirogue down the Niger and then taken from Timbuktu by Tuareg camel trains via the oases of the Great Desert. Fabled Timbuktu! Founded by desert nomads as a place to sell camels, it became a great centre of Islamic learning in the fourteenth century; its university, still operating, was established six hundred years ago. I once stood on the roof of a massive mud-built mosque, to which the faithful have come to pray since 1340, and looked out over this exotic city, unchanged for many hundreds of years but slowly decaying as the desert sand expands inexorably southwards.

Mali, too, eventually decayed and was overrun by the Songhai, based in Gao. Songhai in turn died and in its wake came a host of lesser kingdoms: the Bambara, the Mossi, the not-so-insignificant Hausa. Many of these were swept away in the jihads launched by the militant Fulani, whose short-lived theocracy affected everyone along the southern shores of the Sahara, from the Atlantic to Lake Chad.

Farther east, near Lake Chad, on the borders of Niger and Chad, was the equally fabled kingdom of Kanem-Bornu, the empire that persisted for a thousand years (well, it dimmed and brightened, dimmed and regrouped, until it was finally destroyed by the French colonialists in 1880).

On the periphery of empire (and occasionally in the thick of it) were the desert nomads—the fiercely independent Tuareg, the Berbers of the north, the Moors of Mauritania.

And of course constantly there, inescapable, was the brooding presence that governed all lives in the region, the greatest desert on earth, the endless Sahara.

To this it's come: I leaned over and touched the tomb of B'ton Mamar Coulibal, almost the last of the Bambara kings, ruler of Segou and Segoukoro, faded inheritor of the fabulous Mali emperors, themselves only the heirs of venerable Ghana. Coulibal was laid to rest here in Segoukoro, Old Segou, in 1755. They constructed a royal tomb for him—2 metres (6.5 feet) wide and 4 metres (13 feet) long, with three plastered pillars at one end, the roof of the tomb polished mud the colour of dun. Large enough, no doubt, for himself, his wives, a child or two, and household possessions to comfort him on his long journey, for though he was a Believer, there was no harm at all in a little pagan insurance.

I brushed my hand over the tomb's surface. It was dusty, warm to the touch. The hot wind had been blowing all day from the northwest, from Ougadou, the dusty region where the great desert begins up near the Mauritania frontier. Segou is on the banks of the Niger River about halfway from Bamako, the capital, to the trading city of Mopti, and a third of the way to the Great Bend, where the river starts to curve south, as though afraid of the desert heat—that's where Timbuktu lies. But the Sahara has been moving steadily southwards, and even Segou is no longer immune.

I stared hard at the polished mud, trying to see through to the grinning skull beneath. What would Coulibal tell his ancestors, the illustrious Mansas of Mali, if he were to come across them in the Muslim paradise, as Allah promises? That he had done his best, all his life, with what he had? His kingdom had shrunk to a mere province of Old Mali by the time he came into his own. There were wars on many frontiers. The Fulani were crying for jihad; together with the Tuareg they were tearing Timbuktu apart. (And indeed, a generation later the Fulani would burst out of Mali and sweep across Old Sudan, their waves breaking at last only on the rock of the Kanem-Bornu emperors, far to the east.) Revenues had shrunk too: Segou had been cut off from the gold-fields that had made the Mansas so powerful. It had had to rely on tributes of millet and bitterly resented Customs duties on traffic down the Niger—wasn't that when the Bozo traders first began to travel at night, slipping among the sandbars, cunning as crocodiles?

A faded kingdom, considering what had gone before, but yet not inconsiderable. The explorer Mungo Park arrived in Segou forty-one years later, on July 20, 1796, having struggled for months to reach the Niger, and his notes show he was impressed: "The view of this extensive city; the numerous canoes upon the river; the crowded population, and the cultivated state of the surrounding country, formed altogether a prospect of civilisation and magnificence, which I little expected to find in the bosom of Africa." The Bambara capital didn't much like outsiders, since currents of war were swirling about the countryside and strangers were as likely to be spies as not. The king sent word that Park would not be allowed into the city, nor even to cross it, but would have to put up at a nearby village. On arriving there, he reported, he was met with astonishment and fear. No one would open a door to him. He was hungry, exhausted, and far from well. But "a woman returning from the fields ... perceived that I was weary and dejected and inquired into my situation ... with looks of great compassion she took up my saddle and bridle and told me to follow her [into her hut] ... finding that I was very hungry she ... went out, and returned in a short time with a very fine fish which ... she gave me for supper. The rites of hospitality thus being performed to a stranger in distress, my worthy benefactrice pointed to a mat spread for me and told me I might sleep there without apprehension ... In the morning I presented my compassionate landlady with two of the four brass buttons which remained on my waistcoat; the only recompense I could make her."[1]

The considerable empire of Mali had shrunk almost to nothing by the time Coulibal reigned. Today, the sizeable town that Park visited, Coulibal's capital, has itself shrunk almost to nothing. Segou has become Segoukoro, Old Segou, and a new town has been founded a few kilometres downriver. I spent a night in New Segou, in a pleasant little inn run by two Lebanese brothers. It is a colonial town, largely built by the French, but the oldest part, the "native quarter" in colonialist parlance, has many houses built of mud in the traditional Malian way, and a thriving artisanal commerce of weaving, tinsmithing, carpet making, ceramics, and so forth. Pleasant enough, but I much preferred Segoukoro, or what was left of it.

Segoukoro is made entirely of mud. There are no paved streets—the streets are mud too. The mosque is of mud. The tomb of Coulibal is mud. Most of the houses and streets look—and indeed are—ruins made of mud. The town is a maze of narrow alleyways punctuated by secretive doorways and glassless windows, with intricately carved screens of wood. As I wandered about, I saw at intervals ruined buildings and vacant lots that looked like bomb sites, but the only bomb that had dropped was time and its inevitable consequence, decrepitude. A shrinking population has no money to repair a town made of mud, in which the buildings melt in the wet-season rains unless protected by fresh plaster. The inhabitants are living like the Romans after the Barbarian invasions that led to the Dark Ages, reduced to watching their history slowly fading into the memory of the *griots*. Even most of the trees were dead or dying; the few that were still alive held no more than a twigful of scrawny leaves.

Shrinking population? There were children everywhere, underfoot, taking my hand, shrieking *Babu ça va! Babu ça va!* (White man, how's it going? How's it going, white man?) I had walked down to the tomb of Coulibal like a pied piper, sticky little hands clinging to mine, followed by twenty more children, a cheerful, yelling mob of them. Then they quieted and just stared as I contemplated the bones that lay beneath the cover.

When I left Coulibal to his endless dreams I wandered down to the river past the best-kept building in Segoukoro, a little mud mosque plastered in red, with a pyramidal tower and three smaller cones, the whole not much larger than the average suburban dining-room. Its door was latched shut, but since it was built on a lit-

Mosque at Old Segou, Mali

This little mosque, made of mud, is the best-preserved
building in Old Segou, once the capital of a Bambara
kingdom, and now just a faded trading town on the Niger River.
The world has left Old Segou behind, and even New Segou, a
little farther downstream, is fading around the edges, like an
early photograph exposed to too much ultraviolet light. Just after
taking this picture I sat down under an old mango tree and ate
grilled fish with a group of men who had been lounging there.
No one in Old Segou is any longer in any hurry.

The market at Mopti

The market is remarkable for many reasons, not the least of which is that its methods and commerce have changed hardly at all in the last five hundred years. The pirogues are still made just out of town, by Bozo craftsmen segregated in their own boat-building village; they are still made in the same way, pieced together from hand-hewn boards, nailed up by Bozo-made spikes. Their design is identical to that noted by Arab travellers in the twelfth century—long, up to 20 metres (22 yards), needle-nosed, with a shallow draft and very stable, roofed with arching boughs covered with thatch (occasionally tarpaulins, now). These boats ply the river as they always have, travelling from Segou and Segoukoro to Mopti, Mopti to Timbuktu, and Timbuktu to Gao.

Council chamber, village of Sangha, Dogon territory

The toguna is the men's meeting place among the Dogon, the local "parliament", where the elders sit and grumble and decide the villagers' fate. As a stranger, of course, I wasn't allowed in. Like all Dogon artefacts, the toguna is rich is symbolism: its eight carved pillars represent the eight founding ancestors; there are eight levels of thatched roof; the building is built low to the ground, with not much more than a metre of headroom (mostly to prevent hotheads springing to their feet to harangue the other elders—banging your skull on a beam has a calming effect). In the evening the ancestors enter the building, and it is in their presence that all important decisions are made.

Timbuktu streetscape

Timbuktu is all duns and beiges and dusty browns, for the threatening Sahara is pressing in and its fine desert dust penetrates everything. The only colour is the robes of the Tuareg nomads and the finely wrought opal and silver jewellery still to be found in the markets, between the stalls selling tethered chickens and heavy slabs of Sahara rock salt. The buildings are all of mud dredged from the Niger River. The sloping facade at right is part of an ancient university dating back to the fourteenth century, now a national monument—Timbuktu was once an important centre of Islamic learning. The protruding poles are built-in scaffolding; mud buildings must be replastered after the rains.

Valley in the Atlas Mountains

The High Atlas are stark and forbidding, prone to violent storms and unexpected blizzards in the winter. Once, near the top of the infamous Tizi-n-Tichka pass through the mountains, I saw a long row of stopped trucks, maybe a hundred of them. The pass had been closed the previous night—a freak storm had dumped torrential rains along the Atlantic coast, washing out roads and fields, and had deposited half a metre (about a foot and a half) of snow. The pass, at 2200-plus metres (7,200-plus feet), was open again, but only just—the roads remained uncleared and the surface was treacherous. I passed a few truckers who were just starting out. "Insh'Allah", they would say, God willing, we'll get over in safety, but their white knuckles and terrified expressions were not reassuring. Berber villages, remote and inaccessible, are scattered through the valleys. Most of the Berbers are no longer nomads, but they still tend their flocks of sheep and goats and wild camels on the stony slopes, and their lives have changed little over the centuries.

Moroccan farmer's market

Berber markets are common all up and down the Atlas, and well into the desert. At Tagounite, over the small but precipitous pass called Tizi-Beni-Selmane, the nomads come with their donkeys laden with dates. At Asni and Amizmiz and Azilal and Guemassa the shepherds come down with their flocks from the High Atlas as they have been doing since ancient times. This one was on the outskirts of Marrakech. Muddy alleys pierced the warren of stalls, and the place stank of foul water, animal excrement, urine, and slightly rotting food. Later that day I went to another market in the Atlas foothills, only slightly less muddy; the open lot where the donkeys were tethered was called in high irony, le parking pour Mercedes. I walked down a smoky alley; on charcoal braziers savoury lamb and chicken stews were cooking in the clay pots called tagines, and bits of goat were grilling on skewers. In a small alcove to the right a dozen men were drinking mint tea, squatting on mats or sprawling on benches, entertained by three itinerant musicians, with tambour and lyre. I listened, entranced, as the plaintive music drifted through the smoke and over the hubbub of the market, the music of the nomads preserved through centuries of Islamic disapproval.

The faithful gathered to venerate the Ark of the Covenant, Axum

According to Ethiopian Christian belief, the Ark of the Covenant has been kept safe by their priests ever since it disappeared from the Temple of Jerusalem, in the days of Solomon the Wise. This is the very same Ark built by the wandering Jews to God's specifications to house the Tablets brought down by Moses from the mountain, an artefact of supernal and supernatural powers. It was said to have been taken from Jerusalem by Menelik, the illegitimate son of Solomon and the Queen of Sheba. This holy thing is now housed in an old church in the city of Axum, once the capital of a powerful empire. Seven days in the year it is brought out by the priests who guard it, and taken, shrouded and hidden from sight, to the town square, where the faithful gather to venerate it. The rituals and the prayers that accompany this procession have changed hardly at all in a millennium; only the amplified drone of the priests betray the technological presence of the twentieth century.

The Kasubi tombs, Uganda

This is the Great House of Kasubi, repository of the bones of the last four of the Baganda kings (hidden from view behind a bark-cloth curtain). I was shown through it by an old woman, descendant of King Mwanga II; she lived in a small hut nearby in order to tend to the necessary rituals to propitiate the ancestral spirits. She came, she told me, in an unbroken line from the legendary Kintu, in the lineages the first of the thirty-five kings of Baganda. She had the sniffles and mumbled a lot, but was descended from a demi-god, and talked of the old kings as though they were uncles newly departed. This Great House had been built as a courtroom by Mtesa I, the king who had welcomed the first of the European explorers, among them John Hanning Speke, who was searching for the source of the Nile. Mtesa governed what was, next to Burundi, the most powerful kingdom of the region. A mere four generations later it was all gone, destroyed by the uncomprehending brutality of colonial armies.

tle plateau above the river it afforded a pleasant view, up towards Bamako, and down towards Segou itself. Freight canoes plied the water, and Bambara fishermen were casting their nets. Although it was the dry season and the river was low, there was still plenty of it.

I joined a group of men lounging in the shade of a mango tree below the mosque, and they succeeded, at last, in shooing the giggling children away.

We sat there for a while, in silence, and then one of them fetched two fish he called "capitaine" from a basket at the river's edge, and sold them to me so we could all eat. He grilled them on mango twigs, and served them on leaves. I fetched a couple of bottles of warm Guinness from the car, and after a while we snoozed there in the shade, unheeding as the Niger River commerce passed by to Timbuktu and Gao, as it had done for millennia.

....

To get to Koumbi Saleh, the capital of the First Empire, Ghana, you have to travel north from Bamako, the capital of Mali, through the old Bambaran heartland in what is now the national park called the Bouclé de Baoulé, and then farther north into the desert scrub. The land flattens out in the Ougadou, devolves into folds and wrinkles in the Valeé du Serpent, and, at Nara, the last town south of the Mauritanian border, turns into arid stonelands and dunes. Koumbi Saleh is about 50 kilometres (30 miles) or so into Mauritania, but nothing is left except a few unimpressive ruins and the camps of resident archaeologists. Even M'banza Congo had more than this.

Still, descriptions exist. In the middle of the eleventh century, the Cordoban geographer Abu 'Ubayd al-Bakri described the capital in some detail. It was by then made up of two towns, a stone-built one inhabited by the Muslim traders and a mud-built one of the locals, in which the king had his walled palace. Their centres were 9 kilometres (6 miles) apart, but the whole thing was built up, in what sounds oddly like a medieval version of suburbia, complete with malls—the considerable population was supported by the produce of surrounding farms, which were irrigated from wells. Al-Bakri described the court as displaying "many signs of power, and the king had under him a considerable number of satellite rulers." Much of his revenue came from taxes on trade, and the basis of trade was gold. Ghana's own merchants brought the gold from the south and traded it for salt, which the northerners brought in from deposits in the Sahara.

When was it founded? Even the archaeologists can only guess. There are theories that it was built by Berbers in the fourth century, but by the time the Islamic proselytizers got there in the eighth century it had long been ruled by a Cisse dynasty. The earliest extant Arabic reference to a kingdom of Ghana dates from the close of the eighth century.[2] At the height of its power, in the tenth century, Ghana's influence stretched from the Atlantic to the lakes situated to the west of Timbuktu, and from Taganit in Mauritania south to the Niger River. It remained an animist society until near the end of its existence, though one of its eminent kings, Tounka, allowed Muslim merchants to build mosques there in the tenth century.

This was not the only city in the Empire of Ghana. It may not have been the largest. It may not even be the oldest. A few days later I went to Djenne, a trading city of some twenty thousand people on the Bani River, in the Niger flood plain. Djenne is a picturesque little town now famous mostly for its magnificent mud mosque and its fabric weavers, who make the extraordinary Malian "mud cloth," but, like Segou, Djenne is relatively "new": 3 kilometres (2 miles) away are the ruins of Djenne-Djenno, Old Djenne, a major city that was mysteriously abandoned almost seven hundred years ago, and which now is little but a heap of eroded mud brick, glass beads, tantalizing fragments of metal, scraps of pottery, and small statuettes. Old Djenne has been dated to somewhere around 200 B.C., and was a thriving city by A.D. 300, when jewellery, copper objects, and decorative ceramics were being mass-produced. This was long before North African Arabs penetrated the Sahara in the ninth century. Old Ghana had a network of markets, a developed agriculture, a sophisticated art, an evolved politics, and—yes, the evidence points to it—a tax-collecting bureaucracy, before the Europeans emerged from the Dark Ages.

How far back in time? Leo Frobenius reports the existence of a "vellum manuscript," which he said recorded the names of seventy-four rulers before the Fulbe dynasty in Ghana, "which there occupied the throne in 300 A.D., running through twenty-one generations."[3]

Djenne-Djenno may have been abandoned when Ghana fell, and the upstart Muslim Empire of Mali associated the city with corrupt pagan practices. Or maybe they just liked the new neighbourhood 3 kilometres away better.

....

So black Africa had towns and cities and empires before the Arabs arrived with their Islamic notions of forced assimilation, before, indeed, the birth of the Christian era. *What's the theory of their development?*

Theories, actually, for there are many and they conflict.

The earliest, and now discredited, was the "Hamitic theory," in which Libyan Berber tribes speaking Hamitic languages (the dominant peoples of North Africa before the Arab conquest) were supposed to have drifted south across the Sahara, teaching the "natives" as they went. This was a convenient explanation among those who found it hard to believe black Africans could invent anything for themselves.

The second relies on archaeological evidence, and puts forward the notion of a cattle-herding and agricultural economy among a mixed population of Libyan

Berber and black peoples in the Sahara by at least 4000 B.C., more or less the same time things were getting going in the Nile valley. This theory has it that the desiccation of the Sahara somewhere between about 8000 and 2000 B.C. must have caused the population to drift away towards the southern savannah, where the need to control the limited land and water led to the development of powerful kingdoms.

The third theory gives the nod to the need to control the long-distance trade. Horses, luxury goods, and salt, scarce in West Africa except along the coasts, were traded for gold, ivory, and slaves.[4]

A more recent and more widely accepted theory was summarized neatly in the book *Art of a Continent*, published as a catalogue to a major exhibition of African art in the mid-1990s. The archaeologist John Sutton had proposed a pre-desert Aquatic Civilisation of Middle Africa, composed of settled communities of fishing people along the then-fertile watercourses of what is now the Sahel region. This theory is now regarded as overly simple, but the basic facts on which his argument was based have been generally accepted.

It's known that there were people in the Sahara "genetically close to [the people] now inhabiting sub-Saharan Africa" who were dependent upon fishing and on gathering wild grains like sorghum. Among other things, these people had developed a distinctive pottery, recognizable by a "dotted wavy line" patterning. Digs in the central Sahara site of Amekni, dating from about 6000 B.C., yielded up evidence that such pottery was independent of ancient Egypt (which began producing ceramics later than both Western Asia and the Sahara region). From about 4000 B.C., perhaps in response to the drying up of the Saharan region, there was a shift to a cattle-keeping pastoral economy in the central Sahara. These cattle-keepers drifted southwest, putting pressure on the fishing culture of the Aquatic Civilisation, forcing the locals to become farmers. The same thing was happening at the same time in the Nile valley, which led to pre-dynastic Egyptian civilization.[5]

Archaeologists have now also proved to their satisfaction that African iron-working techniques were not introduced by the Phoenicians, Egyptians (via Meroë), or Arabians (via Axum), as was commonly thought. (The confusion came about partly because of racist assumptions about black African abilities and partly because those Africans seem to have skipped the earlier copper-working phase, passing directly from Stone to Iron.) Indeed, there is evidence for African smelting as early as the seventh millennium B.C.

All of which means what? Merely that the Africans developed their kingdoms without any help from "outside." The same civilization that led to the great empires of West Africa was also substantially responsible for ancient Egypt—and so ancient Egypt is no longer as mysterious in its origins as popular myth would have it, being merely another African civilization that grew out of the heart of black Africa, just as Ghana did and Mali after it.

Trade routes crossed the desert before there was a desert, which means that there was already something in the south worth trading for. So the coming of the desert didn't create the routes—they were already there. The desert only meant that trans-Saharan trade had to be better organized, and would have to take place in larger and more careful expeditions. Herodotus had long ago written that by about 500 B.C., the Sahara was being crossed in horse-drawn chariots, a notion confirmed this century by the discovery of drawings of chariots on rocks in the desert. The trails used by medieval Islam were therefore following much more ancient ones—"the distribution of Saharan rock art paintings and engravings, plotted on a map, shows crossings uncannily like the western and central trade routes of the Arab traders."[6]

There were two main traverses: from Morocco and from Egypt. Both led to the Upper Niger, and thence to the gold-fields of Senegal and Ghana. Egypt and Middle Asia were greedy for gold, and it was gold that built Ghana and Mali. The power of the kings of ancient Ghana was based on controlling the export of gold from the Senegal and Niger valleys.

....

In a small alleyway in Djenne I came across two young Fulani boys, about ten years old, sitting on a mud ledge outside a doorway. They had across their knees smooth wooden boards about 20 centimetres (8 inches) wide by 40 (15 inches) long, and a copybook. They were copying Koranic texts onto the wood, using an ink their class had made that morning from ground charcoal and gum arabic. These were the school's star pupils, sent outside for independent practice of their art.

I heard chanting, and stuck my head through the doorway to hear more clearly. Inside a small room, about twenty other children were sitting on the floor. At the head of the class was a greybeard, their teacher, leading them in their lessons. They were learning the sacred texts, as their fathers had before them. I leaned briefly against the doorway, feeling the tough-textured wood of the frame, scarred and pitted from the centuries—this school had been here, in continuous existence in this same building, since the ninth century: for more than a thousand years, students had passed through this modest portal to study the esoterica of Islam and the mysteries of numbers.

The teacher, whose name was Fazad, saw me there and invited me in, and for a while the chanting faltered as the children stared at the *babu* in his strange gear.

After a while Fazad took me up onto the roof of the school to look at the town. Like the building itself, the roof was mud. I looked down. A couple of children were walking in the alley, a small girl balancing a basket of boxes on her head. A woman sat on a chair, her orange dress a startling contrast to the dun-coloured street and houses. Beside her on the ground were two large bowls of fresh peanut butter for sale.

In the other direction I could see what looked like desert. The school was near the edge of town. A few trees peeked up above the buildings, but beyond the town boundary—nothing. The land was flat, featureless, treeless, grassless, baking in the noonday sun.

Fazad saw me staring. "It's not what you think," he said quietly. "In the wet season the river still rises, and the plain becomes a marsh. The annual miracle of the Niger still keeps us going. It may not rain here anymore, but in the hills of Guinea where the river rises, the rains still come."

"You are used to long traditions, I guess," I said.

"It is human traditions that are important."

"Isn't it important that this building has itself seen so many hundreds of generations?"

"A building is just a place," he said, a little impatient at my slowness. This was "new" Djenne, after all. I guessed new in this context meant a thousand years old. There was a long silence as I looked across the town, contemplating the centuries. In the distance was Djenne's famous mud mosque. I had tried to get in earlier, but had been turned away—it is not open to casual visitors, only to devotions, and then only to Muslims. Visits had once been allowed, but had been cancelled after an Italian crew shepherded their models inside and did a "fashion shoot": how the West cannibalizes cultures in the service of commerce! The mosque isn't very old—it was built in 1904—but is an exact copy of a much earlier building on the same site, and it's almost certainly the largest building made of mud anywhere. The people of Djenne are still taxed to keep it in a good state of repair—every year after the wet season it must be replastered.

I turned back to Fazad. "Do you teach the children to read? Is yours the only schooling they get?" And I added hastily, because this didn't seem to come out right: "I mean, your vocation is to teach Islam, and that's what your school does. Do they learn secular studies as well?"

He looked away. "Few," he said, "only very few. Their families keep them out of school. They say the children are needed to work, but there is no work here. So they go down river to Mopti, or up to Bamako. I don't know what happens to them there."

Djenne is on an island, and you have to cross the Bani River to get to it. The highway traffic to Djenne is carried on one small ferry whose motive power is four men with poles. Obviously, Djenne is no longer a major source of commerce. Even the river markets have shifted north, to Mopti.

"I must go back to my class," Fazad said, and led me downstairs. From below, I could hear the buzz and chatter of children. Teacher was away and the kids did what kids everywhere do.

I had spent a few days at Mopti earlier, hitching rides on the great commercial pirogues and poking about the city's remarkable market, which is arranged around a deep basin set into the banks of the Bani River at the southern end of the city, a few kilometres before it joins the Niger. The market is remarkable for many reasons, not the least of which is that its methods and commerce have changed hardly at all in the last five hundred years. The pirogues are still made just out of town, by Bozo craftsman segregated in their own boat-building village; they are still made in the same way, pieced together from hand-hewn boards, nailed up by Bozo-made spikes. Their design is identical to that noted by Arab travellers in the twelfth century—long, up to 20 metres (22 yards), needle-nosed, with a shallow draught, and very stable, roofed with arching boughs covered with thatch (occasionally tarpaulins, now). Similar but smaller "canoes" act as ferries, carrying families to and from the pottery-making village on the far side. These boats ply the river as they always have, travelling from Segou and Segoukoro to Mopti, Mopti to Timbuktu, and Timbuktu to Gao.

In the dry season the market spills down the cobbled sloping sides of the basin itself. Everywhere there are pirogues, hundreds of them. Merchandise is stacked on the cobbles. I saw two men wrestling an ancient refrigerator onto the roof of a sturdy cargo pirogue. There were huge piles of calabashes, bundles of firewood, stacks of lumber (some of it being made into furniture on the riverbanks), plus the usual accoutrements of an African market: piles of dried fish, bloodily butchered lambs, mounds of mangoes, pyramids of peanuts, heaps of manioc and other roots. And off to one side, spread over an area 20 metres (22 yards) long by as many wide, great slabs of Saharan rock salt, brought by camel caravans out of the deep desert, traded in the markets of Timbuktu, and brought down here to Mopti, whence they will make their way to the refineries and factories of the capital. The salt slabs weigh 100 kilos (220 pounds) each and are stacked in bundles of four or five, tied with cord and piled on sticks laid on the cobbles. They are the colour of dirty cream, flecked with grey.

A merchant saw me staring at the salt slabs, and came over to find out what I wanted. "You want to buy some?" he asked in French.

"No," I said. "What would I do with them?"

"Turn them into money," he said, grinning. "That's what they're for."

"Where do they come from?"

He shrugged. "The Tuareg bring them in from the desert," he said. "I don't care to go and see, myself. What does it matter? They always come."

I stared again. They always come, and they always have. These slabs, brought two to a camel from the Saharan salt mines, have been a staple of Niger commerce since the days of Old Ghana, nearly two thousand years ago.

I sat with the merchant for a while in companionable silence, gazing out to the mouth of the basin and the Bani beyond, watching the boats come and go. Below us, three men poled a heavily laden pirogue off the cobbles and heaved their way out to the open river. In shallow waters they would pole this boat all the way to Timbuktu; when the water was deeper, they'd paddle. It could take five days or longer, and they'd sleep along the way on the banks, near remote villages, as they had always done. The Ghanaian traders had done the same, and when their time had gone, their successors, from Mali the Great and the Songhai of Gao, had carried on the tradition.

I tried to remember why Old Ghana had, at last, faded.

Troubles had started on their northwest frontier as early as the ninth century.

Berber nomads had been drifting south from the Moroccan oases since the Arab conquest several centuries earlier. By the ninth century these desert chieftains had formed themselves into a loose and fractious confederacy that controlled at least part of the Atlantic Saharan caravan routes and, in the dispassionate language of the military historian, "now and then inflicted defeats on the more settled agriculturists of the Ghanaian empire." Hah! These terrible nomads boiled out of the desert with their silver scimitars seemingly as long as a camel's leg, killing the farmers, then the farmers' protectors, then whole caravans of traders who had headed north across the sands with saddlebags of gold ... But the confederacy was short-lived: they had nothing to unify them except a sense of historic grievance and an ethos that glorified robbery as conquest, and they soon fell to fighting among themselves.

In the tenth century the Ghanaian kings reasserted themselves and once again took control of the oases and the caravan routes, pushing the nomads back, and subduing those who could be subdued. The rest remained in the deep desert, out of sight, nursing their anger, developing their legendary mastery of the shifting sands, biding their time. Their raids provoked reaction, reaction fuelled more anger, more partisans to conduct new raids ... And so the pattern repeated itself. The tribes began to cohere once more, into a loose confederation called the Sanhajah, whose centre was around Audaghost, just north of the northern frontiers of the Ghanaian kingdom.

It wasn't until early in the eleventh century that this new confederation took on a more menacing form. A chief of the time, Yahya ibn Ibrahim, made a pilgrimage to Mecca and brought back with him an Islamic scholar from Morocco, 'Abd Allah ibn Yasin, with the thought of improving his people's rather hazy notion of Koranic correctness. Yasin, by all accounts, was filled with the righteous zeal so common in relatively new and militant religions. At first, his teachings went well, and his ideas—a more militant, puritan faith with little room for backsliders and apostates—spread rapidly. Still, many of the Berber tribes resisted, and when Yasin's scholastic choler finally boiled over he resorted to force. He was supported by a Sanhajah chief whose partisans came to be called the Almoravids.

That ever-so-convenient Islamic notion of the jihad, the holy war, of the righteousness of forced conversions to the faith and the holiness of killing enemies of the faith, united the tribes as nothing else had been able to do. In the middle of the century they were united enough to turn their attention to the still-pagan rulers of Ghana, and they began to conquer the productive lands on either side of the western Sahara. In 1076 they occupied the Ghanaian heartland, suppressing pagan practices, building mosques and schools, burning statuary, and smashing clay idols. It was the end of the old empire.

The Sanhajah occupation lasted only twenty years, after which the Berbers, responding to an urgent appeal from their Moroccan brethren for help against their enemies, the Zanatah, departed whence they came. (They left only remnants behind: the Gudala, the most westerly and southerly of the Sanhajah, survive today as the Igdalen of Spanish Sahara.) But by that time the moral authority of the Ghanaian kings had been fatally compromised. Perhaps that wouldn't have mattered had not the Almoravids' raids and constant fighting also undermined the country's agriculture, and thus its prosperity. Whatever the ultimate reasons, the empire began to break apart, and satellite kingdoms such as the Mande gradually began to assert their independence.

Eventually, in 1235, the Mande clan called the Keita, kings of Mali in the uppermost Niger valley, took control and incorporated what was left of Ghana into their own, considerably more extensive, and militantly Islamic, empire.

Suniata, of the country of Mema southwest of Timbuktu, of the Tungara tribe, emir of Malinke, kin to the Songhai of Gao, became the first Malé, the Ruler.

THE KINGDOM OF MALI

This is what the bards say of Suniata:

"This Suniata was a powerful child, though weak on his feet, and the bards asked, 'Why doth thy Suniata always slip about the ground?' In those days there was but one great Sira tree in all of Mande. Whoever swallowed a pip of the fruit of this tree became King of Mandingoland. Suniata went to this tree with his people. Many had tried to get one of its fruits by hurling up cudgels at it, but none could throw sufficiently far. Now instead of a cudgel, Suniata picked up a man, and the man so thrown up struck against a fruit, broke it off and hurled it down. Suniata gulped down the whole fruit, thus hindering the birth of any rival to his might. And then he seized the whole gigantic tree, plucked it out of the ground as another would have torn up a little plant, carried it into town and planted it in his mother's compound."

His father was reported to have said (as well he might): "Haha! Suniata has arrived at man's estate and now one may set about his circumcision."

Nevertheless, Suniata was forced to flee his country for his own protection. He asked the sand oracle to divine his fate. The oracle replied: "Before thou arrivest where thou wouldst thou wilt thrice be stirred to wrath. Yet, if thou let not thine anger overcome thee, thou shalt be king of Mandeland."[7]

Presumably, though the bards are silent on this point, Suniata successfully suppressed his wrath, because ruler of Mandeland he indeed became.

....

Suniata and his successors, now the kings of the Islamic Empire of Mali, began systematically to expand their domains. They developed a new trade route southeastward from Djenne towards new gold-fields that were being opened along the Black Volta and farther south still, in what is modern Ghana. They extended their power beyond what had been the eastern frontiers of Old Ghana, to the then-thriving cities of Timbuktu and Gao, which were the terminuses of the shortest trans-Saharan routes. They began sending caravans laden with gold across the desert to Egypt, which was then more stable than Morocco. The Niger River became their east–west conduit. Soon, Malian merchants were trading as far south as modern Ghana and as far east as the city-states of Hausa, between Lake Chad and the Niger, and to the newly thriving market town of Kano, in northern Nigeria.

For the next few centuries Mande traders, by now Muslims all, extended the reach of their rulers to Central Africa, to the Guinea coast, to the eastern Sudan, and to the centres of Islam around the eastern Mediterranean and the Gulf of Arabia. Universities were founded at Timbuktu, Djenne, and Segou—the one at Timbuktu had more than twenty thousand students in its glory days, though it is shrunken now in stature, funding, and real estate. One of the great scholars of Timbuktu, Ahmed Baba, had a library of sixteen hundred books. Islam spread with the traders, and the Hausa converted *en masse*. The arts flourished; jewellery of rare delicacy has been found in the ruins of Djenne-Djenno. The country became wealthy, so wealthy that the kings were profligate with money, as though it were in inexhaustible supply.

A map published in medieval Europe shows the extent of the kingdom, its lands sprawling from the coast into the hazy interior. "This Negro lord is called Mansa Musa, Lord of the Negroes of Guinea," the cartographer wrote. Its capital was located at Niani, or Niani-Niani, on the Sankarani River in Guinea, a small and unimportant tributary of the Niger, but close to alluvial gold-fields. It is said that the gold once stuck up out of the ground in large cones, there for the taking.

Musa, sometimes called Kanku Musa, made his hajj to Mecca in 1324. He took with him a massive entourage—some reports, surely exaggerated, say he ordered sixty thousand of his subjects to go with him. But what most astonished the scribes of Alexandria, where he paused on his route, were the hundred camels laden with gold that trailed after him. Indeed, the Mansa showered so much gold on the economy that the value of the currency in the whole region was still debased a dozen years later. Europeans had pretty well ignored Africa since Carthage had fallen, but there were Venetian and Genoese trading firms in Alexandria, and these alert and hard-headed gentlemen paid serious attention to the Mansa's extravagant spending; soon reports of Mansa Musa and his immense wealth quickly spread through southern Europe.

The most curious souvenir of this extraordinary voyage, however, was a conversation the Mansa had with the son of the sultan of Cairo, the gist of which was published by the Cairo encyclopaedist, Al-Omari, in 1340. "If I have become the master of Mali," Kanku Musa confided to his host, "it is only because my predecessor refused to believe that the ocean was infinite."

The predecessor in question was Abu Bakari II, the Voyager King. This restless and energetic monarch had travelled the length of his growing empire and had spent—or so the *griots* say—too many hours staring out over the Atlantic, which he came to see as a barricade to his more or less infinite expansion. Somewhere out there must be other lands for a king to conquer. "Therefore," Mansa Musa said, "my predecessor sent a preliminary reconnaissance fleet of four hundred ships towards the unknown and shadowy horizon. Only one returned, but that one told stories of a mysterious river in the middle of the ocean."

I've watched the pirogues pushing through the surf on beaches all up and down the Atlantic coast of Africa. The fishermen still go out every day from Dakar, the Senegalese capital, which is almost certainly where Abu Bakari's astonishing fleet departed for their great adventure. Like the boats of the Niger, the fishing pirogues of Senegal are huge, pieced together from thick planks hewn from the giants of the rain forests; it took a dozen men to bully them through the surf to the smoother ocean beyond. I've seen them disappear over the horizon and return, nets bulging with fish. But four hundred vessels! Lost in the middle of the great ocean, caught in the oceanic currents that ... that what? Drift across to Brazil?

In any case, that story of the river in the middle of the ocean was enough. For Abu Bakari, his fate was decided.

"Not in the least discouraged," Mansa Musa said, "the emperor ordered the building of two thousand more vessels, a thousand for the men, a thousand for supplies." When the fleet was ready, he led his entourage once more down to the coast. There, he placed himself in the lead boat. "He assigned to me his authority and power until such day as he should return, but to this day no one has ever seen him again."[8]

Abu Bakari II set sail for America somewhere between 1310 and 1312. Did he ever get there? On this subject the *griots* are, of course, silent. Historians of the Americas are similarly silent, and except for a few African-looking statues in fifteenth-century Mexico, and a few Spanish texts describing "black men from Ethiopia" near the Darien isthmus in 1513, which may or may not have anything to do with any of this, Abu Bakari's hubristic journeying has vanished from memory.

SONGHAI

No matter how rich, the Mali Empire could not last forever. The distances were too vast, other ambitions too strong. Their power was dependent on control of the Niger, which in turn meant they had to control a non-Mande people called the Songhai, who monopolized the commerce downstream. But the Songhai had an independent monarchical tradition of their own that predated Mali, and the Mali kings kept only erratic control of the Songhai capital, Gao.

The Songhai origins are obscure. There are theories that they had arrived many centuries before from Libya, or even Yemen, but no one knew for sure. The first of the rulers to come to outside attention was a king called Zá-Kasí, who ruled about the year 400 of the hegira, or in the beginning of the eleventh century A.D., and was already the fifteenth king of the dynasty of the Zá.

From this old tradition, a usurper eventually arose, This was Sonni Ali, and his emotional appeal was to the paganism of his people, which he set against the "false cosmopolitanism" of the Mande's Islam. Ali reigned for nearly thirty years, from 1464; early in his rule, his cavalry began raiding even to the Malian heartland, several times entering Niani, the capital. This was the beginning of the city's long decline; archaeologists picking through the bones of Niani now can track how the city began shrinking in the fifteenth century, until it was finally abandoned a hundred or so years later. Ali destroyed the Mali Empire by his ceaseless warfare, and reigned in its stead, from his capital at Gao.

While the Mali kings were defending their heartland against the Songhai, the Tuareg of the desert saw their chance and overran Timbuktu, which they had themselves founded some hundreds of years earlier. This impudent occupation didn't last. Sonni Ali, once he had consolidated his power, wrested it back from the nomads with immense slaughter in 1488. In 1493 power passed to one of Sonni Ali's former generals, Al-Hajj Mohammed A'skia, who was, ironically, both a Mande and a Muslim.

The Songhai were never strong in the west, where the rump Mali kingdoms such as the Bambara asserted their own independence. They did better in the east, however, where the older kingdom of Kanem had declined during the fourteenth and fifteenth centuries following internal dissension after fierce Fulani raids on their border. (Eventually the Kanem kings re-established their state in their former province of Bornu, close to Lake Chad.) To the south, the Songhai exerted their influence over the Hausa, who began to grow in power and importance. South of the Niger bend, the kingdoms of the Mossi-Dagomba were emerging, founded by renegade bands from the northeast.

Songhai power continued to provoke resistance. Their control of the salt mines close to the Moroccan borders upset the balance of trade, and in 1591 provoked retaliation from the Sa'adi dynasty of Morocco. A force of four thousand soldiers, many of them Spanish recruits from Andalucia under the command of Sultan Ahmed al-Mansour, was sent across the Sahara, where it sacked Gao, Timbuktu, and Djenne. But the sultan, having looted the Niger cities, departed hastily back home, where his fiscal mismanagement had provoked revolts. The four thousand men he left behind, no matter how well armed, couldn't hold together an empire. Indeed, they were unable even to control the network of trade routes within West Africa that brought gold and other produce to the Niger cities. The main beneficiaries from the Moroccan conquest were therefore the Tuareg, who filled the vacuum they left behind and were able to demand tribute from the descendants of the Moroccan soldiers, who had come to form the military cast of the Niger cities.

> A'skia had one stroke of luck in his rise to power: the pretender Mohammed Bánkorí was on his way to Gao with a formidable army to contest the throne, when he passed by Timbuktu, and was induced by the Kádhi ruling there to give up his quest for material gain in exchange for a life of contemplation and study—much to the fury and astonishment of his army, who had expected bloody battle followed by rich spoils.
>
> From Barth, Travels and Discoveries in North and Central Africa, p 294

None of this did the ancient city of Timbuktu any good at all. As the German traveller and geographer Heinrich Barth put it, "during the age of anarchy which succeeded the conquest of the country by the [invaders from Morocco], and owing to the oppression from the Tuareg on the one side and the Bambara and Fulbe on the other, the state of affairs could not be very settled; and the town [Timbuktu], shaken as it was to its very base by that fearful struggle of the inhabitants with the Khadi Mustapha, with massacre, rapine, and conflagration following in its train, could not but decline greatly from its former splendour."

The domination of the western Sudan by the Ghana/Mali/Songhai, which had persisted for at least five centuries, was at last ended. The Songhai declined, shrinking in power until they ruled only their original homeland of Dendi (close by Borgu), and the Mande power shrank until only little kingdoms remained, kingdoms like Segou, whose ruler, Mamar Coulibal, I had visited in Segoukoro.

KANEM-BORNU

The last of the great empires of the Sahel were Kanem-Bornu, which spilled over the borders of what are now Niger and Chad, near Lake Chad; the Hausa of Kano, in northern Nigeria; and the chaotic Fulani "empire" in the middle. I had already spent some time around Lake Chad, going there in order to see the Kanem heartland. I had come up from Cameroon, once again passing through Bamenda and Bafoussam and the toy kingdom of the Bamum, and travelled northwards via the Fulani towns of Ngaoundéré and Garoua. Ngaoundéré was an ugly little town, pleasantly situated, and its palace, called the Palace de Lamido ("Lamido" being the local name for ruler), is a splendid example of traditional architecture. I passed through Garoua, stopping only long enough to watch a parade. This was the home of the former Cameroonian dictator Ahidjo, which explains why it has an international airport and so many buildings built in that curiously characterless international style dating from the sixties. There were, but are no longer, direct flights to Paris once a week.

I spent a day around Rumsiki, in the Kapsiki Mountains, a barren landscape of huge basalt outcroppings that André Gide had once called one of the ten most beautiful places in earth, a quote the grateful Cameroonian tourist authorities are still using. Quarrel with him or not, it is a slightly surreal, rather moonlike landscape, into which the Kirdi people were driven by the Kanem-Bornu and their Fulani successors. Up on the cliffs and inaccessible hillsides are the Kirdi's tiny, pointy houses of mud, which are utterly adorable. The houses are round, unlike the square ones of the Bamiléké, but just as tall. They are so small, people must almost have to sleep curled up. The Kirdi— the Kapsiki, Matakam, and some others—are poor, and have been for centuries. Their hostility to the Fulani is legendary, which is not so surprising, since Fula slave hunters drove them into the mountains centuries ago. Nevertheless they mingle freely with the Fulani in the markets, which is an odd sight, because the Fulani, men and women alike, are conservatively draped in voluminous Muslim gear, whereas the Kirdi remain as naked and as close to nature as any tribe in modern Africa.

The Kapsiki Mountains are close to the Nigerian border and very picturesque. The week I was there, the Harmattan was blowing steadily. The sky was hazy, and visibility poor. Most of the Kirdi I saw were wearing some tattered version of Western clothing, but occasionally, in the villages and along the less-travelled highways, women could be seen walking to water, dressed only in earrings and a minuscule apron. I never saw the famous Kirdi cache-sexes, the intricately styled, chain-mailed and leather-thonged pubic patches, which are now mostly to be found in markets as souvenirs; President Biya's prudish government has banned them as unseemly.

The road journey from Maroua to the border town of Kousséri took only a few hours. I wanted to see if I could get to Lake Chad from the Cameroon side, so I took a road that skirted the Nigerian border as it curved around to a village called Fotokol. From there, a track led to Ngouma, on the Serbewel River, which flowed directly into the lake. I was sure I could hire a pirogue there. I had a four-wheel-drive Nissan, so I didn't expect any problems. But well before Fotokol, there was a police barricade, and no amount of cajoling would move them. They even turned down a "cash incentive," an unheard-of thing in rural Africa. I had read that Lake Chad was a "sensitive area," but no one could tell me why. Although it was shared by Nigeria, Chad, Niger, and Cameroon, I didn't see why that would make it sensitive; the fighting has been over for some years.

As I pulled up at the border-crossing to N'Djamena in Chad, the wind picked up. By the time I had crossed the bridge over the Chari River, a gale was blowing. Half the Sahara seemed to be passing overhead. Visibility was less than 100 metres (330 feet). The Harmattan, the Hot Wind of the Desert, was strengthening.

It was 42° Celsius (107° Fahrenheit).

That night my hotel in N'Djamena, described in Alex Newton's almost always useful Central African guidebook as having "air-con. rooms," had neither air-con. (the power was off) nor water (the water was off). Neither of these things was the hotel's fault, and I wasn't resentful, only disappointed. N'Djamena was still recovering, after all, from twenty-five years or so of warfare. Unfortunately, in an extra effort to be helpful and to "air out" the room, someone had left a window slightly ajar, and my bed was covered with a gritty film of Sahara sand. When I closed the window to keep out the sand, the temperature climbed even further, and soon passed 50° Celsius (122° Fahrenheit). Every half hour or so after that, until the small hours of the morning, an apologetic staff member kept knocking on my door to advise me they were working on the situation.

In the morning, there was no problem getting to Lake Chad, "the great sea-like komádugu, the Tsád or Tsáde," as Heinrich Barth had called it. The problem was finding Lake Chad when I got there.

I had read about the lake in many places and was eager to see it. It was known to Ptolemy, and was the subject of legend in the European Middle Ages, but to the African traders it was no legend: one of the most ancient caravan routes across the Sahara from Tripoli teases the lake at its northwest corner. I remembered fragments of reports from the Denham–Clapperton–Oudney expedition of 1823: "The great Lake Tchad, glowing with the golden rays of the sun in its strength ... within a mile of the spot on which we stood ... On the shores ... there were prosperous little villages, most of the houses having a cow or two, some goats, and chickens in the yard and the lake itself was thronged with birds and animals ..." All was not, however, as peaceful as it seemed, for the villages were subject to constant raids, not only by the Tebu in the north, but from the warlike people who inhabited the islands of Lake Chad and controlled the waters from their battle canoes.[9]

Once, the lake was immense, bigger than Britain; on some maps it is still shown twice its actual size, for it is shrinking fast, almost 100 metres (330 feet) a year. These days, it's less a lake than a large bathing pool for hippos, and if you're a reasonable size and don't fall into a hole, you can wade across it. In the drought of the eighties it once dried up altogether, except for a few pools where the desperate wildlife gathered (the fishermen simply starved). To its north, in the Kanem region, there are huge dunes, among which dwell a secretive fisher folk, the Yedina. In the south the shores are flat and swampy. What water is left is divided into two lobes separated by a ridge; only one channel now pierces that sandy barricade.

The gale had stopped, but its effects had not. Visibility was still only a few hundred metres. I carried a case of Cameroonian Tanguy mineral water with me and went through three litres that day. Everything was gritty. Clothing felt abrasive. I was developing a rash. I thought I was getting a low-grade fever but couldn't really tell, it was so hot and uncomfortable. I had rented an air-conditioned Toyota, but the desert heat outclassed it, and I gave it up and opened the windows. Little drifts of sand piled up in the back seat. We reached Dougia, which Alex Newton had described as a "restful, shady place by the Chari river with a refreshing pool in good order and lots of thatched paillotes." No doubt correct. But the season was obviously wrong. The Frenchman who built the place was in Paris and had been temporarily replaced by a surly Berber from the north, by his attitude a veteran of many a desert campaign and not yet reconciled to comfort-seeking infidels. The paillotes were there, but the place was empty. No one would sit outdoors anyway, for fear of being sandblasted. Thirty kilometres (19 miles) farther on there were supposed to be motorized boats for hire, but there were none. And in any case, there was no sign yet of the lake, and the Chari River was nearly empty.

Nonplussed, I pressed on. Twenty kilometres (12 miles) or so farther, I rounded a bend and saw a dugout canoe paddling gently among the reeds and papyrus beds, the muddy marsh that marked the edge of Lake Chad proper, and a hippo, with its enormous mouth wide open and a bird pecking away at its teeth. The paddler took me out for an hour or so, but I saw nothing more than mud and swamp and islands of reeds. If there was a lake somewhere, it was hidden in the grass and the haze. Nor did I see any Yedina, the last surviving permanent residents, remnants of the glorious Empire of Kanem. Perhaps they had sensibly stayed home to drink tea.

Once, Lake Chad helped feed the Nile. Soon, unless things change, the Chari River will run into dust, and the desert will have won another victory.

For a few days afterwards I wandered about the N'Djamena hinterlands. I poked about the village of Gaou, a small hillside town that is supposed to be the ancient capital of the Sao people. The Sao no longer exist, but have left behind artistic traces in the form of terracotta heads and figures and decorative bronzes. If they were giants, as the legends say, there is no sign of it here; the gaily painted wattle-and-daub houses are, if anything, smaller than usual. The local theory about these painted walls is that they are a revival, that they were once a traditional art form. There is scant evidence for this, but the locals are so pleased with the idea that it seems churlish to argue. Pottery seemed to be the main industry in town, some of it slyly advertised as "ancient," and maybe some of it is. The Sao were supposed to have originated in the Nile valley, which is possible, since Lake Chad once connected to the Nile. It is also possible they were related to the Nuer of the Sudan, and other Nilotic people.

Sometime around the ninth century salt traders began moving into the area from the Nile valley, intermarrying with the Sao, who eventually disappeared. One of these traders established himself as king and founded the state of Kanem, which under the Sef dynasty was to last for another thousand years before it finally succumbed to the deadly technologies of the West. Through all its long history, Kanem, and later Kanem-Bornu, served as a point of contact between North Africa, the Nile valley, and the sub-Sahara region; the trade in salt, copper, cotton, gold, and slaves brought the Sef kings to the attention of Muslim merchants, and by 1200 Islam was the dominant religion. The empire's first capital was at Njimi, northeast of Lake Chad. It was moved to Bornu, to the west of Lake Chad, in modern Niger, in the late fourteenth century, driven there by raiders from the Bulala tribe. The empire languished, dormant, until it was roused again in the sixteenth century, pushing out the interlopers and retaking Kanem. Under the greatest of its kings, Idris Alawma (1571–1603), the empire was expanded and consolidated; Alawma developed a strong cavalry force, complete with chain-mail, quilted armour, and iron helmets, and had a small force of musketeers trained in Turkey. I had seen something of the remnants of this cavalry in the post-Ramadan festivals I had watched in northern Cameroon, which had been part of the empire in the old days. It was Kanem-Bornu, alone of the old empires, that later resisted the Fulani jihads, launched from the land of the Hausas.

The kingdom was still going strong when Clapperton and Oudney arrived in 1813. Their expedition had crossed the desert from Tripoli, "and included two hundred soldiers and a number of Arab merchants anxious to travel to Bornu in the safety of an armed party. The physical hazards—excessive heat by day, sandstorms, rocky hills, choked-up wells—were on the whole less frightening than the human hazards." Any caravan was liable to attack by the nomadic, though fortunately gunless Tebu, and safety was unreliably procured by bribes to various minor chiefs through whose territory they passed. "After two months of very hard going the harsh frown of the desert began to fade."[10]

They travelled down the western bank of the lake to the capital of Bornu, and were received there by Sheikh El-Kanemi, a highly capable ruler who had succeeded in preserving his independence from the expanding power of the Fulani in the west. It wasn't until December that Clapperton and Oudney were reluctantly released by the sheikh, and continued their journey towards Hausaland.

When Heinrich Barth passed through the Bornu heartland in 1854, "Zurríkulo was once a large town [but] it has gradually been decaying and is now half deserted. The neighbourhood of the town is full of wild animals; and great fear was entertained by my companions for our beasts ... The roaring of the lion was heard during the night ... Here begins a zone characterised by sandy downs from 100 to 120 feet high, and exhibiting on their summits a level plain of excellent arable soil, but with few trees, while the dells ... which often wind about in the most anomalous manner, are in general richly overgrown with a rank vegetation, among which the dúm-palm and the dúm-bush are predominant. This curious formation, I fancy, has some connection with the great lagoon, which in a former period must have been of much greater extent ... All was silent with the exception of a distant hum, becoming more and more distinct as we wound along the side of an exuberant meandering valley. The noise proceeding from the considerable town of Déffowa, which we reached at a quarter past seven o'clock ... Lively music never ceased in the town till a late hour."[11]

Barth's journey was complicated by the chaos of a civil war that broke out in Bornu, caused, he speculated, "in the circumstance of the coffers and slave-rooms of the great men [of Bornu] being empty."

....

I strolled around Gaou for much of a morning. There was a market in town tenanted mostly by Bagirmi traders, who had controlled a substantial kingdom in the area about two centuries ago. The women in the market wore leather jerkins made from goatskin, and kilos of brass around their ankles and wrists and necks; they had their hair pulled up into cornrows so tight they lifted the scalp into tiny furrows, into which small black beads were pressed. I'd seen pictures like them years before and had read about them. Nothing had changed.

The Bagirmi had been slavers, for slavery in Chad predated European incursions by many centuries. The decentralized polities of the Chad basin were no match for the Arab and Bagirmi raiders; Chadian slaves were so common that even relatively poor Fulani owned two or three. The population of the country began to shrink. Caravans of slaves went stumbling across the desert, and many of them perished along the way, leaving a trail of skulls to Tripoli; for every slave that survived the trip, it was said, ten more had died. It was in this era that the Sara women south of Lake Chad began the practice of self-mutilation, inserting huge plugs into slit lips to make themselves repellant to slavers. It is still possible to see old women in the market, plugs now removed, their lips distended in a great loop, looking for all the world like leather shoelaces growing on their faces. There are young women, too, who have inserted small plugs like buttons; these are now high fashion.

....

I went back to N'Djamena. It looked dusty, and tired, and the bullet holes from so many years of war could still be seen, though most of the fighting had taken place many kilometres to the north.

This had been called Fort Lamy once, and the French colonialists had regarded it as a romantic outpost of empire (although hellish hot for the serving officers of *la force étrangère*). In those innocently arrogant days the French believed that "whoever holds Fort Lamy holds Africa," and declared it to be "the first fort for the defence of Cape Town," though against what sinister invading force from the far north was never specified.

The French had made themselves immediately popular in the Lake Chad area by putting an end to the slave raids. Popularity didn't last, however, as they shipped out entire communities of Sara peoples to build the railway in the Congo. They also set up cotton plantations, which amounted to the same thing: French overseers fixed artificially high cotton quotas and bullied the village chiefs into coercing labour from their people. By the time Chad became independent in 1960, the French had built only three schools in the entire country.

Independence was merely a prelude to a prolonged civil war between the northerners, backed by Libya, and the southerners. In the middle of all this the Chadian president, François Tombalbaye, in a bizarre episode of transatlantic cultural reseeding, became addicted to voodoo practices, not from Togo and Benin, where they had begun, but from Haiti, where they had mutated, in the absence of cultural controls, into something entirely more vicious. Tombalbaye forced all civil servants to undergo voodoo initiation rites; those who resisted were shot. In 1975 the army, fed up with the killings, shot Tombalbaye instead. The war went on, until the Libyans were finally forced to retreat by a horde of civilians in minivan taxis, heading north in an insane rush from N'Djamena. Even then, it was not over. Hissène Habré, the leader of a northern splinter group, took the fighting to the capital itself before he was finally subdued and fled into exile in Senegal. From that great distance, in 1992, he launched an attack on the Lake Chad area and captured two towns before he was repulsed. French paratroopers were sent in to help drive the rebels away.

But the divisions remained. The president, Idriss Déby, was forced to promise political pluralism in order to hold the country together (and to retain French support). As of early 1997, the promise was still just a promise.

THE TUAREG AND TIMBUKTU

O*f course, I needed to visit Timbuktu, the ancient city that had been at the centre of so much of the turmoil that the empires had wrought—and yet which had for centuries been an eminent centre of Islamic learning. There, I would visit the Tuareg, the founders of the city. I had been told in Bamako that it was once again "safe" to visit Timbuktu, but that I would have to surrender my passport and obtain a police permit when I got there. "Safe" was a code-word in this context. It meant that the Mali government had settled—for the moment—the Tuareg rebellion that had been simmering since the early eighties. Convoys were still being attacked occasionally, in the far north of both Mali and Niger, by Tuareg bandits posing as separatists. I could go, but I should be careful, the Bamako people told me gravely. The Tuareg are very touchy.*

I was thinking of that great hazy emptiness to the north and of caravans laden with gold as I sat in the desert in a Tuareg tent, drinking sweet mint tea. Mohammed Ali had been telling me a story of an oil prospector he called "the Texaco man," who had spent some time out in the desert with the Blue Men, as the Tuareg are known, for their faces and hands are often stained from the indigo dyes of their robes. This Texaco prospector had left a large sum of money in his tent when he went away for a few days, somewhere down to the coast. All the money was still there when he returned. But the point of the story wasn't the honesty of the desert nomads—no, didn't their own legends and poems celebrate thievery, usually glorified as the manly art of raiding? Everyone had known of this money, Ali said. Everyone in the desert was talking about it—it was one of the tales told when caravans met. The point was that the Tuareg, who are afraid of nothing, are afraid of money. Money is soft. Money is a settled life in the cities, where there is sickness and filth and poverty. Money is corruption. Money is the killer of cultures. The Tuareg want to keep their culture alive at all costs and they haven't survived for so long in the desert by being soft.

But there is softness and softness. I hadn't been with these people ten minutes before a young boy trotted up beside my camel and told me in passable French that he was the first of his family to go to school. I gave him a pen, a small gift with big consequences. In return, he gave me a ring he had made himself, and later his big brother did me a favour, when I came across a surly group of men in the desert who had spread out "souvenirs" on a dune, and were insisting, with increasing levels of peremptoriness, that I buy something. Their attitude was pretty straightforward. They, or rather the Bella (a reference I didn't yet catch), had made these things, and it was my duty to buy them. That these souvenirs were utterly beautiful (inlaid-ebony jewellery, silverware, hand-wrought silver swords) was beside the point. Big brother, a commanding

My Air Mali flight to Timbuktu via Mopti had been cancelled because the plane had gone to Guinea instead, where there were more important people to pick up. This was the Air Mali "large plane," holding forty passengers, as opposed to the two others in the fleet, which were the "small planes," with room for seventeen passengers each. All were elderly aircraft of dubious provenance, nominally Czech but with Russian markings, and flown by slightly shop-worn Russian pilots. "Perhaps the next day?" Jean-Marie from the booking agency asked. "No?" Well, he explained there was a 12:30 to Mopti, but it was overbooked and it didn't go to Timbuktu, in any case. Still, it would be worth trying to get on—after all, Mopti was halfway to Timbuktu … On the morrow we arrived at the airport prudently early, at 8:30. The check-in crew didn't show up until 11:45. Jean-Marie disappeared into an office marked Taxes and emerged thirty minutes later, triumphant. He had a cousin at the airport, a man who worked in "*contrôle*." He had explained the dilemma to his cousin and had persuaded him to persuade the controllers to send the flight an hour farther and take me to Timbuktu. Not for the first or last time, I appreciated the African sense of family.

As we waited in the terminal, the Russian engineer, dressed in a red beanie, Hawaiian shirt, shorts, and beach flip-flops, walked from the plane to the terminal and returned with a stepladder. He propped it against a wing, climbed up, and unscrewed a stopcock. After refuelling, he scrupulously put the ladder back in the terminal building. There was a Fulani family on board whose grandmother had to be hoisted into the plane by the entire crew and several passengers, and who was much too fat for a seatbelt. The Malian stewardess just shrugged. The luggage was secured with bungee cords at the back, blocking the door to the only washroom, and had to be shifted in flight when a large man in voluminous robes stripped off his coverings down to his bloomers and demanded to be able to go *faire pipi*. Inflight service was a Coleman cooler filled with cans of Fanta and plastic bottles of mineral water. A baby threw up on the shoes of an Ismaili woman from the U.N. The pilot yelled at another baby to shut up, and its mother pushed a breast into its mouth, which worked better than the pilot's yelling. Despite all this, the passengers were amazingly cheerful.

We stopped at Mopti, where everyone else got off. But the plane rapidly filled up again with delighted passengers heading for Timbuktu—it was never explained how they'd learned that the flight would be continuing—presumably they had cousins too. We stopped one more time between Mopti and Timbuktu, to let a family off at a town called Goundam. The authorities hadn't expected a flight, and the airport was closed—there was no one there, not a single person or vehicle, only buzzing flies and a few locusts and, high overhead, a circling hawk. For twenty minutes or so the Russian crew stood in the shade of a wing and waited, but then they wearied of it, moved the baggage to the side of the runway, and we took off, leaving the family huddled forlornly in the middle of the landing strip in the 40° Celsius (104° Fahrenheit) heat. The town was 15 kilometres (6 miles) away.

From the air, the Niger River was a beautiful blue-green in a sea of dun. Such vegetation as there had been higher up, towards Bamako, thinned out on the way to Mopti, and the desert appeared, a lovely reddish golden beige. In this low-water season the Niger was no more than a few hundred metres wide; in the wet season the river overflows its banks and makes swamps and shallow lakes. With proper timing, it's possible to grow rice in the newly made paddies, harvesting just as the water recedes again after the rains.

From the air, Timbuktu was the same golden brown as the desert that surrounded it, a secretive maze of brown houses in brown streets. I could make out the small towers of a mosque, and in a sandy depression children were playing, and camels wandering. I could even see a police jeep spinning its wheels in the sand. Far to the south, I could just make out the Niger, on its way to Gao. To the north, there was only haze.

presence in a sweeping blue robe, helped me fend them off. Particularly the hand-wrought-steel-sword guys who, when I told them I had no use for a hand-wrought steel sword, were threatening to turn ugly. Afterwards, he introduced me to his sister and his mother, asked me in for mint tea, and invited me that night to a wedding.

His name was Ahmed, he said, and he introduced himself to me as Mohammed Ali's nephew. He was a *caravanier* by trade—made his living fetching salt from the mines at Araouane.

"Next time we'll go to the salt mines together," he said.

"How far is it?"

"Twenty days out, twenty days back," he said.

I declined the forty days, but I went out with him into the desert anyway. We swayed across the dunes, the camels plodding and snorting like old men with heartburn, their front feet kicking up little bow waves of fine sand. The sky was luminously clear and you could see forever. How different from the humid, claustrophobic, fecund swamps of the south! This is the Endless Desert, home of the Berbers, the Bedouin, the Tuareg, and the Toubou, Muslims who deny descent from Mohammed, and who share the mountainous and craggy central desert with the Hadjerai, "men of the rocks," one of the few cultures isolated enough and fierce enough to have successfully resisted Islam. In that arid, secretive north with its lunar craters, deep gorges, and volcanic massifs, memories of ancient blood-feuds still fester; there are strange rock paintings which date back past the early days of ancient Egypt into the dim mists of man's ancestral memories, but they are hidden from sight, guarded by tribal animosities and suspicion of outsiders; very few visitors now risk the trip and of those who do, not all survive.

An hour out of Timbuktu the sun went down in a flare like a star burst. The temperature dropped twelve degrees, to 32° Celsius (90° Fahrenheit), and a full moon appeared, throwing the ripples in the dunes into sharp relief, etching the scrub thorns on the sand, indigo against sable.

Ahmed's family lived (until the seasons changed and they moved again) with about thirty others in an encampment scattered along the slopes of the dunes north of Timbuktu. Their round goatskin huts were pitched in the sand, each out of sight of the others. There were no trees, only a few scrubby thorn bushes, and the Tuareg must make do without shade. Or they make their own—over the top of each tent, pegged to four stakes, was a large flat cloth for shade and ventilation. Goats wandered freely and there were camels everywhere. But there were no cattle—the cattle were 100 kilometres (60 miles) away in a wadi. Ahmed twitched aside the goatskin door and motioned me inside. I stooped low and sat awkwardly on a tightly woven rug. On pegs and wooden hooks were the accoutrements of nomad life—silver ornaments and jewellery, daggers, knives and swords, a polished vintage rifle, rugs and clothing, cooking pots, everything arranged with a fanatical neatness. A tea service waited on a cushion.

Like all the Tuareg men of the desert, Ahmed was dressed in indigo robes, the *gandoma*, that swept the ground as he walked. Around his head and lower face was a 6-metre (20-foot) length of indigo cloth called the *tagelmoust*. It was designed for the desert life, protection against sun and blowing sand, but even at home it is kept in place, and when a man drinks tea the cup is passed under the veil, keeping the mouth covered. The higher the Tuareg's social status, the more likely he is to remain covered when meeting strangers. When I first met Ahmed, he kept his *tagelmoust* hitched over his mouth and half of his nose; only his eyes could be seen, black and penetrating. As we'd become more comfortable talking, he'd allowed the covering to slip to his chin.

I'd been talking earlier to Mohammed Ali about the Tuareg way of life, and he'd mentioned the thorny problem of schooling. Ahmed admitted, a little sheepishly, that he could neither read nor write, but his father considered him schooled anyway. What Ali meant was schooling in the ways of the tribe, knowledge of the rituals and traditions, familiarity with the Koran, and a deep, practical knowledge of the desert and its caprices.

"It's why," Ali said, "a man should have only one wife. You can't educate your children properly if they are scattered in too many tents."

"How many children, on average?"

"Only five, no more. The life is not easy."

As I sipped Ahmed's mint tea, I thought of the Tuareg women. Unusually for a Muslim society, the men are veiled, but the women are not. A Tuareg woman is free to choose her husband and divorce him, but the husband cannot divorce his wife without her consent. I'd asked Ali about this matter of one wife. Was this by female demand? "You're entitled to four? Isn't that what the Prophet allowed?"

"But only if you treat them all equally, and fairly," Ali said. He laughed. "And it's not just that you think you're treating them equally—they must think so, all four of them. The thing is impossible."

Ahmed was still unmarried. His sister had slipped from the tent when we entered, and I could hear her singing with the other women a short distance away. She had reminded me of a phrase from Angela Fisher's *Africa Adorned*, in which she referred to "the strange wild beauty of the Tuareg women, unveiled and free," with their startling blue eyes and fair skin burnished to old ivory by the Saharan sun, "evidence of their Berber ancestry."[17] I'd come across her earlier, dancing in the sand with her mother and other women, their feet shuffling, singing an ancient Berber love song, a dozen women in black or green robes, along with giggling children and one old man, dreamy in a white robe with sky-blue *tagelmoust*, keeping time by beating the sand with an ancient sword. They saw me watching, and let me take pictures, but the pictures do nothing to capture their boldness and their beauty. Ahmed's sister was in green, with skin like cream. Her eyes were not blue but deep black, bold, and mischievous. Around her neck she wore a single strand of blue beads and a talisman called a *khomissar*, a fertility symbol. As she stood straight, her head covering, kept in place by a silver pin, trailed down her back.

The Tuareg, like the Moors, are descended from the Berbers. They left their fertile homelands in the north about a thousand years ago, migrating into the desert to escape the invading Arabs, who had made their way into Africa in the seventh century. The Moors headed southwest, into what is now Mauritania; the Tuareg made their way across the dunes and gravel deserts of Algeria to the central mountains, and eventually to the Sahel, picking through the dry riverbeds and mountains of sandstone and volcanic rock, from oasis to oasis. Their lives were fine-tuned and intricate: the desert came to be Home, and they the masters of it. They took to breeding camels up there in the rocky fastnesses. They disdained intermarriage with the locals, unlike the Moors, and submitted to no man's control, not even the Mali kings'. A group of Tuareg founded Timbuktu about nine hundred years or so ago.

> Timbuktu was never supposed to be a town, only a market. The original market was presided over by an old woman of fierce and chastising ways. *Tin'Buktu* in Tuareg, Place of the Old Woman.

The Tuareg adopted Islam, but on their own terms. Theirs is an inclusive Islam, not at all fundamentalist. They make music as part of their worship, and the music they make is all their own; even today you won't find cassette players or boomboxes here. Much of their singing is extemporaneous and poetic. I asked Ahmed about this business of their poetry celebrating thievery. But Ahmed denied it. They celebrate daring, he said—it is the action, not the result, that is celebrated: a Tuareg would take by force, never by stealth. They now look down on the Berbers for having adopted settled ways, and for intermarrying with Arabs. Their own society is hierarchical, being divided into nobles, vassals, and religious men. Haratines, or freed slaves of mixed blood, cultivate the oases, and are paid in produce. Traditionally, Bantu slaves did the menial labour, and, indeed, still do. I was walking around Timbuktu with Ali and came across a group of grass huts among the rectangular mud buildings, and asked him what they were used for.

"Those," he said, as casually as though he was pointing out the post office, "are where the slaves live."

The slaves were the Bella people. Actually, they were freed by the Mali government in 1963, though I suspect not all of them have been told. It is one more source of grievance among the Tuareg that Outsiders would interfere with the proper regulation of society.

When dark fell, the Tuareg women started to sing again, a plaintive sound I thought, songs of the desert, songs of life, songs of history, songs of longing—Ali and Ahmed translated what they thought I should hear. Afterwards, the women stared and giggled among themselves, and then the whole group settled back on cushions and told stories. Ali's mother was on one side of me and Ahmed's sister on the other, shadowy in the moonlight, smelling faintly of spices and jasmine and fresh mint. They told stories of water, of wells 40 metres (130 feet) deep, of the great emptiness of the north. I thought of my ancestors trekking across the Thirstland of the Kalahari, but from here it didn't seem so formidable—the Sahara is the greatest desert on earth, 2,000 kilometres (1,243 miles) across, sand and gravel and desiccating heat stretching all the way up to Carthage.

Dinner was couscous and goat-meat sauce, eaten communally with the hands from a large bowl, and mint tea, very sweet, in tiny cups. Ahmed's sister picked out morsels of goat and fed them to me. Afterwards we plodded back to Timbuktu on our camels, by the light of the moon. I dropped my camera at the hotel, and an hour later Ahmed and his sister came to take me to the wedding, which I could already hear in the souk across the sandy depression where the kids play soccer in the sunlight. The marriage ceremony itself was over by the time we got there. The tambours were out, and the dancing had already begun, formal but wild, intricate but improvised, every movement pregnant with symbolism. The night was absolutely clear, and the stars were blazing hot in the desert sky above. It was 35° Celsius (95° Fahrenheit), there in the sands of Timbuktu.

THE FULANI

The Fulani, the other people who had so filled up the interstices of Sahelian history (they had no "empire" to speak of, only radical theocracies), I had already met briefly in Cameroon. They had moved there in centuries past, driving the native Kirdi, whom they despised as primitives, up into the mountains. They had recently settled down into a more or less bourgeois existence. Now, they are spread out over the whole Sahel, as far as the Senegal coast; there are said to be more than six million altogether in Senegal, Mali, Mauritania, Burkina Faso, Niger, Nigeria, and Cameroon, though no one knows for sure.

I bought some earrings from a young Fulani woman in a busy little market in the village of Yangasso, which is near Bla, which in turn is near Segou, in Mali. The earrings were massive, great clumsy things formed in the shape of a double crescent moon, tied together with a red cord, and heavy enough to tear the lobes. Or they would have, had they been made of gold, in the traditional manner—these were authentic, because they had been made by Fulani craftsmen, but were of tin covered with gold leaf instead of the real thing.

The young woman had already married her third husband, as she told me, and was clearly a woman of substance in the community. Ah, she was beautiful! Skin the colour of milk chocolate, haughty and tall, features aquiline.

I asked her who had made the earrings I bought, and she motioned to a man hovering protectively nearby. I asked her where she came from, but she wouldn't say, and when I started to ask other questions the man stopped hovering and chased me away. Perhaps he was husband number three, already wary of number four.

German explorer Leo Frobenius, whose views are not always trustworthy (coloured as they are by his apparently ingrained belief that the black Africans were incapable of originating anything themselves) but who may have got the Fulani origins right, put it this way: "In considering the Fulbe [Fulani] tribe, two eminently distinct types must be kept strictly apart in one's mind, namely, the emigrant [westward-moving] and returning [eastward-moving] types ... I call the emigrant Fulbes the remains of that migration of peoples which at some pre-historic epoch led them from some part of East Africa toward the west ... while the bulk of the wanderers reached the Upper Niger up to Senegambia, some portions of it broke off and remained on the road ... These detached fragments ... are partly preserved in their particular purity and partly intermixed with the back-flow of the Fulbe ..." The rest of the Fulani, much more mixed ethnically, were the backflow that resulted when the first wave crested somewhere around western Guinea or Senegal, and turned back east. Frobenius also had a word to say about the Fulani's notorious ideological purity: "... the Fulani had in early times been fanatical about racial purity until the point, primarily in the westernmost of their migrations, where they adopted the Muslim faith and their fanaticism transferred in that direction," he wrote.[13]

The preconditions for the emergence of the Fulani theocracy was the disintegration of the ancient empires, and the unhappiness of the Fulani pastoralists at the constant taxation and vexation of the petty successor kingdoms. The precipitating event was the arrival in West Africa and the Sahel of a mystic and militant version of Islam, the *tariqah*, which held that the forced conversion of pagans was for the glory of god and an urgent duty. The *tariqah* spread through Fulani society like a desert storm in the late seventeenth century, and the first of the Fulani jihads was launched by Karamoko Alfa near the source of the Niger, in central Guinea, in 1720. This led to a small theocracy that persisted until 1881, when it was finally brushed aside by the French.

It was only a taste of the agitation to come. In 1790, a Fulani holy man, Usman dan Fodio, who lived in the northern Hausa state of Gobir, began to preach sedition against the kings, whom he accused of being little more than pagans. His jihad charged through Hausaland and engulfed Adamwa, Nupé, Yorubaland to the south, the three old Hausa kingdoms of Kano, Katsina, and Zaria, and the adjacent one of Daura, and swept up tribal chiefdoms in what is now northern Cameroon and southern Chad. As we have seen, only the armies of Kanem-Bornu, secure against Lake Chad and trained in battle against the erratic nomads of the central Saharan mountains, were able to resist. After the old kingdom of Gobir was destroyed, two major military encampments, Sokoto and Gwandu, emerged as the twin capitals of a new Fulani empire. Sokoto, the more powerful, was the last of the empires of the Sudan.

The commanders of the jihad, Usman dan Fodio's brother Abdullah and his son Muhammed Bello, became the viceroys of the new empire, which combined the three former Hausa kingdoms of Kano, Katsina, and Zaria with the smaller rump kingdom of Daura. Abdullah ruled the western half, from Sokoto and Bello, the eastern half from Gwandu. But their hearts weren't in the militant mullah business, and when Usman died the standards once again decayed, the people seduced by the softer life of the Hausa, and the Hausa tongue, forbidden by the theocrat, returned as the language of state.

A few decades later, in 1818, a Fulani cleric called Agmadu ibn Hammadi launched another jihad patterned after the conquests of Usman dan Fodio. There was resistance even among the Fulani. The local chief called on his ruler, the Bambara king of Segou, for help, but to no avail—Bambara was only a pale imitation of its former glorious self, and the Segou army was crushed. A new theocratic state was set up that included Segou, Djenne, and Timbuktu. The Tuareg seethed in the desert, waiting their chance.

There was a European witness to all this. In 1825, after three months' silence, Major Alexander Gordon Laing wrote to his wife from Timbuktu explaining that his bad writing was the result of a cut finger. The truth related later by one of his camel drivers was far worse. A party of Tuareg from Ahaggar, ostensibly acting as escort, attacked Laing in his tent one night, having first gained possession of his ammunition. Laing was "cut down by a sword on the thigh, he ... jumped up and received one cut on the cheek and ear and the other on the right arm above the wrist which broke the arm, he then fell to the ground, where he received seven cuts, the last being on his neck." His attendants were killed. An unexpectedly charitable Tuareg sheikh sheltered Laing while he recovered somewhat from his wounds, and generously provided him a strong escort to assist him to Timbuktu.[14]

Laing spent a difficult month in the city, despite being generally well treated by the inhabitants. His timing wasn't great, though. The Fulani who governed Timbuktu were still preaching holy war (and treating the inhabitants with a mixture of cruelty and contempt) and Tuareg raiders had isolated the city. (Better Laing should have stayed, but after a month he set out with an ostensibly friendly Tuareg chieftain towards the Senegal. They hadn't gone far before Laing was murdered as an infidel. His skeleton and that of an unnamed Arab boy travelling with him were exhumed by the French authorities in 1910 and reburied in Timbuktu.)

The city struggled on. In 1844 the Tuareg drove the Fulani completely out of town after a battle fought on the banks of the river, in which a great number of Fulani were slaughtered or drowned. This victory was of no avail either, "and only plunged the distracted town in greater misery; for, owing to its peculiar situation on the border of a desert tract, Timbuktu cannot rely upon its own resources, but must always be dependent upon those who rule the more fertile tracts higher up the river; and the ruler of Macina [Fulani] had only to forbid the exportation of corn from his dominions to reduce the inhabitants of Timbuktu to the utmost distress."

In 1852 it happened all over again when yet another jihad, the third of the nineteenth century, was launched by a Tukulor cleric called Al-Hajj Umar, who had been seduced by the new puritanism of the Wahhabis in Arabia. He was appointed the West African caliph of a relatively new activist brotherhood, formed a community of his own, and in 1852 came into conflict with nearby Bambara chiefs. He launched a jihad northwards through the gold-bearing valleys across the upper Senegal, then west down the river towards his own homeland in the Hausa kingdom of Gobir, and its French trading posts, where he was repulsed. After 1859 he sought to enlist the Fulani of Macina in taking on the more powerful Bambara kingdom of Segou, but they refused. He conquered Segou anyway, and continued downriver until he was able to assert control over Timbuktu. This, too, was as short-lived as other Fulani polities. The old established Muslim towns and Fulani communities regarded the Tukulor as upstarts, and Umar was killed trying to suppress a Fulani rebellion in 1864.[15]

The Fulani creation myth:

At the beginning there was a huge drop of milk,

Then Doondari came and created the stone.

Then the stone created iron;

And iron created fire;

And fire created water;

And water created air.

Then Doondari descended a second time.

And he took the five elements

And he shaped them into man.

But man was proud.

Then Doondari created blindness and blindness defeated man.

But when blindness became too proud,

Doondari created sleep and sleep defeated blindness;

But when sleep became too proud,

Doondari created worry and worry defeated sleep;

But when worry became too proud

Doondari created death, and death defeated worry

But when death became too proud

Doondari descended for the third time

And he came as Gueno the eternal one

And Gueno defeated death.

Translation by Ulli Beier, in African Poetry, *1966*

The Fulani of Senegal and Mali have settled down now, their pastoral ways forgotten, their holy wars barely remembered. The Fulani of Chad and Nigeria intermarried with the locals, and have also settled down, becoming farmers or traders; and the Fulani in Cameroon have become a modern political force. Only in Niger, in a rough triangle from Agadez to Ingal and Aderbissinat, do the nomadic and pastoralist Fulani remain, fiercely attached to their herds of zebu cattle, independent, scornful of settled ways, contemptuous of people who make their living by *making things*, as slaves do ... These people call themselves the Wodaabe, people of the taboo (that is, those who adhere to the old ways). The city folk, on the other hand, refer to them as "people who live in the bush and don't wash."

In August and September, the rains come to Ingal, and leach to the surface a quantity of subterranean salt; and each year (rebellions and revolts permitting) thousands of Tuareg and Fulani herdsmen make their way to the oasis for the *cure saleé,* the salt cure: their beasts eat the fresh salty grass; the men and women celebrate with camel races, dancing, singing, feasting, and rites of seduction. The *cure saleé*, nowadays hosted by the sultan of Aïr, ruler of the bleak mountain district north of Agadez and Ingal, is still one of the grand festivals of Old Africa. The festival only resumed recently, in 1994, after a hiatus of several years caused by Tuareg rebellion in Mali, which also affected Niger. It was resumed more to facilitate census-taking, the dissemination of regulations, and the vaccination of cattle than as a celebration, but the participants don't seem to mind.

The opening ceremony, before all the grandees of the desert, is an extraordinary spectacle. In front are the Fulani, in their gaudy make-up and costumes, white ostrich feathers on white turbans, black kohl lips, black tunics with coloured plaits, and jewellery of all descriptions, including ornaments made from key chains and other everyday bric-à-brac. At the rear are the Tuareg, in traditional costume. The women perform a dance of welcome to the shrill sound of the sultan's orchestra; behind them come the men on their camels, demonstrating their control of their mounts with elaborate displays of dressage. Camel races follow, and great bouts of feasting and dancing and fighting and all-round good fellowship.

After three days the Tuareg fade back into the desert, and the Fulani *gereewol* gets under way. The young men spend the mornings getting ready. Appearance is important, beauty a necessity. The Fulani believe they are the most beautiful people on earth, and so important is this notion that a man will sometimes allow his wife to sleep with a more attractive man to sire a more attractive child. They shave their hairline and plait their hair. A lipstick of kohl blackens the lips, and a yellow paste made from a friable stone called *polla* is spread over the face. Each man adds circles and dots in red and white, according to his own idea of what will work with the girls. They assemble in the afternoon to perform the *yaake*, a dance of celebration in which they display their beauty and charm for the assembled women to admire—the idea is to seduce the prettiest girls with erotic looks and grimaces. "Before the dance they drink stimulating concoctions made from pulverised bark, which enable them to perform for hours in a trance-like state. Teetering on tiptoe, they turn their heads from side to side and part their kohl-black lips to reveal their teeth. To emphasise the whites of their eyes they roll their eyeballs, holding them in a fixed stare for added effect."[16]

What works, works. The most seductive guys get the girls. Marriage is not necessarily the goal, but sometimes marriages result.

After the *gereewol* is over, the nomads retire their finery and return to the bush. The jewellery is stored in leather boxes for the next year, and they return to their normal decoration, a small leather amulet to promote virility among the boys and fertility among the girls, and a set of charms to protect their herds, consisting of talismans like teeth and claws of powerful beasts, and verses from the Koran. No harm in insurance.

THE HAUSA KINGDOMS

T he last of the great Sahel people to fill up this swirling timescape of history were the Hausa. The old Hausa kingdoms of northern Nigeria and Niger are gone now, and only pale copies of ancient rituals survive—that, and a few remnant taxes collected by a gaggle of sultans and emirs with no power other than symbolism. Who, in any case, has power in the chaotic landscape of modern Nigeria unless it is whatever band of generals the army chooses to elevate?

Like Timbuktu, the Niger city of Agadez was founded as a market town by the Tuareg, and in the fifteenth century was the seat of a Tuareg sultanate. Although it was a flourishing town of more than thirty thousand people and possessed one of the oldest Arabic schools in Africa, the city was virtually unknown to the Europeans until Heinrich Barth passed through on his way south from Aïr to the Hausa centre of Kano. It was grand, though, at one time! In the markets of Agadez, salt once traded ounce for ounce with gold, and in 1906 a caravan of twenty thousand camels left the city to fetch the salt from the oasis of Bilma, some 600 kilometres (375 miles) to the northeast. Agadez has been decaying slowly for several centuries, and now has a kind of faded and melancholy charm, like Timbuktu itself.

The road south from Agadez to Zinder, and thence to Nigeria and the Hausa heartland, crosses 400 kilometres (250 miles) of stony sand called the Great Nothing, which is as good a name as any. The plains are featureless, the monotony broken only by the precious signs, every 50 kilometres (30 miles) or so, "Abelama: Good water, 24 metres," "Tchin-Garagen: Sweet water, 31 metres," "Gézawa: Good water at 47 metres," the wells getting just a little deeper with every passing decade as the land gets older and its veins, so deeply hidden, constrict. The convoys of four-wheel-drive Toyotas with their cisterns of water pass the wells by, but you can still see camels there, their masters lounging under the shade of the spare dúm-dúm

> T he Tuareg, like all the desert people who can afford to do so, wear silver, "the pure metal blessed by the Prophet" in preference to gold, the metal of the devil, which is feared and believed to bring bad luck. The cross of Agadez is the most popular of the Tuareg crosses—a cross of life, similar to the Egyptian ankh. In the drought of the 1970s the Tuareg traded much of their jewellery in Sahel market towns in order to survive.
>
> From Fisher, Africa Adorned, pp 193–94

palms as they wait out the Saharan sun (the nomads prefer to travel by night, "with the guidance," as Ali had put it in Timbuktu, "of the heavens themselves").

South of Zinder, everything changes. Watercourses appear, dry it is true for eleven and a half months of the year, but in the rainy season there are actual pools—water on the surface, a thing of marvels.

There were also, in early 1997, many police checkpoints. The Nigerian border was nearby, and everyone was watchful of Nigeria. Nevertheless, the Niger border formalities at Matameye, a dusty little town of no consequence, were lackadaisical, and the Nigerian authorities not much stricter. The first town of any consequence inside Nigeria is Daura, the spiritual home of the Hausa people.

Daura might not be the oldest Hausa town, and it was never very eminent—Kano was more powerful, and so were Katsina and Sokoto and Zaria, and even little Bida, in its time, all of them trading cities that performed better than Daura. But Daura is old, none the less, and venerated for its legendary role in the Hausa beginnings. It was founded by a queen, the *magajiva* Daura, sometime in the ninth century, and was ruled thereafter by women for some hundreds of years (the senior princess in the household of the emir of Daura even now holds the title *magajiva*). In the declining years of the queens, it is said, the Bayajida (or Abuyazidu), a son of the king of Baghdad, killed Sarki the fetish serpent at the town's well and married the reigning queen. Their six grandsons and a son of Bayajida's other wife, a princess of Bornu to the east, became the Seven Rulers of the Hausa *Bakwai*, the seven true Hausa kingdoms. Sarki's well is still there, and women draw water from it every day for the daily chores of Hausa life.

The Hausa kingdoms were subject to the fluctuations of power in the great empires to the north and east. The kingdom of Kano, founded in 999 but located in its present spot only since the reign of King Gajemasu (1095 to 1134), was converted to Islam when scholars from Mali set up centres of learning there in the 1340s. A little while later the kingdom was defeated in battle by its rival, Zaria, and King Kanajeji renounced the faith, blaming its "softness" for his shameful capitulation. The Malians persisted, and when new teachers arrived fifty years later, Islam once again became the official creed. Camel caravans brought prosperity under Mohammed Rumfa, the greatest of Kano's Hausa kings (1463–1499). When the Mali Empire itself disintegrated, Kano was taken by Songhai raiders in 1513, and became a tributary state. By 1734 it was paying tribute to another master, this time the resurgent Empire of Kanem-Bornu; and in 1807 it was taken in the Fulani jihad launched by Usman dan Fodio.

Still, by the 1820s Kano had outlasted them all and had become the greatest commercial power in West Africa, an independent state of perhaps half a million people, able to field an army at a moment's notice of ten thousand horsemen and twenty thousand men on foot. On January 20, 1824, Hugh Clapperton reached Kano, which until then was known to Europeans by name only. He estimated the city had thirty to forty thousand inhabitants, more than half of them slaves. In the market he bought, for three Spanish dollars, an English green cotton umbrella, "an article I little expected to meet with, yet by no means uncommon."[17] The markets also sold calicos and cotton prints from Manchester, French silks and sugar, beads from Venice and Trieste, sword blades from Solingen, and all manner of imported goods.

Heinrich Barth has left us a vivid description of Kano's principal market: "... here a row of shops, filled with articles of native and foreign produce, with buyers and sellers in every variety of figure, complexion, and dress, yet all intent upon their little gain, endeavouring to cheat each other; there a large shed, like a hurdle, full of half-naked, half-starved slaves torn from their native homes, from their wives and husbands, from their children or parents, arranged in rows like cattle, and staring desperately upon the buyers, anxiously watching into whose hands it should be their destiny to fall. In another part were to be seen all the necessaries of life; the wealthy buying the most palatable things for his table; the poor stopping and looking greedily upon a handful of grain: here a rich governor, dressed in silk and gaudy clothes; mounted upon a spirited and richly caparisoned horse, and followed by a host of idle, insolent slaves; there a poor blind man groping his way through the multitude, and fearing at every step to be trodden down."

Kano's Kurmi market is still there, still the city's major attraction and still a centre for craft work and manufacturing, including gold, silver, and bronze, fabrics, and leather work. Outside the market's gate on Kofar Mata road are the Kano dye pits, which have been there, as far as anybody knows, for eight centuries. It's an open terrace of clay, "with a number of dying-pots, and people busily employed in various processes of their handicraft: here a man stirring the juice, and mixing with the indigo some colouring wood in order to give it the desired tint; there another, drawing a shirt from the dye-pot, or hanging it up on a rope fastened to the trees; there two men beating a well-dyed shirt, singing the while, and keeping good time; men and women making use of an ill-frequented thoroughfare as a 'kaudi tseggenábe' to hang up, along the fence, their cotton thread for weaving; close by, a group of indolent loiterers lying in the sun and idling away the hours." That was Heinrich Barth's description in 1854, but nothing has changed. You can still find men on that same open terrace with their hands and arms stained indigo, dipping fabrics into the vats, just as they have done for so very long. By contrast, the emir's palace next door is positively new: it was built for the twentieth emir, in the fifteenth century.

Usman dan Fodio's militant Islam soon ran out of juice in the sophisticated atmosphere of commercial Kano. "The Fúlbe [Fulani]," Barth reported soon afterwards, "marry the handsome daughters of the subjugated tribe, but would not condescend to give their own daughters to the men of that tribe as wives. As far as I saw, their original type has been well preserved as yet, though by obtaining possession of wealth and comfort, their warlike character has been greatly impaired, and the Féllani in Kanó have become notorious for their cowardice throughout the whole of Negroland."

Kano's great rival, Katsina, lies to the northwest, hard by the Niger border. During the reign of Mohammed Korau, in the late fifteenth century, monthly camel caravans crossed the Sahara from Ghadames, Tripoli, and Tunis to Katsina, and brought such prosperity that the state became caught in the rivalry between the great empires of Songhai and Bornu. In 1513 the city was conquered by the Songhai; in 1554 they defeated Songhai itself, and then Kano; in 1591 it became a tributary state of Bornu. For a while, Katsina replaced Timbuktu as the chief West African centre of Islamic studies, and as Barth noted, "[became] the chief city of this part of Negroland, as well in commercial and political importance as in other respects; for here that state of civilisation ... seems to have reached its highest degree, and as the Hausa language here attained the greatest richness of form and the most refined pronunciation, so also the manners of Katsina were distinguished by superior politeness from those of the other towns of Hausa."

Alas, it was not to last. The Fulani took this town as well in the jihad of Usman dan Fodio, after a long and bloody war. "Indeed, M'allem Ghomáro had carried out an unrelenting war against the town for seven years before he at length reduced it by famine; and the distress in the town is said to have been so great that a dead vulture (impure food which nobody would touch in time of peace) sold for five hundred kurdi. Afterwards the town declined rapidly, and all the principal merchants migrated to Kano."[18]

Katsina is still worth a visit. Parts of the old walls are still there, and so is the emir's palace. You can climb the fifteenth-century Gobir minaret and poke about some old Hausa burial mounds. But the only sign of its former glory is at the festival of Durbar that ends Ramadan, when the nobles carefully unpack their ancient finery, get themselves up on horseback, and charge around the playing fields north of town, faded ghosts of the glorious cavalry of the Elder Days.

COLONIAL SAHEL

T*he colonial history of the Sahel lacks, after all this, a certain ... drama, although the French "conquest" of a territory so vast had its own fine madness, and French paras are still living off the epic myths of* la force étrangère.

Independence duly came to Niger in 1960 with Hamari Dori, a French puppet, in charge. He survived until the great droughts of 1973, but when stocks of food were discovered in the homes of some of his government's ministers, he was overthrown in a bloody but popular coup led by Seyni Kountché. Kountché reinvented the imperial Bornu notion of direct rule, and took a sensationally hard line on corruption, occasionally surrounding a ministry with armed troops until its books balanced, to much popular acclaim. Kountché survived until 1987, when he died after a long illness.

After that there was a cautious edging towards an ever-fragile democracy, with aborted coups and almost-coups a fact of political life. By early 1997 there was a government that seemed merely cobbled together from anxious minorities, and a still-fractious Tuareg minority.

And the camels still wandered down the wide boulevards of Niamey, the capital.

....

Mali, too, became independent from France in 1960 (after a few months of federation with Senegal). The country then went through the apparently inevitable flirtation with socialism and its corollary, Soviet "advisers," which ended in an army take-over in 1968, under Moussa Traoré. After continuing agitation for multiparty democracy, food and other riots, a deteriorating economy, and reports of Traoré's stash in Zurich, he was himself overthrown by another army coup in 1992, under Amadou Toumani Touré, aka ATT.

Nothing, so far, very surprising.

Except that in June 1992 Touré fulfilled his promise of holding multiparty elections, and, when Alpha Oumar Konaré was invested as president, he resigned as promised. And then there were the Tuareg.

French colonial policy had discouraged nomadism, by the simple expedient of taxing the Tuareg into submission, but all through the long Fulani wars and through the colonial period, Tuareg tribal leaders had never given up their search for control over their own affairs. During the droughts and food shortages of the 1980s, it had been the Tuareg who had suffered most, and there were many complaints that U.N. food aid had been unfairly diverted to other, and in the Tuareg view, ethnically inferior, regions. In 1990 Tuareg rebels attacked army posts in the Timbuktu and Gao area. The army retaliated, and a civil war seemed inevitable. But early in 1992, before he resigned, ATT signed a "declaration of national reconciliation" with the Tuareg, and except for sporadic raids and random acts of violence by small hunting bands, the northern frontier region north of Timbuktu was, by early 1997, quiescent.

....

The history of Mauritania, the only country in Africa governed by nomads, has been relatively uneventful since the conquest of Ghana (the empire, not the modern country) by the Almoravids from Morocco in 1076, and the consequent spread of Islam. The successor states to the empires of Ghana and Mali were governed by Moors, descendants of Berber–Arab–Black mixing in the first millennium. However, relatively little happened until the colonial period, when in 1814 France declared its right to explore and control the coast.

Mohktar Ould Daddah, the post-independence leader, got the country into hot water by callously agreeing with Morocco to divide up Spanish Sahara, and the inhabitants of that arid land protested in a bloody guerrilla war led by Polisario rebels. There was a coup in Mauritania in 1978, followed by a palace revolt in 1984 and the installation of the Colonel Sid'Ahmed Ould Taya, an Islamic militant.

The most significant social problem of recent decades has been the thorny question of race. The Moors believe that the whiter they are the better, and they look down on the blacks, mostly Soninké from Senegal. The blacks, in turn, think of the Moors as capricious, cruel, and unjust. This led to race riots in 1989, sparked by grazing disputes. Mauritanian (that is, Moorish) businesses were looted, and the consequent reaction was brutal, verging on genocide—entire villages were driven into the desert without any supplies at all, and left there to die of thirst. Almost a hundred thousand people were forced into exile. The repression continued up to and through 1992, when Taya finally allowed more or less free elections, which he won handily with 63 per cent of the vote.

The simmering race problem, however, persisted.

And in Burkina Faso? The Songhai penetration of the old Mali Empire had allowed the emergence to the south of small kingdoms of the Mossi tribe, centred in the modern capital of Burkina Faso, Ouagadougou. The legends say the city was founded around 1050 by the *morho naba*, the Overlord of the Mossi, but as kingdoms they probably date from the fifteenth century, when horse-borne conquerors arrived from the northeast and merged with the local tribes. There came to be four kingdoms in all, hierarchically organized, the ruling castes a military élite with an almost Panzer-like ethic—strike fast, hard, and often, and victory will be yours. They actually sacked Timbuktu in the fourteenth century, but from about 1400 they acted as trading intermediaries between the forest and the Niger. Mossi society was feudal in nature; the king's court contained hereditary nobles and high officials, and numerous bodyguards, pageboys, and eunuchs; his wives lived in special villages, all of whose male inhabitants had been castrated.

Confined as they were by the Songhai from about 1600, territorially the Mossi kingdoms didn't amount to much. Still, they maintained their tenacious independence for five hundred years until the French colonial conquest near the end of the nineteenth century. The French skilfully exploited the kingdoms' internal rivalries, and in 1919, when Upper Volta became a formal colony, they had destroyed the confederation. The Ouagadougou king survived, however, and returned to the colony after "agreeing" to a French protectorate. The French then partitioned the king's lands, giving half of them to the Côte d'Ivoire and the other half to Mali and Niger. After that they followed the pattern they had set elsewhere and built a railway from Ouagadougou to the coast, using the Mossi as slave labour. Many thousands perished.

After the French restored the colony of Upper Volta and granted it independence in 1960, five coups, of various degrees of bloodiness, followed.

The most interesting leader to emerge came from the 1983 coup, when the Fulani Thomas Sankara came to power, changed the country's name, and embarked on a Mao-style grass-roots revolution. To a great deal of Western consternation (because the Western cliché is that Maoism, like all communism, is economically unfeasible), he not only remained popular through all this but actually improved the economy, seeing the GDP grow from an average of 3.1 per cent to 4.6 per cent. Even today, though agriculture is still small-scale peasant farming, employing 90 per cent of the population, Burkina Faso is a net exporter of food. Sankara became even more popular when he waged a five-day war against Mali over an ancient and mostly forgotten border dispute (sixty people were killed, and the war stopped because both sides ran out of ammunition). Alas, this giddy period of Burkinan optimism didn't last. Sankara was shot by army rebels in 1987 and replaced by a junta headed by Blaise Campaoré, son-in-law of the Côte d'Ivoire's Houphouët-Boigny. Presidential elections were held in 1992, but since Campaoré was the only candidate, that he won was hardly surprising. Only 38 per cent of the people bothered to vote.

The *naba*, or king, of the Mossi, was still living in Ouagadougou in 1997, holding court there every Friday morning in a ceremony that dates back five hundred years.

....

Both Guinea (sometimes called Guinea Conakry) and Guinea Bissau were part of Old Mali, as we have seen. And in 1997 they both represented a countervailing presence to the dreadful examples of Liberia and Sierra Leone. In Guinea, since the unlamented death of the dictator, Sékou Touré, in 1984, the current of democracy has flowed freely. In Guinea Bissau, the popular leader Nino Vieira continues to improve both the economy and the mood of his people.

Neither country got there easily.

Guinea was the first French colony to become independent. Sékou Touré, who was Malinké and said to be a descendant of the legendary hero Samori Touré, had led the fight, and when de Gaulle offered French colonies the unenviable choice of "sovereignty" within a Franco-African alliance or immediate independence, Touré, announcing that he would prefer "freedom in poverty to prosperity in chains," opted for independence. De Gaulle, in a fit of unstatesmanlike pique, immediately withdrew everything the French had installed, even the telephone system. Colonists looted what was left, and the economy duly collapsed, as de Gaulle had hoped it would.

Touré turned to the Russians for help, but was soon throwing them out for interference. For the next dozen years, arrests and torture became aspects of approved statecraft. In the mid-1970s Touré launched a Soviet-style purge against the country's Fulani citizens, charging them with collective treason. However, after a historic revolt by market women in 1977, who were angry at his attempts to collectivize commerce, he started to dismantle his authoritarian practices and most of the Marxist notions of government. He died in 1984 before the process had gone very far, and the military leaders who took over in a coup shortly afterwards released several thousand political prisoners and, amid rousing condemnations of everything Touré had stood for, promised elections and economic freedom.

By 1992, after several false starts, seventeen political parties were legalized, and in December 1993 elections were duly held. After some accusations of vote fraud, the military leader, Lansana Conté, was elected. He promptly promised elections for 1998.

Guinea Bissau, which in the late nineties is widely regarded as the friendliest, safest country in West Africa, had a tougher road to travel to independence. The Portuguese, whose colony this was, stubbornly held on to it and the result was one of Africa's longest liberation struggles, conducted by a joint alliance of Guinean and Cape Verdean guerrillas. In 1973 the rebels were secure enough to hold elections in the "liberated" areas, and Louis Cabral was elected president. The following year Salazar was overthrown in Portugal, and the last metropolitan troops were withdrawn.

Louis Cabral was a hard-line socialist, and was overthrown by João Vieira in 1980. By the middle of the decade the Soviet advisers had been sent packing, and Vieira started privatizing the country. He survived three early but somewhat half-hearted coup attempts, and in 1994, after postponing elections several times, he was duly and freely elected president. By 1997 the economy was improving. Guinea Bissau was still one of the world's ten poorest countries, but the country was actually exporting food, and the mood in the capital was heady.

Gambia (or, more pretentiously, The Gambia) is only 35 kilometres (22 miles) wide and 300 (186 miles) long, and is entirely surrounded by French-speaking Senegal. After independence the two countries briefly linked up in a federation called Senegambia, but this didn't work. (Though the countries are ethnically similar, both consisting largely of leftover Malinké from Old Mali, Fulani, and Wolof, one was British in culture and the other French.) The federation was dissolved in 1989.

Gambia had one of the best and most democratic reputations in Africa, and its president for several terms, Dawda Jawara, was exceptionally popular (being easily elected to a sixth term in 1992), so the military coup in July 1994 seemed more than ordinarily inexplicable. The military, as usual, promised an early return to civilian rule, but no one seemed to know when this would be, and in late 1996 the new regime was "confirmed in office" by the voters. Meanwhile, in a comic-opera series of accusations and counter-accusations, the new president, Captain Yahya Jammeh, and one of his ex-cronies, Ebou Jallow, alternately accepted and rejected responsibility for an errant $300 million (U.S.), paid—of course—into a Swiss bank account. Jallow, it turned out, had a further $20 million in several other accounts. A short while later, seven tons of marijuana addressed to the Ministry of Agriculture in the Gambian capital, Banjul, were seized in nearby Mauritania. About these "supplies" Jammeh had nothing to say.

Senegal, Gambia's former spouse, was part of both Ghana and Mali in the old days; it is from a Senegalese port, supposedly, that the great fleet of Abu Bakari set sail for the Americas so long ago. When Ghana dissolved in the attacks of the Sanhajah confederation, Islam took over as the dominant religion of the region. The earliest known Fulani jihad occurred in Senegal in the seventeenth century, when Fulani clerics briefly succeeded in taking political power from the Mande rulers. Early in the following century the pattern was repeated, and by 1750 a Muslim theocracy had been erected whose leaders engaged in organized trade with the upper Guinea coast.

At the same time, the continuing desiccation of the Sahara drove the Fulani and the Wolof further into the territory. The Wolof, a tall, slender, and deep black people (whose women are renowned for their elaborate hairstyles, abundant gold ornaments, and voluminous dresses), had an empire of their own once. It lasted for two hundred years, from the time of Mali's decline until the European incursions, and dominated what is now inland Senegal. Around 1440 it was drawn into a profitable trading partnership with the Portuguese, based primarily on slaves, and then into a brief political alliance. Nevertheless, the Wolof remained sufficiently independent to repel Portugal's attempts at hegemony.

> The Wolof are fond of what they call "dilemma tales." These are told for entertainment; the audience is supposed to supply the ending. An example: Three brothers journey to a strange land and are married to the same girl. She is murdered by a robber, and the eldest brother, with whom she was sleeping, is condemned to death on suspicion. He begs leave to visit his father before he dies. When he is late returning, the second brother offers to die in place of him. The third brother steps forward and "confesses." But the eldest rides in, just in time to embrace his fate. Which of the brothers, the listeners are asked, is the most noble?
>
> Adapted from Encyclopaedia Britannica
> 1:238

In 1556 the nobles of Caylor, a Wolof dependency, threw off their masters and cut off Wolof access to the sea. After the Portuguese, came the Dutch. And then the English. And, finally, the French, who used Senegal as a military staging-post into their vast colonial holdings.

And so it remained until the twentieth century, when Léopold Senghor, poet, agi-tator, journalist, and classmate of the later French president Georges Pompidou, began to build a political power base in the colony. He became the new country's first president, in 1960. Unusually, he refrained from autocracy, and remained president for twenty years, through somewhat turbulent economic times, before resigning in 1980 and passing power to a hand-picked successor, Abdou Diouf.

Diouf and the main opposition leader, Abdoulaye Wade, have been feuding ever since. Wade was briefly in exile, returned to run in the presidential elections of 1993, lost, went on trial in 1994 for conspiracy and attempted murder, was acquitted, and in 1997 remained a political force.

The capital, Dakar, is still a major transportation hub in Africa, and although there are many petty annoyances, it's one of the pleasantest cities in West Africa, an intriguing combination of French and African.

THE DOGON

Some time after I left Timbuktu, slightly dazed by its long history of conquest, vendetta, holy war, blackmail, and slaughter (interspersed, true enough, with a long and eminent history of scholarship and learning), I found myself on the Bandiagara cliffs, on the southern edge of Mali, towards the border with Burkina Faso. There, I encountered the Dogon, and learned again that Africa is not only a his-tory of wars and conquests. One of the other great themes of African life is endurance, or persistence, an adherence to traditional ways.

Islam swept through the Sahel like a gale, but there were pockets of resistance. Not through warfare, but through a belief system so attuned to the lives of the people who practised it that it remained impermeable not only to the proselytizers of Islam, but to the Christian missionaries who followed them.

The Dogon are not the only people between the desert and the forest who have cho-sen to withdraw from modernity. The Kirdi people of Cameroon, who like the Dogon withdrew from Islamization, are similarly looked down on by Muslims as being "uncivilized." There are others, too, like the Lobi and Kasena people, who withdrew into the territory where Ghana and the Ivory Coast and Burkina Faso meet. To the south of the Bandiagara cliffs live the Mossi and Bobo. But the Dogon people might be unique, in both the seamlessness and the thoroughness of their complex belief system and in the fact that those who do make the crossing into a modern urban culture still seem immune to that culture's blandishments.

The cliffs of the Bandiagara escarpment are a natural wonder. They drop precipi-

tously from plateau to plain, sheer for hundreds of metres, and are pierced by numerous caves. In these, the early people took refuge.

Was this for security from human predators? Both Mossi and Songhai raided here, in the fifteenth century, looking for slaves. But surely one can be as secure in a cave 15 metres (50 feet) off the ground as 50 (165 feet)? Having seen the place, and watched the Dogon swinging down the cliffs on fragile ropes (or climbing up like spiders), I lean to the theory put forward by the mountain climber David Roberts, who said, "Maybe, just maybe, the Tellem [who lived here before the Dogon] undertook the effort for its own sake, because it was clever and beautiful. By the end [of his trip to the cliffs] I wanted to believe that aesthetics alone had driven the Tellem to their mastery." [19]

The Toloy people were, as far as anyone knows, the first to dwell here, around 300 B.C. They were followed by the Tellem, who lived in the cliffs and in the perilous caves for five hundred years before they, too, vanished, pushed out by the current incumbents. The Dogon originated upriver, near where Bamako is today; they began to migrate when Islam began to take hold among the people, about six hundred years ago. They retreated with their own cosmology to the rugged cliffs, building their own peculiar villages clinging to the cliffside.

The Dogon are known to the world mostly through the teachings of their most famous son, the sage called Ogotemmêli. For me, they are the essence of enduring Africa. There are mosques in Dogon country now, and a few churches—the churches fed the people in the famines and demand their pound of spiritual flesh. A few Dogon attend church. "But at night," my friend Guiré, himself a Dogon, said, "they remain Dogon."

I got into a bizarre conversation about the virgin birth of Christ with one of Ogotemmêli's grandsons, who runs a souvenir stand in the village of Sangha. He was interested in the Christian theory of origins—contrasting it with his own more complicated and much more interesting theory—but I'm an ignorant exponent of the Christian belief, and I rather floundered when it came to Mary. "Is it true," he asked, "that the supreme being came down to earth disguised as a man, and had intercourse with this Mary?" I protested that it wasn't quite so, she was virgin even at the time she gave birth, and he gave me one of those "oh come *on*, we're guys here, we know how it works" looks and rested his case. He seemed to think God's congress with Mary (he was the Father, after all) a reasonable if still implausible notion. In the Dogon universe, God wouldn't deign to do these things himself. He has his agents for corporeal duties like impregnation, making rain, and so on. When he pushed me, I had to admit it wasn't much of a stretch, plausibility-wise, to an angelic impregnation rather than a divine one.

At this point he savoured his triumph and tried to sell me an ancient carved Dogon door. Since he had a poster from the Malian government in his shop warning about strict penalties for attempting any commerce in antiquities, I demurred. He sat for a while, then came back to another point that bothered him. God created one man and then one woman from his rib, of all things, and that was all—how do you avoid the abomination of incest? I had to confess I didn't know. No, he said, it is as we say: god

Amma created the celestial twins, the Nummo, and these serpent-like creatures, hermaphrodites, in turn gave birth to four further sets of twins, male and female in each one, and that way there came into being the four founding lineages of all mankind. I wasn't going to argue with him. I knew that in Dogon lore every child is born both male and female, the foreskin being the sign of the female in men and the clitoris that of the male in women. It was only after circumcision among men or clitoral excision among women that they could take their place in society as full members. I thought there was very little to choose between the two myths. In both cases, there was a supreme being, and in both Dogon and Christian versions, God's universe got away from him, in the Christian variant through the revolt of Lucifer and the hubris of Woman, in the form of Eve, and in the Dogon's through the improprieties of Jackal, whose intercourse with the earth caused so many calamities, including the imperfections of menstrual blood. (To this day women are secluded in "their own house" during menses, as far from the men's quarters as possible. The house is usually decorated with representations of Lébé, the serpent who plays a role in the founding myth, and pictographs of huge and distended female genitalia.)

When a Dogon passes another he knows, he must be greeted properly. These greetings are so long that they begin when the two are still three or four metres (10 feet) apart and finish only when they have passed each other by and can barely hear the responses. But the form is important, and followed to the letter.

How is your day?

Fine.

How is your health?

Fine.

Your parents?

Fine.

Your family?

Fine.

Your children?

Fine.

Your crops?

Fine.

And so on and so on. "Fine" (Sever) is the required response. Even if your father has just died, when you are asked in the greeting about your father's health, the proper response is still "Fine." Afterwards, you can explain that your father is dead, if it seems appropriate.

I never learned his name—he was just Ogotemmêli's grandson, for Ogotemmêli is perhaps the most famous sage of all the Dogon, made famous by the French ethnographer Marcel Griault, who, after spending fifteen years or more with the Dogon, produced reams of academic papers and one popular book, *Conversations with Ogotemmêli*.[20] The sage's "conversations" with the European had made him justly famous, I thought, because, among other achievements, Ogotemmêli put paid once and for all to the simplistic notion that animist religions are basically guff about "ancestor worship"—the Dogon don't "worship" their ancestors; they only use them as conduits to higher authorities, much as Christians use priests or saints or prayer. Ogotemmêli conducted his conversations in an elliptical style aimed at illumination rather than instruction, and he had an apt pupil in Griault, who recorded faithfully, and then pieced together the lessons. Dogon religion has an arcane symbolism as esoteric as mathematics. Each action, word, or even omission is rich in meaning. To take a trivial example, a Dogon granary is a place to store grain, a symbol of the divisions between men and women, a repository of female lore but also the repository of earthly masculine power, and is constructed in a way that mimics the creation of the universe and the creation of the original four couples, the Dogonish Adams and Eves.

It was from Griault that I learned more of the Dogon beliefs. Ogotemmêli's grandson did not speak easily of the Nummo or the invention of speech or the advent of blacksmithing, or of the dual nature of all humans—not because those are secrets, but because they are too intimately tied to daily life. You can't just go blundering in. There must be an apprenticeship first, and proper respect, then the mysteries must be understood, not just learned, and only a long apprenticeship can achieve that. The equivalent would be for the casual visitor from another country to ask the most intimate questions—when a man lies with a woman, how is it done? The Dogon are unique in that their lives are both practical and entirely symbolic. Even their houses and sleeping platforms and granaries are constructed to conform to their religion. And yes, the way the man lies with the woman is arranged and laid out in lore—the man must lie this way and the woman that, and the thing must be done in the prescribed fashion. The gift of speech came from the Nummo, too, and a woman's mouth is the symbol of the loom from which language was derived (speech began by threads being drawn between the sharp points of the Nummos' teeth, and the Dogon still sometimes file their own teeth to recall the origin of language).

Later, Guiré took me to the *toguna*, the men's meeting-place, the local "parliament" where the elders sit and grumble and decide the villagers' fate. As a stranger, of course, I wasn't allowed in. Like all Dogon artefacts, the *toguna* is rich in symbolism: its eight carved pillars represent the eight founding ancestors; there are eight levels of thatched roof; the building is built low to the ground, with not much more than a metre of headroom (mostly to prevent hotheads springing to their feet to harangue the other elders—banging your skull on a beam has a calming effect). In the evening the ancestors enter the building, and it is in their presence that all important decisions are made.

On the subject of Ogotemmêli, I rather got the impression that his descendants thought the old chap a bit of a windbag, albeit an eminent and famous old wind-bag—*their* windbag.

....

There are perhaps 400,000 Dogon scattered in several hundred villages over some 8,000 square kilometres (3,000 square miles). There are plateau villages, cliff villages, and plains villages, and among them more than thirty dialects are spoken—so intensely inner-focused are the Dogon that many of these dialects are mutually incomprehensible. The cliff villages are the most extraordinary, almost inaccessible. And above those are the Tellem burial caves, still in use by the Dogon.

From the foot of the cliff I stared upwards. It arched out overhead for hundreds of metres. Halfway up I could just make out small openings in the rock. These were the Tellem caves. How do the Dogon climbers reach them? A villager pointed to a black pole protruding out from a cave, about 15 metres (50 feet) overhead. The trick was to throw a rope over that pole, haul yourself up, haul your rope up after you, edge out on a small ledge, throw your rope over another pole another 10 or 15 metres (30 or 50 feet) overhead, and—do it again, and there you were, 60 metres (200 feet) off the ground ... As David Roberts had been earlier, I was aghast and impressed. To bury their dead, they trusted their lives to poles stuffed into the cliff almost seven hundred years earlier by the Tellem! Which begged the question, How did the Tellem get up there? To this, the Dogon have no answer.

The Dogon also have burial chambers closer to home, which are used in times of drought when many are dying and people are too weak to haul the bodies halfway up a cliff.

They are agriculturists, with millet as the chief crop. Since soil and water are so scarce, they build their tiny houses and pointy little granaries on top of boulders. Soil is guarded like the treasure it is—some fields, especially those near water, are some-times as little as a metre square, intricately laid out, carefully surrounded by dry-stone walls set with a mathematician's precision. Over the centuries Dogon have carried soil to rocky outcrops near water, and there have constructed new fields. There are even "fields" in shallow depressions on top of large boulders. In these plots they grow rice, onions, millet, and maize, often coaxing two crops a year from the reluctant soil.

Men and women till the fields, but the family's granaries are a man's business—Dogon society is profoundly sexist. Women don't dance, for instance, because it is said to make them infertile. Women take no part in governance. Women can't inherit property. Women are for work. Women go to market. Women are for procreation and for men's recreation. And women aren't allowed near the primary granaries—they have their own. Every day the man of the house will allocate to the woman her ration of grain. She grinds it, then stores it in "her" compartment of the women's granary, along with spices, peanuts, oil, and whatever else she uses for cooking. There she also stores her personal possessions, such as they are—no one can go into her compartment without her permission.

Each granary has an intricately carved door rich in symbolism. These Dogon doors are much sought after by Western art collectors, and because the belief system is so strong, the doors are still being made.

....

I visited the Dogon villages of Sangha, Ogoly, Ogol du Haut, Ogol du Bas, Diaminina, Diamini Gora, Dini Bongo, Baru, Engele, Sangui. Each was different, and yet the same, the same neatness, the same granaries with their topping of thatch, the same mud-made family compounds. Cooking is by wood and charcoal. Lighting by palm oil or kerosene. Water by well. Sanitation by gravity. Sleeping is done on mats, although women sometimes have straw beds on poles. In each village was a hogon's house, the home of the chief spiritual adviser to the village. The position of hogon is not inherited. To be a hogon you don't need to be of a particular clan or family, only old. A hogon must stay in or near his house for the rest of his life, once appointed—he can move a few hundred metres here and there, but not far. Each night the serpent Lébé is said to visit the hogon and lick him clean from head to toe, cleansing him spiritually for the following day's work. When the hogon dies, the next-oldest man in the village becomes hogon.

In Sangha I went by the women's house, the hogon's house, and a small misshapen building with four conical humps on the roof, decorated in a chequerboard pattern and closed shut with a slab of rock. This was a "temple," where sacrifices are made. The humps were covered with stains from millet porridge and animal blood.

Sacrifices are still made on ritual occasions, or when the times are needful. Most sacrifices these days are chickens, rabbits, goats, or, rarely, cattle. In the old days human sacrifice used to be relatively common. I asked a Dogon elder about this. He looked amused. "Not any more," he said. "Or if it is, it must be very discreet."

....

In the calm before the dusk, the diviners do their work.

Each village diviner has a small plot of land near the village perimeter, marked off by stones, its fine sand smoothed with a brush. This plot is subdivided into smaller plots, no larger than 20 centimetres by 40 (8 inches by 16). Each subplot represents a "question" the diviner will ask the spirits. If your crops are failing more than they should, you ask the diviner and he will inscribe the appropriate symbols in the sand. If you are ill, there will be another set of symbols. If you suspect your wife is unfaithful, yet another set. In each case, the diviner will interrogate the complainant before asking the right question. These interrogations are rapid-fire and as complete as necessary: I was told they could ask "a thousand questions an hour" if they were needed.

The questions are easy. But how are answers received?

Just before nightfall the diviner will scatter peanuts across the "question field" in prescribed patterns. They will be left there for the morning. Sometime during the night a jackal will be attracted by the nuts, and in the pattern of its paw prints the answers can be found. It's in the interpretation of the patterns that the diviner's skills lie. And it's in his authority that his effectiveness resides.

Usually, a sacrifice will be required. And of course a payment.

I asked Sangha's diviner whether the project I was working on would go well. The jackal's answer was unequivocal, but still enigmatic: you have an enemy on this project, the paw prints said.

It cost me a chicken.

Each Dogon village has a market that takes place once a week—every five days in the Dogon calendar. Women run the markets. They can be seen early in the morning, walking into the village, sometimes from as far as 20 kilometres (12 miles) and more away. For sale is the usual mélange of trinkets, household utensils, clothing, fabrics, shoes, and foodstuffs, including an array of more-or-less dried fish, usually pretty rank in the hot sun. There are large tubs of peanut butter, dark brown and delicious. Packets of spices. Dried medicinal herbs. Fresh herbs for cookery. Cucumbers, okra, and other greens. Mangoes, yellow and green peppers. Magi bouillon cubes, the apparently universal seasoning of Bantu Africa.

Each market has a fast-food section, where grilled goat ribs can be had cheap, and a pub, for men only, serving millet beer from a calabash, about a litre and a half (one-third gallon) at a time. It's common for the men to get drunk on market day. The women do the work but the men go to gossip, and to get and give messages for and from friends and family in other villages. Later, at night, the women walk home with huge bundles on their heads. The men ride donkeys or mobylettes, or sleep it off until the morning.

One day in Sangha, I came across a rehearsal for the harvest festival. An orchestra of drums was leading about thirty masked dancers through a series of choreographed movements in the dust of the village square, down by the solar-powered well, gift of some European quango. Dogon masks are famous in Africa, and are much copied in the souvenir shops. They are used on many occasions, the most extraordinary being the *sigi*, the festival that happens only every sixty years, commemorating some now-forgotten celestial event, when the Dogon perform sacrifices and the Dance of Miracles to renew their world. Generally, the masks are kept safe in caves along the cliff, and brought out only for special occasions. They are, indeed, extraordinary: there were men in cowry-shell masks topped with monkey skin; there was a fellow with a metre-tall head-dress on top of which sat a metre-long carved statue of a female with enormous breasts; there were men wearing the Dogon cross, its four points representing the heavens, the earth, and the universe in between; there were masks representing the vigour of man, the fecundity of women, the generosity of the earth. The dancing was ferociously energetic. Perhaps the most interesting movements are performed by the men in the masks representing the founding lineages. These are 2 metres (6.5 feet) of pliable wood strapped to the head, and a skilful dancer can sweep his head in a circle so that the highest tip of the mask just brushes the ground, kicking up a little pile of dust. Failure (either smacking the ground or missing it altogether) brought jeers from the assembled old men, who stooped and pinched dust in their fingers, throwing it into the air as encouragement. The rehearsal drew a substantial crowd, but, since it was a working day, most of them were either old or children, though there was a decent sprinkling of nubile young women, there to admire all this pounding male energy.

I was the only Outsider present, and afterwards they invited me to join them for a photograph. I still have the picture. There are three rows of the dancers in their gorgeous finery, the front row kneeling on the ground, the men on stilts at the rear. I'm in the middle, between two men bearing the cosmos on their heads. It looks eerily like a school team photo. Team Dogon, 1996.

<hr />

One evening, after we had gotten to know each other a little, Guiré told me his own story.

He comes from a poor family in a village on the Dogon plateau. During the colonial years his uncle had been one of the rare ones to attend school. It came about like this: The French colonial governors, perhaps seeing independence coming, or possibly just in one of those colonialist fits of bureaucratic good conscience, decided that what the country needed were some educated people. *Alors!* Build some schools! And so they did, but none of the people came. Dogon children were too busy helping to bring in the harvest and generally making themselves useful. An edict was therefore issued to all village chiefs: select a dozen kids and be prepared to send them to school, or else.

This presented an awkward dilemma for a conscientious chief. On the one hand, he had to obey his colonial masters—the French didn't appreciate the natives not appreciating being appreciated. On the other hand, to a chief the idea of schooling represented child abuse.

In Guiré's village, the chief came up with what must have seemed an elegant solution—send the kids of the poor to school, and let *them* suffer through this thing called education. Not having enough millet to persuade the chief to turn his attention elsewhere, Guiré's grandparents submitted, and his uncle went off to Bandiagara, several days' walk away, where the French had built a school.

There, it turned out, the young boy had an aptitude for numbers. He sailed through primary school and won a scholarship to a high school in Bamako, the capital, where he soon graduated and became an accountant. Within a few years, independence came, and Guiré's uncle rose to become chief accountant at the new Mali embassy in Paris.

For the family, this was a triumph. Uncle knew his duty to the family and kept the money flowing to the village, enabling them to buy supplies and pay the independent government's burdensome new taxes. Education therefore turned out to be an unexpectedly Good Thing—the poor became less poor because of it, and their status increased. The lesson to be drawn seemed clear: in every generation, be prepared to sacrifice a child to the system, so he could go out into the world and send money home.

For the chief, it was somewhat less of a triumph. He had missed a source of wealth for his own family.

In due course, Guiré was born, eldest son and first born of his father. Within two months of birth, as was the custom, his parents tied a black string and a cowry shell around the wrist of a new-born girl in the village, which signified their intention to bind the girl and Guiré in marriage. Guiré, of course, recalls nothing of this. By the time he was seven he remembers how people would say of the girl as she passed, "Ah, there is your wife!" He would shake his head and cry, no, no! But he knew it was so. (She, it turned out, used to run away when people pointed out her husband—it sometimes cuts both ways, even in a society as profoundly sexist as the Dogon. She didn't like Guiré much, and she let it show.)

Uncle to the rescue. In a letter to Guiré's parents, he pointed out that he himself was growing old. When he was gone, or not able to work, who would continue to send money to the family? It was time to train someone as his successor. He suggested that Guiré should begin his schooling.

This was a tough decision. Guiré was the first-born, the eldest, and he should carry on the family. But ... he was clearly smart, and the family obligation did demand money. He would have to make the sacrifice.

After finishing primary school he was sent to live with his uncle in Bamako. There he finished his schooling and earned his bachelor's degree. Uncle was not satisfied: a man must be properly educated. So he paid for Guiré to go to Lagos, in Nigeria, where he could take a course in tourism management and public relations, and at the same time learn English—Guiré had an aptitude for languages, and already spoke two dialects of Dogon, Bozo, Bambara, and French. He eventually got a job in the tourism industry, shepherding foreigners around his exotic country, and more recently helped form a new tourism company.

But what of his marriage? The girl to whom he had been promised had grown up. If they had followed custom, she would have been formally married to Guiré at the time her breasts began to grow, usually around fourteen or fifteen. Nor had the girl had any schooling. She and Guiré were not only apart, but different. Once again, Uncle came to the rescue. Guiré could not marry in any case until he had finished his schooling, he said, so Guiré's parents released the girl from her obligations and she married one of Guiré's cousins, a nice industrious boy of no obvious intelligence.

"What about you?" I asked Guiré, after he recounted this tale. "Were you free to marry whomever you chose then?"

Not entirely, it turns out. His uncle laid out the conditions: finish schooling, then find someone you really like. It could be anyone, for the uncle was an enlightened man. Any tribe—even a white person, if one took his fancy. But not, of course, the daughter of a smith, a Bozo, or a *griot*.

I was curious. "Why not them?"

"The *griots*," Guiré said, "are a form of beggar, a low form of life." His attitude was similar to the common Western one about, say, political handlers or flacks—*griots*, who are the tribe's storytellers, would tell anyone anything for money, and had no regard for honour or verity. The Bozos? Well, the Bozos were, not to put too fine a point on it, decent fishermen but inferior human beings. About the smiths he was more evasive. Smithing is the only full-time job in Dogon society. The weaving is done by men too, but only in the agricultural off-season. Smiths hold a peculiar position in Dogon mythology, too. They have influential, and even unsettling, connections with the spirit world. Smiths came down from heaven and gave the land its life force, bringing with them grain and the techniques for shaping iron, which made tilling the soil possible. A smith's own life force is constantly diminished, and he must restore it by diligently striking the anvil every day. It sounded to me as though marrying a smith's daughter would be a perilous thing, and the attitude towards them rather like that of a pious Puritan in colonial Salem towards marrying a witch's daughter—why deliberately put yourself in the way of possible spiritual harm?

Guiré was to bring his chosen girl to Uncle for approval. If she wasn't on the proscribed list, and if in the uncle's judgement Guiré really liked her, and she him, his blessing would be forthcoming. He really was an enlightened man.

As it happened, Guiré met and fell in love with a fellow Dogon, a girl from the plains. They live now in Bamako. They would prefer to live in the village, but they can't afford it. Instead, they send money home. The money they send is their duty.

Maybe the chiefs were right, after all. Education is sacrifice. Of what value, then, is schooling?

Says Guiré: "We are a communal people. We don't go against our families. The family is right because it's the family. The parents are right because they gave you life."

Part VII

....

The Maghreb and the
Barbary Coast

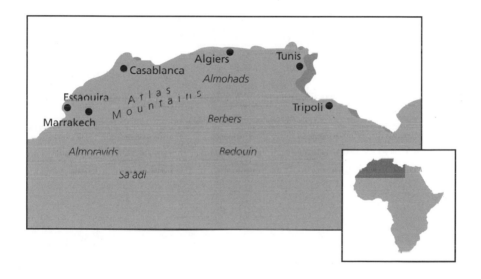

THE OLD MAGHREB

I started in Morocco, for no good reason except that my last memory of Timbuktu had been of the camel trails to the north, some of them heading for Cairo and for Leptis, Tripoli's neighbour in Tunisia, but most of them setting out on the perilous journey to Moroccan Zagora and the perfumed gardens of Marrakech ... The Tuareg I had met on the sands north of Timbuktu had pointed out the way, and there were many historical reports of travellers' relief at seeing, after so many days in the parched and arid interior, the first palm trees in the oases of the Moroccan Drâa.

The Maghreb, being Arab North Africa, has ancient links with the south. They go back to Old Ghana, long before Mali the Great emerged to dominate the Sahel. Even the Phoenicians knew about Ghana's gold, and came looking, planting their settlements along the northern Atlantic coast.

Planeloads of pre-packaged tourists now fill the resort hotels and the beaches from Tunis to Agadir, insulated by sophisticated concierges from the strange and exotic history of the Barbary Coast, as the southern Mediterranean shore was once called. The Barbary pirates have long gone, but this is not to say the Maghreb coast is altogether safe. In early 1997 the Polisario guerrillas of the western Moroccan desert (Spanish Sahara) were quiescent, but still watchful; the fundamentalist cadres of Algeria were locked in a death struggle with the military "democratic" government; the ever-mercurial Colonel Gaddafi of Libya could still be counted on for unpleasant surprises. I watched the Scandinavians and the Germans basting on the Atlantic beaches while pale-skinned Berber waiters flitted among them with towels and pseudo-Hawaiian cocktails—descendants of the same Berbers who had been desert nomads when the Phoenicians settled along the coast somewhere after 1000 B.C. The North African coast has been the nexus of cultural cross-pollination for three millennia, and possibly longer, and it's far from over: just as the eco-animism of the First People was overrun by worship of that sullen and angry god Baal; just as Baal and Ishtar of Carthage struggled with the People of the Book, so is Islam today locked in an ideological struggle with the subversive ideas of the secular West. The Maghreb's is a history of savagery and sophistication, of primitivism and high culture, of glorious conquests and inglorious retreats.

Carthage was the first Outsider colony in Africa, Nelson Mandela has said, and the Afrikaners the last.

Well, maybe. The Berbers were supposed to be the indigènes *around here, descended from the Neolithic peoples of the central Sahara, but their own legends tell of a crossing from Egypt, Arabia, Uzbekistan, Afghanistan, no one really knows whence. We do know that rural Berber tribes remained relatively autonomous until the twelfth century, when invading Bedouin Arabs wrecked their peasant economy and converted many of the settled tribes to nomads. The Berbers are often classed as Mediterraneans, a slippery term for ethnographers. Some Berber groups in the Moroccan Rif, middle Atlas Mountains, and the Jebel Nefusa of northwestern Libya include many individuals with fair skin, blue eyes, and light hair, particularly in their beards. Curiously, their blood types are northwestern European, and in some tribes of the Moroccan middle Atlas the Rh-negative gene reaches a frequency elsewhere found only among Basques. Whatever their origins, the Berbers are a wonderfully exotic mix of desert nomad, Phoenician trader, Arab invader, Andalucian and Roman and black African genes.*

The other two players in the region are the Bedouin and the Moors.

The Bedouin are Arabic-speaking nomadic tribes who came into Africa from Arabia in several waves. Nobles of the nomad tribes trace their ancestry back for centuries to one of two branches of Arabs: those recorded as descendants of an ancient patriarch named Qahtan and called "true Arabs," and those who trace their descent from Ishmael, son of Abraham, and called "arabized Arabs" because they were from farther north and became Arabs by adoption.

The Moors are rather harder to define. As we saw in Part VI, the word was first used by the Romans, from the Latin Mauri, *to describe the inhabitants of the Roman province of Mauritania, comprising the western portion of modern Algeria and the northeastern portion of modern Morocco. It was later used by the English to describe the former Muslims of Spain, of mixed Arab, Spanish, and Berber origins, who created the Arab Andalucian civilization and subsequently settled as refugees in North Africa between the eleventh and the seventeenth centuries.[1]*

The Phoenicians hardly penetrated the North African interior. They founded Carthage in 814 B.C. and explored the coast, making at least two epic voyages, one of them up to Brittany, at the time home to Celtic savages, and the other around Africa's Bulge, possibly as far as Cameroon.

Carthage fell to the Romans in the Punic Wars of 146 B.C., and, when Rome itself was overrun by the Visigoths, the Maghreb for a brief while became part of the Byzantine Empire before it was conquered by the triumphant armies of Islam, as the Arabs invaded all of North Africa.

The eleventh and twelfth centuries saw the great flowering of Almoravid and Almohad civilization and its rich infusion of Andalucian culture. The great monuments of Islamic art, the palaces and mosques of Toledo and Seville and the Alhambra, the Royal cities of Fez, Meknès, Rabat, and Marrakech, were all built during this extraordinary period.

In Iberia much was subsequently destroyed by the Christian hordes. From the perspective of North Africa, the Song of Roland, *that great Christian hymn to battle-fever, can be more easily seen as a surrender to barbarism than as a liberationist hymn against the threat of Unbelief.*

In the sixteenth century, most of the Maghreb became part of the Ottoman Empire, and three hundred years later Western European powers gained control.

Thirty years ago, the last of the colonists finally departed.

I stumbled down a dune high as a house, a shifting thing, treacherous underfoot. The usual midmorning wind was picking up, and the dune's edges, until then sharply etched against the cobalt sky, became blurry. The wind was doing its implacable work, slowly shifting the Sahara northwards. Ahead of me, anchored in the lee of another massive hill of sand, were a few ragged Berber tents. There was no sign of people, but footprints led off across the plain. Behind me, just out of sight, was the dusty little Moroccan town of Mhamid, last stop before … before nothing—there was nothing between Mhamid and Timbuktu, fifty days' journey by camel, but sand, sear scrub, stones, and secretive caves in the Hoggar and the Tibesti mountains, in which Early Man had left memories of better days. And of course oases. It was the occasional oases that made the desert traffic possible.

This is where the caravans always passed. And all the invaders to and from Mali, Mauritania, Old Ghana—the Almoravids, their successors the Almohads, the Sa'adis who wrecked Timbuktu. The nomads still come in through Mhamid from the desert to Tagounite on market days to socialize, to find wives and husbands, to trade camels and goats and dates and tall tales. (Other kinds of tall tales are told here as well. Up the road, at Ouarzazate, are the Atlas Sound Studios. The Atlas Mountains have recently doubled on the silver screen for Arabia, Nepal, Egypt, the Holy Land, and many other places—at Ouarzazate, right across the road from the old Kasbah, is a new "Tibetan palace" cobbled together from plywood and Styrofoam, courtesy of Hollywood.)

Up the Drâa valley and its ribbon of oases came the nomads with their puritan ways.

At the top of the first pass to the north is a sentinel fort on a lonely mountain peak, where they have been watching for invaders for more than two millennia. The view is magnificent, north and south, east and west, as well it should be—they needed all the warning time they could get. At the top of the second pass, on the craggy cliffs of the Jebel Bani, Bani Mountain, is a military microwave station and communications post, where they still watch warily for Polisario tribesmen from the Spanish Sahara, against whom the old Moroccan dynasty was until recently waging a deadly desert war. Not to mention also watching for the Algerians; the southern border of Morocco is not supposed to be still in dispute with the Algerians, but, if that is so, why does every map and every authority draw a different line?

There are camel tracks on the stony banks and the soft bottom of the usually dry Drâa River. And also the oily stains of tracked vehicles, armoured divisions more potent by far than all the Almoravid armies.

It was in the Drâa valley that the traders from the Hausa and Mali and Kanem-Bornu saw their first trees in almost two months of travel across the unforgiving Hamada, the stony plain that makes up so much of the Sahara. At Zagora they stopped for a while to savour the waters before proceeding over the Anti–Atlas Mountains to Ouarzazate, and then over the High Atlas to the fleshpots of Marrakech, with its legendarily hard-nosed traders (now, alas, reduced to hustling carpets to the innocent busloads of tourists from the more orderly world of Europe).

I slid down the dune to the bottom. To the right, already surrounded by shifting sand, was a set of clay Berber ovens, and a midden. But the portable village that had been there had stolen away, only the few tents left. I could smell mint tea brewing. A few people had emerged. The men lounged on the sand in the sun, the women peered curiously from within.

The modern coexists with the old. It doesn't do to become too sentimental. At the bottom of the dune my foot tangled in the shreds of a pair of partly degraded nylon pantyhose, half buried in the sand. And I woke late that night in Zagora to the sounds of a party of drunken French singing, for a reason never discovered, "Auld Lang Syne."

....

Berber markets are common all up and down the Atlas, and well into the desert. At Tagounite, over the small but precipitous pass called Tizi-Beni-Selmane, the nomads come with their donkeys laden with dates. At Asni and Amizmiz and Azilal and Guemassa the shepherds come down with their flocks from the High Atlas as they have been doing since ancient times. I had a guide for one of the markets who called himself Hassan le Magnifique, but he disappeared because I didn't fall for his hustle, which was for him to gain commission on the sale of Berber rugs. That market was on the outskirts of Marrakech, but was in all ways typical, the locals buying and selling in the manner of African markets everywhere. Muddy alleys pierced the warren of stalls, and the place stank of foul water, animal excrement, urine, and slightly rotting food. Later that day I went to another market in the Atlas foothills, only slightly less muddy; the open lot where the donkeys were tethered was called in high irony *le parking pour Mercedes*. Even here they were peddling "Berber jewellery," mass-produced in some offshore factory. But I saw a tall, grave shepherd from the high hills giving his two children a few dirhams to spend as they saw fit, an early lesson in the economics of the marketplace, and a treat on a rare visit to a town. I walked down a smoky alley; on charcoal braziers savoury lamb and chicken stews were cooking in the clay pots called *tagines*, and bits of goat were grilling on skewers. In a small alcove to the right a dozen men were drinking mint tea, squatting on mats or sprawling on benches, entertained by three itinerant musicians, with tambour and lyre. I listened, entranced, as the plaintive music drifted through the smoke and over the hubbub of the market, the music of the nomads preserved through centuries of Islamic disapproval. In a shed tucked up against the wall of a mosque, barbers plied their trade, one of them scraping away at a greybeard's chin, the steel razor gleaming, as sharp as a scimitar—the Berbers have always had a good way with steel (though the actual work was traditionally done by Jews and captured blacks—as with the Tuareg, the Berber nomads consider manual work a matter for lesser beings).

There were no women in this market. As elsewhere in Islam, women have little place in public life.

I looked around as much as I could without offending the Berbers' often prickly sense of personal dignity. I knew that their society was tribal, in the limited sense that they thought of themselves as an assembly of men stemming from a legendary common ancestor, whose name they continued to bear, but I also knew that their society was small-scaled and intensely libertarian. Very small-scale in most cases: the typical Berber grouping often consisted of little more than two or three hundred households occupying an area of not much more than 20 or 30 square kilometres (8 or 12 square miles). These tiny statelets were managed by a council of family heads and temporary magistrates. Among the nomads, the *douar*—people who lived and migrated together—was often even smaller. A tribe could be as few as ten family groupings, and was chiefless except in wartime. Tribes would confederate for battle, but these larger units never held for long—every observer of Berber life remarked on its obsessively libertarian character and its almost perverse mistrust of political power. They are hospitable to a fault—no doubt a product of their excessively inhospitable homelands—but seldom trusting. Innocent inquiries are often treated as intolerable interference.[2]

Trace elements of the first colonizers, the Phoenicians, are rare along the coast. Even in their capital and greatest city, Carthage, all signs of their activities have vanished. The Romans made sure of that. After nearly a hundred years of grinding wars, the Romans finally prevailed and sacked Carthage. So determined were they that nothing would survive of the Phoenician scourge that they destroyed the town brick by brick, stone by stone, salted the remains and cursed the ruins.

The Phoenicians' original homeland might have been—no one knows for sure—somewhere in the region of the Persian Gulf; their language, certainly, was kin to Hebrew and Moabite. The capital of their empire for many years was Tyre, in Lebanon.

"For many years" is an understatement. The Phoenician hegemony lasted as long as glorious Rome; and when Tyre faded after the predations of the Babylonians and Greeks and Romans, its protégé, Carthage, became the centre of empire in its turn.

The Phoenicians, in fact, were not looking for empire; they mostly needed staging-points on the trade route to Spain and other far-flung places. Few of their settlements grew to any size, and they made little effort to subdue native tribes. Yet from the sixth to the third centuries B.C. Carthage controlled the coast from the Gulf of Sidra to Atlantic Morocco, its ships sinking intruders, its mercenary armies demanding—and getting—tribute from powerful kings. The number of gold coins minted in Carthage at the time far exceeded the coinage of similar states elsewhere. Meanwhile, the towns of Leptis, Sabratha, and Oea (Tripoli) became rich through trans-Saharan trade; Leptis was the terminus of one of the shortest routes across the Sahara, linking the Mediterranean with the Niger.

The Carthaginians were a harsh people, who are said by a Greek historian to have "admired not those governors who treated their subjects with moderation but those who exacted the greatest amount of supplies and treated their subjects most ruthlessly." Their wars were renowned for their atrocities against the civilian population, and their god, Baal, seems to have demanded the sacrifice of human children for his appeasement (thousands of urns containing burned infant bones have been found in various Carthaginian sanctuaries). Carthaginian religion was unrelievedly sombre, the central belief being one of human weakness and frailty in the face of the overwhelming and capricious power of the gods.[3]

Those other military adventurers, the Romans, finally overtook the Carthaginians in the ruinous Punic Wars. Tens of thousands of men were killed in the first war, which lasted twenty-three years, until 241 B.C. Carthage was defeated, and in response set up a new empire under Hamilcar Barca in Spain. Hamilcar's son, Hannibal, was the hero of the second Punic War (218 to 201 B.C.) in which he led his famous charge of forty thousand troops and three hundred elephants into Italy from the north, over the Alps, inflicting a stunning defeat on the astonished Romans. But—war took time in those days—Hannibal dallied in southern Italy for seven years or so, waiting for reinforcements that never arrived, and when Rome attacked Carthage itself, he was forced to return and his army was destroyed by the Roman general Scipio. The third Punic War was the shortest, lasting only three years, and ended with the sacking of Carthage in 146 B.C.

I sat at a small outdoor table near the grillers of fresh sardines and calamari in the Moroccan port of Essaouira, and flipped through my notes on Hannibal and the Carthaginians. I had of course read about Hannibal at school, but my memory was hazy, and in any case my Latin lessons were biased—the Romans were the good guys then. It all looked different from an African perspective.

Essaouira was once called Mogador by the Portuguese, but it was already old by the time the Iberians arrived. The Phoenicians had set up a trading station here, for a very particular reason. I looked up. Beyond the Portuguese-built fortified breakwater were two scruffy islands, now sanctuaries for birds, but in one of their previous incarnations the site of a prison. Before that, though, the Phoenicians used to collect snails on the islands which they used for making a popular purple dye. It was not likely Hannibal had come here—his last name, Barca, indicated his family were Libyans, possibly tribal Libyans and not immigrants. I knew other native Libyans had commanded troops in the Punic Wars. Was Hannibal then a native African? It was possible.

Most of the fishing fleet had returned an hour earlier, and the men were already setting up their trays of fish along the breakwater, piles of the Atlantic *loup*, eels, shrimp, dogfish, squid and cuttlefish, baskets of sardines. The smells of grilling fish, salt water, rockpools, and rotting weed were the same smells the Phoenicians would have known—only the reek of diesel fuel was new. The sounds drifting across the docks were Arabic—new since the Phoenicians—and Berber, ancient when Carthage was born. After Carthage died there had been an interregnum of sorts before Rome asserted its control. A few native kingdoms briefly flourished: the Mauri, who gave their name to Mauritania and the Moors; and the Numidae, west of the former Carthaginian homeland. There was also a third group, the Gaetuli, a nomadic people of the desert fringe. The Numidae, or Numidians, had a series of formidable kings; one of them, Bocchus II, died in 33 B.C., bequeathing his kingdom to Rome. The emperor, Augustus, had small interest in so large and backward an area, and in 25 B.C. he installed Bocchus's grandson, Juba II, as king. Juba ruled until his death about A.D. 24; and along the way married Cleopatra Selene, daughter of Mark Anthony and Cleopatra VII of Egypt. He was a prolific writer in Greek on a number of subjects, including history and geography. His son Ptolemy succeeded him, but was executed by Caligula in A.D. 40, for reasons unknown—Caligula didn't often need a reason for his mad doings. A brief revolt followed, and the kingdom was divided into two provinces, Mauritania Caesariensis and Mauritania Tingitana.

Carthage was refounded by Augustus as a Roman colony. For two hundred years it was a significant centre of Roman influence, and dominated the whole of the Maghreb. In the first century Carthage was ruled by several men who subsequently became emperor. Agriculture improved. African exports of grain provided two-thirds of the needs of the city of Rome by the end of the first century A.D., and African fruit, including figs and grapes, appeared in the markets of the capital. The production of olive oil became a massive industry by the second century, particularly in southern Tunisia. In the third century, however, Africa became a military and cultural backwater, and in the fourth century Rome was itself overrun by Aleric and the Visigoths, who sacked the city in A.D. 410. Africa escaped, but only for a while; the Vandals were attracted by its wealth, and led by king Gaiseric, eighty thousand of them crossed into Africa from Spain in 429, overrunning the whole coast. One eminent casualty of this invasion was St. Augustine, born Aurilius Augustinus in A.D. 354 at Tagaste, in what is now northeastern Algeria, to a pagan father and a Christian mother.

I wandered out to the end of the stone breakwater, staring at the remaining fishing fleet far out to sea and reflecting on this turbulent history. The Vandal rule was, again, largely coastal, and independent kingdoms emerged in the interior, largely of Berber character. Nor did the Vandals last. The Byzantine emperor Justinian took back the Maghreb in 533 with only sixteen thousand men (though it was another twelve years before the interior was pacified). But Byzantine rule was, well, byzantine, and collapsed into petty quarrels, small tyrannies, and tribal fiefdoms. By the time of the Arab conquest—the next great wave of immigrants and conquerors—city life had decayed into nothing, and agriculture had virtually collapsed.

It's not hard to see why the colonizers and conquerors coming in from the sea failed to make it past the North African coastal ranges—the Atlas ranges and the Moroccan Rif—to the hinterland.

It's about 40 kilometres (25 miles) from Marrakech to the foothills of the Atlas Mountains, then a steady climb, then another climb. At the top of the second ascent, and before the pass itself, the infamous Tizi-n-Tichka, I saw a long row of stopped trucks, maybe a hundred of them. The pass had been closed the previous night—a freak storm had dumped torrential rains along the Atlantic coast, washing out roads and fields, and had deposited half a metre (about a foot and a half) of snow on the High Atlas. The pass, at 2,200-plus metres (7,200-plus feet), was open again, but only just—the roads remained uncleared and the surface was treacherous. I passed a few truckers who were just starting out. "Insh'Allah," they would say, God willing, we'll get over in safety, but their white knuckles and terrified expressions were not reassuring. On the other side I dropped down to Ouarzazate, to face the craggy and forbidding Anti–Atlas. Once past that, I descended to the Drâa valley, a series of oases with kasbahs and picturesque villages among the palms; on this chilly winter's day rows of Berber men in their *djellabas* were propped against the Kasbah walls in the sunlight, snoozing.

The coast itself is inhospitable, with few natural harbours. The mountains, the Atlas and the Anti–Atlas, run parallel to the coast, with their highest elevations in the High Atlas themselves. There are few places where crossing is easy. Not surprisingly, the early settlers opted for the coastal plains or the valleys between the mountains.

I spent a couple of days poking about the ancient monuments of Marrakech and dodging carpet sellers, hustlers of still more "genuine" Berber jewellery, and water sellers in quaint costumes who allow their photos to be taken for a "mere trifle." The souks and markets of Marrakech are notorious for their rip-offs, though there are bargains to be had—if you have dental problems, for instance, you can pick out a single tooth, or a whole set, neatly laid out on carpet in the main square, the Djemaa el-Fna, the city's crooked commercial heart. There is good leatherwork to be had, though it's easier to buy if you haven't already visited the appalling dye pits and tanneries, where young men work up to their thighs in lye, amidst the stench of rotting hides, sewage, and offal. Still, the city can be rewarding. Much of the old rampart walls are still there, and traces of the old palaces can still be seen.

In every direction, there are minarets.

The Islamic conquest of North Africa had been swift, in historical terms. After overrunning Syria, Mesopotamia, and Egypt, Arab Islamic troops surged into Cyrenaica and Tripolitania. In 670, Uqbah ibn Nafi penetrated Tunisia and as far as southern Morocco. Finally, from 703 to 711, Musa ibn Nusayr brought all North Africa and Spain under Islamic domain.

The whole conquest, in retrospect, might seem to have an air of inevitability about it, but in reality it was a conquest more fractious than most. No more than 100,000 Arab soldiers actually invaded, and their tyrannical ways soon led to revolt. Opposition revolved around Islamic leaders. Within two years rebel forces had retaken all of North Africa, and ten years later managed to depose even the ruling Umayyad caliphs, replacing them with the Abbasids, based in Baghdad.

In the chaotic political conditions that followed, three major kingdoms emerged, roughly corresponding to the three modern countries of Morocco, Algeria, and Tunisia.

All three kingdoms were religiously Orthodox, having embraced the majoritarian Sunni version of Islam. Only the Berbers of northern Algeria adopted the schismatic and more fundamentalist Shiite sect (which, among other things, held that Islam should always be ruled by a descendant of the Prophet through his daughter, Fatima). Their power soon spread, and under Ubayd Allah they set up a Fatimid kingdom. After defeating the Egyptians, Ubayd's successor, Al-Mu'izz, founded the city of Al-Qahira, or Cairo, in 969.

It too didn't last. Backsliding occurred even at home, and when the Berber tribes reverted to Sunnism the Fatimids of Cairo sent in the northern Egyptian tribes for revenge; within a few decades North Africa and its cities were systematically reduced to rubble.

....

A new force, however, was slowly gathering strength in the Sahara. A loose confederation of Berber tribes called the Sanhaja began to wage wars in the Anti–Atlas and the fertile oases of the Drâa. Under the charismatic Abdallah bin Yasin they became known as "the people of the fortress," the *al-murabitin*, the Almoravids.

Marrakech was founded in 1062 by the Almoravid sultan Youssef ben Tachufin. Youssef and his son, Ali, conquered all of the Maghreb, and Ali secured Spain, defeating the Christian hordes in 1085 at Toledo. The irrigation canals that still water Marrakech's famously perfumed gardens were built by Ali. No doubt Ghanaian gold, brought by camel from the Niger ports, helped finance the magnificence.

The Almoravids were succeeded by the purist Almohads, who destroyed Marrakech along with the Almoravid Empire in 1147. The Almohads were fundamentalists in religion but not necessarily in architecture: their synthesis of simplicity and Almoravid opulence created some of the world's most beautiful buildings. They rebuilt the empire in their own image. The tallest and most magnificent mosque of Marrakech, the Koutoubia, was Almohad-built in the twelfth century to rival their other edifices in Rabat and Seville. The Almohads controlled all of North Africa for a brief but glorious time.

Marrakech fell into decay when the Almohad Empire collapsed in 1269, and the successor dynasty, the Merenids, moved the capital to the new city of Fez.

Moroccan politics in the following decades were chaotic. After 1428 a dynasty of viziers—the Banu Wattas (Wattasids)—attempted to rule the country, but were obeyed only in parts of northern Morocco. The Portuguese showed up on the coast, and after 1480 began to settle at various points from Oum er Rbia to Sous. Sufism, an ascetic and mystical view of Islam intolerant of foreign influences, spread through the region; it was Sufi brotherhoods who resisted the Portuguese. From the fifteenth century the *marabouts*, as the Sufi religious leaders were called, challenged the power of the sultans, and anarchy resulted. Morocco essentially split in two, into the *Bled Makhzen* (land under control) and the *Bled Siba* (land of dissidence), where the mountain people organized their own lives while limiting their contact with the cities and the plains.

Marrakech became the capital of Morocco one more time, under the Sa'adian dynasty, a puritan sect that had boiled out of the Drâa oases in the fifteenth century.

One day just before dusk I went to see the tomb of the Sa'adian ruler Abu Yusuf Ya'qub al-Mansur, known as "the Golden One," buried with sixty-six of his relatives in a necropolis near the Kasbah Mosque. I remembered him from Timbuktu, where he is still ill-favoured—Ahmed al-Mansour, as his name is rendered there, was the ruler who had come across the Sahara in the late 1400s with four thousand Andalucian soldiers and had put Timbuktu, Djenne, and Gao to the torch. The Golden One is buried with his son and grandson in the Hall of Twelve Columns, twelve pillars of Italian marble in a room so harmonious, so elegant, so *complete*, that it stands as one of the great monuments to Moroccan–Andalucian aesthetics.

Outside the Tombs, a vendor tried to bully me into buying a carpet containing the putative likeness of Mansour himself. I declined, and he cursed bitterly.

....

For the next several centuries North Africa was the squabbling-grounds for a mess of empires and cultures—the Ottoman Turks, the Holy Roman Empire, the Sicilians, the Spanish and Portuguese. In the sixteenth century, Spain and Turkey fought a series of inconclusive wars there. In 1578 the famous Battle of the Three Kings was fought, when Abd'al-Malik, the ruling sultan and a poet of note, defeated a coalition of Portuguese forces and dissident Moroccans under a dethroned sultan, al-Mutawakkil. This led to a substantial decline in Portuguese influence in North Africa (and the dream of another crusade). In the seventeenth and eighteenth centuries, the Barbary pirates, operating largely from Algiers, made commercial shipping in the Mediterranean almost impossible. The Americans, who were trying to build up their trade with Europe, reacted angrily. From 1803 the Americans made war against the beys. In one episode in 1805 American Marines marched across the desert from Egypt into Tripolitania, giving rise to the famous line in the Marine anthem "From the Halls of Montezuma to the Shores of Tripoli." Washington forced the bey of Tunis to pay $46,000 in compensation for sinking American ships, and in Tripoli he also extracted a fine and secured the release of American, Danish, and Neapolitan slaves.[4]

From 1830, when the French overran Algeria, North Africa was a European protectorate, though formal occupation often came later. In 1881 the French occupied Tunisia, and in 1911 the Italians expelled the Turkish government from Libya. The process was completed by the Franco-Spanish occupation of Morocco, which followed the signing of the Treaty of Fez in 1912. Independence came to the North, as it did to the rest of Africa, after the chaos of the Second World War and the rebirth of nationalism. Libya became an independent state in 1951; Morocco and Tunisia became independent in 1956. In 1960 a new state, Mauritania, was created to the south of Morocco; and, last of all, in 1962 Algeria achieved independence.

MOROCCO

The corniche road from Agadir and the south comes in past the affluent suburbs of commercial Casablanca and terminates … here …at the plaza of the new Hassan II mosque. I stood on the marble-mosaic plaza—big enough for fifty thousand worshippers—and stared up at the minaret, towering over me, 100 metres (320 feet) or more. At dawn the amplified voice of the muezzin had boomed out, through a state-of-the-art speaker system, the familiar words:

Allahu Akbar, allahu Akbar
Ashhadu an la Ilah ila Allah
Ashhadu an Mohammed rasul Allah
Haya ala as-sala
Haya ala as-sala …

I had heard the muezzin's words every morning from my parents' house in Cape Town when I was young; most recently I had heard them outside an international "chapel" in the departure lounge of New York's Kennedy Airport, after which my seat-mate-to-be had unrolled a small prayer mat and had unselfconsciously performed his necessary devotions—Islam connects with its adherents in a way First World Christianity seldom any longer does. The mosque, finished in 1993, is a grandiose thing, rival in hubris to the Ivory Coast's extraordinary Basilica de Notre Dame de la Paix, and one of the tallest structures in all of Islam. But it is beautiful as well as grandiose. I leaned on the seawall listening to the Atlantic breakers pounding the stones below and stared upwards once more. The tower of the Hassan II minaret is massive, square, but so tall it looks fragile. Far overhead is a swirling band of blue and green mosaic, formal and intricate, a delicate tracery of colour in the morning sky. They say that worshippers who choose their place carefully can stare straight down into the green Atlantic—the mosque is built on the shore.

Hassan named the mosque after himself, as well he might. He's been in power since 1961, but there is more to his legitimacy than longevity. He's the latest in a dynasty, the Alawites, who have been at least nominally in charge since the seventeenth century; he is not just king but Commander of the Faithful, for he is also *sherif* of Morocco, claiming descent directly from the Prophet himself, through his grandson, Al-Hassan bin Ali.

The Alawites had slipped into power as the Sa'adians declined. Moulay ar-Rashid was the first of the dynasty to be declared sultan, and his successor, Moulay Ismail, was famously cruel, famously vindictive, famously busy—his capital, Meknès, was built by Christian slaves, and he spent most of his reign in wars against the desert and mountain tribes. (It was said of him that "he tortured his slaves and pampered his camels.")

For a century after his death, the country was marked by increasing European intervention. In the Treaty of Fez, signed in 1912, the French formally declared Morocco a protectorate, though it took another twenty years for them to subdue the Berbers in the high mountains and the Rif, who waged ferocious battles against French units until well into the 1930s.

After the Second World War ended, the Free French had little thought of freedom for the colonies, Morocco included. Naturally enough, nationalist sentiment grew. Boycotts, suppressed, led to terrorist reprisals, which led inevitably to more repression. Mohammed V, the sultan, supported the nationalists and was briefly deposed. But it wasn't to be: the era of colonialism was winding towards its end, and in 1955 Mohammed returned to a rapturous welcome. He died in 1961, and his son Hassan II, the current king, succeeded to the throne.

Hassan, I remembered, had survived two early coup attempts, but had made himself enormously popular at home when he orchestrated the so-called Green March of 350,000 unarmed Moroccans into what had been the Spanish Sahara, until Madrid abruptly abandoned it in 1974 following sixteen years of occupancy. It was hard to see why anyone wanted the place. Most of it was desert, inhabited since medieval times by Sanhajah Berbers and Arabic-speaking Bedouin. The Green March may have been popular at home, but the Popular Front for the Liberation of Saguia al-Hamra and Rió de Oro (aka Polisario) objected strongly to this unsought exchange of foreign masters, having no particular connection to the Alawite rulers of Morocco. They embarked on a long and difficult guerrilla war that ended only with a U.N.-sponsored cease-fire in 1991. There was supposed to be a referendum in the territory in 1995, but it has been postponed indefinitely while the two parties try to sort out who will be allowed to vote. Will it ever take place? *"Insh'Allah,"* God willing, the Berber who had guided me into the dunes near Mhamid said, his voice heavy with irony—meaning, probably not, let's hope not, leave well enough alone, what does it matter ... The Polisario has not been disbanded; it would take very little for it to start up again. It had only been three years since army patrols were withdrawn from the highways along the southern flanks of the Anti–Atlas, and as I had seen for myself there were still watchful units in the high hills, waiting for the Polisario to return.

Meanwhile, Hassan toughed out a World Bank–sponsored austerity program in the 1980s (surviving sporadic urban rioting) and was trying to set up a free-trade agreement with the European Union. The smart money in early 1997 was betting that he would succeed. The same money was laying long odds that if his son, a nice young man properly trained in all the spit and polish at fancy European military schools, ever succeeded to the throne, it would very likely be as a king along the European model, the figurehead ruler of a parliamentary democracy.

But the smart money has been wrong in the Maghreb often before. The same Islamists who were bringing terror to Algeria were, by the late nineties, active in Morocco too. Hassan banned the most extreme group, the euphemistically named Justice and Charity, and its leader, Abdelsalam Yassine, from active politics—despite the fact that Yassine declared himself in favour of pluralist democracy, a declaration that was greeted with incredulity among the Moroccan élite. Rioting broke out in the universities and there were grumblings in the countryside. Some of the richer Moroccans were already buying Canadian passports, just in case.

ALGERIA

All through the long and bitter war of independence waged by the Front de Libération Nationale (FLN) against the French (and through the subsequent revolt of the colons against what they saw as de Gaulle's betrayal), the most potent symbol of nationalist aspirations and colonial insensitivity was the Great Mosque of Algiers. Well, not so much the mosque itself, but the atrocity at the top of the minaret. The French had appropriated Arab and Berber land, expropriated their businesses, suppressed their culture, razed their medinas, closed their medersas, their holy schools, and then, the crowning indignity, converted the Great Mosque to the Catholic Cathedral of St. Philippe. At the very top, where the muezzin had exhorted the faithful to prayer, they installed a cross.

The modern "European" period of Algeria began when a British battleship, the hundred-gun HMS *Queen Charlotte*, showed up in the outer harbour of Algiers determined to teach the bally corsairs (as the Barbary pirates were popularly called) a lesson once and for all. Algiers was still, officially at least, a province of the Ottoman Turkish Empire, and the beys or pashas were appointed by and responsible to the sultan in Constantinople. But Ottoman control was nominal at best, and the pirates paid little attention to edicts from the East. The British vessel anchored 100 metres (110 yards) out, and as soon as the first defender's guns opened up, the commanding admiral gave orders to begin the bombardment. For decades previously, Algiers (along with Tunis and Tripoli) had been notorious for preying on "Christian shipping" in the Mediterranean. The Barbary pirates, using as their excuse a fundamentalist interpretation of Islam, kidnapped Christian "livestock" from Italy, Malta, Sicily, Sardinia, and Corsica, and from the ships of all nations sailing the Mediterranean. The principal sources of income were kidnapping, hostage taking, slavery, and ransom. At one time Algiers held as many as 25,000 Christians as slaves.[5]

The British battering changed nothing, and it was left to the French to sort things out. The French arrived in earnest in 1830, when they attacked Algiers, in response to some fancied slight against a French consul. In 1834 the *sherif* Abdelkader, the nationalist leader who controlled the west and the south (and who is still in popular imagination the greatest of the Algerian freedom fighters), was officially recognized by the French in a series of cavalierly signed treaties, as equally cavalierly broken in 1839, after which he waged a six-year war against the Christian invaders. He lost, and spent the next thirty-six years in exile, dying in Damascus in 1883.

For the following hundred years or so, Algeria was considered an integral part of *la France métropolitaine*. By the time the war of independence started, in October 1954, more than three million French were living in Algeria, and all Algerians had the right to live and work in France itself. None of this counted for much with the partisans of the FLN, who wanted nothing more than to get France out of their country. By the time they succeeded, more than a million people had been killed and the economy was in ruins. Fewer than thirty thousand French remained in Algeria after independence.

Not that independence helped much. The bungling socialist government of Ahmed Ben Bella was succeeded by the creeping caution of Colonel Houari Boumédienne and the lumberingly bureaucratic rule of Chadli Benjedid, all of them centralist, secular, and intolerant of opposition.

After riots against food shortages in 1988, constitutional changes were made which were intended to permit a gradual shift to multiparty government and away from the FLN monopoly on power. But when local elections in 1990 ended in overwhelming support for FIS (the Front Islamique du Salut), a hitherto forbidden Islamic extremist party, followed by another landslide in the elections to the National Assembly, the army had finally had enough—it deposed Chadli and replaced him with rule by army council. After Lamine Zeroual was installed as supreme leader in January 1994, the country slid into civil and sectarian warfare. Non-Muslim foreigners were being killed, and bombs were once again going off in Paris (France was being blamed for propping up the FLN militarists). At the end of 1996, the country's prime minister, Ahmed Ouyahya, asserted that all but "remnants" of terrorism had been crushed; entirely predictably, the terrorist massacres in the villages and towns promptly escalated. In an effort to prop up its sagging reputation in the countryside, the regime then announced that Arabic would become the sole official language by 1998, prompting furious denunciations not only from French-speakers, but from the Berber population as well. By early 1997, the chances of a peaceful settlement seemed remote, and Ramadan was, as the Islamists had promised, "a time of horror," filled with massacres and brutal killings.

TUNISIA

The beys who ruled Tunisia after 1830 did their best not to give Europe any excuse to intervene—outlawing piracy, encouraging Westernization and secularization, hiring French advisers—but to no avail: Europe was carving up all of Africa, and Tunisia was not to escape.

In 1881 the French sent in an army, ostensibly to control raids into neighbouring French Algeria, and two years later the bey signed a convention acknowledging French protection.

Settlement followed, but with some restraint—French settlers took the best farm land and the best raw materials, but their numbers were relatively few, and, although there was a short-lived nationalist movement early in the century, it wasn't until Habib Bourguiba formed a true opposition party in 1934 that matters started to heat up.

The French helped things along by banning Bourguiba and his party. After the Second World War, from exile in Cairo, Bourguiba brilliantly orchestrated a resistance campaign, and in 1955 he returned to Tunis in triumph to form the first post-independence government.

The new government was secular and socialist to its core; among other things, Bourguiba closed the Islamic schools, and forbade the wearing of the *hijab* for women. None of this went down very well in the hinterland, but it wasn't until he attempted to persuade the mullahs to exempt Tunisians from the fasting of Ramadan under the altogether slippery rationale that they were needed for a "jihad against underdevelopment" that organized Islam finally turned on him.

In 1981 Bourguiba was persuaded to call elections. However, he didn't allow his newly developed democratic urges to get the better of him. He banned the Islamic parties from participating, and shamelessly rigged the results, emerging with the usual 99 per cent of the vote. His National Front took all 136 seats in the national assembly.

As time went on, Bourguiba seemed to become more and more erratic, and after he had carelessly rigged a few show trials against dissidents in 1987, his foreign minister, Zine al-Abidine bin Ali, got together a gaggle of eminent physicians who declared the eighty-three-year-old leader too unwell to govern. He was bundled off to his palace in Carthage in permanent "retirement."

Bin Ali was about as much infused with democratic enthusiasm as his predecessor. In the 1989 elections, he too came up with the magic number of 99 per cent of the vote, after preventing the Islamic opposition party, the Hizb al-Nahda, from participating. Following the Gulf War (in which Bin Ali supported the U.S.-led alliance, to popular disapproval), he suddenly "discovered" that Al-Nahda had plotted to overthrow his government and would perforce have to be immediately banned.

In 1994 elections were held again, with the same monotonous results. And that, in early 1997, was where matters stood. Bin Ali had scored some points with militant Arab regimes by covertly helping Gaddafi circumvent a U.S.-inspired air boycott, while at the same time allowing the Americans to supply his armies. He seemed to be firmly in control. But he would be wise to be looking over his shoulder. In the Maghreb, fundamentalist successes have a long history.

LIBYA

L ibya I thought I was already familiar with. I had seen the results of Colonel
Gaddafi's mercurial foreign policy in Chad, where proud citizens were still
wont to point out the holes made by Libyan shells, and recount their own no
doubt exaggerated exploits in helping to repel the Gaddafian invaders. The Libyan
desert—the place was mostly desert, and still is, and had been generally worthless until
they discovered vast reservoirs of oil underneath it—had been a favourite topic of
literary bragging since Herodotus. In his Histories he recounted how he had heard a
"story from some people of Cyrene ... These men declared that a group of wild young
fellows, sons of chieftains of their country, had on coming to manhood planned among
themselves all sorts of excessive adventures ... one of which was to explore the Libyan
desert, and try to penetrate further than had ever been done before."[6]

Many European explorers dared the same desert.

In 1799 one Friedrich Hornemann, disguised, at least to his own satisfaction, as an
Arab, set out from Tripoli southward across the desert, heading for the still-legendary
(to Europeans) kingdom of Bornu. In seven weeks he was in Murzuk, where he wrote
to Joseph Banks of the African Association in London: "Being in an excellent state of
health, perfectly inured to the climate, sufficiently acquainted with the manners of my
fellow-travellers, speaking the Arabic language, and somewhat of the Bornu tongue,
and being well armed and not without courage, and under protection of two great
Shereefs, I have the best hope of success in my undertaking ..."Alas, Hornemann disappeared, though he is believed on scant evidence to have reached Bornu and the Niger
before succumbing to one or other of the myriad African diseases.[7]

In 1822, the Denham–Clapperton–Oudney expedition to Lake Chad also set out
from Tripoli. They, too, reached Murzuk. There, however, they were prevented by
the bey from proceeding. While they waited, they "discovered" the Roman ruins at
Germa/Garama, and received a friendly reception from the dreaded Tuareg.
Eventually, they departed, a large expedition of two hundred soldiers and a number
of Arab merchants eager to travel to Bornu with an armed escort.[8]

Heinrich Barth, the great survivor, nearly succumbed in southern Libya. He was
between Murzuk and Ghat, and was determined to visit a rocky protuberance some
way off ... but the distance proved to be greater than he had originally imagined,
and when he at last reached a crest, in a state of the utmost exhaustion, there was no
sign of the caravan he had left. Nothing gave shelter from the sun and he had very
little water. The Bedouin had told him a man might last in the desert without water
for twelve hours ... He crawled about, frantically seeking shade under a stunted, leaf-
less tree. Desperate with thirst, he sucked blood from his own veins, then fell into a

sort of delirium. Sometime later he regained consciousness and heard nearby the cry of a camel ... A solitary Tuareg, searching for him over the pebbly ground where there were no footprints, heard his croaking call for water and hastened to his aid.[9]

Libya is the fourth-largest country in Africa, but has no rivers except a few "intermittent" streams. Ninety per cent of the population live in the narrow coastal belt around Tripoli and to the east, between Benghazi and Tobruk. In the south are the Tibesti Mountains, vast barren peaks rising more than 3,000 metres (9,840 feet), still home after all these centuries to bandit refugees from long-gone Kanem-Bornu, and not safe for travellers. There are extraordinary rock paintings in the mountains, dating to Neolithic times and before, recounting stories of a Sahara verdant and lush with life. Deep under the desert are massive fossil aquifers, said to be more than 3 billion cubic metres (106 billion cubic feet)—enough to supply the whole country for half a century. Gaddafi, never a man of small vision, set about constructing a pipeline from the desert to bring the water to Tripoli. The Great Man-Made River, in early 1997 still under construction, is the largest building project on the planet, estimated to cost nearly $30 billion (U.S.)

In fifty years, the aquifers, which are not being replenished, will have been sucked dry. And then what?

At the start of the nineteenth century Libya had been in the hands of quasi-independent rulers for several hundred years—most latterly the Karamnli dynasty—and had prospered by giving refuge to the Barbary pirates. But by the 1830s the Americans and the French had put an end to piracy, and in 1835 the Ottoman Turks sent a fleet to assert a rather more direct control. Still, all they managed was to dominate the coastal strip; in the interior, administration was in the hands of their surrogates, the Senussi movement, a mystic form of Islam akin to Sufism that sought to "restore" the "purity" of society as they imagined it had been at the time of the Prophet.

In 1911, though, Libyan self-rule was abruptly ended when the country was brutally invaded by the Italians. Under their tyrannical regime, the Libyan population fell by 50 per cent, through either extermination or forced exile. What there was of fertile land was expropriated and handed over to Sicilian peasants, imported for the purpose.

In the Second World War, Libya was a major theatre of battle, and the massive minefields laid by both sides during the great desert tank battles have still not been entirely cleared. After the war, Libya was placed under U.N. trusteeship and in December 1951 became an independent monarchy, under King Idris, an elderly nonentity from the interior, chosen because he was a grandson of the Great Senussi, the movement's founder.

Eighteen years later, in 1969, a twenty-seven-year-old army officer called

Muammar Gaddafi seized control of the state radio station and announced: "In the name of God, the Compassionate, the Merciful, O Great Libyan People! To execute your free will, to realize your precious aspirations, truly to answer your repeated call demanding change and purification, urging work and initiative, and eager for revolution and assault, your armed forces have destroyed the reactionary, backward, and decadent regime ..."[10]

There was more in this vein, but the drift was straightforward enough. Libya was no longer to be a client state of Britain and America. The oil revenues were going to stay in the country. Those who didn't like it could lump it.

A few years, later Gaddafi disappeared into the desert to emerge with his *Green Book*, his "radical alternative to capitalism and communism," most of which meant abolishing political parties and operating through a tiered series of peoples' committees, with Gaddafi at the top. He even went so far as to propose abolishing the army and substituting a people's militia run by revolutionary committees (his relationship with the army has been uneasy ever since).

Gaddafi expected his political credo to be rapidly adopted by other countries, since it was self-evidently superior as political philosophy, and was confounded when that didn't happen. He believed in Arab unity, and at various times announced the formation of political unions with an array of countries, including Tunisia, Egypt, Sudan, Morocco, Syria, and Chad, none of which ever came to anything (in the case of Egypt it almost came—twice—to war, and in the case of Chad, it did). He supported freedom fighters everywhere, and seemed unable to distinguish between the genuine thing and disaffected criminals. He was bamboozled by Idi Amin's professed conversion to Islam into handing over millions of dollars to the Ugandan looter supremo. On the other hand ... despite the privations caused by Libya's political isolation, and despite the drying up of the formerly endless oil-revenue stream, it's probable that Libyans are better off under his rule than they were before the colonel began his curious and idiosyncratic dash to immortality.

Part VIII

The Longest River

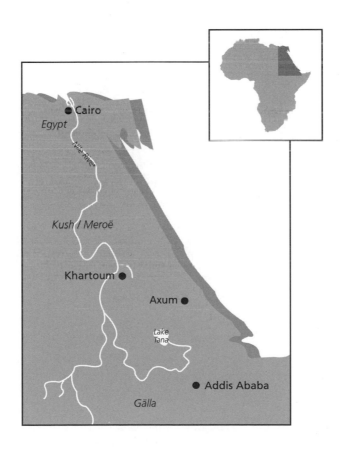

EGYPT

In the Nile mouth below me, a pair of dolphins splashed, a silvery glitter that was gone in an instant. I was leaning on the stern railing of a passenger vessel headed for Suez and Mogadishu and beyond. It was the first time I had seen the Nile. I don't know what I expected, but here it was, sluggish and black in the Egyptian night. Across the harbour I could hear the sound of a rough-hewn diesel, pukkapukka, in the channel. There were low murmurs from the quay, where a group of Arab men in djellabas smoked and gossiped. The dolphins splashed again. They had swum in from the wine-dark sea, here where it meets the Emerald River, flowing down from the Mountains of the Moon ... Is there any more romantic spot on earth than this? Did not Mohammed, the Prophet of God himself, say that the "Nile comes out of the Garden of Paradise, and if you were to examine it when it comes out, you would find in it leaves of Paradise"?[1]

The Nile, the longest river on the planet, would take me full circle, up the Great Rift Valley, that massive wound in the earth, to the African heartland. It would take me past Kush and its old capital, Meroë, in the Sudan. These old civilizations had infected black Africa through the southwards migrations of Nilotic speakers; and in turn they infected and were infected by Egypt. The White Nile and its many branches would carry me south to the Great Lakes, to Jinja on Lake Victoria, to Burundi (where the Nile is really born) and beyond. The Blue Nile would take me to Lake Tana and into Ethiopia, whose culture goes back to the time of Solomon the Wise, King of the Jews. It is the annual drenching of the Ethiopian highlands that spills over into the Nile, and the annual deposit of silt in the Nile that enabled the fecundity of Egyptian civilization.

Stanley, on his travels, recounts many legends of the Father of Rivers, most of them from early Arab manuscripts: "As for the Nile, it starts from the Mountains of Gumr ... Some say that word ought to be pronounced Kamar, which means the moon, but the traveller, Ti Tarshi, says that it was called by that name because the eye is dazzled by the great brightness." And again: "Other explorers have said that the four rivers, Gihon, Sihon, the Euphrates and the Nile arise from one source—from a dome in the gold country, which is beyond the dark sea, and that that country is a part of the regions of Paradise, and that the dome is of jasper. They also say that Hyad, one of the children of Ees, prayed God to show him the extreme end of the Nile. God gave him

power to do this, and he traversed the dark river, walking upon it with his feet over the
water which did not stick to his feet, until he entered that dome." And: "Others say
that the Nile flows from snowy mountains, and they are the mountains called Kaf.
That it passes through the Green Sea, and over gold and silver and emerald and ruby
mines, flowing on ad infinitum until it reaches the lake of the Zingh, and they say
were it not to enter into the salt sea and be mixed up with the waters thereof, it could
not be drunk for great sweetness."²

Legends, lost in the suburban pages of history. But true enough. The Nile is the Father
of Rivers, the Seed of Civilization. Modern engineers, at the urging of the pan-Arabist
Gamal Abdel Nasser, finally put a stop to the Nile Delta's infusions of silt by building
the High Aswan Dam. No one yet knows the consequences of this act of hubris.

I did all the usual Cairo things. I apparently bumped into each of Al-Qahira's eigh-
teen million citizens at least once, visited the frenetic bazaars and the chaotic souks,
and poked about the old Islamic quarters between the medieval gates and the
Saladin's Citadel. I visited the City of the Dead (where beggars are very much alive);
I saw the last surviving southern gateway, called Bab Zuweila, through which Mansa
Musa had entered in triumph after his long journey from Mali; I went to see Old
Cairo (older than Islamic Cairo but not nearly as old as the Pharaohs), which is now
the centre of Coptic Christianity; I ate grilled pigeon with pine-nuts and yoghurt
in a vaulted room cool with blue tiles and lazy fans and filled with the murmur of
Berber, Aramaic, Arabic, Ge'ez, and Persian; I watched the boats plying the Nile,
piled with goats and palm nuts, and dates, not very different from the boats and car-
goes depicted on the frescoes on the tombs at Thebes, and not different at all from
the boats I had seen on the Niger at Djenne; I watched, as much as I dared, the daily
dance with death of the Cairo traffic (a bus driver, his patience running out at last,
wrenched his vehicle off the highway and made a mad rush down a parallel stretch
of paving—the runway of a military airport). I had declined a visit to the Egyptian
Museum—who hasn't seen enough Egyptian mummery to last a lifetime?—but of
course had duly taken the trip out to the Sphinx and the pyramids at Giza.

The Sphinx—its undeniably *African* features worn down by the passing of forty
centuries and abraded by the pollution spewed by eighteen million citizens—is a sad
thing, battered, more street-weary tomcat than leonine majesty. But the pyramids,
now, the pyramids are a different thing altogether.

A short way up the south *col* of the Great Pyramid of Cheops there is an opening, a gateway, and from there, bored at an angle upwards into the rock (no, that's
wrong—*constructed into* the rock), is a passageway, a pathway to the burial chamber of the pharaoh. This passageway is not for the faint of heart and most definitely
not for the claustrophobic—it's almost impossible, as you crawl up on hands and
knees, not to think of the millions of tons of rock hanging over your head, gravity

defied only by the ingenuity of unknown engineers. My knees were scraped and it was hard to breathe, the air as desiccated as a mummy's bones. The passageway must be a hundred metres (330 feet) long, though it's devilish hard to tell there in the bleak black (shadows only partly rent by the tenuous light of a few paltry lamps).

The burial chamber must be very close to the centre of the beast itself, millions of tons of rock below you, millions above, millions on every side. So easy, here in this amazing place, to be seduced into mysticism. So great was the labour involved, so heroic the very conception, that it's easy to come to believe in the intercession of gods, of the mysterious Other, or to "understand" that the "ancients" must surely have had access to esoteric secrets of science far beyond ours—how else build something so perfect, and at the same time so *infernally heavy*? Surely they must have levitated the blocks into place? This thing cannot just be a tomb, can it, a place for royal bones; it must have another purpose, a celestial observatory, a beacon to the Alien ... And so on and so on—how many books have been written undertaking a solution to the curse and the promise of the pyramids? (Of course, the best antidote is to visit Saqqara, 24 kilometres [15 miles] south of Cairo, the old pharaonic capital of Memphis, which is now a barren plain littered with temples and pyramids of all kinds and conditions and degrees of inclination. Here were the proving grounds for the pyramid builders—surely gods wouldn't have needed to *practise*? The early pyramidist the Pharaoh Snefru, in 2613 B.C., was something of an experimenter himself, and many of his failed pyramids can still be seen, built with varying degrees of incompetence.)

A little later I fell into conversation with a sharp-nosed South African, a thin and disapproving woman of the old colonial school, who thought most wog customs more or less disgusting, and the wogs themselves like children, only dirtier. She, of course, was convinced that the "ancient Egyptians" were a different sort of people altogether, a much finer, saner, smarter (and probably whiter) lot than the present incumbents. The current lot couldn't possibly have built those great monuments, the temples of Karnak, the pyramids, the rest ... Her views would hardly be worth recounting, banal and myopic as they are, except that so much of both Western and Arab writing about old Egypt has glossed the interesting and irreducible fact that ancient Egypt was an African civilization. Even the best of the guidebooks, the Lonely Planet series, which is almost always as even-handed and as sceptical as possible, isn't above suggesting that Ancient Egypt, through its trade missions and travellers, probably nudged other African civilizations into being, never considering that it might have been a two-way street.

Well, some things are known, others not. Around 3000 B.C., the conventional histories go, Menes unified the kingdom of the Delta with the kingdom of the Nile valley, thereby reaching a critical mass that made an advanced technical civilization possible. After that, of course, things are well enough known: thirty-odd dynasties and three thousand years-plus of continuous indigenous rule. But it still begs the question, Who were the ancient Egyptians?

You want "evidence"? Greek historians of the first millennium B.C. commonly thought Egyptian and Ethiopian were synonyms, and there's at least one early Greek writer who asserted that it was Ethiopians, led to the Nile delta by the (Greek, of course) god Osiris around 3000 B.C. who founded the Egyptian civilization. Moses's wife, according to the Bible, was an Ethiopian (and—some things never change—he was roundly criticized by his brother Aaron for it). Khufu, the great pyramid builder of Egypt, was described as a "thick lipped and woolly haired black," which possibly implies the others weren't. During the twenty fifth and twenty-sixth dynasties, beginning around 720 B.C., Egypt was governed by Nubian rulers. An Arab manuscript of fairly recent vintage (1686) says the following: "Achmed, son of Ti Farshi, in his book of the description of the Nile, says historians relate that Adam bequeathed the Nile unto Seth, his son, and it remained in the possession of these children of prophecy and of religion, and they came down to Egypt (or Cairo) and it was then called Lul. So they came and dwelt upon the mountains. After them came a son Kinaan, then his son Mahaleel, and his son Yaoud, and his son Hamu, and his son Hermes—that is Idrisi the prophet [Enoch]. [And] Idrisi began to reduce the land to law and order ... He is the first man who regulated the flow of the Nile to Egypt. Idrisi gathered the people of Egypt and went with them to the first stream of the Nile, and there adjusted the levelling of the land and the water by lowering the high land and raising the low land and other things according to the science of astronomy and surveying. Idrisi was the first person who spoke and wrote books on those sciences. It is said that in the days of Am Kaam, one of the kings of Egypt, Idrisi was taken up to Heaven, and he prophesied the coming of the flood, so he remained on the other side of the equator and there built a palace on the slopes of Mount Gumr. He built it of copper, and made eighty-five statues of copper, the waters of the Nile flowing out through the mouths of these statues and then flowing into a great lake and thence to Egypt."[3] This recounting is so similar to the ancient legends of the Baganda, up there at the Great Lakes near the Mountains of the Moon, that Stanley, who made a hobby of collecting stories of the Nile, made the connection between Idrisi and Kintu, the legendary founder of the Baganda kingdoms, who was said to have come up to Uganda from the Nile regions. What, also, to make of pottery shards being found at Axum, in Ethiopia, which also date to around 3000 B.C.? And so on and so on—there is, as you can see, much anecdotal evidence for the African origins of Egypt, and you can be as convinced by the evidence as your preconceptions will allow.

More interestingly, the Egyptians themselves believed they originated elsewhere, in a land called Punt. The name came up in inscriptions dating to the third millennium B.C. Much later, a curious queen, Hatshepsut, decided to go see for herself, and mounted an expedition in 1500 B.C., but seems to have lacked proper secretarial help, and its conclusions are not known. Punt lies somewhere along the Indian Ocean coast, but whether only as far as the old Axumite port of Adulis in Eritrea, or in Somalia, or even somewhere beyond, maybe in old Azania or the land of the Zanj, no one knows.

Perhaps none of this matters. We know that there are civilizations, like the pre-Axumites and the Kushites in Ethiopia and Sudan, almost as old as Egypt. We know they fought each other, often married each other, mixed with each other, and went on with their lives. Perhaps that's enough.

....

The pharaonic dynasties finally fell into decay and disarray around the fourth century B.C., when Egypt was overrun by the Persians. In 332 B.C. the Persian usurpers were themselves defeated by Alexander of Macedonia, self-styled the Great (among his many less-than-savoury inventions, Alexander was the first exponent of biological warfare—he had plague victims hurled into a besieged city with catapults). Egypt welcomed Alexander as a liberator, and after he was told by the oracle of Amon that he was, indeed, Amon's son, he became godlike enough to become pharaoh.

When Alexander died nine years later, it took his generals less than a week to carve up his divine empire. Egypt became the property of Ptolemy I, son of Lagus of Macedonia. The Ptolemies ruled for several centuries, but eventually their power faded and they became clients of the Romans (Cleopatra VII, African lady of legend and romance, was the consort both of Julius Caesar, whose son she bore, and Mark Anthony, whose daughters she bore—after Mark Anthony's navy was defeated by his rivals at the battle of Actium, in 31 B.C., Cleopatra and her consort committed one of history's best-recorded and beloved double suicides). Divers are still pulling up splendid Graeco-Roman statuary from the mouth of Alexandria harbour, site of the famous Pharos lighthouse of antiquity.

Roman Egypt was a place of little importance. The Romans treated it like a backward provincial satrapy, and the main evidence of their passing was extensive vandalism of the ancient culture's monuments. In A.D. 640, Egypt was conquered by the invading armies of Islam and became a centre of Islamic learning and culture under the Fatimids.

After that it was part of the Turkish Empire, but as the Turks declined, so did Egypt, and it sank into corruption and incompetence. Bonaparte came, conquered, overthrew the Mamelukes, provoked a popular uprising, and went back to France, where pseudo-Egyptian style became all the rage, feeding off the treasures Napoleon looted. The British threw the French out, and, when they in turn left, the Ottomans returned. The second-in-command of the Ottoman forces was one Mohammed Ali, who came from Albania, as did his troops. Within two years he had formed a populist alliance with the artisans of the bazaars, the Cairo poor, and the students of the al-Azhar university, under the tutelage of their rector. In 1805, at a word from Ali, all the shops shut; the Cairo poor rose, forming themselves into a street militia; the *ulemas* of the al-Azhar set up religious war chants; and Ottoman rule collapsed ignominiously.

Ali became viceroy. He expelled his predecessor, sent his chief henchman and tame demagogue, Umar Makram, into exile, butchered the last of the Mameluke warlords, and even cowed his own supporters by his ferocity and willingness to inflict pain. He was perhaps the biggest dealer in slaves in the world during the second and third decades of the nineteenth century, drawing them from the entire Sudanese-Nile basin as well as East Africa. With the connivance of the French consul general, he set up a system of conscription which forced large numbers of peasants into his army.

Edward Lane, an English mathematician and engraver who spent much of the 1820s in Egypt, described a despotism uniquely pervasive for its time. The country was run by the secret police. "They had no distinguishing uniform, and their first task was to visit the coffee shops and listen; their second was to enforce the tax system. The Wali, or head policeman, ran the 'public women' all of whom paid taxes to Ali ... If the Wali heard of a woman committing adultery, the woman was promptly classified as a prostitute and taxed. [A] curfew was imposed an hour and a half after sunset, at which point anyone outside his house (other than the blind) had to carry a lantern ... On night patrol the Wadi was always accompanied by a torchbearer ... and an executioner." Curfew breaking was punished by a beating on the spot and "the Chief of Police [had] an arbitrary power to put any criminal or offender to death without trial." By day the markets were toured on horseback by an officer called the Mohtesib ... checks for evasion of economic laws or taxes were made on the spot, and floggings carried out the same way. In 1825, Lane said, the Mohtesib frequently clipped the ears of offenders ... and "a butcher, who had sold some meat wanting two ounces of its due weight, was punished by cutting off two ounces [of flesh] from his back."[4]

Ali's essentially secular rule provoked revolts led by the *mahdis*, fundamentalist preachers with a narrow Islamicist bent. Later, the British faced the same kind of fundamentalist backlash in the Sudan, a popular revolt that led to the Battle of Omdurman in 1899.

The ship ploughed steadily through the Suez Canal, the deserts of Sinai to the left and the Arabian Desert of Egypt to the right, the Red Sea ahead. Before Ferdinand de Lesseps built the canal for his Anglo-French shareholders last century, this had been dry land—malarial, swampy, but relatively dry. Why hadn't Moses and the Israelites headed north and then east, crossing into Sinai here, instead of getting trapped farther south between the Eastern Desert and the Red Sea? Wouldn't it have been better advice for the God of the Jews to steer them here rather than working up a lather to generate that East Wind that parted the Red Sea? Better advice, but perhaps not so good as drama. I went downstairs to the ship's library, and borrowed their Bible. The Old Testament Lord was always ready for the Grand Gesture, I remembered, and there it was: "And the Lord spake unto Moses, saying, Speak unto the children of Israel that they turn and encamp before Pihahiroth, between Migdol and the Sea, over against Baalzephon: before it ye shall encamp by the sea. For Pharaoh will say of the Children of Israel, They are entangled in the land, the wilderness hath shut them in. And I will harden Pharaoh's heart, that he should follow after them, and I will be honoured upon Pharaoh and upon all his host, that the Egyptians may know that I am the Lord."

The sequel, of course, is well-enough known: the Lord was "honoured" upon pharaoh in a big way, drowning his army in the sea.

The Egyptian tanks crossed here without effort in the Six Day War of 1967, and were beaten back.

It was another day before we sailed through the Gulf of Suez. Mount Sinai was off in the desert to the left; it was there Moses had spent forty days and nights with his God. On the western side of the gulf, the Nile wandered through the Eastern Desert, passing all the grand places of Egyptian history, Deir Mahwas, Qena, Qus, Luxor, Aswan, Abu Simbel. Up there was Lake Nasser and the Aswan Dam. Nasser had skilfully played off the Soviets and Americans to get the funding he needed for this grandiose scheme, and then persuaded the U.N. to pay for the shifting of the Great Temple at Abu Simbel, Ramses II's monument to his own deification—the moving of this monument out of the way of the waters of Lake Nasser rivalled in its engineering skills the original conception.

Nasser was succeeded by Anwar Sadat, who made peace with Israel and was killed for his trouble. His successor, Hosni Mubarak, profited from the Gulf War, has settled Egypt's long-simmering dispute with Syria, and has calmed the unrest with Sudan on his southern borders, but his World Bank–mandated economic retrenchment has hurt the *fellahin*, the ordinary Egyptians, and in the middle of the decade radical Islamicists declared their intention of remaking the secular state into one governed by the Islamic *shari'a*, the code of conduct laid out in the Koran. The *mahdis* of Mohammed Ali's day have their own inheritors.

On Lake Nasser, formed by the Aswan High Dam, the feluccas ply the waters as they have done the Nile for forty centuries. Higher up the Nile, at Lake Tana, they are called *tankwas*. Both are made of papyrus, and are identical in style to the boats depicted on the frescoes at Luxor and Karnak. You can sit by the Nile at Aswan and, if you're lucky, you may see the feluccas drifting by in the light of a blood-red tropical moon.

MEROË AND KUSH

One of my earliest memories of Africa outside of the country in which I was born is now just a snapshot image. It was a Nuer tribesman of the Sudan fishing in the equatorial swamps of the Sudd. The countryside was flat, featureless, and bland. He was standing in a small channel between two reed banks no more than half a metre or so higher than the water. The water itself was milky brown, and not very deep—the Nuer was tall, but not that tall, and the water barely reached his knee. He had something knotted in his hair, an improvised cap of some sort, and thrust into the knot was half of an old and rusty pair of scissors, which doubled as his hunting knife. He carried a long spear and was standing on one leg, like a stork, one foot wedged tightly against the other knee. Apart from the "cap," and a leather thong around his waist with a small pouch slung on his hip, he was quite naked. He had the most enormous penis I had ever seen, almost reaching his knee.

Later, at college, the Nuer figured in my social-anthropology classes, and I learned about their intricate kinship patterns, with their concentric circles of consanguinity and clan linkages. The Nuer, along with their associated tribes the Dinka, the Acholi, and the Lango, have among the most subtle set of social taboos of any tribe in Africa; their lives are simple in the extreme, consisting of little more than cattle-herding and fishing, and perhaps in compensation one of their art forms is lawmaking. They have constructed an edifice of prohibitions and sanctions, mostly related to what can and cannot be done with or to relatives, that a genealogical software/database package for a computer would have a hard time tracking.

Not for the first time I learned an important lesson about this continent: Africa is always more complicated than it seems: beware of the beguiling stereotype!

The Sudan (bilad as-Sudan, *land of the blacks*, in Arabic) is Africa's largest country, almost 8 per cent of Africa's land mass, and one of its poorest. Like Cameroon, it straddles black Africa and the Arab north. Unlike Cameroon, it has ancient links with Egypt and Ethiopia; it's possible, and even plausible, that ancient Nubia, as northern Sudan and southern Egypt were sometimes called, influenced Old Egypt as much as Old Egypt affected ancient Nubia. Nubian is still commonly spoken in the north; the Beja, another surviving Sudanese ethnic group, are known to have lived in the eastern Sudan somewhere between 4000 and 2500 B.C., and are said to be "similar in ethnic origin to the pre-dynastic Egyptians."

Some have placed Punt here, rather than on the coast. But no one really knows.

The pharaohs pushed south, passing Abu Simbel and Dongola and the Second Cataract, as early as 2300 B.C., conquering the already settled kingdoms they found there. By 1100 B.C. Nubia was firmly in Egyptian control, and had been incorporated into the Egyptian state with quasi-colonial status. As the gold trade increased, the southern towns became wealthier, and with wealth came dreams of both independence and conquest. Near the modern town of Merowe, at the Fourth Cataract, a city grew, which became the centre of the empire the Egyptians called Kush. By 900 B.C. the Kushites were powerful enough to send an expeditionary force down the Nile. Egypt itself fell to the invasion, and the Kushites ruled the whole empire from their capital, which they called Napata. This was Egypt's XXVth dynasty. They were explicitly "negroid" in features.

For three hundred years, Napata flourished, becoming one of the Old World's most significant trading centres. Gold, ivory, ebony, animal skins, and slaves flowed down the Nile to the markets of the north.

When Egypt was attacked by the Assyrians in 666 B.C. and a few of its southern towns destroyed, the Kushites prudently moved their capital southwards to the royal city of Meroë, close to the modern town of Shendi.

Meroë gave its name to a new empire, which flourished in the Sudanese heartland for more than six hundred years, a very long time in human history. The people of Meroë were black Africans, either Nilotes or Kushites; it was probably they who inspired the ancient Greeks to call them *Aithiopiai*, "burned faces," an early version of "Ethiopia." Eventually Meroë traders began bumping against new rivals, traders from the Ethiopian kingdom called Axum, and in the fourth century A.D. Ethiopia's King Ezana, the first Christian emperor of Axum, sent an army into the rival empire, sacking the royal city. Nothing very much survives from the pre-Axumite Empire but a few slag heaps, assorted pyramids not very impressive in size, scattered temples at Meroë and Napata, and the still uninterpreted Meroitic hieroglyphs and cursive script.

As Axum's influence waned, two Christian powers arose in the Middle Nile, the kingdom of Nubia, with its capital at Dongola, and the kingdom of Aloa, with its capital at Soba, near modern Khartoum. These states were coherent enough and powerful enough to resist the Arabs, who had seized Egypt in A.D. 641; in 651, however, Dongola was besieged and the Nubians signed a treaty with the Arabs that lasted until the Mamelukes took Egypt in 1250. Again, hardly anything survives of the Nubian states except the language, and a few ruined churches.

The third and final Middle Nile power was the Fung Sultanate of Sennar, which lasted from 1504 to 1821. Its achievement was to merge with the invading Arab tribes in a loose confederacy, an arrangement still surviving in the main tribal alignments and ruling families of the Sudan. Under the sultanate, Islam spread through most of northern Sudan, distributed by itinerant holy men.

The Fung confederacy fell apart in 1821, partly through internal squabbles but mostly because Mohammed Ali of Cairo sent in mercenaries to set up his own fiefdom, from which he could draw profit, in the form of gold and other minerals, as well as slaves for his armies and his estates. The effects were predictable: the Sudan's population was halved by slave raiders, and disease and chaos were everywhere evident.

After Ali's death, control of northern Sudan became disorganized and corrupt. There were more and more European intrusions; the British in particular were meddling in Egypt and interfering in Sudan in a typically imperial mix of profit-taking, high-mindedness, and an eye for the main chance, which was control of the Nile. With Egypt by now bankrupt, matters became even worse, and in 1881 the Sudanese finally rebelled in a fervent religious and political uprising called Mahdism, led by Mahdi Mohammed-Ahmed, who preached a version of Sufism. Among his victories was the massacre of the British general "Chinese" Gordon's army at Khartoum in 1885. The Mahdi ruled until 1898, when he was defeated and overthrown by an Anglo-Egyptian army under Lord Kitchener (who the following year was summoned to the Cape to wage war on another revolution by another set of Puritans, the Boers).

The post–Second World War history of the Sudan has been dismal. Shortly after independence in 1956 the non-Muslim south, disappointed in its secessionist efforts, revolted, and the country sank into a bitter civil war that was to last for the next twenty years.

There was a coup in Khartoum early in the 1960s, followed by elections, which were won by a grandson of the Mahdi, Sadiq al-Mahdi. Five years later there was another coup, led by Colonel Jaafar Nimeiri. He ruled for sixteen years and survived several coup attempts, but only made things worse—first he granted a feeble autonomy to the South, then abruptly withdrew it and imposed the strictest Islamic *shari'a* over the whole country. The Sudanese Peoples' Liberation Army reacted by taking control of much of the south. Nimeiri was ousted in a coup in 1985, Sadiq al-Mahdi got a second chance, muffed that one too, and the army came back, in the person of General Omar Ahmed al-Bashir, who once again set off on a process of radical Islamization. As though he didn't have enough to do at home, he immediately began stirring up the Islamic jihad movement in Somalia, hoping it would in turn infect Ethiopia, whose Islamic minority had been growing restless.

Which is where, in early 1997, matters still stood. The south was a war zone, home not only to Sudanese rebels, but to the remnants of both Idi Amin's and Milton Obote's forces, driven into sullen exile by the successful revolt in neighbouring Uganda. In an improbable odyssey, several hundred Sudanese refugees walked and hitchhiked 4,000 kilometres (2,500 miles) to Ghana, of all places, where they were promptly denied refugee status on the nicely bureaucratic grounds that the U.N. rules allow refugee status only to those who flee next door. Al-Bashir agreed early in 1997 to a "transitional council" to govern the south, but no one took it seriously. The only trade still flourishing in the Sudan was the one in weapons. Of those, there seemed to be an endless supply.

AXUM AND ETHIOPIA

*S*ometime later I found myself in Ethiopia, in Tigrai province, up near the
Eritrean border, in Old Axum, the Holy City, ancient capital of a civilization
not very much younger than the Egyptians.

*I walked up the dozen or so worn stone stairs to the front door of Makeda's ruined
palace, and paused on the landing. To the east were the hills that surrounded Axum
itself, and beyond them the barren cliffs and deep gullies of the Great Rift. To the
north, hidden from my view by the slopes of a nearby hill, were the mountains of
Tigrai and the route through Sudan to Old Egypt, a fact well-enough known to
Makeda, who had travelled there and beyond. Some way to the west was the Blue
Nile, on its long journey from Lake Tana to the sea. I scuffed the worn stone of the
steps, and laid my hand on the rough-cut walls, now not much more than a foundation, the four-storey palace having crumbled over nearly three millennia. These were
rubble walls, like Zimbabwe's, but the stones were smaller, and neater, with squared
lintels, corners, and thresholds. I thought of Zimbabwe and laid my cheek to the
stones, and then my ear, but the stones were quiet, and I could hear nothing but the
click of a pick from workmen on the far side of the ruins. The stones, if they were
telling their stories, were doing so in a way beyond interpretation.*

*I wondered what Makeda had thought as she returned home again to Sa'aba from
her visit to Solomon the Wise. Did she know she would make it into the Jewish chronicles (and therefore into Christian doctrine) as the mighty Queen of Sheba, who had
brought with her to Jerusalem gifts of red gold, and exotic spices, and with whom
Solomon had built a palace and sired a son? Did she climb these stairs with babe in
arms? Solomon's child, soon to be King Menelik I and to lead, in unbroken succession,
to the 237th and last of the line, the Lion of Judah, Haile Selassie, beloved of the
Rastas, the world's longest-lasting dynasty, overtaken finally by the forces of Marxist
darkness under Mengistu Haile Mariam.*

*Unbroken continuity is the hallmark of Ethiopian civilization. Menelik I is said to
have gone back to Jerusalem as a young man, and returned home with a holy thing,
believed by the Ethiopians to be the original Ark of the Covenant built by the Jews to
contain the Tablets of Stone Moses had brought down from Mount Sinai, tablets writ
by the Finger of God, a holy thing indeed. And this holy thing is still guarded by
monks at the church of St. Mary of Zion, a few kilometres to my east.*

Makeda, Queen of Sa'aba, Sabea, Sheba, the stolen Ark of the Covenant ... What
to make of all this? On the other side of Axum is an old reservoir to which the people still come for baptismal water (and, indeed, to swim on occasion). It is said to
have been the Queen of Sheba's bath. The story recounted above, of the great

queen's fruitful visit to Jerusalem, has been accepted for millennia by Ethiopians, but has never been taken seriously by historians, who have usually located the Queen of Sheba somewhere in Yemen. The evidence for the Ethiopian case is chiefly anecdotal, and in prosecutorial terms largely circumstantial. Some of the dates, for example, are slippery. Makeda, if she were indeed a contemporary of Solomon's, would have lived in the ninth century B.C., but the ruins of "her" pre-Axumite palace were originally dated to a few centuries A.D. That seemed conclusive. Then other archaeologists pushed the probable building date to 500 B.C., "maybe further," no one really knows. If the Ark of the Covenant really came to Axum, it would have arrived several centuries before the place was founded ... Or would it? Originally archaeologists believed Axum dated from the fourth century of our era, which is when Ethiopia officially adopted Christianity, but now they think it's a thousand years older than that, which makes the Ethiopian legend more plausible. And the story is far from complete: fewer than 10 per cent of the archaeological sites in Tigrai have even been catalogued, never mind excavated and studied.

There is a pre-Axumite stone temple in Yeha dating back to 1500 B.C. There are still dwellings and rock-hewn tombs scattered all through the north, many of them going back to pre-Sheba and pre-Solomon times. Early Egyptian artefacts have been found in Tigrai, which means that Axum had trading links with the north in Middle Kingdom times. The Axumites owned Yemen for a period, and many links have been found between the two places, including astral religion, the notion of a sacred royalty, a distinctive architecture, and art. Yemeni writing was adopted in Ethiopia to transcribe a language almost identical to that of the Arabian Sabeans, a language and writing still preserved by the Ethiopian church in the form of Ge'ez. The ancient Greeks, too, came here, to trade for gold.

The story of Sheba and the theft of the Ark is recounted in an old Ethiopian text, written in Ge'ez, the *Kebre Negest*. This claims to be a copy of a much earlier fourth-century text, but it was more probably written when the "Sheban" or "Solomonic" dynasty was reasserting its power after an interregnum lasting several centuries, and is more likely to be an act of deliberate propaganda on the part of the newly restored monarchs, filled as it is with legends and marvels and praise-poems.

And yet ...

After I visited the ruins of Makeda's palace I went to see a few of the other sites excavated around the town. At the top of the hill to the northeast is a fourth-century crypt, tomb to the early Christian kings Kaleb and his son, Gabre Meskel. The old burial place has a magnificent view over the surrounding mountainscape, looking north towards Egypt and south towards Addis. Meskel was a mystic. Three kilometres (2 miles) due north of Axum is a hilltop with stone stairs carved into it, and a hole the size and shape of a deep barrel excavated into the solid rock. Meskel handed the throne of Axum and Yemen to his son and spent the last twelve years of his life in this hole, contemplating eternity. From there I visited the tomb of King Bazen, who reigned from 8 B.C. to A.D. 9, and has entered Ethiopian legend as the king who dispatched one of the Three Wise Men to Bethlehem.

The Axumites were engineers on a massive scale. Some of their tombs are made of slabs of rock 15 metres (50 feet) square. In the centre of town are funerary stelae, monoliths larger and taller than anything similar on earth, one of them weighing more than 600 tons, dwarfing any of the Egyptian monoliths, quarried miles away and brought here, to be carved and set on end as though they were mere fence-posts. As well, they thought nothing of hewing churches from the solid rock. Northeast of Axum, on a stony mountaintop with sheer cliffs on all sides, is a rock-hewn church and monastery, the monks fed by produce hauled up on ropes made to resemble serpents. There are several hundred other such churches scattered through the country, and, at Lalibela, there are an even dozen of them, wondrously preserved, carved from bedrock, painted—and still used.

....

The following day I was supposed to fly to Lalibela, but, when I got to the little gravel-strip airport with the bullet-riddled corrugated iron "terminal," there was no plane. It had been cancelled, there being only two passengers. It wasn't worth sending a plane for us. Maybe tomorrow ...

This was either lucky or unlucky. Lucky, I guessed, because as I wandered through town I found the way blocked by a dense throng of white-robed pilgrims, most of them women, listening intently to a priest with a megaphone. I recognized him. I had seen him the previous day outside the St. Mary of Zion Church, the very one where the Ark was supposed to be kept. He was the Ark's chosen custodian. He had allowed me to photograph him under a sacred red umbrella, and then, for a donation of sixty birr, about six dollars, he had unlocked a case where the church keeps its temporal relics—bishops' mitres (one of them dating to the fourth century) and other imperial gear, the usual gold and jewel-encrusted artefacts of royalty, looking a little battered and the worse for wear. I asked him if the Ark itself was in the crypt behind him, and he had smiled, and said yes. Of course, I would not be allowed in to see. No one is ever allowed in, not even royalty, no one except the guardian himself, who must keep within a few metres of the Ark for the rest of his life.

"Is that the real Ark of the Covenant, not a more recent copy?"

"The same."

"The one that came from Jerusalem in the time of King Solomon?"

"The same. It came up the Nile. To Tana. To Axum."

"Has it ever left?"

"It is always protected," he said evasively, and would say no more.

Now here was the custodian, out in the open, and under a tree, in the shade and shielded by umbrellas, was the Ark itself. It couldn't be seen—it was draped with a grey cloth, and it was impossible to make out its shape, or whether it was really, as the Bible said, made of shittim wood so many cubits by so many, and covered with real gold. The Bible had given oddly exact measurements for the thing, this tabernacle to hold the holiest of Jewish artefacts, the Tables of Law given to Moses. I knew that even then the Ark had to be covered. The Bible said it was a dangerous artefact. Ethiopian legends agree.

I asked Tesfay, a guide who had just shepherded a World Bank delegation around town, what it was doing in the open.

"Seven days each year it is brought out for the people to venerate," he said, "on holy days. This is one."

I went back to watching the crowd. Except for the megaphone, it was a scene with deep roots into antiquity. There were no vehicles to be seen, only donkeys. The white robes of the worshippers were identical to those worn in biblical times. The priests, their robes either white with black shoulder capes, or green and red swirling with golden threads, wore vestments unaltered for sixteen hundred years. Later would come the deep throbbing of the *kebero*, the oval drum of the Ethiopian church, and the monks would start to sing hymns in the lost language of Ge'ez, giving silvery emphasis to the words with the waving of the *sistrum*, which gives off a clear, bell-like sound.

That evening I went back to the texts.

The *Kebre Negest* had asserted Menelik's removal of the Ark from Jerusalem. Not only did Solomon let him go, having been told by God that it was his will the Ark be removed, but he ordered each of the twelve tribes to send a thousand people along, and each of his commissioners to send their eldest sons. On Menelik's return, his mother Makeda abdicated in his favour, and the Solomonic dynasty was born. Uniquely among Christian churches, every Ethiopian church still has a holy of holies in which is stored a replica of the Ark, called a *tabot*. It is just one of many Jewish referents still present in Ethiopian lore and custom.

The authenticity of the legend of the Ark has yet to be tested. I watched the service in the streets at Axum for a while longer. Among the faithful, the debates are pointless, as debates among the faithful always are. They *know*.

....

A little later, in Addis Ababa, I ate *zilzil* and *doro wat* at the Addis Hilton and watched a "folkloric show" consisting of "traditional instruments" (electrified, however) and a quintet of dancers. The music, updated and changed and simplified for the tourists, nevertheless had thrilling roots deep into Africa, with echoes all the way down to the Zulus—anyone who says Ethiopian culture is not African has never listened to the music. Even there in the Hilton I could catch the authentic threnody of Africa, and in every Ethiopian church there is the same haunting association, transmuted into Christian liturgy.

Axum was a going concern, as an empire, by the start of the first millennium. The Greek travel book *Periplus of the Erythraean Sea* described it in A.D. 60 as already stretching from Port Sudan south to Berbera, and inland as far as the Nile. Adulis, the Eritrean port, was already several centuries old, and a major trading village. In the third century the Iranian religious leader Manni called the Axumite Empire "one of the four greatest existing kingdoms of the world" (the others were Persia, China, and Rome).

Christianity arrived very early. Queen Candace, who ruled both Ethiopia and Meroë from A.D. 42 to 52, is said to have heard of the new faith from her treasurer, who had gone to Jerusalem on a pilgrimage and was baptized there by Philip the Apostle. The treasurer is never named, but is described in the Bible as "a eunuch of great authority under Candace, queen of the Ethiopians, who had the charge of all her treasures, and had come to Jerusalem to worship."

The Axumite Empire became officially Christian in A.D. 320. The Axumite emperors Ezana and Saizana, kings at the time also of Kush (or Meroë), ruled the kingdom jointly for twenty-seven years. Early in their reign they were baptized and asked the Holy See of St. Mark, in Alexandria, to send them a bishop. His name was Frumentius, but the Ethiopians called him Bringer of Peace.

It was the mitre of Frumentius I had seen in the lockbox outside the church of St. Mary of Zion, in Axum.

The last few Felasha, the black Jews of Ethiopia, were airlifted to Israel in the seventies, ending a very long chapter of Jewish influence on the country.

The Felasha, who also claim descent from Solomon, were commonly thought to be descended from a group of Yemeni Jews who uprooted themselves in the first few years of the Christian era and moved across the Red Sea to Ethiopia. But in 1973 the chief rabbi of Jerusalem, who had been asked to rule on whether the Felasha were true Jews or not, concluded they were, and that their many archaic practices, such as animal sacrifices and their ignorance of the Talmud, should be interpreted as their having been cut off from the main body of Judaism since before the Josiah reforms, which happened in the seventh century B.C. It's much more probable, therefore, that the Ethiopian Jews were the descendants of the Egyptian Elephantine community who fled southwards along the Nile and the Tekaze rivers and took refuge around the Lake Tana region. Whether or not they brought with them the Ark is not the point, though the Felasha histories assert that they did, and that it was "stolen" by Axumite Christians in the fourth century.

Their name, Felasha, means "exile" in Ge'ez.

All through the first millennium, Ethiopia's Jews prospered and spread, but they made little impact on the chronicles of the time. That changed in the tenth century with the emergence of the Felasha Queen Judith (Jodit), daughter of Gedeon. She was known to history as *Esat*, or *Esato*, the Monster, and as *Isato*, Fire.

Jodit launched her war against the Ethiopian Christians of Axum when the king, Anbessa Wudim, was a boy of ten. The court fled as her armies approached. Axum was reduced to rubble, its churches destroyed and its holy things looted—except, the legends say, the Ark, which was carried by monks far to the south, to an island in Lake Zewai. Jodit ruled for the next forty years, a reign of great cruelty, in which many thousands of Christians were killed. Only the rock-hewn churches of Tigrai, almost impossible to destroy, survived. The terrible queen is said to have died while returning to her palace after an expedition to burn a few more churches. God, it is said, misdirected her to a place called Adi Nefas, and there a whirlwind lifted her high in the air and dropped her to her death. Her grave is at Ade Kaweh near Wukro, and is marked merely by a heap of stones.

In subsequent centuries, despite accusations of being *buda* ("evil eye") by the Amharas, and despite being deprived of heritable land and political independence, the Felasha survived. In the hundred years before their retreat to Israel, however, they had become a despised and feared occupational caste, with their own concepts of impurity reinforcing separation from other groups.

Few Felasha resisted the call "home."

The Muslim presence in Ethiopia is also very early. In 615 several of the Prophet's followers, his own wife among them, took refuge in Axum. They were treated kindly by the king, and granted land at nearby Negash. Mohammed, in gratitude, warned his followers that the Ethiopians were not to be touched, an edict that lasted through several uneasy centuries until it was finally broken by Ahmed Gragne, "the Left Handed," in 1528. The *entente cordiale* was helped by the Ethiopian church's subscription to a version of Christianity called the Mono-physite heresy (a technical Christian argument having to do with the indivisibility of divinity); their split with Rome on this matter allowed the Muslims to treat them as a slightly better class of unbeliever, and to leave them alone.

In many places I had visited in Africa, I had come across traces of early European explorers looking—in vain—for the home of the legendary Christian king Prester John. At every major river they'd come to—in Cameroon, Congo, Angola, the Zanj coast—up went the Portuguese, looking for Prester John. Up the Congo went the Portuguese, the Dutch, the Spanish, chasing rumours. In Angola, they'd been looking for Prester John's gold mines. In Zimbabwe, he was "known" to have built great palaces out of rock.

The quest was a matter of avarice (the Christian king was reputed to be fabulously wealthy), curiosity (all the Christian kings were curious about potential rivals), and need (another Christian army would be helpful in the Crusades against the Muslim unbelievers).

But was there really such a person, and did he really have such a kingdom?

Was he Ethiopian?

There were tantalizing fragments of historical evidence. A report by Bishop Hugh of Gebal in Syria, in 1145, asserted that John, a wealthy and powerful "priest and king," had defeated the Muslim kings of Persia in battle, stormed their capital at Ecbatana, and intended to proceed to Jerusalem but was unable to cross the Tigris River.

A thirteenth-century chronicler recounted the story of a letter supposedly sent by Prester John in 1165 to several European rulers, in which his realm is described as "the three Indies, a land of natural riches, marvels, peace, and justice administered by a court of archbishops, priors, and kings."

Two Ethiopian kings were supposed to have visited Jerusalem; word might easily have filtered back to Europe about the existence of Christian African kings. And the Ethiopian church was in regular contact with the Copts in Alexandria, from whom they still drew their bishops. Ethiopia, then, soon became identified with the land of Prester John, though Europe seemed only to have a hazy idea where Ethiopia was. The legend sometimes located both Prester John and Ethiopia somewhere in Asia and sometimes described him as a king-priest reigning in the Far East "beyond Persia and Armenia."

In 1487 one Pêro de Covilhã was sent by the Portuguese king, John II, on a mission to India while his compatriot, Alfonso de Paiva, was sent to seek Prester John. Hearing news that his companion had died, Pêro, on his return from India, set out for Abyssinia himself. He was received by Emperor Eskender and was well treated and made governor of a district. He reported back occasionally to his king, but was never again allowed to leave the country.

The legend of Prester John was one of the driving forces behind Portuguese exploration, and it was Prester John that finally brought them to Ethiopia in 1520. This was fortuitous, for it was only a few years later that the Muslim fanatic Ahmed Gragne unleashed his war on the Ethiopian Christians. He was finally defeated with the help of Portuguese arms.

In the aftermath of the Gragne campaigns the country fell once more into chaos, and out of the chaos came the Galla, now called the Oromo, the wild pagans of the south and southeast. The Galla never were powerful enough or unified enough to rule the country, but they helped keep it in political turmoil for several centuries thereafter, through much of the so-called Gonder period, which lasted until the mid-nineteenth century. Ethiopia became a loose alliance of quarrelsome fiefdoms only nominally ruled by an emperor.

This period wasn't all bad. Gonder, north of Lake Tana, became the capital of Ethiopia under King Fasil, in 1632, and despite the ruler's political weakness was the centre of a cultural and artistic renaissance. During this time dozens of splendid castles and monasteries were built, many of them still standing.

For a hundred years the rulers remained weak, controlling only about a third of the modern state of Ethiopia, but they were relatively popular, and their smaller kingdom was prosperous. Then in 1730 the energetic figure of Ras (Prince) Michael emerged onto the political scene. Michael quite literally became a king-maker, though he was a king-killer first (he had two emperors assassinated and replaced). The Scottish explorer James Bruce, who spent years in Ethiopia and at the Gonder court, found him intelligent, with an attractive personality but rough-and-ready ways, suitable for a turbulent time. He was certainly a man who knew which polit

ical end was up: when Ras Michael read one of Bruce's introductory letters, which asked him to ensure the traveller's safety, he was scornful. "Safety! Where is that to be found? I am obliged to fight for my own life every day." At his court, Bruce reported, any display of pity was interpreted as a sign of weakness. There was no need for the Scot to feed his hunting dogs, he reported; they foraged happily among the corpses strewn about Gonder. When Ras Michael returned from warfare, he brought with him the severed testicles of his defeated enemies as trophies.[5]

And the Galla ... the wild Galla? They were still wild to this century. In the 1930s Evelyn Waugh, travelling on the Djibouti Addis Ababa railway, reported that trains travelled only in daylight, so that the driver could see whether the Galla had ripped up the rails to make spear-heads.

From Mountfield, African Exploration, p. 61

Rough and ready Ras Michael may have been, but he was the epitome of cultivation compared with the Galla chief, Guangoul. Bruce recounted the story of Guangoul's arrival at the Ethiopian court with five hundred of his followers: "He was a little, thin, cross-made man ... his legs and thighs being thin and small for his body, and his head large; he was a yellow, unwholesome colour, not black or brown; he had long hair plaited and interwoven with the bowels of oxen, and so knotted and twisted together as to render it impossible to distinguish the hair from the bowels, which hung down in long strings ... He had likewise a wreath of guts hung about his neck, and several rounds of the same about his middle, which served as a girdle, below which was a short cotton cloth dipped in butter, and all his body was wet, and running down with the same; he seemed to be about fifty years of age, with a confident and insolent superiority painted on his face ... He was then in full dress and ceremony, and mounted upon a cow, not of the largest sort, but which had monstrous horns ... Whether it was necessary for the poising himself upon the sharp ridge of the beast's back, or whether it was meant as graceful riding, I do not know, being quite unskilled in cowmanship; but he leaned exceedingly backwards pushing his belly forwards, and holding his left arm and shield stretched out on one side of him, and his right arm and lance on the other, like wings. ... An insufferable stench of carrion soon made everyone in the tent sensible of the approach of this nasty sovereign, even before they saw him. The king, when he perceived him coming ... could not contain himself from an immoderate fit of laughter, which finding it impossible to stifle, he rose from his chair, and ran as hard as he could into another apartment behind the throne."[6]

Life in Ethiopia was not for the squeamish. In 1770, shortly after leaving Axum, Bruce's party encountered three men driving a cow, and tried to buy it. The men said the cow was not wholly theirs, so they would not part with it; but they were willing to sell part of it. "They tript up the cow, and gave the poor animal a very rude fall upon the ground, which was but the beginning of her sufferings. One of them sat across her neck, holding down her head by the horns, the other twisted the halter about her forefeet, while the third, who had a knife in his hand ... got astride upon her belly before her hindlegs and gave her a very deep wound in the upper part of her buttock ... I saw, with the utmost astonishment, two pieces, thicker, and longer than our ordinary beafsteaks, cut out of the higher portion of the buttock of the beast ... one of them still continued holding her head, while the other two were busy curing the wound. This too was not done in an ordinary manner; the skin which had covered the flesh that was taken away was left entire, and flapped over the wound, and was fastened to the corresponding part by two or more small skewers, or pins. Whether they had put anything under the skin, between that and the wounded flesh, I know not; but at the riverside where they were, they had prepared a cataplasm of clay, with which they covered the wound; they then forced the animal to rise and drove it on before them, to furnish them with a fuller meal when they should meet their companions in the evening."[7]

As the Galla/Oromo plainly show, Ethiopia is not all urbanized old-line Christians. On the lower Omo River, near the Kenya border, are a score or more of isolated tribes, some of them now on the endangered list, being down to fewer than five hundred individuals: groups like the Mursi—like the Sara of Chad, their women still wear the extended lip plates introduced to scare off the slavers (now transmuted into vanity)— the Karo, whose wild dances are among the most colourful in Africa; the Bumi, whose patterns of scarification are among the most intricate on the continent. These are all cattle-herders, semi-nomads, isolated, immune to education, ignorant of the long civil war, ignorant of Addis Ababa and its ways, uncaring about the passionate debates in the Assembly at Addis, debates that will in the end shape their fate, willing or no.

The great unifier of modern Ethiopia was a bandit chief called Ras Kassa, who had himself crowned King Tewodros II in 1855. He did many things right. He modernized the state, abolishing feudal remnants and turning fallow church lands over to the peasants. He created a modern army and a strong central government, though his peremptory manner and brutal methods kept him unpopular. He tried to manipulate the British government into helping him solidify Ethiopia's sovereignty, but succeeded only in antagonizing the British envoys. In 1867 the British sent a military force against him, under the command of Sir Robert Napier, Tewodros retreated to a fortress at the top of Makdela Hill, wrote a long and rambling letter to Napier complaining about his ungrateful countrymen and listing his own many failures. Then he shot himself

His successor, Yohannis IV, helped the British against the Mahdist uprising in the Sudan and was promptly betrayed, the British inserting Italy into Ethiopia as a reward for help in Egypt. Yohannis was wounded in battle and died. He was succeeded by Menelik II, the King of Kings, who moved the capital to Addis Ababa, defeated the Italians in a famous battle at Adawa, increased the size of the empire by annexing the Ogaden desert from the Somalis, moved in on Galla territory in the south, and shepherded his country into the twentieth century as an independent power.

After the First World War Ethiopia became a member of the League of Nations. Which didn't stop Mussolini moving in to exercise his armies in 1936. The Italians remained until 1941, when they surrendered to an Allied Force. Ethiopia has been independent ever since.

Menelik died of old age in 1913. His supposed successor, Iyasu, managed to annoy almost everyone by flirting with Islam and attempting an alliance with the "Mad Mullah" who had revolted against the British and Italians in Somalia, and was deposed in 1916. Zauditu Menelik, the daughter of Menelik II, became empress, with the grandson of an earlier monarch, Ras Tafari Makonen, as regent. "This ambiguous relationship was resolved in 1930, when the empress's husband was killed in rather murky circumstances in a civil battle. Two days later, Zauditu herself succumbed, apparently to that most Victorian of maladies, heartbreak. Ras Tafari was crowned under the name Haile Selassie in November 1930."[9]

It was Selassie who survived the Second World War, and lived to see the exodus of the Italians. It was also Selassie who reannexed Eritrea in 1962. The Red Sea territory had been part of Axum, and had been under the sporadic control of Ethiopia's rulers through the centuries. But the Italian invaders had administered it separately, and after the Italians were driven out the British ran it until 1952, when the U.N. encouraged it to be "federated" with Ethiopia, a move much resented in the territory. After Selassie unilaterally incorporated it into Ethiopia, a thirty-year civil war followed.

> The Djibouti–Addis railway, built early in the century and remembered so fondly by Evelyn Waugh, has fallen into disrepair, but is being rehabilitated by a European Union grant. No one really knows why: Djibouti, granted its independence from France only in 1977, has been racked by a mini (though still brutal) civil war since 1991. But it's Ethiopia's only railhead to the sea.

Selassie ruled until 1974 when he was deposed by the Derg, a cabal of junior military officers with radical Marxist and dictatorial leanings, under the sinister influence of Mengistu Haile Mariam. Despite Mengistu's attempts at social engineering (including the forced transfer of populations that led to a series of horrific famines), his regime's control was never complete. The Eritrean guerrillas continued their war, and were soon joined by the Tigrai People's Liberation Front. In May 1991, with rebels only a few kilometres from the capital, Mengistu fled the country and took refuge in, of all places, Zimbabwe. Eritrea gained its hard-won independence. A coalition of rebel groups under Meles Zeawi took control of a country with an empty treasury, a moribund economy, and a ruined agricultural sector. Despite this, they announced multiparty elections and a program of economic reform.

By early 1997, the government was still popular. But there were already rumblings. There were too many powerful people from Tigrai in the government. Perhaps a looser federation would be better . . .The regime responded by charging more than five thousand people, including a former Olympic gold-medallist, with genocide for complicity in the Red Terror killings in the seventies.

The process continues.

Part IX

The Great Rift

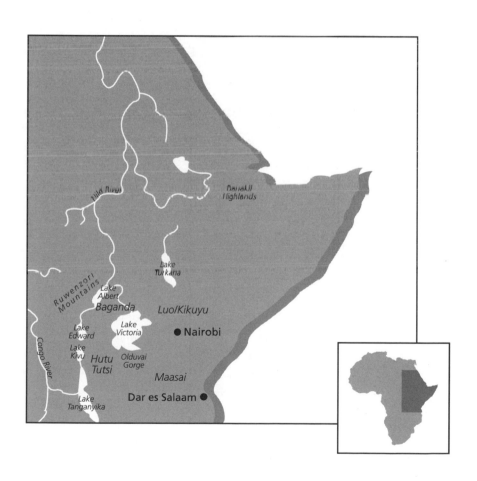

THE BAGANDA KINGS

And so we come full circle ... Up the Nile, from Aswan and Kush and Axum, into the Great Rift and its myriad extensions, into the Great Lakes and the Mountains of the Moon. Many millions of years ago a series of violent convulsions changed the shape of East Africa forever. The earth rose up in a great dome to create huge volcanoes, and as it swelled it split, forming a massive depression in the west (which became Lake Victoria) and a slash that stretched for 5,600 kilometres (3,480 miles) from Jordan to Mozambique, the Great Rift Valley. This great gash divides into two branches, the western branch spotted with deep lakes, the eastern with shallow alkaline lakes and a series of volcanoes, of which Kilimanjaro is the most famous. The Rift finally dwindles to nothing very much in Malawi and Mozambique.

The highlands born in the convulsions created a rain shadow to the leeward, and the forests began to disappear. In their place came a new phenomenon—savannah grasslands. Eventually, some ape species on the fringes of the vanishing forests moved onto the new grasslands, and, in time, one of these species evolved into early hominids, our ancestors. In the Rift Valley, then, mankind finally shook off the dust of his ape-like ancestors, picked up his tools, and set out on his long march into history. It's the simple truth, then, to call this the Cradle of Mankind.

I followed the westerly branch of the Rift around the top of Lake Victoria into the interlacustrine highlands. Full circle indeed ...In these fertile plains developed some of the earliest and most successful Bantu kingdoms; it is out of the rivalries of these sophisticated polities that the restless and the discontented, possibly the soon-to-be Luba among them, migrated southwestwards into Shaba and Kivu, and set off, through diffusion as well as migration, the changes that eventually helped create the distant kingdoms we saw in Section IV, the Kongo. The Luba and their associates took with them skills and theories of organization that eventually spread all the way to Angola. And so the swirling patterns of Africa are begun and repeated and confirmed.

I sat on my haunches in the Great House of Kasubi, contemplating the bones of the last four of the Baganda kings (hidden from view behind a bark-cloth curtain). Beside me squatted my guide, an old woman, descendant of King Mwanga II, who lived in a small hut nearby in order to tend to the necessary rituals to propitiate the ancestral spirits. She came, she told me, in an unbroken line from the legendary

Kintu, in the lineages the first of the thirty-five kings of Baganda. She had the snif-fles and mumbled a lot, but was descended from a demigod, and talked of the old kings as though they were uncles newly departed.

The four men whose bones lay here had presided over a radical transformation of Great Lakes Africa. The first, and the man who had used this Great House as a courtroom, was Mtesa I; it was Mtesa who had welcomed the early European explorers, among them John Hanning Speke, whom the wily king liked mostly for his guns. Mtesa governed what was, next to Burundi, the most powerful kingdom of the region. A mere four generations later it was all gone. Mtesa II, the last of the Baganda kings (jollily if patronizingly known in England as "King Freddie"), became the first president of the independent post-colonialist state of Uganda before run-ning afoul of the atrocious Milton Obote, the precursor, patron, victim, and suc-cessor to the even more atrocious Idi Amin. The last king died in sad exile in a flat in London in 1969, no doubt pining for the Seven Hills of his old capital, Kampala.

....

This part of Africa—meaning eastern Zaire, Uganda, Rwanda, and Burundi, north-western Tanzania—is shrouded in legend and governed by demigods. And no won-der: this is the Root of Africa, the home of the Mountains of the Moon, of the Virunga volcanoes, of the Source of the Nile, of the Impenetrable Forests where the mountain gorillas have been pushed to make their last stand, of the Crater Lakes, sulphurous and unplumbable, from which secret channels are said to connect, deep underground, to the Great Lakes, a place of magic where the spirits are restless and quick to anger. Not all legend, either: on the dusty floor of the Rift, in northern Tanzania, there are mas-sive stone-built irrigation channels, abandoned centuries ago. They run for kilometres along the escarpment—more than 2,000 hectares (12,355 acres) were carefully cul-tivated in this fashion by agriculturists, themselves long gone. And at Bigo ("the defended place") in Western Uganda, great earthworks were constructed near the swamps of the Katonga River—in places trenches were hewed 5 metres (16 feet) into the rock, 10 kilometres (6 miles) long, enclosing more than 300 hectares (740 acres), a mighty bulwark against a danger now lost in the mists of time.[1] No one knows what Bigo was. Some of the legends say it was where Mugenyi of Chwezi fame kept his magical herds; others say it was a royal capital of an empire long vanished.

Chwezi fame? Almost everyone accepts that there was an ancient kingdom that ruled here, whose influence extended to Uganda, Rwanda, Burundi, and north-western Tanzania. But whether the Chwezi, or BaChwezi, really existed no one can now tell. After all "these Bacwezi were not like other men but were gods, for although they were born of women they had unending life and knew neither sick-ness nor death. During their reign on earth these Bacwezi conquered and ruled the countries of Ankole, Toro, Bunyoro, Baganda, Karagwe, Kiziba, Busoga and Bukedi.

They eventually decided to leave the kingdom of the world because they thought it had been defiled ..."[2]

Earlier that morning I had inspected the penis and testicles of Kibuuka, the Ganda god of war, a curious sensation. The desiccated penis was encased in a leather sheath, decorated with cowry shells, the balls all shrivelled and shrunken and sewn up with more shells. These important relics had been miraculously preserved since 1580, or thereabouts, surviving many wars, including being looted by the British and taken back to London, to be gawked at in the British Museum, before being returned to the land where they had done their original business. Kibuuka was the brother of the BaChwezi lake god, Mukasa, and a contemporary of Mugenyi. He was betrayed by a woman and was shot out of the sky. His body landed in a tree and the relics were taken. Now they're sitting in a neat little cowry-lined basket on a shelf in the Kampala Museum.

But even the Chwezi were not the first here, the legends say.

The legends of all the people of the Great Lakes have a common theme—a struggle for power between "natives" and an alien group which established itself as an aristocracy with a king at its head and which maintained its authority by virtue of its prestige until secession of the outlying counties weakened the kingdom and allowed another group to seize power.

Of course legends, as we have seen, are reliable only if not taken literally.

The Bunyoro legends, for example. The Bunyoro were rivals of the Bagandas, but with a similar history. Their traditions are linked to three dynasties, the Batembuzi, the Bachwezi, and the Babito. As usual, aboriginal hunter-gatherers amalgamate with an influx of grassland cultivators. They are later overtaken by an invasion of pastoral people, who enter the country from the northeast in search of grazing land. The pastoralists are more united, and look to one man for leadership—the notion of the king. All these early peoples are loosely grouped in legend as the Batembuzi. There is the usual shopping list of Batembuzi kings, in this case twenty of them, not really kings but individual heroes—gods, in fact, embodying the myths of creation and of the validation of social and political organization.[3]

The last of these gods was Isaza, and when he disappears from the scene the reign of the gods gives way to the rule of the demigods, the BaChwezi.

The remarkable thing about the BaChwezi—apart, that is, from their reputed superhuman knowledge and skill, their possession of immense herds of cattle, and their odd diet, which consisted entirely of milk—was the dynasty's brevity. It lasted only two generations before their auguries failed and their prestige dissipated in the thin highland air. It was a time, the legends say, of chaos and great dismay.

Could it be from this time that the Luba emigrated? It would match their own stories.

One of the third generation, a MuChwezi, whose name is not recorded, married a woman of the Luo group of Nilotic-speaking peoples of the southern Sudan and

Uganda. They in turn established a ruling Bunyoro dynasty known as the Babito, who carefully copied the kingship customs of the BaChwezi and so inherited their kingdom. Babito traditions go back nineteen generations, putting the disappearance of the BaChwezi between 450 and 550 years ago. The Babito extended their power to the east of the Nile, southeast along the shores of Lake Victoria, and maintained pressure southwards on Ankole and Rwanda. For about ten generations the Babito dynasty, centred near Mubende, was the dominant power in the region between the Great Lakes.

"As soon as King Ndahura had established Chwezi rule over Kitara he moved his capital to Mubende Hill so as to have a clear view of his kingdom." Mubende Hill is still there, of course, now mostly a depository for broken bits of pottery and other artefacts, but on a clear day you can see the glaciers of the Ruwenzori from its summit, as well as Lakes Albert and Victoria in opposite directions. In this sense, Mabende is the very centre of Great Lakes Africa. A "witch tree" grows on the summit, 40 metres (130 feet) tall and more than four hundred years old; priestesses, descendants of the legendary founder's wife, Nyakaima, still attend a shrine tucked between its buttress roots, and make small offerings and sacrifices of white chickens.[4]

And then came the Bagandan kings.

Although "then" is a tricky word in this context. There were Ganda in the neighbourhood contemporaneous with the BaChwezi; thirteen clans had come into the country under the leadership of the mythical First King, Kintu, from somewhere beyond the eastern bank of the Nile. Kintu himself is supposed to have disappeared in mysterious circumstances. One version of the legend says that he had killed his deputy, Kisolo, with a spear, the first murder in all the world, and was so distraught that he disappeared. "By that time he was one hundred and twenty Kiganda years old. That is, sixty two years of the European calendar."[5]

The sniffly old lady, who was recounting this history for me, pointed to the barkcloth curtain that hid the coffins of the four dead kings. "That's the forest," she said. "The bark represents the forest into which the great Kintu vanished one day, never to reappear. We still call this curtain *kibira*, forest. It's where the spirits of the dead kings are."

With Kintu gone, the Bunyoro saw their chance. They took over and were absorbed in turn.

And so the familiar African patterns repeat themselves: migration, conquest, absorption, the creation of new tribes and kingdoms, more migration, new conquests ... And so on and so on.

....

On the way out of the Kasubi tombs, we shuffled past Mtesa I's pet leopard, stuffed after his death and looking a touch mouldy these days. The old lady led me to the thatched hut where the royal drums are stored, off to the side of the guardhouse.

She mumbled something I didn't catch.

"What was that?" I asked.

She gave me a withering look. "This place, these tombs, this palace, is called *Muzibu-azaala-mpanga* in Luganda," she said. "That means, 'the cock begets its own heir to the throne . . .'"

"Oh," I said, rather at a loss.

Every Baganda king, or Kabaka, chose a hill and built himself a palace there, giving the capital a new home and a new name. After his death, the court moved again, and the old palace became a shrine; the jawbone of the dead king was preserved, a talisman for his spirit. This constant shuffling of capitals didn't prevent some magnificent palaces being constructed—at the apogee of their power, the Bagandan kings, or Kabakas, commanded considerable wealth. (An early European explorer, one Johnston, who came across their settled and orderly communities, called them "the Japanese of Africa," and meant it as a compliment—they were among the most organized societies he had seen, their cities neat and prosperous, the kingdoms replete with functioning bureaucracies, their legal codes sophisticated, their agriculture superior.) The capital was described in 1889 as "one of the greatest of Africa," even though it was constructed totally of grass, wood, and other organic materials, and moved frequently.[6]

John Hanning Speke, along with James Augustus Grant, showed up at the Kabaka's palace in 1863, and left a lurid account that was a *succès d'estime* in England, where they were agog at every savage detail. His accounts of Mtesa's acts of arbitrary cruelty showed a deft hand for the telling detail—how Mtesa tested a new rifle by instructing an attendant to go outside and shoot someone with it; how he wanted to club a woman to death for merely offering him fruit (Speke of course intervened); how his ritual sacrifices of literally hundreds of people served his political purpose. The Baganda he described was a frightening country, its court existing "in a state of semi-hysteria."

Mtesa was one of many sons of Suuna II; he was so afraid of a rebellion that he imprisoned all his brothers in a great trench, where many of them died. After that, unsurprisingly, Mtesa "became a very powerful king, and so many people curried his favour that he was given more wives than any previous king: he had eighty-four official wives and many hundreds of women in his harem."[7]

Early in his reign Mtesa adopted a few selected practises of Islam from Zanzibari traders, who had finally made it to the area in the reign of his father. After Speke arrived, Mtesa summoned Christian missionaries, but became irritated when the Anglicans from England showed up with a gift of a lamp and two chairs instead of guns, and seemed incapable of teaching the king the things he really wanted to learn, which were the skills of construction, manufacture, and warfare. (Mtesa's successor went one better and had thirty-two Christian converts burned to death in 1886. They're still known as "the Ugandan Martyrs.")

By the late nineteenth century the Bagandan kings had presided over what John Sutton called a "spectacular demographic increase," followed by military, economic, and political success. So much so that the British adopted the Swahili form of Baganda, Uganda, for a chunk of Africa much larger than the Bagandans actually occupied.

And so the politics of the present flow directly out of the configuration of the recent past.

Richard Twimo, a southerner from Kibale, near the Rwandan border, expressed a common Ugandan view that the horrors that followed independence were substantially the fault of Britain.

"They ruled through the Bagandas. Anyone who wanted a job in the civil service had to be Bagandan. They educated the Bagandas, but they didn't really trust them. So the northern tribes, the Lango and Acholi, went into the army. Then the British used the army to control the civil service and the south. The potential for trouble was always there. The British made it certain."

Milton Obote was a Lango. He won independence for Uganda after he brokered a deal in which he agreed to recognize Bagandan sovereignty within the new country, and the Bagandan Kabaka became the new country's first president, with Obote as prime minister. But within months Obote had turned on his supposed colleague and driven him into exile, using his army chief of staff, Idi Amin, to do so; Obote then rewrote the constitution to give himself all power, abolished formal opposition, and nationalized foreign assets. The economy started its long and dismal nose-dive.

Within a few years, Obote himself was ousted by Amin, and the country began to deteriorate into blood-letting, looting, and all-round savagery. Before he was done, Amin killed more than 300,000 Ugandans, many of them for no very good reason. He looted from foreigners, looted from the resident Asian community, which he drove into exile, and looted from any native Ugandan with anything at all. Whole villages were eliminated by his death squads. Almost everyone with a university degree was killed. The screams of the tortured could be heard reverberating through the capital. He had his tanks ruin the road system to the borders with Zaire, ostensibly to stop smuggling but mostly because he was afraid of invasions. His soldiers machine-gunned most of the country's wildlife, which is now only just beginning to return.

The story is well-enough known from the grisly news reports. The economy collapsed to the degree that Amin could no longer pay his soldiers, and he chose a diversion—a war with Tanzania—instead. Julius Nyerere's ragtag army of untrained villagers put Amin to rout, and he fled to take refuge with Gaddafi of Libya (who soon tired of his primitive guest, and threw him out). Unfortunately, that wasn't the end of the story. Tanzania turned out not to be the good guys after all, and looted the country of everything Amin had left behind. The result was a Nyerere-installed puppet who was forced to make way for a "military commission" which reinstalled Milton Obote, who reinstituted authoritarian rule ...

The cycle was broken at last by guerrilla leader Yoweri Museveni, whose disciplined, well-drilled revolutionary force, the National Resistance Army, slowly took over the country.

By 1986 Museveni was firmly in control, and the remnants of Obote's partisans were merely sniping at him from the sanctuary of Sudan. Almost half a million refugees returned from abroad. The economy picked up. Farmers planted crops, manufacturers tooled up their factories. Uganda, so fertile and productive, got going again.

Among the returnees, back to regain their property, were some of the Asians Amin had so summarily and disastrously expelled.

....

Rohit M. (he didn't want his name used), whose family was expelled from Uganda by Amin and has now returned to reclaim their land and many businesses, picked me up in his Mercedes and took me to Jinja to see the source of the Nile. He lives in a huge mansion outside Kampala, but he's hardly ever there, apparently running most of his businesses, which include a brewery and sugar operations, from his car phone. In between bursts of order-giving and deal-doing, Rohit talked about his community's cautious return from their Amin-made exile. By early 1997, only a relative handful of the seventy thousand expelled Asians had come home.

"Museveni said everyone should come back, but of course not everyone could. Only the big businessmen came back. The small shopkeepers couldn't afford to return. And in the end, maybe this isn't such a bad thing. See, that the Asians ran the businesses the blacks dealt with was a bad source of friction. Now blacks are being exploited by other blacks, so its all right. It removes a big source of resentment."

Rohit is optimistic about Uganda, he says, if it can get its population under control and not get caught up in the war going on to the southwest and in Zaire. "For a guerrilla leader, Museveni has a good understanding of politics. He understands that what the country needs is economic stability and political liberty." He hesitated, then slowed the car so he could make his point clearly: "Even his adventurism in Rwanda was understandable. He had to do something about the Rwandan refugees in Uganda. Habyarimana just wouldn't take them back. He had to do something ..."

There had been a quarter of a million Tutsi refugees squatting in southwestern Uganda, victims of the ongoing tribal conflict in Rwanda. In 1991 Museveni's patience gave out and he helped a rebel force of Tutsis mount an invasion. It was beaten back, with an assist from Belgium, France, and Zaire, and for a short time the pogroms that followed only made matters in Uganda worse. However, in 1994 the rebels returned, and this time they took control. The refugees began to drain away ... only to return in 1996, as Rwanda began to make war on the disintegrating giant of Zaire, and the fearful once again began to move.

While Rohit stayed in his car, making continual phone calls, I peered at the little plaque marking the source of the Nile (a claim, as I was to see, hotly disputed by Burundi, where there is a small village defiantly named Le Source de Nil. In fact, there seem to be many claimants for ultimate headwater, and Uganda itself now somewhat tactfully only claims to be the source of the "Nile proper.") Speke, when he visited King Mtesa I, was still looking for the Nile's source, but when the king blandly offered to show him a way home that would be less than a month's travel (that is, the Nile itself) Speke dismissed him as an ignorant savage. The Nile, for all its romance, is not very impressive at Jinja, feeding almost directly into a very unscenic hydro-electric scheme. There was a small busload of German tourists snapping away with insta-cameras, and three Russians with fishing poles, staring morosely at their empty bait buckets.

THE MOUNTAINS OF THE MOON

The next day I went down to the Virunga volcanoes and the Bwindi Impenetrable Forest to look for gorillas. Only about six hundred mountain gorillas are left on the planet, and more than half of them are in Bwindi, now cut off from their cousins in Zaire. How can they possibly survive? Just a few kilometres away are the borders of Zaire and Rwanda; in 1997 the villagers around here could still occasionally hear artillery barrages from the Rwandan side. Worse, the population pressures and the refugee crisis meant that intensive cultivation was now just a few hillsides away, and the gorilla habitat was protected only by the will of the bureaucrats in Kampala. The fierce motherliness of the game wardens and trackers will count for nothing unless the authorities continue to intervene.

To get to Bwindi we travelled for a hundred kilometres over narrow mountain roads slick with mud and strewn with boulders. It was overcast, damp with recent rains, and it was dark, very dark. There are few places blacker than the African countryside at night, for the villagers still rise and sleep by the rhythms of the sun, not having any source of light but the fires they use for cooking. Occasionally, in the dark, our headlights picked out pathetic convoys of refugees, walking through the blackness in search of an elusive sanctuary, massive bundles balanced on their heads; they stared as we rumbled past, their eyeballs gleaming in the reflected headlights, small frightened moons in the African night. Several times we were stopped by armed Ugandan patrols, who searched the car for contraband weapons before waving us on.

In the early morning, with just a stain of light in the night sky, two trackers led a small group of us up a steep mountain slope and into the thick jungle. We had already been carefully screened. A woman with a bad cold was turned away, although she had come thousands of kilometres—and paid a substantial sum—to have a chance to see the magical gorillas in their native habitat. No children under fifteen were permitted. The gorillas were horribly vulnerable to human diseases, and the wardens were taking no chances that they would become infected.

For three hours we climbed steadily, 500 metres (1,640 feet), 1,000 metres (3,280 feet). The vegetation was dense, the visibility only a few metres—you could barely see the tree trunks for vines and creepers. Ahead of us the trackers were cutting a path with pangas; underfoot, the tangled vines were over a metre thick, a treacherous cladding that snagged and tugged—it was easy to slip through until you were waist deep in tangled vines, many of them with ugly thorns. The air was heavy, and humid, and there were clouds of biting flies and creatures that stung, bit, and scraped at the skin. We came to a small opening at the top of a rise, and I could see across the lush valley to the mountains beyond, similarly impenetrable. It was obvious, I thought, why slash-and-burn became the clearing technique of choice around here—the forest felt claustrophobic, oppressive.

A few minutes later one of the trackers called in a low voice. He had found a nest the gorillas had made the previous night. Around it the vegetation had been crushed. There were new droppings in the vicinity. For another twenty minutes we followed their path, the evidence of their travel easy to see, even for amateurs.

"Hssst!," the lead tracker called. He had found them. He turned back, and confiscated the walking-sticks he had given us at the start of the trek. What did he think we'd do? Try to assault the gorillas? In fact, that's exactly what he was afraid of. He feared some edgy Westerner mistaking the playfulness of a juvenile gorilla for an aggressive charge and taking a whack at it. That would attract the attention of the adults, and after that things could get ugly … I was contrasting this with the gorillas' benign image, when I turned around and there, staring at me curiously from no more than 4 metres (13 feet), was a silverback, an alpha-male gorilla. He was semi-upright, one huge arm thick as a tree trunk grasping a vine. We stared at each other, two apes across an impenetrable divide, then he turned aside, losing interest, and began munching on leaves. At his feet two junior gorillas rolled and wrestled, oblivious to the intruders. I looked around. We were in the middle of the troop. There must have been fifteen gorillas to the six of us humans.

Our guides had disabled camera flashes and had told us not to point—pointing the finger is, in gorilla etiquette, apparently a no-no. Still, it was hard not to do so, as another gorilla wandered past, trailing lunch, paying us no mind.

I spent that night at the Mweya Lodge, a government-run place wonderfully sited at the end of a peninsula between Lake Edward and the Kazinga Channel, which leads to the smaller Lake George. The channel is said to be home to more than 100,000 hippos, a claim that seemed exaggerated, but that evening I was sitting on the terrace, admiring the view towards Zaire and the Mountains of the Moon, when a hippo wandered across the lawn, cropping as it went. Later a pack of hyenas set to growling and howling outside my room, but after an hour or so they obviously smelled something tastier elsewhere and left. After that I had only to deal with the immense spiders and fast-moving attack centipedes, and when a passing troop of mongooses invaded the patio the next morning it seemed almost normal.

At midmorning I took a boat out into Lake Edward to Izinga Island, a kilometre or so offshore, where the Ugandan park authorities had set up a sanctuary for orphaned chimps, most of them confiscated from poachers. I wasn't allowed ashore—the chimps are afraid of humans, with good reason—but we moored a few metres out and watched them feed. There were about a dozen animals. Although chimps are social beings, these were taken from their parents too young to be able to fend for themselves. Only one had ever learned to make a nest, and she mostly made a botch of it. The rest had discovered a cave on the other side of the island, and were excavating it deeper to make a shelter—like human children, they were afraid of the dark.

Sometimes they cry themselves to sleep at night, and break the game warden's heart.

From the village of Nyakalengija I hiked into the Ruwenzori National Park. The great peaks and glaciers of these romantic mountains were hidden; dark purple thunderclouds scudded in from Zaire, lightning flashed, jagged and dangerous, and peals of thunder rolled through the valleys. The ancients had known of these mountains. Ptolemy wrote of the Mountains of the Moon. The Nile was thought to rise here, once. Stanley himself acknowledged this in his own fruitless quest for the great river's source: "we have not much to boast of; that the ancient travellers, geographers, and authors had a very fair idea whence the Nile issued, that they had heard of the Lunae Montes, and the triple lakes, and of the springs which gave birth to the famous river of Egypt ... what the chartographers [sic] of Homer's time illustrated of geographical knowledge succeeding chartographers effaced, and what they in their turn sketched was expunged by those who came after them ..."[8] So many legends! This was the home of the talking great apes, of gorillas the size of elephants, of savage queens with diamonds on their toes, where houses were built of gold ...

A day or so later I headed off to Kibale Park, where there are more primates than anywhere else on earth—chimps, colobus monkeys, blue monkeys, red-tailed monkeys, L'Hoest monkeys, olive baboons. On the way I stopped for a Nile beer at the town of Ibanda. I sat at the back of the rudimentary café and stared northwest towards the Ruwenzoris. Briefly, as the clouds parted, I thought I saw a mountain top. I looked at my map. That must be the Portal Peaks, 4,300 metres (14,168 feet), but as I looked up the mountain once again drew its veil, and a storm broke across its face. In the café a little scarlet bird perched on my chair, and overhead bright yellow weavers were constructing their nests. There were swallows everywhere, and storks and pelicans in the lake, some of them enormous. Only that morning we'd passed a crater lake that smelled strongly of hydrogen sulphide, but its water was stained pink with flamingos. Another crater lake nearby was shaped like Africa, and was supposed to be connected with the Kazinga Channel, an hour's drive away. In this region are groves of bananas whose fruit no one unauthorized will pick, for the sap is said to run blood red on the hands of thieves. If you take fruit from a roadside stall without paying, you'll never reach your destination—you'll be run down by a truck, eaten by hyenas, murdered by agents of the spirit world: the solutions vary. So the legends of Africa persist. But as I was leaving a nervous young man came up to me to tell me he was the first of his family to be educated, he was the only child to get his O levels, and didn't I think that was splendid? He didn't want anything, only to be told he was doing the right thing. I congratulated him most sincerely, and he told me he was from a small village on the slopes of the Ruwenzori. He was twenty-six years old, but not yet married and therefore treated by his family as though he were still a child. His English was poor, but his life was full of hope. In modern times, he said, parents are no longer choosing spouses for their children. He was hopeful they would also see the value of education.

RWANDA AND BURUNDI

*I*n Rwanda and Burundi the familiar African patterns can be plainly seen: migration followed by conquest, followed by ... but here the sequence breaks down. Here the migration and conquest was not followed by absorption at all, but by feudal rule, hatred, and genocide. The Tutsis (aka WaTutsi) blame the colonial administrations. The Hutu, in their own legends, speak of a historic enslavement of their people by the Tutsis. More than anywhere else in Africa, the past poisons the present.

"Sure you can pick 'em out," the American aid worker was saying. "Put 'em in a lineup, pick 'em out every time. Tutsis lighter, taller, thinner; Hutus shorter, stockier, darker. That's what everyone says. That's what the rebels say—Hutus kill the tall ones, Tutsis the dark ones ... But know what? We tried it in our village. Our village is mixed, Hutus and Tutsis living all in a heap for centuries. Know what? We picked out five, got five wrong."

He was a leathery young man, whipcord strong, with a ponytail and a cynical air. He was leaning up against a Toyota Landcruiser, banging his boot against the wheel rim. Little cascades of mud fell to the road at each kick. We were just inside Rwanda. The Ugandan border post was within sight, the town of Kisoro a few kilometres up the road. The Zairian border was not very far away, to the west. We were on the road to Goma. It was an uneasy place to be, in this time of ethnic revolution. There were army patrols everywhere, and it wasn't always clear which army was which.

I stared at the crowd of people streaming past us. It was impossible for me to tell who was who. Like any African crowd, the palette was random, from black to café au lait; they came in all shapes and sizes. An army jeep growled by. I stared again. These would be Tutsis, since this was Rwanda in 1996. They didn't look any different from the rest of the crowd. Better dressed, maybe, sleeker and better fed, but otherwise no different.

"The killers with guns seem to know who is who," I observed.

"If you're a Tutsi with a gun, the ones who run away are Hutus," the young man said brusquely. "It's not hard."

Well, it's simpler than that, and not so simple.

Everyone accepts that the Twa pygmies were the original inhabitants of Rwanda and Burundi, and that they were gradually displaced around the start of this millennium by ... someone. Almost certainly these were the ancestors of today's Hutus, who came from ... somewhere, possibly Chad or Niger. The Hutus' own legends are silent on this point: it is in their interests to gloss this matter of migratory origins, since in their politics they were the *owners of the land* who were conquered by invading Tutsis. The conventional wisdom is that the Tutsi were cattle-herders who came into the country in a long migration around the fifteenth century, presumably from the Sudan or possibly Ethiopia, and set up kingship over the agricultural Hutu. Tutsi legends don't disagree with this: only the malignancy of their rule is in dispute. Under ordinary African circumstances, a blending of populations would have followed, but in the case of Rwanda and Burundi, this never happened. The Tutsis, 10 or 12 per cent of the population, set up centralized states under a series of *mwamis*, kings, and maintained their political stranglehold over the majority, the rural Hutus. The rule was more direct, and more peremptory, in Rwanda than in Burundi; it rather resembled the feudalism of medieval Europe. Other Tutsis settled in the Kivu province of Zaire.

Is this really what happened? Perhaps even the simplest outline is not so simple: "It is commonly held that ... the cattle-keeping minority has always been separate from the ... cultivators. Distinct origins have been assumed, the cattle keepers often regarded as conquering invaders of several centuries ago. That is how Speke ... understood the social and political situation in the 1860s ... He neatly summed it up with a chapter-heading 'Theory of conquest of inferior by superior races' ... This notion of a separate northern origin for the pastoral elites of the interlacustrine region has persisted. And these elites have had of course an interest in perpetuating it. Yet persuasive historical evidence to support this line is difficult to find, and the linguistic situation argues strongly against it. The Hima and Tutsi minorities share the Bantu language of the Iru and Hutu cultivators, and no one has detected traces of a Cushitic substratum in the region related to Oromo [Speke's theory] or any other Ethiopian tongue."[9] Once again, the notion of intractable tribalism being at the heart of African conflict is, at best, suspect.

As I had noted elsewhere in Africa, hardly anyone any longer blames the European colonizers for the mess Africa is in. But it also seems clear that in Central Africa the Europeans—Germans in the nineteenth century and Belgians after the First World War—made bad things worse. Only Tutsis were allowed education and administrative posts: the European notions of bureaucracy reinforced and cemented the ethnic divisions. And then, of course, the Europeans brought what colonizers had given other parts of Africa: the alien idea of an immutable nation-state, the notion of majority rule in a rigid and centralized structure, and the higher technology of murder.

In Burundi, faced with a majoritarian Hutu rule, the Tutsis attacked before independence, murdering Hutu political leaders. The result was a regime of Tutsi army officers and the ruthless suppression of any sign of rebellion. In Rwanda, a renegade Tutsi clan seized power in 1959, following the death of Mwami Matara III, and set about murdering Hutu leaders. This led to a massive Hutu uprising in which some 100,000 Tutsi were killed; hundreds of thousands of Tutsis fled as refugees into nearby countries. Many of them ended up in Uganda. The result was a Hutu regime in which Tutsis were excluded from power.

There were almost a quarter of a million Tutsi refugees in Uganda, living on the steep hillsides in the mountainous southwest, stretching the resources of their hosts and severely trying their patience. Because the governments of Obote and Amin confiscated many of their meagre goods, they joined the rebel armies of Museveni. For some years after Museveni's triumph, they waited. Eventually, their patience snapped and in late 1991 they invaded Rwanda with a five-thousand-strong guerrilla force, the Rwandese Patriotic Front, armed and supported by Museveni. With the help of Belgian, French, and Zairian troops, the invasion was beaten back, and, after four more years of stalemate, Hutu extremists, almost certainly under government direction, set about the genocide of Rwanda's Tutsi population. More than 800,000 were slaughtered in a few weeks, mostly by roving gangs of youths armed with machetes and small arms. Eventually, however, the RPF triumphed, and 2 million Hutus fled into neighbouring Zaire and Tanzania. By some accounts, nearly 7 million of the 9 million people in Rwanda were affected.

The blundering West stepped in without understanding the on-ground politics.

Relief agencies set up massive camps in eastern Zaire, into which the Hutu extremist army melted, protected by a huge civilian population and fed by a blatant and open "diversion" of Western aid into arms-buying binges. More than $2 billion poured into the camps, a substantial proportion of it going to protect the gang of genocidal maniacs who had escalated the blood-letting.

It was here that the fighting in 1996 began once more, made worse by Zairian discrimination against its own Tutsi civilians. Late in 1996 the Rwandan army permitted Hutu refugees to return home, but no one believed the trouble was over. The Tutsi governors wanted the killers punished, and, in the town of Cyangugu, all the Hutus were rounded up and forced to stand in a soccer stadium under appalling conditions, without food or water, until they agreed to identify the *génocidaires* among them. It was an ominous sign of more reprisals to come.

In Burundi, the ethnic cleansing went on apace. Tutsis drove Hutu from the towns, Hutu drove Tutsis from the countryside. The president, quite properly afraid of being murdered, took refuge in the U.S. embassy, and Pierre Buyoya, the army commander who had handed power back to an elected government in 1993, took over once more. Under his leadership, the Tutsi army swelled, while in the countryside the Hutu rebels began to attempt a stranglehold on the capital, Bujumbura. The outside world imposed sanctions, hoping this would somehow mysteriously drive Buyoya to negotiate. Instead, they have made him more recalcitrant. His recalcitrance is driven also by fear—if the Hutu take over, will genocide once again follow?

....

In southern Zaire, as we saw in Part I, the Zairian government deliberately precipitated a pogrom against Shaba's Luba citizens, mostly to destabilize a rival power base to Mobutu's, and to head off any Shaban thoughts of secession. In Kivu province, across the border from Rwanda, the same pattern was repeating itself in 1996—one more cause, if more were needed, for the popularity of the rebels under Laurent Kabila. The Zairian government had never attempted to disarm the génocidaires, *and Kivan politicians used their presence to inflame the always-simmering rivalry between the "original" inhabitants of the region and the "invading" Tutsi and Hutu—although the "invaders" had been settled for several hundred years. Mobutu may have been away in Switzerland for cancer treatment, but the system he had set up was quite capable of initiating pogroms on its own. This is divide and rule with a vengeance. The point—largely ignored in the West despite a U.N. Human Rights Report that accused Zaire of "government-sponsored massacres"—is that the troubles have been deliberately fomented.*

....

In North Kivu, the Hutu and Tutsis are known collectively as the Banyarwanda, and, although they have long been a majority in the province, political power has remained in the hands of other tribes. For twenty years this has resulted in a series of small but ugly wars, as the Banyarwanda fight the locals while continuing to fight each other. The Banyarwanda are treated as foreigners; in 1995 they were forbidden to hold government jobs, and their property was confiscated. Mobutu's agents—those who hadn't fled before the rebels—were still fomenting trouble in 1996, and were widely believed to be behind the Maji Maji Ingilima militia, which has attacked Banyarwanda settlements, and has used grisly witchcraft techniques to mark its passage.

In the Mulenge Mountains of South Kivu, the Tutsis are known as the Banyamulenge. They have been there for generations, but late in 1996 the governor of the province announced that they had a week to leave or be hunted down like criminals. The given reason was that both Burundi and Rwanda had been supplying the Banyamulenge with weapons and encouraging them to revolt against Zaire, which was almost certainly true. The governor was promptly fired by Mobutu, and for a while no one seemed to be in charge. Zairian army units fought each other for control of food supplies; Kinshasa, given Zaire's chaotic transportation, couldn't afford to send reliable units to intervene; local politicians were making both secessionist and loyal noises while fomenting unrest to give their followers a chance to seize Banyamulenge property.

THE KENYA HIGHLANDS

I t was a relief, finally, to leave the Great Lakes and its turbulent, chaotic, violent politics. I went east, to the Rift proper, heading up around Lake Victoria and crossing into Kenya just past Tororo, then down the highway for Nakuru and the Equator.

I'd been to Nakuru some years before. I'd come up from the Aberdare Mountains, one of the most beautiful landscapes in Africa, and had gone on to Eldoret, in what used to be called, in less knowing times, the White Highlands. From there I hitched a ride with Ibrahim, a former game warden. I was to visit a tea plantation 20 kilometres (12 miles) away, one of the last holdovers of Kenya's great bwana estates, Karen Blixen's spiritual descendant. I'd been eager, then, to talk to a bwana or two; they were hard to come by as the independence struggle faded into the past, and their way of life seemed curiously fossilized, as though they were denizens of a kind of Bwana Park, a preserve where the fauna could be studied by the perverse at heart. On the other hand, the farms of the remaining bwanas were the most productive in the country. I was to see the same pattern in Zimbabwe.

I remember his old Renault roaring and straining as Ibrahim pushed it to the limits of its design tolerance. We weren't going very fast—he hadn't shifted out of second in all the kilometres since Eldoret—but it seemed fast enough, for the red dirt road was very narrow, it was pitch dark, his headlights weren't working well, and the dense bush whipped by centimetres from my window. In any case, Ibrahim had volunteered to take me there, having arranged it with the bwana in question in some mysterious fashion I never quite understood (the phone lines were down again). Ibrahim was employed by the Kenya wildlife service, and was a government loyalist and a declared foe of oppositionists of all kinds. He was particularly against poachers. He devoted much of his life to frustrating them.

"What happens when you catch them? What are the penalties?"

His habitually fierce little face looked even fiercer. "If I'm alone and there are not too many of them, I shoot them," he said.

"You *shoot* them?" I said stupidly.

"If they are many and I am alone, they would shoot me if they could," he said, with implacable logic.

"You have shot many?"

"Some, yes."

He hauled the wheel to the right, then even harder to the left, to avoid a black-on-black *thing* in the middle of the road—a log, a body, a rock, a something.

"What happens to those you don't shoot?" I asked, after this manoeuvre was over.

"If we are many and they are few, we break their guns, burn the ivory if there is any, and take them to jail. You wouldn't," he said, with a sidelong glance, "like our jails. We let the guards beat them a little," he amplified.

He let me chew on this while he concentrated on keeping the straining Renault out of the elephantine ruts. I knew most of the poachers weren't organized criminals, though they might sell to organized criminals from Hong Kong or New Orleans, but local tribesmen displaced for one reason or another by some national Work or some grand Scheme. They were generally both resentful of the amount of land held aside for the protected pachyderms and desperate for some way, any way, of making a living and feeding their families. Shooting them, or letting them be beaten up in jail, didn't strike me as calculated to win their hearts. But Ibrahim's view was simpler and more direct. There were very few elephants, and soon, if the poachers had their way, there'd be none, and to prevent that a little localized unpopularity—along with a little unauthorized mayhem—was a minor matter. No one knew then that within a few years in Zimbabwe and Botswana and Zambia rampant elephant overpopulation would become the biggest threat to other wildlife.

He was expounding on this theme when the car crested a small but steep hill, and suddenly there was a band of men running full tilt at us, no more than twenty paces away, as fleet as cheetahs. As Ibrahim slammed on the brakes, I caught a horrified glimpse of them, the whites of their eyes caught in the headlights, their black skin glistening with sweat. They were stark naked, and I saw their bulging eyes and their heaving chests and their penises whipping with the effort of their sprinting and their pumping legs and then they were upon us and around us, looming up like a threatening storm, and then they were gone, disappearing into the dark behind us, disappearing as fast as they'd come, and within a few seconds it was over. There'd been no chance to react, no time to shout, no time to duck or even flinch.

Ibrahim pushed open the door and scrambled out. With a long cry that sounded something like "*Wehnah! Wehnah!*" he sprinted after them and he, too, disappeared into the black.

I turned off the motor and the headlights. It was utterly black. I could barely see the steering-wheel. I felt for the door handle, and got out.

There was no sound of the running men. At first, there was no sound at all. I thought I'd gone deaf. But then I heard heavy rustlings in the bush. It could have been the wind—it very likely was the wind—but I thought of the many predators and noxious creatures creeping about in the equatorial bush, and hurriedly got back into the car.

I thought I heard rustling in the back seat, too, but I knew it was an overactive imagination and ignored it as best I could. What could be back there? I tried not to think of spiders the size of dinner plates. A tarantula had fallen on my knee in an outhouse not that long before, and I still had palpitations at the thought of that disgusting, hairy thing with its cold black eyes.

Turn on the radio? No! Listen to the night ... I thought of my friend Peter's story about the group of silent lions that had surrounded his car near Augrabies Falls down south; fortunately he'd left the engine running and got out of there in a big hurry. "What would they have done to your car?" I asked him. "Torn it to pieces and me with it," he said. Well, there were no lions here. Were there? Lions liked the plains, and besides, the few that had made their way up here the hunters had chased away years ago. Still, I left the radio off.

After about ten minutes Ibrahim returned, grinning broadly. He got into the car, started the engine. The headlights flared, then settled into their habitual dim glower.

"Who were they?" I asked.

Naked men running through the African bush! Were they hunters off on some atavistic ritual, some ancient rite of passage? Or the hunted, fleeing god knows what peril?

"So who were they?" I asked again, now free to feel irritation.

"Rangers," said Ibrahim, grinning even more broadly.

"Rangers? Park rangers?" Hell of a way to chase poachers, I thought.

"No," he said, with a whinnying giggle, *xheexheexhee!* "The Rangers. The Eldoret Rangers."

"What are they?" I demanded, wanting to shake him.

"Soccer team, out for a training run!" he yelled, and howled with laughter, slapping the wheel. "Their clubhouse is only about a kilometre from here."

Then he looked at me, the grin still on his face but frozen there. A hard look came into his eye. "What did you think? Mau Mau ghosts from the past? Come to kill you with their pangas? Cut up the white boy, leave his guts on the ground?" He laughed again, without humour, and put the car into second gear, starting off with a series of jerks. He left it there for the next kilometre or so, then for no reason at all shifted into third, where he stayed. White paranoia, his silence said, is itself an evil ghost from the past.

A while later I heard the rustling from the back seat again. This time there was no mistake; I could hear it above the howl of the engine. There were also creakings, as some heavy weight shifted. I didn't look back.

"There's something in the back," I said.

"Oh," said Ibrahim, "I meant to tell you. That's Brenda."

"Brenda? Who's Brenda?"

He gave me a flashlight and I turned around. Coiled on the rear window ledge was a very large python. I don't mind snakes, but I yelled anyway. I wasn't very steady.

"She's sick," he said. "I'm taking her to the doctor."

I kept my flashlight on Brenda. She paid no attention. But after a while she gave a little ladylike sneeze, and her body quivered. Her lidless eyes looked warm and a little sorrowful. I hoped she got well soon.

THE WORLD ACCORDING TO MOI

W hen I left the north, I travelled to Nairobi on the Colour Me Badd Video Coach Dream Machine. These small taxi minivans are called daladalas in Tanzania and matatus in Kenya, and they're the universal rural transport in Africa—one of the signs of the transition to black rule in South Africa was the burgeoning presence of such taxis there. These minivans are always jammed with humanity, since for most people they're the only transport they can afford, costing the equivalent of a few cents for an intercity ride. They are also unsafe, unregulated, generally filthy and driven by incompetents, often unlicensed. Not a week goes by in which one of these matatus doesn't overturn, killing everyone on board. Still, I would take my chances.

I waited at a rural bus stop with a press of others—Chaggra, Maasai, men, women, all intensely curious why a mzungu would choose to ride this way. They are more used to white people sailing by in their eight-person safari vans, which, unbelievably, contain only eight people.

The first to arrive was a "video coach," which as usual was without the advertised video—truth in advertising isn't high on a matatu driver's must list. Sometimes these coaches are called "sleeper coaches," which usually isn't true either, unless you can sleep standing upright in a crush. The trip from, say, Nairobi to Dar es Salaam calls for an overnight stay somewhere, since it is illegal for public transport to travel after ten at night. So the long-distance coaches stop at one of the many rudimentary overnight "hotels," such as the Butcher Shop and Happy Holidays Hotel just north of the Tanzanian border in Kenya, a truly useful place but somewhat disgusting to the fastidious Western eye (and nose). It consists of a small concrete-brick and tin "dorm" with a pit latrine out back and greasy, foul-smelling bedding. But these hotels are cheap, and common, and the owners are generally hospitable. Like the markets and the *daladalas*, they serve an essential function in the country's economy.

Most of the intercity taxis have slogans painted at the rear, usually in English and often of a quasi-religious nature. In theory there are schedules, but no one knows what they are, nor are they posted. It would be a waste of paper to post them, in truth, for they are never adhered to. The rarity of these free-lance transporters accounts for their famous motto: Always Room for One More. It is certainly the best way to travel shoulder to shoulder, buttock to buttock, breast to breast, and nose to nose with the local people.

I waited two hours to go on a journey of less than a hundred kilometres, chatting desultorily to the other waiting passengers, most of whom were going home to Nairobi. The journey itself took about four hours.

Once I had been shoe-horned in (helped by a hefty and impatient shove from the rear by a woman bearing an immense bundle tied in a sack), I couldn't move. There wasn't any place to sit, but I didn't exactly stand either—we all sort of floated free, unable to go up or down or sideways. Everyone of course wanted to know where I was from, and why I was there. More important, everyone wanted to warn me that I should never go anywhere on my own in Nairobi.

When we were finally disgorged in the city, half a dozen of my fellow passengers insisted on walking with me until we found a taxi to take me to the Norfolk Hotel. I wished later that we'd been within walking distance of the hotel—I would love to have seen the look on the face of the top-hatted doorman as my unruly crowd of escorts came up to the door. It was a simple lesson in privilege. I was as filthy and ragged as my new friends, but I was white and they were not, and even in Nairobi this still made a difference—I was armoured with an attitude that brooked no inter-ference, while they were merely poor. The Norfolk was full of tourists courtesy of Abercrombie & Kent, visiting businessmen from America or South Africa, upwardly mobile Kenyans with servants, and a group of nuns drinking tea and eating cream scones. They barely noticed as I walked past the courteous doorman.

Everyone I spoke to in Nairobi warned me about the thuggishness of the city. Foreigners were advised not to go out alone, even in daylight. The papers were full of stories of violence—carjackings, muggings, murders, rapes, not to mention accidents caused by the Kenyans' cavalier disregard for the rules of the road. The day I arrived a group of armed men forced their way into the Argentine embassy and made off with all its cash. The same papers, tamed as they are by Daniel arap Moi's equally thuggish security police, were nevertheless full of dire warnings about the escalating political violence, tribal clashes, and a generalized national level of heightened irritation.

President Moi's police are omnipresent, political opposition and the media are tightly controlled, and the government's fury when it lost a by-election (as it did just before I got there) was real, and its reprisals quick. Any opposition must perforce be from "people who want to destroy the country." Elsewhere, clans were killing each other, and government politicians accused the Kikuyu of wanting to monopolize the presidency—Moi and many of his cronies are from the minority Kalenjin tribe, and are intensely suspicious of both the Kikuyu and the other major tribe, the Luo. Guards were placed around the home of a politician who defected from the opposition party, FORD (Forum for the Restoration of Democracy), to the governing and until recently the only party, KANU (Kenya African National Union). There were political riots in Nakuru after Richard Leakey, one of the founders of the opposition not-yet-allowed party, Safina, was beaten by government thugs. Safina was not even allowed to register candidates for the election due late in the decade. Early in 1997 the governing party itself began to fracture, and various candidates vied for the presidential succession: Moi was not supposed to run again, according to the constitution. Student leaders were arrested and killed in Nairobi, and, when they rebelled, the institution was shut down.

This is Kenya, the most stable polity in East Africa and its most muscular economy, the West's best friend? I asked a Kenyan journalist what was going on. I showed him a mere two days' worth of newspaper clippings, which gave ample indication of the fractiousness of Kenya politics. "In a way," he said, "this only proves the country's relative stability—because there *is* opposition, and it *is* vocal, and it *is* permitted, if only at the insistence of the World Bank."

I remembered what another journalist, a woman who toiled for a toady newspaper, had said: "Kenya-style democracy is based on personalities, not ideologies."

There were other ways to put this. The opposition calls it *nyayo* politics. *Nyayo* literally means "footsteps," but it has come to mean following closely in the president's footsteps. Moi himself had put this point of view chillingly, I thought: "I call on all ministers, assistant ministers and every other person to sing like parrots. During Mzee Kenyatta's

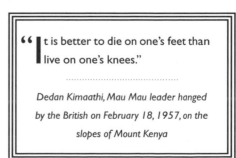

" **I** t is better to die on one's feet than live on one's knees."

Dedan Kimaathi, Mau Mau leader hanged by the British on February 18, 1957, on the slopes of Mount Kenya

period, I persistently sang the Kenyatta tune until people said: this fellow has nothing to say, except to sing for Kenyatta. I said: I did not have ideas of my own. Who was I to have my own ideas? I was in Kenyatta's shoes, and therefore I had to sing whatever Kenyatta wanted. If I had sung another song do you think Kenyatta would have left me alone? Therefore you ought to sing the song I sing. If I put a full stop, you should put a full stop. This is how the country will move forward. The day you become a big person, you will have the liberty to sing your own song, and everybody will sing it."

This is Moi's vision of caucus discipline.

Of course, he believes multiparty elections are "bad for Africa."

On Kenyatta Avenue in Nairobi I heard an American tourist complaining about African leaders' penchant for naming the *grandes allées* after leaders of the liberation struggle (Kenyatta Avenue, Kaunda Boulevard, Nyerere Road) and after themselves (Moi Street).

"I guess they'll get over it," she said.

"About as soon as the U.S. abandons Washington and Independence Avenue," I muttered, not expecting to be heard.

"It's not the same thing," she said snappishly. "They were given their independence by Britain. We won ours by fighting for it, and we started the whole process. Even the French followed us."

"Then who or what were the Mau Mau?" I asked.

"Terrorists," she said.

I remember chatting to a storekeeper in Narok about his family. He had ten children, "so far," five with one wife and then five with another.

Had the first wife died?

"No, she was used up. So I put her aside and got another."

Kenya has 6.7 live births per woman, and the population is growing at 3.3 per cent, the world's fastest, according to the Kenya National Museum in Nairobi. Even if the economy grows at a respectable rate, Kenya is likely to become poorer, not richer.

The museum has a permanent display on the population problem, which it calls the country's most serious. There are cases showing the various birth-control methods and exhibits explaining the procreation process. Busloads of eager young schoolchildren, in their British-legacy school uniforms, are toured through the exhibits every day, bussed in from surrounding villages. The museum regarded this education task as far more important than the history it displays in other exhibition rooms.

I told the curator of the population exhibit what I had read in Johannesburg.

There, the black population has historically been growing at a much faster rate than the white; popular expectations were that it would continue to do so, and that population growth would continue to worry the politicians. But to the experts' surprise, the black birth rate had fallen dramatically in the past few years, to a point where it is now just at replacement level.

"Yes," the curator said, "this is because all the girls are going to school. Teach the girls, and the problem is halfway to being solved. It can happen here too." She looked out at the chattering, eager schoolchildren. "Too bad," she said, "what they really want to see is Ahmed." (Ahmed is the skeleton of the giant elephant that became a national institution in the 1970s; Kenyatta had even gone to the lengths of protecting him through a special presidential decree.)

I looked outside. She was wrong. The boys wanted to see Ahmed. The girls were clustered around the birth-control cases. Their small black faces, round and eager, were rapt. Boys will be boys, but these girls would control the future.

OLDUVAI AND LUCY'S KIN

From the future . . . to the very distant past. Before I left Ethiopia I'd gone on a pilgrimage to the National Museum in Addis Ababa to see Lucy, whose bones were perhaps the most famous in Africa. Lucy was a little bipedal female, not much taller than a metre or so, with a delicate skeleton. She is somewhere around 3.5 million years old. Her remains were unearthed by Donald Johansen in Hadar, in the Danakil region of northern Ethiopia, and she was assigned to an entirely new species, australopithecine afarensis. She's resting now, in the parlance of funeral operators, in a small glass case in a badly lit room near the main entrance of the museum, surrounded by skull and bone fragments from others of her kind.

Lucy is famous not for her size or even her age, remarkable as it is. She's famous because she and her kin were almost certainly the ancestors of . . . everyone.

Since I'd respectfully made her acquaintance, they'd discovered near Aramis some bone fragments—not enough to anthropomorphize with a name—Luke?—a full half a million years older. A recent dig in the Danakil found a whole community of little hominids, seventeen of them in various stages of disrepair, about 4.4 million years old. All along the bony ribs of the Rift escarpment, in the Danikil, on the barren shores of Lake Turkana, in the dusty plains of Kenya and Tanzania, archaeologists are at work, sifting through the fossil record, piecing together the story of our species, for the whole history of evolution played itself out along this ancient valley, up to and including the dramatic shift from homo erectus to homo sap. One of the most famous of all these sites is between Serengeti and Ngorongoro.

The Olduvai Gorge is some 80 metres (260 feet) deep and nearly 85 kilometres (55 miles) long, with two branches. It's an unimpressive place, rocky and barren, but to archaeologists it is close to heaven, for in an accident of fate the gash in the earth has exposed five levels of sediment from different epochs, each rich in fossils—this is the British Museum, the Smithsonian, of the fossil world.

The most charming thing about the Olduvai fossils is that they were discovered only by the sheerest accident. A dotty German professor called Katwinkle was clambering after butterflies, waving his net, when he quite literally stumbled over a few of them—among them fossils of hominid bones. Later, of course, the butterfly hunter was followed by the Leakey family and their inspired lunge for the main chance. It was in 1926 that an autocratic, eccentric Kenyan called Louis Seymour Bazett Leakey, having seen Katwinkle's fossils at an exhibition in Berlin, began to dig into the East African soil. A few years later he married Mary Douglas Nicol, and the two of them spent the next few decades decoding the runes left in the volcanic ash that had preserved an astonishing number of stone tools, hominid bones, ape and animal fossils going back almost 25 million years. The results of their work are, in a way, a new Book of Revelations on the early history of our species. The major finds, so far, have been a broken but complete skull of *Australopithecus zinjanthropus*, the Nutcracker Man, which Mary Leakey found in 1953, and remnants of *Homo habilis*, dating back some 1.75 million years, *Homo erectus*, 1.5 million years, and the extraordinary hominid footprints, which are dated back to 3.6 million years. A team of Americans and Tanzanians have recently uncovered 302 bones of an adult female that they have dated back some 1.8 million years.

The Olduvai museum is a small stone building whose exhibits include explanatory charts, a few bone fragments, a plaster cast of the *Zinjanthropus* skull (the original is in Dar es Salaam), casts of the Laetoli footprints, photos of the jolly Leakeys at work and at play, and a box earnestly requesting donations. Outside, Maasai women lounge about and their men sell trinkets, beadwork, and some beautifully made artefacts. From the look-out point, an open hut described as the visitor reception centre, you can clearly see all five Olduvai levels, and how the earliest were preserved by layers of volcanic ash.

The Olduvai Gorge is now in the hands of the Tanzanian Department of Antiquities, and access to the site is, very properly, restricted to those in the company of a warden. Teams of archaeologists are licensed to continue surveying the gorge system for more fossils, though everyone assumes that the glory days are over—the focus has now shifted to the east side of Lake Turkana, in Kenya, and to the highlands of Ethiopia, whence came Lucy.

But of all the finds, whether in Olduvai or Turkana or on the Ethiopian highlands, the eeriest and most evocative are the tracks called the Laetoli footprints, named after the branch of the gorge in which they were found. There, left in a muddy stream bank and subsequently fossilized, are imprinted the bare feet of our earliest ancestors. Three of them passed by that day so long ago, leaving two large sets of prints and a smaller one, presumably two adults and a child. They stride purposefully across the mud, surrounded by the prints of creatures much larger and more dangerous than they. These marvellous impressions have been carefully covered over again to preserve them from the ravages of nature, but it is possible to superimpose in your mind the site, at the bottom of a broken, stony gorge, and castings of the footprints, and get a mental picture of the three little upright hominids as they made their careful way up the path (perhaps hand in hand, for the small tracks are parallel to the larger).

Here walked our ancestors, 3.6 million years ago, dreaming no doubt their wary dreams of warmth and wealth and well-being, bequeathing their dreams as well as their genes to the endless generations to follow. It is a humbling thought that all the world's saints and all the world's sinners, down over the endless millennia, can be seen in these tiny impressions—every warlord who was ever born, every mystic, every murderer, every poet, and every politician descended, somehow, from the people who left behind these small traces, and their kin. How *old* this place is! The Bushmen, who bequeathed us their marvellous cave paintings so many millennia ago, were to these little people (for they *were* people) still the unimaginably distant future. The three of them passed this way only once. But once was enough to make them immortal. I like to think they were a family, going home, making their way carefully through the many hazards that beset them. I hope for their sakes they had full bellies, and that they made a fire that night, to comfort them, there in the African night.

Notes

....

PART I: MONOMOTAPA

The material in this chapter was collected from on-site visits and interviews, from the many excellent general histories (especially the UNESCO series), from Peter Garlake's and Ken Mufuka's work at Great Zimbabwe. (The white colonial regime once fired Garlake from the Historical Monuments Commission for declaring unequivocally that Great Zimbabwe was the work of the Shona forebears.) For the traveller and non-specialist, the various Africa guidebooks produced for Lonely Planet contain digested histories that are a model of their kind, especially for their even-handedness with post-colonial development. Numbered passages in the text are from:

1   History adapted from Murphy, *Rhodesian Legacy*
2   Adapted from Randles, *The Empire of Monomotapa*
3   Quoted from Mountfield, *A History of African Exploration*, p. 136
4   Lonely Planet, *Africa*, 6th edition, 1992
5   This sentence and some details in following page from Lonely Planet, *Africa*
6   Lonely Planet, *Africa*
7   Graham and Beard, *The Eyelids of Morning*

....

PART II: THE LAND OF THE ZANJ AND THE BIRTH OF THE SWAHILI

Again, much of the information in this section came from personal visits by the authors. There is a rich legacy of travellers' tales on the Swahili coast; among the most interesting were the redoubtable Ibn-Battuta, who visited the coast in the fourteenth century, and other Muslim travellers. The Portuguese have left many records behind of their long and violent occupation of the coast. Later, the equally redoubtable traveller Richard Burton passed many a month on Zanzibar, and left vivid recollections of his travels. Much of the best writing on the coast has been collected and published by G. S. P. Freeman-Grenville in his excellent book, *The East African Coast*. Many of the specific passages marked in the text are from Freeman-Grenville. Edward Rice has collected the most interesting of Burton's tales. The other citation in this chapter comes from one of Basil Davidson's many books on Africa. All writers on African history owe a debt of gratitude to Davidson, the passionate populariser, who has been attempting to persuade readers for four decades that Africa was more than it seemed to the prejudiced Western eye.

1   Freeman-Grenville, *The East African Coast*, p. 241
2   Ibid., p. 150
3   Ibid., p. 146
4   Ibid., p. 60
5   Davidson, *The African Past*, p. 138

6   Rice, *Captain Sir Richard Francis Burton*, p. 281
7   Lonely Planet, *Africa*
8   Freeman-Grenville, p. 60
9   Ibid., p.120
10 Some details in this paragraph and on following page from Lonely Planet, *Africa*

PART III: TOWARDS AZANIA

As noted in the text, many hundreds of books have been published on South Africa. Most noteworthy among them for our purposes are: The series of historical journeyings and memoirs published by the Van Riebeeck Society in Cape Town; the general histories written by Leonard Thompson and Monica Wilson; the writings of Richard Elphick and Hermann Giliomee; on Lesotho, (again) Leonard Thompson; on Botswana, Mary Benson's *Tshekedi Khama;* the excellent work done by David Hammond-Tooke and others. For the rest, the text is derived from more than twenty years of authorial wanderings. Specific references in the text:

1   Hammond-Tooke, *The Roots of Black South Africa*
2   Thompson, *Survival in Two Worlds*
3   Ibid.
4   Reprinted with permission from *Encyclopaedia Britannica,* 16:791

PART IV: KONGO

The histories of the Mbundu kingdoms, the Kongo empire, the Vili of Loango and the Luba-Lunda-Songye kingdoms of the interior (inheritors of the legendary hero Kongolo) have been the subject of hundreds of volumes. Among the best, for specialist and non-specialist alike, are the many books of David Birmingham, who has specialized in Angola and the Congo, and the French ethnographer Georges Balandier.

1   Balandier, *Daily Life in the Kingdom of the Kongo*
2   Adapted from Birmingham, *Trade and Conflict in Angola*, p. 6, and Balandier, *Daily Life in the Kingdom of the Kongo*
3   Balandier, *Daily Life in the Kingdom of the Kongo*
4   Ibid.
5   From Bassani and Fagg, *Africa and the Renaissance*
6   I bid., p. 203
7   Axelson, *South African Explorers*, p. 44
8   Bassani and Fagg, *Africa and the Renaissance*, p. 47
9   Adapted from Birmingham, *Trade and Conflict in Angola*
10 Ibid., p. 29
11 Ibid., p. 27
12 Ibid., p. 36
13 Ibid., Gouveia material from Ibid.
14 Ajahi and Crowder, *Historical Atlas of Africa*
15 Birmingham, *Trade and Conflict in Angola*, p. 89
16 Adapted from *Encyclopaedia Britannica*
17 Boulger, *The Congo State*
18 Lonely Planet, *Africa*

19 UNESCO, *General History of Africa*, p. 563
20 Fagg, *Tribes and Forms in African Art*
21 The accounts of the Luba "beginnings" are from Birmingham, *Trade and Conflict in Angola*
22 Details from Cunnison, *The Luapula People of Northern Rhodesia*, p. 37
23 *The Economist*, March 22, 1997
24 Birmingham, *Trade and Conflict in Angola*, p. 9

PART V: THE GULF OF GUINEA

UNESCO's general history, with its dozens of contributors, is of mixed authority, usefulness and read-ability. It is, however, very good on West Africa and its old kingdoms, especially Ife and Oyo; the *Encyclopaedia Britannica* is reliable for those who want a more potted version. David Mountfield's splendid popular anthology, *A History of African Exploration*, is invaluable. A constant travelling companion in the region was Alex Newton and David Else's thorough, sympathetic, and reliable *West Africa*, published by Lonely Planet. For specific references in the text:

1   Cable, *The African Kings*
2   Philips, *Africa: The Art of a Continent*, p. 37
3   The *Encyclopaedia Britannica* is good for a short history of Ife and Oyo.
4   Cable, *The African Kings*
5   Bassani and Fagg, *Africa and the Renaissance*, p. 173
6   Mountfield, *A History of African Exploration*, p. 81
7   Ibid., p. 81
8   Ibid., p. 79
9   Reprinted with permission from *Encyclopaedia Britannica*, 5:420
10 Radin, et al, *African Folktales and Sculpture*, p. x
11 Lonely Planet, *West Africa*
12 Anti, *Kumasi in the Eighteenth and Nineteenth Centuries*
13 Reprinted with permission from *Encyclopaedia Britannica*, 19:764
14 Fisher, *Africa Adorned*
15 Anti, *Kumasi in the Eighteenth and Nineteenth Centuries*
16 Ibid.
17 Fisher, *Africa Adorned*, p. 70
18 Ibid.
19 Bassani and Fagg, *Africa and the Renaissance*, p. 49
20 Johnson, *The Birth of the Modern World Society*, p. 332
21 *The Economist*, January 20, 1996
22 William Shawcross, *London Daily Telegraph*, March 15, 1996

PART VI: THE SAHEL: THE GOLDEN EMPIRES OF THE SUN

Muslim travellers have been criss-crossing the Great Desert since . . . since there *were* Muslims. Ibn-Battuta was here, as elsewhere. And African travellers have been visiting Egypt and the Muslim holy places since the twelfth century. European explorers, too, were diligently making their own crossings, if rather later: David Mountfield has collected many of the best. Thus, many accounts have been left behind, and much is known. Some of these travels the authors have also made themselves.

1   Mountfield, *A History of African Exploration*, p. 69
2   From *Encyclopaedia Britannica*
3   Frobenius, *The Voice of Africa*, p. 495
4   Many sources, including *Encyclopaedia Britannica*, 19:762
5   Philips, *Africa: Art of a Continent*, p. 328
6   I bid., p. 328
7   Frobenius, *The Voice of Africa*, pp. 451-66
8   Story recounted in *Le Roi d'Afrique et la reine mer*, by Jean-Yves Loude
9   Mountfield, *A History of African Exploration*
10 Ibid., p. 74
11 Barth, *Travels and Discoveries in North and Central Africa*, p. 561
12 Fisher, *Africa Adorned*, p. 192
13 Frobenius, *The Voice of Africa*, p. 421
14 From Mountfield, *A History of African Exploration*, p. 78
15 Reprinted with permission from *Encyclopaedia Britannica*, 19:774
16 Fisher, *Africa Adorned*, p. 154
17 Mountfield, *A History of African Exploration*
18 Barth, *Travels and Discoveries in North and Central Africa*, p. 475
19 David Roberts, "Below the Cliff of Tombs," *National Geographic*, October 1990
20 Griault, *Conversations with Ogotemmêli*

PART VII: THE MAGHREB AND THE BARBARY COAST

All the colonizing powers except perhaps the Carthaginians have left their own versions of North African history; the *General History of Africa* steers a usefully neutral course. For specific references in the text:

1   From *Encyclopaedia Britannica*
2   Details from *Encyclopaedia Britannica*
3   Reprinted with permission from *Encyclopaedia Britannica*, 13: 148
4   Johnson, *The Birth of the Modern World Society*, p. 288
5   Ibid, p. 286
6   Quoted in Cooley, *Libyan Sandstorm*
7   Mountfield, *A History of African Exploration*, p. 74
8   Ibid., p. 74
9   Ibid., p. 91
10 Cooley, *Libyan Sandstorm*

PART VIII: THE LONGEST RIVER

The source of the Nile, such an enduring mystery to the Victorian explorers, was well known to ancient travellers. Ptolemy, whose Africa was hazy at best, seemed to know it welled up in the Mountains of the Moon, which is not far from the truth. The Baganda kings, of course, knew from whence it came and where it went. Much of the material in this section came from the general histories and from personal visits. The number of books on Egypt are too many to count, and while there are fewer on Axum, they would still fill a shelf or two in a good-sized library. Philip Briggs's *Guide to Ethiopia* contains an excellent if short history of that country, and is properly sceptical on the Ethiopian church's claim to possess the ancient Jewish Ark of the Covenant.

Specific references:

1   Stanley, *In Darkest Africa*, p. 449
2   Ibid.
3   Ibid., p. 487
4   Story and details from Johnson, *The Birth of the Modern World Society*, p. 685
5   Mountfield, *A History of African Exploration*, pp. 61–64
6   Ibid., p. 64
7   Ibid., p. 58
8   Briggs, *Guide to Ethiopia*

....

PART IX: THE GREAT RIFT

Tanzania's Department of Antiquities has published widely on the fossil finds in east Africa and the Olduvai Gorge area; so have the Leakeys. The archaeologist John Sutton has published much ground-breaking work. Graham Connah's *African Civilizations* is invaluable in the scope and breadth of its commentary. The *Uganda Journal* has published dozens of significant articles. Specific references in the text are attributed to:

1   Sutton, *A Thousand Years of East Africa*, p. 8
2   Z. C. K. Mungonya, *Uganda Journal*, vol. 22
3   Dunbar, *A History of Bunyoro-Kitara*, p. 1
4   Sutton, *A Thousand Years of East Africa*, pp. 12–13
5   *The Kings of Buganda*, M/S.M. Kiwanuka, p. 3
6   Connah, *African Civilizations*, p. 214
7   Mugerwa, *The Kasubi Tombs*, p. 2
8   Stanley, *In Darkest Africa*, p. 476
9   Sutton, *A Thousand Years of East Africa*, p. 15

Selected Bibliography

Abbate, Francesco. *African Art and Oceanic Art*. London: Octopus Books, 1972.

Abrahams, Roger D. *African Folktales*. New York: Pantheon, 1983.

Ajahi, J. F. Ade, and Michael Crowder. *Historical Atlas of Africa*. Cambridge: Cambridge University Press, 1985.

Andrews, Edward M. *The "Webster" Ruin in Southern Rhodesia*. Washington, D.C.: Smithsonian Miscellaneous Collections, 1908.

Anti, A. A. *Kumasi in the Eighteenth and Nineteenth Centuries*. Accra: Damage Control Limited, 1996.

Axelson, Eric, ed. *South African Explorers*. Oxford: Oxford University Press, 1954.

Ayittey, George B. N. *Africa Betrayed*. New York: St. Martin's Press, 1992.

Ayot, H. O. *Topics in East African History 1000-1970*. Kampala: East African Historical Bureau, 1970.

Bacon, Edward. *Vanished Civilizations of the Ancient World*. New York: McGraw-Hill, 1963.

Baines, Thomas. *The Gold Regions of South East Africa*. Cape Colony: J. W. C. MacKay, 1877.

Baker, Samuel White. *Pasha Ismailia: Expedition to Central Africa for the Suppression of the Slave Trade*. New York: Harper and Bros., 1875.

Balandier, Georges. *Ambiguous Africa*. London: Chatto & Windus, 1966.

———. *Daily Life in the Kingdom of the Kongo*. New York: Pantheon, 1968.

———. *The Sociology of Black Africa*. New York: Praeger, 1970.

Bannister, Anthony, and Peter Johnson. *Namibia: Africa's Harsh Paradise*. Cape Town: C. Struik, 1978.

Barbosa, Duarte. *The Book of Duarte Barbosa*. Liechtenstein: Kraus, 1967.

Barth, Heinrich. *Travels and Discoveries in North and Central Africa*. London: F. Cass, 1965.

Bassani, Ezio, and William B. Fagg, eds. *Africa and the Renaissance: Art in Ivory*. New York: Prestel-Verlag/The Center for African Art, 1988.

Ibn-Battuta. *Travels in Asia and Africa* 1325–53. New York: Robert McBride & Co., 1929.

Benson, Mary. *Tshekedi Khama*. London: Faber, 1960.

Bierman, John. *Dark Safari: The Life Behind the Legend of Henry Morton Stanley*. New York: Alfred A. Knopf, 1990.

Birmingham, David, ed. *The History of Central Africa*. vol. 1. London: Longman, 1983.

Birmingham, David. *Trade and Conflict in Angola: The Mbundu and Their Neighbours Under the Influence of the Portuguese 1483–1790*. Oxford: Clarendon Press, 1966.

Boaten, Barfuo Akwasi Abayie I. *Akwasidae Kese: A Festival of the Asante, People with a Culture.* Accra: National Commission of Culture, n. d.

Boulger, Demetrius C. *The Congo State.* London: W. Thacker and Co., 1898.

Bowles, Paul. *Their Heads Are Green and Their Hands Are Blue.* Hopewell, N.J.: Ecco, 1984.

Braffi, Emmanuel Kingsley. *Silver Jubilee of Otumfuo Opoku Ware Ii: Asantehene and Some Aspects of Asante History.* Kumasi: University Printing Press, 1995.

Bredin, Miles. *Blood on the Tracks: A Rail Journey from Angola to Mozambique.* London: Picador, 1994.

Briggs, Philip. *Guide to Ethiopia.* Chalfont St. Peter, U.K.: Bradt Publications, 1996.

Brode, Heinrich. *Tippu Tip: The Story of His Career in Central Africa Narrated from His Own Accounts.* Chicago: Afro-American Press, 1969.

Brown, Monty. *Where Giants Trod: The Saga of Kenya's Desert Lake.* London: Quiller, 1989.

Burton, A. W. *The Highlands of Kaffraria.* Cape Town: C. Struik, 1969.

Burton, R. F. *Lacerda's Journey to Cazembe in 1798.* London: John Murray, 1873.

Cable, Mary. *The African Kings.* Chicago: Stonehenge Press, 1983.

Camelopardalis: Carteret. London, 1769.

Camerapix, Inc. *Spectrum Guide to Kenya.* Nairobi: Westland Sundries Ltd., 1989.

Camerapix, Inc. *Spectrum Guide to African Wildlife Safaris.* New York: Facts on File, 1989.

Cameron, Trewhella. *Nuwe Geskiedenis van Suid-Afrika.* Cape Town: Human & Rousseau, 1986.

Capello, Hermenegildo. *From Benguella to the Territory of Yacca.* New York: Negro University Press, 1969.

Carey, Margaret. *Myths and Legends of Africa.* London: Hamlyn, 1970.

Center for African Art. *Art/Artifact: African Art in Anthropology Collections.* New York: CAA, 1988.

———. *Perspectives: Angles on African Art.* New York: CAA, 1987.

Chaffin, Alain, and Francoise Chaffin. *L'Art Kota.* Self published, n. d.

Chesi, Gert. *The Last Africans.* New York: Rizzoli, 1977.

Childs, Gladwyn Murray. *Umbundu, Kinship and Character.* London: Dawson, 1969.

Chillick, H. Neville. *East Africa and the Orient: Cultural Synthesis in Pre-Colonial Times.* New York: Africana Publishing Co., 1975.

Clerc, Pierre-Olivier, and Hubert Maheux. *Pouvoirs: Les Sociétés Traditionnelles dans la Région de la Cuvette.* Brazzaville: Ministry of Culture, Congo, 1992.

Connah, Graham. *African Civilizations.* New York: Cambridge University Press, 1987.

Cooley, John K. *Libyan Sandstorm: The Complete Account of Qaddafi's Revolution.* New York: Holt Rinehart Winston (now Henry Holt and Co.), 1982.

Couzens, Tim. *Tramp Royal: The True Story of Trader Horne.* Johannesburg: Ravan, 1992.

Cubitt, Gerald, and Johann Richter. *South West.* Cape Town: C. Struik, 1976.

Cunnison, I. G. *The Luapula People of Northern Rhodesia.* Manchester: Manchester University Press, 1967.

Davidson, Basil. *Africa in History.* New York: Collier, 1991.

————. *The African Awakening*. London: Jonathan Cape, 1955.

————. *The African Past*. London: Penguin, 1964.

————. *Guide to African History*. London: Allen & Unwin, 1963.

————. *Old Africa Rediscovered*. London: Gollancz, 1965.

————. *The Search for Africa: History, Culture, Politics*. New York: Random House, 1994.

de Almeida, Antonio. *Bushmen and Other Non-Bantu Peoples of Angola*. Johannesburg: Witwatersrand University Press, 1965.

de Guingand, Sir Francis, ed. *Africa South of the Sahara: An Assessment of Human and Material Resources*. Oxford: Oxford University Press, 1951.

De Njoya à Njimoluh: cent ans d'historire bamoum. Foumban: Éditions de Palais, 1984.

de Villiers, René, ed. *Better Than They Knew*. 2 vols. Cape Town: Purnell, 1972.

Duffy, James. *Portuguese Africa*. Cambridge: Harvard University Press, 1968.

Dunbar, A. R. *A History of Bunyoro-Kitara*. Nairobi: Makarere Institute of Social Research, 1968.

Edwards, Adrian C. *The Ovimbundu under Two Sovereignties*. Oxford: Oxford University Press, 1962.

Encyclopaedia Britannica. 15th edition. Chicago: Encyclopaedia Britannica Inc, 1975.

Eksteen, M. C. *Lesotho in Uitwaartse Beweging*. Johannesburg: Perskor, 1972.

Elphick, Richard. *Khoikhoi and the Founding of White South Africa*. Johannesburg: Ravan, 1985.

Eyongetah, Tambi, and Robert Brain. *A History of the Cameroon*. London: Longman, 1974.

Fage, J. D. *A Short History of Africa*. London: Penguin, 1962.

Fage, J. D., and Maureen Verity. *An Atlas of African History*. 2nd ed. London: E. Arnold, 1963.

Fage, J. D., and R. A. Oliver. *Papers in African Prehistory*. Cambridge: Cambridge University Press, 1970.

Fagg, William. *African Majesty from Grassland and Forest*. Toronto: Art Gallery of Ontario, 1981.

————. *The Sculpture of Africa*. New York: Hacket, 1978.

————. *Tribes and Forms in African Art*. New York: Tudor, 1965.

Fagg, William, and Margaret Plass. *African Sculpture*. New York: Dutton, 1964.

Farson, Negley. *Behind God's Back*. London: Gollancz, 1940.

————. *Last Chance in Africa*. London: Gollancz, 1949.

Fisher, Angela. *Africa Adorned*. New York: Harry N. Abrams, 1984.

Fitzgerald, Mary Anne. *Nomad: Journeys from Samburu*. London: Sinclair-Stevenson, 1992.

Forde, Daryll, and P. M. Kaberry. *West African Kingdoms in the 19th Century*. Oxford: Oxford University Press, 1967.

Frazer, Sir James George. *The Native Races of Africa and Madagascar*. London: Percy Lund Humphries, 1938.

Freeman-Grenville, G. S. P. *The East African Coast: Select Documents from the First to the Earlier Nineteenth Century*. Oxford: Clarendon Press, 1962.

————. *The New Atlas of African History*. New York: Simon and Schuster, 1991.

Frobenius, Leo. *The Voice of Africa: Being an Account of the Travels of the German Inner African Exploration Expedition in the Years 1910–1912*. New York: Benjamin Blom, 1968.

Gailey, H. A. Jr. *History of Africa in Maps*. Chicago: Denoyer-Geppert, 1971.

Garlake, Peter. *Great Zimbabwe, Described and Explained*. Harare: Zimbabwe Publishing House, 1982.

Gebauer, Paul. *Art of Cameroon*. New York: Portland Art Museum and Metropolitan Museum of Art, 1979.

Gibson, J. Y. *The Story of the Zulus*. London: Longman, Green & Co., 1911.

Giday, Belai. *Ethiopian Civilisation*. Addis Ababa: Self published, 1991.

Gide, Andre. *Travels in the Congo*. Hopewell, N. J.: Ecco, 1994.

Giliomee, Hermann B. *Zimbabwe: The Short and Long Term Socio-Political Prospects of a New State*. Research Paper, University of Stellenbosch, 1980.

Graham, Alistair, and Peter Beard. *Eyelids of Morning: The Mingled Destinies of Crocodiles and Men*. New York: A & W Visual Library, 1973.

Graves, Robert. *New Larousse Encyclopedia of Mythology*. London: Hamlyn, 1959.

Green, Lawrence G. *Under a Sky Like Flame*. Cape Town: Howard Timmins, 1954.

———. *Where Men Still Dream*. Cape Town: Howard Timmins, 1945.

Greenberg, Joseph Harold. *The Languages of Africa*. Bloomington, IN: Indiana University Press, 1966.

Griault, Marcel. *Conversations with Ogotemmêli: An Introduction to Dogon Religious Ideas*. Oxford: Oxford University Press, 1965.

Gros, Felix. *Rhodes of Africa*. London: Cassell, 1956.

Guidoni, Enrico. *Primitive Architecture*. New York: H. Abrams, 1978.

Guillaume, Paul. *Primitive Negro Sculpture*. New York: Hacker Art Books, 1968.

Gunther, John. *Inside Africa*. London: Hamish Hamilton, 1955.

Guy, Jeff. *The Destruction of the Zulu Kingdom*. Johannesburg: Ravan, 1984.

Hailey, Lord. *An African Survey*. Oxford: Oxford University Press, 1956.

al-Hakami, Umarah ibn Ali. *Yaman: Its Early Mediaeval History*. London: Edward Arnold, 1892.

Hallett, Robin. *Africa to 1875 & Africa since 1875: A Two Volume History*. London: Heinemann, 1970.

———. *The Penetration of Africa*. London: Routledge and Paul, 1965.

Hamilton, James. *Wanderings in North Africa*. London: J. Murray, 1856.

Hammond-Tooke, David. *The Roots of Black South Africa*. Johannesburg: Jonathan Ball, 1993.

Hancock, Graham. *The Sign and the Seal: The Quest for the Lost Ark of the Covenant*. Toronto: Doubleday, 1993.

Hatch, John. *Nigeria: The Seeds of Disaster*. Chicago: Regnery, 1970.

Hollis, Alfred Claud. *The Maasai: Their Language and Folklore*. Oxford: Oxford University Press, 1905.

———. *The Nandi: Their Language and Folklore*. Oxford: Oxford University Press, 1909.

Hourani, Albert. *A History of the Arab Peoples*. Cambridge, MA: Belknap/Harvard, 1991.

Hull, Richard. *West African Cities and Towns Before the Europeans*. New York: Norton, 1976.

Hunter, Monica. *Reactions to Conquest*. Oxford: Oxford University Press, 1936.

Inskeep, R. R. *The Peopling of Southern Africa*. Cape Town: David Philip, 1978.

Jahn, Janheinz. *Muntu: The New African Culture*. New York: Grove, 1961.

Johnson, Paul. *The Birth of the Modern World Society 1815–1830*. London: Phoenix, 1992.

July, R. W. *History of African People*. Prospect Heights, IL: Waveland Press, 1992.

———. *The Origins of Modern African Thought*. New York: Praeger, 1967.

Kagwa, Sir Apolo. *The Kings of Buganda: Historical Texts of Eastern and Central Africa*. Nairobi: East African Publishing House, 1971.

Kalck, Pierre. *L'histoire de la République Centre-Africaine*. Paris: Éditions Berger-Levrault, 1974.

Kiwanuka, Semaula. *A History of Buganda, from the Foundation of the Kingdom to 1900*. New York: Africana Publishing Corp., 1972.

Klotchkoff, Jean Claude. *Le Congo Aujourd'hui Librairie*. Brazzaville: Raoul, 1987.

Konczacki, Janina M., ed. *Victorian Explorer: The African Diaries of Captain William G. Stairs, 1887–1892*. Halifax, NS: Nimbus, 1994.

———. *Kumasi: The City of Kumasi Handbook, Past, Present and Future*. The Institute of African Studies, University of Ghana, 1992.

Kwamena-Poh, Michael, et al. *African History in Maps*. New York: Longman, 1982.

Lamb, David. *The African*. New York: Random House, 1982.

Laye, Camara. *The Guardian of the World*. New York: Vintage, 1984.

Legum, Colin, ed. *Africa: A Handbook to the Continent*. London: Anthony Blond, 1961.

Leiris, Michel, and Jacqueline Delange. *African Art*. New York: Golden Press, 1968.

Le Vaillant, M. *Voyage de M. Le Vaillant dans l'Interieur de l'Afrique 1780*. Paris: Chez Leroy, 1789.

Levtzion, Nehemia. *Ancient Ghana and Mali*. London: Methuen, 1973.

Listowel, Judith M. *The Other Livingstone*. Lewes, UK: Julian Friedman, 1974.

Livingstone, David. *The Last Journals of David Livingstone in Central Africa Including His Last Moments As Related by Chuma and Susi*. Westport, CT: Greenwood Press, 1970.

———. *Narrative of the Expedition to the Zambezi and Tributaries, Including Lakes Shirwa and Nyassa 1858–64*. London: Chatto & Windus, 1956.

———. *South African Papers 1849–1853*. Cape Town: Van Riebeeck Society, 1974.

———. *Travels and Researches in South Africa*. Philadelphia: J. W. Bradley, 1870.

———. *The Zambian Collection at Livingstone Museum*. Livingstone, Zambia: The Museum and Indiana University Press, 1990.

Lonely Planet Guides: *Africa* (edited by Geoff Crowther, et al); *Central Africa* (edited by Alex Newton); *West Africa* (edited by Alex Newton and David Else); *Morocco* (edited by Geoff Crowther and

Damien Simonis); *North Africa* (edited by Damien Simonis, et al): Hawthorn, Australia, 1995.

Luhikula, Gratian. *Tourist Guide to Tanzania*. Dar Es Salaam: Travel Promotion Services Ltd., 1985.

Macmillan, W. M. *Africa Emergent*. London: Penguin, 1938.

Manhyia Palace Museum & Jubilee Foundation. *Otumfuo Opoku Ware Ii*. Kumasi: University Printing Press.

Marquard, Leo, and T. D. Standing. *The Southern Bantu*. Oxford: Oxford University Press, 1939.

Marnham, Patrick. *Fantastic Invasion: Dispatches from Africa*. London: Penguin, 1988.

Marsh, Zoe, and G. W. Kingsnorth. *A History of East Africa: An Introductory Survey*. Cambridge: Cambridge University Press, 1972.

————. *An Introduction to the History of Africa*. Cambridge: Cambridge University Press, 1957.

McLeod, Lyons. *Travels in Eastern Africa with the Narrative of a Residence in Mozambique*. vol. 1. London: Hurst & Blackett, 1860.

Meyer, P. J. *Trek Verder: Die Afrikaner in Afrika*. Cape Town: Haum, n. d.

Miller, Joseph Calder. *Cokwe Expansion 1850–1900*. Madison: African Studies Program of the University of Wisconsin, 1969.

Monteney-Jephson, A. J. *Emin Pasha and the Rebellion at the Equator*. New York: Scribner's, 1890.

Moore, Ernst D. *Ivory: Scourge of Africa*. New York: Harper & Bros., 1931.

Moorehead, Alan. *The Blue Nile*. New York: Harper & Row, 1962.

Mostert, Noel. *Frontiers*. New York: Alfred A. Knopf, 1992.

Mountfield, David. *A History of African Exploration*. London: Hamlyn, 1976.

Mufuka, Ken, et al. *Dzimbahwe: Life and Politics in the Golden Age*. Harare: Harare Publishing House, 1983.

Mugerwa, R. Kigongo. *The Kasubi Tombs*. Kampala: RMK Associates, 1991.

Muller, C. F. J. *A Pictorial History of the Great Trek*. Cape Town: Tafelberg, 1978.

Mungazi, Dickson A. *The Mind of Black Africa*. Westport, CT: Praeger, 1966.

Murphy, Ian. *Rhodesian Legacy*. Cape Town: C. Struik, 1978.

Murray, Jocelyn. *A Cultural History of Africa*. New York: Facts on File, 1981.

Musée National Du Mali. *Collections Permanentes*. La Mission Française de Coopération et d'Action Culturelle au Mali.

Mutwa, Vusumazulu Credo. *Indaba My Children: African Tribal History, Legends, Customs and Religious Beliefs*. London: Kahn & Averill, 1966.

Mvens, Engelbert. *L'Histoire du Cameroun*. Paris: Presence Africaine, 1963.

Neyt, Francois. *La Grande Statuaire Hemba du Zaire*. Louvain-la-Neuve: U. C. L. Arts Africains, 1977.

Newson-Smith, Sue. *Quest: Stanley & Livingstone As Told in Their Own Words*. London: Arlington Books, 1978.

Niane, Djibril Tamsir. *Sundiata: An Epic of Old Mali*. London: Longman, 1979.

Norris, H. T. *Saharan Myth and Saga*. Oxford: Clarendon Press, 1972.

Nyaratura, J. W. *Anatomy of an African Kingdom: A History of Bunyoro Kitara*. New York: Nok Publishers, 1973.

O'Brien, Conor Cruise. *To Katanga and Back*. London: Hutchinson, 1962.

Okri, Ben. *The Famished Road*. London: Jonathan Cape, 1991.

Oliver, Roland, ed. *The Dawn of African History*. London: Oxford University Press, 1961.

Oliver, Roland, and J. D. Fage. *A Short History of Africa*. Baltimore: Penguin, 1962.

Pakenham, Thomas. *The Scramble For Africa 1876–1912*. New York: Random House, 1991.

Patterson, K. David. *The Northern Gabon Coast to 1875*. Oxford: Clarendon Press, 1976.

Philips, Tom, ed. *Africa: The Art of a Continent*. Munich: Royal Academy of Art & Prestel Verlag, 1996.

Powell, Ivor, and Mark Lewis. *Ndebele: A People and Their Art*. Cape Town: Struik, 1995.

Prins, Gwyn. *The Hidden Hippopotamus: Reappraisals in African History: Early Colonial Experience In Western Zambia*. Cambridge: Cambridge University Press, 1980.

Radin, Paul, et al. *African Folktales & Sculpture, Bollingen Series XXXII*. New York: Random House, 1964. Reprinted by permission of Princeton University Press.

Randles, W. G. L. *The Empire of Monomatapa*. Gwelo: Mambo Press, 1981.

Rasmussen, R. Kent. *Migrant Kingdom: Mzilikazi's Ndebele in South Africa*. London: Collins, 1978.

Ravenstein, E. G., ed. *The Strange Adventures of Andrew Battel of Leigh, Essex*. Liechtenstein: Kraus, 1967.

Reefe, Thomas Q. *The Rainbow and the Kings: A History of the Luba Empire to 1891*. Berkeley: University of California, 1981.

Relation of the Voyage to Siam, performed by Six Jesuits, 1685. London, printed 1688.

Ribaud, Paul. *Adieu Congo*. Paris: La Table Ronde, 1961.

Rice, Edward. *Captain Sir Richard Francis Burton*. New York: Scribner's, a division of Simon and Schuster, 1990.

Riefenstahl, Leni. *Vanishing Africa*. New York: Harmony, 1982.

Ritter, E. A. *Shaka Zulu*. London: Penguin, 1978.

Robbins, Warren M. *African Art / L'art Africain in American Collections*. New York: Frederick A. Praeger, 1966.

Roberts, Paul William. *River in the Desert*. New York: Random House, 1993.

Rosenthal, Ricky. *The Sign of the Ivory Horn: Eastern African Civilization*. Dobb's Ferry, New York: Oceana Publications, 1971.

Rotberg, Robert I. *Joseph Thomson and the Exploration of Africa*. London: Chatto & Windus, 1971.

———. *A Political History of Tropical Africa*. New York: Harcourt Brace and World, 1965.

Rubin, William, ed. *Primitivism in 20th Century Art*. New York: Museum of Modern Art, 1984.

Schoeman, Karel, ed. *Sotho War Diaries 1964–1865*. Cape Town: Human & Rousseau, 1985.

Schreiner, Olive. *Story of an African Farm*. Johannesburg: Dassie, 1949.

Skelton, R. A. *Explorers' Maps*. London: Routledge and Paul, 1958.

Smith, Edwin. *The Life and Times of Daniel Lindley: Missionary to the Zulus 1801–80*. London: Epworth Press, 1949.

Soga, John Henderson. *The Ama-Xhosa: Life and Customs*. Lovedale, South Africa: Lovedale Press, n. d.

Ssekamwa, J. C. *A Sketch Map History of East Africa*. Amersham: Hulton Educational, 1971.

Stanley, Henry Morton. *In Darkest Africa*. New York: Scribner's, 1890.

———. *My Dark Companions and Their Strange Stories*. New York: C. Scribner's Sons, 1893.

Stigand, C. H. *The Land of Zinj*. New York: Barnes & Noble, 1966.

Sundkler, B. G. M. *Bantu Prophets in South Africa*. Oxford: Oxford University Press, 1961.

Sutton, John. *A Thousand Years of East Africa*. Nairobi: British Institute in Eastern Africa, 1990.

Tams, G. *Visit to the Portuguese Possessions in South-Western Africa*. New York: Negro University Press (originally published in 1845), 1969.

Tempels, Placide. *Bantu Philosophy*. Paris: Presence Africaine, 1952.

Thompson, Leonard. *Survival in Two Worlds: Moshoeshoe of Lesotho 1786–1870*. Oxford: Oxford University Press, 1975.

Thompson, Leonard, and Monica Wilson. *A History of South Africa to 1870*. Cape Town: David Philip, 1985.

Thompson, Leonard, and Monica Wilson, eds. *The Oxford History of South Africa*, in two volumes, 1971.

Tomatis, Claudio. *The Jade Sea: Journey to Lake Turkana*. Rome: Self-published, 1992.

Tracey, Hugh. *Zulu Paradox*. Johannesburg: Silver Leaf, n. d.

Tufuo, J. W., and C. E. Donkor. *Ashantis of Ghana: People with a Soul*. Accra: Anowuo Educational Publications, 1989.

UNESCO. *General History of Africa*. 8 vols. Paris: UNESCO; London: Heinemann; and Berkeley: University of California Press, 1984.

van der Post, Laurens. *Lost World of the Kalahari*. London: Hogarth Press, 1958.

Vansina, Jan. *The Children of Woot: A History of the Kuba Peoples*. Madison: University of Wisconsin, 1978.

———. *Kingdoms of the Savanna*. Madison: University of Wisconsin, 1966.

———. *The Tio Kingdom of the Middle Congo, 1880–1892*. Oxford: Oxford University Press, 1973.

Van Noten, Francis. *The Archaeology of Central Africa*. Graz: Akademische Dr., 1982.

Vilakazi, B. W. *Zulu Horizons: The Vilakazi Poems* (tr. by D. McK. Malcolm and F. L. Friedman). Cape Town: Howard Timmins, 1962.

Watkins, Owen S. *With Kitchener's Army: Being a Chaplain's Experiences with the Nile Expedition 1898*. London: S. W. Partridge, 1900.

Wauthier, Claude. *L'Afrique des Africains: Inventaire de la Négritude*. Paris: Éditions de Seuil, 1964.

Webster, J. B., ed. *Chronology, Migration and Drought in Interlacustrine Africa*. New York: Africana Publishing Corp., 1979.

West, Richard. *Back to Africa: A History of Sierra Leone and Liberia*. London: Cape, 1970.

Wheeler, Douglas L., and René Pélissier. *Angola*. New York: Praeger, 1971.

Wiedner, D. L. *A History of Africa South of the Sahara*. New York: Random House, 1962.

Wilmot, the Hon. A. *Monomotapa: Its Monuments and Its History from the Most Ancient Times to the Present*. New York: Negro University Press, 1969.

Womersley, Rev. Harold. *The Legends and History of the Luba*. Berkeley: Crossroads Press, University of California, 1984.

Index

ANCIENT AFRICA

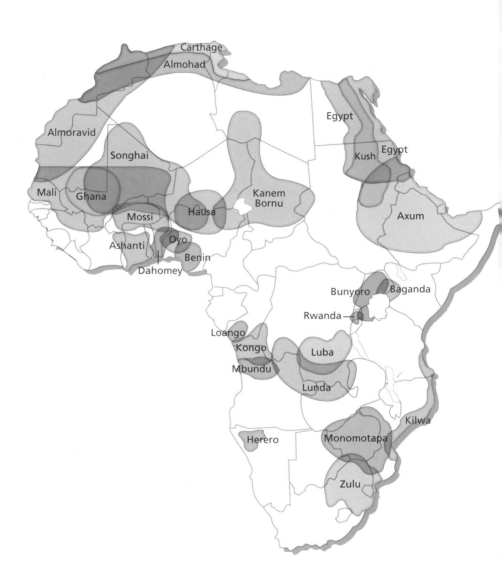